Cloud Native Geospatial Analytics with Apache Sedona

A Hands-On Guide for Working with Large-Scale Spatial Data

Paweł Tokaj, Jia Yu, and Mo Sarwat
Foreword by Qiusheng Wu

O'REILLY®

Cloud Native Geospatial Analytics with Apache Sedona
by Paweł Tokaj, Jia Yu, and Mo Sarwat

Acquisitions Editor: Aaron Black	**Indexer:** BIM Creatives, LLC
Development Editor: Gary O'Brien	**Cover Designer:** Karen Montgomery
Production Editor: Clare Laylock	**Cover Illustrator:** José Marzan Jr.
Copyeditor: Charles Roumeliotis	**Interior Designer:** David Futato
Proofreader: Carol McGillivray	**Interior Illustrator:** Kate Dullea

December 2025:   First Edition

Revision History for the First Edition
2025-12-05:   First Release

See *http://oreilly.com/catalog/errata.csp?isbn=9781098173999* for release details.

978-1-098-17399-9

[LSI]

Table of Contents

Foreword

Geospatial data has become central to our understanding and response to the world around us. From monitoring ecosystems to precise map matching, location is often the key to unlocking insight. However, as the volume and velocity of geospatial data have surged, our analytical tools have struggled to keep pace. Traditional GIS tools excel at analysis but are often limited to single machine environments. Meanwhile, cloud data warehouses offer impressive scalability but often treat geospatial data as an afterthought.

Apache Sedona bridges this divide. Sedona is an open source framework that embeds geospatial analysis directly into distributed computing platforms such as Apache Spark, Flink, and Snowflake. It treats spatial as a first-class concern, enabling complex spatial joins, queries, and raster processing across billions of records. With Sedona, we gain both the depth of geospatial science coupled with the elasticity of the cloud.

I introduced Sedona briefly in my previous book, *Introduction to GIS Programming: A Practical Python Guide to Open Source Geospatial Tools*, where I included a chapter on distributed computing with Apache Sedona. That chapter sparked strong interest among readers, but it could only scratch the surface. Sedona is far too powerful and comprehensive to be condensed into a single section. It deserves a full-length treatment, and that is precisely what *Cloud Native Geospatial Analytics with Apache Sedona* provides.

This book is authored by Sedona's creators and core developers, who not only understand its technical architecture but also know how to make it approachable. It begins with the fundamentals such as the spatial DataFrame and spatial SQL, then advances into topics including distributed joins, raster analysis, and geospatial data lakehouses. It also introduces readers to running Sedona in real environments, from Docker containers to managed platforms like Wherobots Cloud. With Wherobots Cloud, practitioners can quickly launch Sedona clusters, experiment with scalable analytics, and focus on solving problems rather than managing infrastructure. That accessibility lowers the barrier for anyone eager to bring distributed spatial analytics into their work.

Equally important is how the book situates Sedona within the broader ecosystem. Geospatial practitioners often rely on Python libraries like GeoPandas, Shapely, and Rasterio for analysis, as well as visualization frameworks like Kepler.gl for exploration and communication. Sedona integrates seamlessly with these tools, scaling familiar workflows across distributed clusters while adhering to open standards such as GeoParquet and spatial SQL. The authors highlight these connections, making Sedona valuable not only for GIS professionals but also for data engineers and scientists building modern data pipelines.

The timing of this book could not be better. We face global challenges in disaster response, public health, and urban mobility, each of which relies on location-aware data at massive scales. Sedona has already been widely adopted by the geospatial community, and it is being used by organizations including Amazon and the Overture Maps Foundation. By walking through practical examples such as analyzing New York City taxi trips, visualizing Overture Maps building data, or processing global flood hazard maps, the book demonstrates Sedona's versatility and its ability to tackle real-world problems.

For me, this book represents a natural extension of the journey in geospatial analytics. In my *Introduction to GIS Programming* book, I could only provide a glimpse of what Sedona enables. This book delves deeper, teaching not only how Sedona functions but also how to effectively deploy it in scalable production environments.

Whether you are a data scientist enhancing machine learning with spatial features, an engineer designing large-scale ETL pipelines, or an analyst seeking patterns hidden within billions of records, this book is tailored to meet your needs. Even if you are simply curious about the future of geospatial analytics, you will discover why cloud native approaches are essential and why Apache Sedona is a cornerstone of this evolution.

I am delighted to recommend *Cloud Native Geospatial Analytics with Apache Sedona*. It is a technical guide, a practical manual, and an invitation to join a vibrant open source community. With Sedona and platforms like Wherobots Cloud, the future of geospatial analytics is already here: scalable, accessible, and open.

— Qiusheng Wu
Associate Professor at
the University of Tennessee, Knoxville
Knoxville, TN, September 2025

Preface

Welcome to *Cloud Native Geospatial Analytics with Apache Sedona*. Thank you for choosing this book as your learning companion. The following pages introduce what lies ahead, our reasons for writing it, and how to get the most value from your reading.

About This Book

In this book, you will learn how to process and analyze geospatial data with Apache Sedona. Sedona is designed for data engineers and geospatial analysts working with datasets in the physical world, and this book explores the core concepts, inner workings, and practical applications of Apache Sedona. By the time you reach the end, you will have grasped the essentials and possess the practical knowledge to use Apache Sedona effectively in your data projects. You will have learned about how to use state-of-the-art geospatial data processing techniques on different engines and for different types of spatial data. You will learn how to perform spatial joins, run KNN queries, and build spatial indices with different algorithms like R-tree and quadtree. No matter your level of experience, *Cloud Native Geospatial Analytics with Apache Sedona* offers a comprehensive and accessible path to mastering Apache Sedona in the realm of cloud native geospatial analytics.

Why We Wrote This Book

As adoption of Apache Sedona accelerates across industries, a clear need has emerged for a comprehensive technical resource that addresses the complexities of large-scale geospatial data processing. The volume of available spatial data like weather maps, socioeconomic data, vegetation indices, and geo-tagged social media has increased tremendously, and scalable tools like Sedona are needed to extract insights from these datasets. Additionally, the growing ecosystem of spatial file formats, the integration of both vector and raster data, and the demand for scalable spatial analytics have created challenges for geospatial professionals working with distributed systems. We wrote

Cloud Native Geospatial Analytics with Apache Sedona to bridge this gap and provide a centralized, authoritative reference for leveraging Sedona's capabilities in spatial indexing, spatial joins, coordinate system handling, and format interoperability. Our goal is to equip practitioners with the knowledge required to process and analyze geospatial data efficiently in modern big data environments.

What You Will Find Inside

The upcoming chapters will teach you Apache Sedona's fundamentals and operational mechanics, demonstrate how to leverage the framework across different platforms and tools, and share proven strategies for handling geospatial data efficiently with Apache Sedona. Following is an overview of what each chapter covers:

Chapter 1, "Introduction to Apache Sedona"
   Provides a foundational overview of Apache Sedona, explaining what it is, its core capabilities for geospatial data processing, and why it's valuable for modern data analytics workflows.

Chapter 2, "Getting Started with Apache Sedona"
   Walks you through the initial setup and configuration of Apache Sedona, covering installation requirements, environment preparation, and your first basic operations with the framework.

Chapter 3, "Loading Geospatial Data into Apache Sedona"
   Demonstrates how to efficiently load and manage large-scale geospatial datasets in Apache Sedona, covering various data formats, ingestion methods, and optimization techniques for handling big geospatial data.

Chapter 4, "Points, Lines, and Polygons: Vector Data Analysis with Spatial SQL"
   Explores how to analyze vector geospatial data using Apache Sedona's SQL capabilities for spatial operations and geometric computations.

Chapter 5, "Raster Data Analysis"
   Covers techniques for processing and analyzing raster geospatial data using Apache Sedona, including operations on gridded datasets like satellite imagery and digital elevation models.

Chapter 6, "Apache Sedona and the PyData Ecosystem"
   Demonstrates how Apache Sedona integrates with Python's PyData ecosystem, showing how to leverage popular libraries like GeoPandas, Shapely, and Jupyter Notebooks for geospatial analytics workflows.

Chapter 7, "Geospatial Data Science and Machine Learning"
    Explores how to apply data science techniques and machine learning algorithms
    to geospatial datasets using Apache Sedona, covering spatial feature engineering,
    predictive modeling, and analytical workflows.

*Chapter 8, "Building a Geospatial Data Lakehouse with Apache Parquet and Apache
Iceberg"*
    Demonstrates how to construct a modern geospatial data lakehouse architecture
    using Apache Sedona with Apache Parquet files and Apache Iceberg for efficient
    storage, versioning, and querying of large-scale geospatial datasets.

Chapter 9, "Using Apache Sedona with Cloud Data Providers"
    Shows how to deploy and utilize Apache Sedona with major cloud platforms
    and data services, covering integration patterns, configuration options, and best
    practices for cloud-based geospatial analytics.

Chapter 10, "Optimizing Apache Sedona Applications"
    Highlights essential methods for making Apache Sedona applications faster and
    more memory-efficient, with a focus on optimizing spatial join queries, acceler-
    ating Python applications, and efficiently storing data in Parquet and Apache
    Iceberg format.

How to Use This Book

This book is carefully designed to deepen your comprehension and hands-on expertise with Apache Sedona, suitable for both newcomers and experienced practitioners.
Although organized in a progressive sequence that allows you to develop complete
mastery from beginning to end, the structure also supports adaptable study patterns.
Every chapter stands independently, permitting you to jump straight into particular
subjects or scenarios that interest you without requiring prior chapter completion.
This methodology transforms the book into an essential tool for both structured
education and focused, on-demand learning opportunities.

Within these pages, you'll encounter numerous code examples and hands-on dem-
onstrations. To facilitate your educational journey, we have created a specialized
GitHub repository (*https://github.com/wherobots/apache-sedona-book*) accompanying
this book. The repository follows a chapter-based structure, providing convenient
access to all essential resources, code samples, and illustrations relevant to each
section's material. The repository contains more examples than those in the book;
it's the place where we put design and architectural patterns to use Apache Sedona
in production systems or to understand the internals better. For instance, in the
book, we covered Apache Airflow for scheduling your geospatial workflows, but in
the repository, you can find examples with other schedulers, like Prefect. There are
plenty of new upcoming features, or those we can't put in the book, which you can

find in the repository, and they will be updated whenever needed. We will include examples with SedonaDB, including the geography data type, GeoPandas data type, and other new features that will be released after the book's publication. We have a limited amount of space for figures in the book, so we can put many more in the repository. Many of us are visual learners, and we believe that interactive visualizations and figures are the best way to understand geospatial systems and algorithms. All contributions are welcome, including issue reports or example requests.

Whether you aim to comprehend Apache Sedona's technical architecture or need to execute particular features, this repository functions as a supporting resource to strengthen your understanding and implementation of the principles presented throughout the book.

Whether you decide to study this guide from beginning to end or concentrate on specific chapters according to your current requirements, this book serves as a thorough and user-friendly reference for Apache Sedona, enhanced by practical, interactive elements available through our dedicated GitHub repository.

Conventions Used in This Book

The following typographical conventions are used in this book:

Italic
Indicates new terms, URLs, email addresses, filenames, and file extensions.

`Constant width`
Used for program listings, as well as within paragraphs to refer to program elements such as variable or function names, databases, data types, environment variables, statements, and keywords.

`Constant width italic`
Shows text that should be replaced with user-supplied values or by values determined by context.

This element signifies a tip or suggestion.

This element signifies a general note.

This element indicates a warning or caution.

Using Code Examples

Supplemental material (code examples, exercises, etc.) is available for download at *https://github.com/wherobots/apache-sedona-book*.

This book is here to help you get your job done. In general, if example code is offered with this book, you may use it in your programs and documentation. You do not need to contact us for permission unless you're reproducing a significant portion of the code. For example, writing a program that uses several chunks of code from this book does not require permission. Selling or distributing a CD-ROM of examples from O'Reilly books does require permission. Answering a question by citing this book and quoting example code does not require permission. Incorporating a significant amount of example code from this book into your product's documentation does require permission.

We appreciate, but do not require, attribution. An attribution usually includes the title, author, publisher, and ISBN. For example: "*Cloud Native Geospatial Analytics with Apache Sedona* by Paweł Tokaj, Jia Yu, and Mo Sarwat (O'Reilly). Copyright 2026 O'Reilly Media, Inc., 978-1-098-17399-9."

If you feel your use of code examples falls outside fair use or the permission given above, feel free to contact us at *permissions@oreilly.com*.

O'Reilly Online Learning

O'REILLY® For more than 40 years, *O'Reilly Media* has provided technology and business training, knowledge, and insight to help companies succeed.

Our unique network of experts and innovators share their knowledge and expertise through books, articles, and our online learning platform. O'Reilly's online learning platform gives you on-demand access to live training courses, in-depth learning paths, interactive coding environments, and a vast collection of text and video from O'Reilly and 200+ other publishers. For more information, visit *https://oreilly.com*.

How to Contact Us

Please address comments and questions concerning this book to the publisher:

O'Reilly Media, Inc.
141 Stony Circle, Suite 195
Santa Rosa, CA 95401
800-889-8969 (in the United States or Canada)
707-827-7019 (international or local)
707-829-0104 (fax)
support@oreilly.com
https://oreilly.com/about/contact.html

We have a web page for this book, where we list errata and any additional information. You can access this page at *https://oreil.ly/cloud-native-geospatial*.

For news and information about our books and courses, visit *https://oreilly.com*.

Find us on LinkedIn: *https://linkedin.com/company/oreilly-media*.

Watch us on YouTube: *https://youtube.com/oreillymedia*.

Acknowledgments

We would like to thank our technical reviewers of this book, Kamil Raczycki, Kacper Leśniara, and Vladislav Bilay. Your professionalism, creative ideas, and valuable suggestions not only helped us catch errors but also made the book easier and more enjoyable to read. Most of all, thank you to the many contributors to Apache Sedona and its ecosystem. Without their work, this book would not have been possible.

Paweł Tokaj

First and foremost, I would like to thank my close family, especially my wife and my best friend, Zosia, whose support and patience were significant to me. You were my first reviewer of the chapters before they came into Gary's hands. I really appreciate the time we spent together reading all the chapters. You were always asking how the writing was going, and you prepared beverages when I stayed up late writing. Also, a huge thank you to my brother Bartek, who is an inspiration and proof that with hard work, nothing is impossible.

Thanks to the Sedona community, first to coauthor Jia, who accepted my first Python SDK MR back in late 2019. This has been an incredible journey that I never thought would go in this direction. Thank you for all the discussions, MR reviews, and for always being friendly and open-minded. Secondly, thanks to Matthew for early reviews of the book and willingness to help.

I would like to thank Gary for his patience and detailed explanations on the process of writing a book. I learned a lot from you. Thanks for the friendly atmosphere and your professionalism, which made writing seamless and possible!

To all the great engineers I have the pleasure of working with—Filip Mikina, JC Arbelbide, James Burkhart, Przemysław Walczyk, Piotr Bartkiewicz, Marek Wiewiórka, and other great engineers I met in my career at PwC, Allegro, GetinData, and Splunk—I've learned a lot from you and become a better engineer. I am lucky that our paths crossed and we had the opportunity to work together.

To the geospatial community, whose resources were invaluable in writing this book, and especially to Matt Forest and Qiusheng Wu for their efforts in evangelizing geospatial data and making it more accessible and easier to understand.

Last but not least, to all the inspiration I had throughout my career, book authors, blog posts, tutorials, and many more. Still, three that made a huge impact were *Designing Data-Intensive Applications* by Martin Kleppmann, *The Pragmatic Programmer* by David Thomas and Andrew Hunt, and the book that everybody should read, *How to Win Friends and Influence People* by Dale Carnegie.

Jia Yu

This book is a milestone in my journey with Apache Sedona, and I am deeply grateful to everyone who made it possible.

I want to thank the Apache Sedona community—committers, contributors, and users—for building and shaping Sedona together. Every contribution, no matter how small, has helped Sedona grow into what it is today, and I have learned so much from working alongside this incredible group of people.

I am also thankful to the Apache Software Foundation (ASF) for providing the framework of open collaboration and governance that allowed Sedona to thrive. The ASF's values of community over code have guided me not just in this project, but in my broader open source work.

Beyond Sedona, I owe much to the geospatial and big data communities. The standards, tools, and datasets created by so many researchers and engineers laid the foundation for Sedona's capabilities. This book stands on the shoulders of decades of work from those who came before me.

I also want to express gratitude to my colleagues at Wherobots who gave feedback on early drafts and shared their real-world experiences with Sedona. Your support and insights pushed me to refine my thinking and make this book as useful as possible.

Most of all, I thank my family and loved ones for their patience. Your encouragement gave me the strength to finish this work.

## CHAPTER 1

Introduction to Apache Sedona

The open source Apache Sedona project grew out of the need for a scalable geospatial analytics framework capable of working with large-scale spatial data. There's a common saying in the data world that "spatial is special." In other words, working with spatial data implies that due to the unique characteristics and complexities of spatial data, specialized techniques, tooling, and knowledge are required for effective analysis and interpretation of spatial data. While there is some validity to this perspective, it misses the more nuanced truth that many traditional best practices, techniques, tooling, and data formats from the data engineering and data science world are still perfectly relevant when working with geospatial data. However, there are some unique challenges and considerations that arise when working with spatial data.

In this chapter, we will discuss some of the challenges that commonly arise when working with geospatial data and provide an overview of the geospatial data ecosystem, including some of the gaps in tooling that led to the need for a scalable geospatial analytics framework like Apache Sedona.

We will also introduce how Apache Sedona addresses the challenges of working with geospatial data at scale and take a look behind the scenes at the basic architecture and components of Apache Sedona. At the end of this chapter, we should have a clearer understanding of the idea that "spatial is special" and evaluate if there is truth to this common phrase.

Introduction to Cloud Native Geospatial Analysis and Its Challenges

In our increasingly interconnected world, geospatial data and analysis have become essential tools for understanding the complexities of our environment, societies, and economies. Geospatial data shapes our decision-making and problem-solving processes.

Geospatial data refers to information that is associated with specific locations on the Earth's surface and can be represented in forms such as points, lines, polygons, and rasters, which capture features such as roads, rivers, buildings, and terrain. The richness of geospatial data lies in its ability to provide both location information and additional attributes, which enable a multidimensional view of our world.

Geospatial data can come from a variety of sources, such as:

Satellite imagery
> Satellite imagery provides detailed views of the Earth's surface, which is useful for monitoring environmental changes and urban development.

GPS data
> Captured from devices and sensors, this type of telemetry data offers precise location tracking for navigation and logistics.

Census and survey data
> Demographic and socioeconomic information tied to specific locations describes a large amount of geospatial data, often managed by governments.

Aerial photography
> Captured from aircraft, aerial imagery provides high-resolution images for mapping and analysis.

Remote sensing
> Utilizing sensors to detect and measure physical characteristics of an area from a distance, often from satellites, remote sensing is a large and data-rich technique.

Crowd-sourced datasets
> Crowd-sourced datasets, such as OpenStreetMap, which contains a global-scale collection of points of interest, road networks, land cover, and administrative boundary data, provide a rich input for geospatial analysis.

These are just some of the sources of geospatial data that are commonly found in geospatial analysis projects. It is also useful to note that many enterprises generate massive amounts of data that have a geospatial component through normal business operations, such as retail transactions, inventory management, and customer interactions. It is also common to find data derived from the preceding sources, such as those enriched by a commercial dataset provider or as the result of a machine learning process, in geospatial analytic workflows.

> The terms "spatial data" and "geospatial data" are often used interchangeably, but they have slightly different meanings. *Spatial data* refers to any data that has a spatial or geographic component and can describe the location, shape, and relationships of objects in space. *Geospatial data* is a subset of spatial data that specifically pertains to the Earth's surface and features.
>
> Because of the types of insights that can be attained and relevance to common business challenges, the focus of this book is specifically on geospatial data. However, it is worth noting that many of the techniques discussed can be applied to spatial data in general, and Apache Sedona can work with both spatial and geospatial data.

Geospatial data analysis or *geospatial analysis* involves the techniques and tools used to interpret and visualize geospatial data. By applying spatial analysis methods, we can uncover patterns, relationships, and trends that are not immediately apparent. This process empowers us to make more informed decisions, optimize allocation of resources, and predict future outcomes.

Geospatial analysis is crucial because it provides a spatial context to data, which can reveal insights that traditional data cannot. Spatial data analysis helps us understand complex spatial relationships and dynamics, leading to better decision making in fields ranging from environmental conservation to business intelligence. As our world continues to become more data-driven, the ability to interpret spatial data will be key to addressing global challenges. In this section we will explore the foundational concepts, tools, and applications of geospatial analysis used to harness the power of location-based data.

Let's examine some of the complexities that arise when working with geospatial data for analysis that can help us evaluate if the idea that "spatial is special" is really true or not. The first complexity that often arises is in handling the two common types of data representation used to store geospatial information: *vector data* and *raster data*.

Vector data represents spatial features as discrete geometry objects (such as points, lines, and polygons), which are defined by their coordinates and can also include topological data such as connectivity between lines or adjacency between polygons. Vector data typically also includes attributes associated with the geometries such as a unique identifier, name of the feature, or other relevant data. Working with vector data is discussed in more detail in Chapter 4.

Raster data represents spatial information as a grid of cells (or pixels), where each pixel represents a specific geographic location and has an associated value (or values) known as band(s). The raster data representation is typically used to describe continuous data such as aerial imagery, elevation, or temperature. Raster data analysis will be covered in depth in Chapter 5.

Coordinate systems are another complexity of working with geospatial data. Coordinate systems use a model of the Earth's surface to map coordinates to a point on the Earth's surface. Geospatial data can be represented using various coordinate systems (including geographic coordinate systems and *projected coordinate systems*), which may use different units of measure. Projected coordinate systems introduce distortion and often require assessing trade-offs when choosing which projected coordinate system is appropriate for the intended analysis.

Geospatial indexes are used to improve the efficiency of spatial queries and operations on geospatial data by organizing the storage and retrieval of spatial objects based on their spatial properties and relationships. Because spatial data is multidimensional, indexing structures used for geospatial data—such as R-trees, quadtrees, and Geohashes—are specialized for spatial data and differ from index structures commonly used for nonspatial data such as B-trees or hash indexes.

Spatial partitioning, especially in a distributed system, adds complexity and introduces challenges when we factor in "hot spots" that indicate observations are likely not evenly distributed by geographic area. For example, are we likely to find more taxi pickups in Manhattan or Montana?

Now that we have a sense of some of the complexities of analyzing geospatial data, let's take a look at the geospatial data analytics ecosystem to see how tools and libraries have evolved to address these challenges.

The Geospatial Analytics Ecosystem

When evaluating geospatial analytics tooling, it is important to keep in mind the requirements of your project. What type of data will you be working with? Will you be working with vector data, raster data, or both? Are you building an interactive application with transactional data access requirements or will you be defining data transformation pipelines and analytics workflows? Will you be combining data from multiple sources? What scale of data will you be working with? How often is the data changing? What type of spatial querying functionality does your project require? Understanding these requirements will inform how you evaluate, prioritize, and select the tools used to implement your project.

A typical geospatial analytics use case will involve combining multiple datasets or enriching an existing dataset with additional values or aggregates based on spatial relationships. Some component of vector data is typically involved and often both vector and raster data are involved. The scale and velocity of the data (how often the data changes) will depend on the specific use case but will often involve national- or planetary-scale data and therefore will be large scale, especially if we are working with high-resolution raster data.

Based on this description of the typical geospatial analytics project, we can identify some important characteristics to look for when evaluating geospatial data tooling:

Efficiency is important

Because of the scale of the data we will be working with, it is important to consider how efficiently we can process geospatial data. This is a relevant consideration both in terms of the cost of computing resources but also when considering the productivity of our engineering and data teams. Simply put, if an analytics task takes 48 hours to run, our team's product velocity will be slower than if the same task runs in 10 minutes.

Minimize data transfer

Related to the efficient use of computing resources is the efficient use of data transfer. Because of the costs incurred when moving large amounts of data and transforming the data into a format preferred by a different system, we should prefer tools and data formats that don't require this transformation step and can work with data stored in a cloud object storage service such as AWS S3. This concept is often called "bringing compute to the data instead of data to the compute."

Optimize for analytics over transactional workloads

Transactional systems are designed to handle day-to-day operational data with a focus on data integrity and speed of online transactions such as inserting, updating, and deleting data. Analytical systems are instead optimized for handling large volumes of data and complex queries for data analysis.

Support for complex geospatial operations

Since our data processing tasks will often involve combining datasets based on spatial relationships, our tooling must be able to define and efficiently determine these spatial relationships. These relationships can be based on distance but also on more complex spatial relationships such as intersecting, touching, or fully contained geometries and will often involve complex geometries such as polygons.

The geospatial analytics ecosystem has seen significant evolution in previous decades. Specialized Geographic Information Systems (GIS) software were perhaps the first tools to enable geospatial analysis. These tools were largely desktop-driven GUI applications used by analysts and geospatial domain experts. They typically run on a single machine, and the scale of the data being analyzed is limited by the resources of the machine on which they are running.

The open source ecosystem has played an important role in advancing the ability to work with geospatial data. Tools such as PostGIS, GDAL, QGIS, and GeoServer have addressed the need for storage, retrieval, processing, sharing, and visualizing geospatial data. The Python data ecosystem is especially rich in the geospatial domain with libraries such as GeoPandas, Rasterio, and Shapely that enable working with geospatial data in data structures idiomatic to Python. Similar to the specialized GIS software described earlier, much of this tooling runs on a single machine with scalability typically limited by the resources of that machine. However, there are notable exceptions for specialized use cases such as scientific computing.

The tooling that makes up this GIS-specific ecosystem enables very sophisticated analysis and has been hardened over decades of use by the community. However, as data volumes have soared in recent years, especially in the geospatial domain, the need for geospatial data processing at massive scale has arisen as a challenge for many of these tools due to their single machine design and limitations.

For example, one commonly used geospatial tool is the PostGIS extension to the open source PostgreSQL database. PostGIS is an excellent tool for geospatial data storage and spatial queries and analysis. However, since PostGIS is based on the PostgreSQL relational database management system (RDBMS) transactional database, challenges can arise when using PostGIS for large-scale analytic workloads. Scaling PostGIS horizontally for high-volume analytics workloads can be challenging when compared to distributed systems specifically designed for analytics. PostGIS stores data in a row-based format, which may not be as efficient for analytic workloads that benefit from columnar storage. As a transactional database, this requirement of using row-based storage also makes it difficult for PostGIS to leverage cloud storage systems like AWS's S3 service.

Leveraging Cloud Native Architecture

In more recent years the data analytics ecosystem has largely moved to the cloud, taking advantage of the major benefits of cloud native architecture such as distributed compute, elastic scalability, and cloud object storage.

While many cloud-based analytics services such as data warehouses offer scalability and the ability to work with massive amounts of data efficiently, these tools often are not optimized for working with geospatial data, resulting in poor performance when their techniques are applied to spatial data. Users must often deal with missing features and functionality required for working with geospatial data at scale.

The previous section illustrated that there are geospatial tools and libraries that treat geospatial data as a first-class citizen and have extensive geospatial support. However, these tools often have challenges with scalability and may not be able to take advantage of modern cloud native practices like distributed compute, elastic scaling, and cloud native storage.

On the other hand, tools like cloud data warehouses, which are best in class at leveraging cloud native practices that enable scaling to work with massive datasets, often do not treat geospatial data as a first-class citizen and often lack functionality or optimizations for working with geospatial data.

This clearly points out a gap in the ecosystem for tools that are capable of handling the complexities of geospatial workloads with the scale of cloud native analytics tooling like cloud data warehouses, which was exactly the motivation for the creation of the Apache Sedona project.

Apache Sedona Overview

Apache Sedona is a cluster computing system for processing large-scale spatial data. It treats spatial data as a first-class citizen by extending the functionality of distributed compute frameworks like Apache Spark, Apache Flink, and Snowflake. Apache Sedona was created at Arizona State University under the name Geospark.[1]

> While Apache Sedona can work with several distributed compute frameworks, the focus of this book will be using Apache Sedona with Apache Spark. See Chapter 9 for examples of using Apache Sedona with other cloud services.

Apache Sedona introduces data types, operations, and indexing techniques optimized for spatial workloads on top of Apache Spark. Let's take a look at the workflow for analyzing spatial data with Apache Sedona.

Spatial Query Processing

The first step in spatial query processing is to ingest geospatial data into Apache Sedona. Data can be loaded from various sources such as files (shapefiles, GeoJSON, Parquet, GeoTIFF, etc.) or databases into Apache Sedona's spatial data structures (typically the spatial DataFrame).

Next, Apache Sedona uses spatial indexing techniques to accelerate query processing, such as R-trees or quadtrees. The spatial index is used to partition the data into smaller, manageable units, enabling efficient data retrieval during query processing.

Once the data is loaded and indexed, spatial queries can be executed using Apache Sedona's query execution engine. Sedona supports a wide range of spatial operations, such as spatial joins, distance calculations, and spatial aggregations.

---

1 Jia Yu, Zongsi Zhang, and Mohamed Sarwat, "Spatial Data Management in Apache Spark: The GeoSpark Perspective and Beyond," *Geoinformatica* 23 (2019), 37–78.

Apache Sedona optimizes spatial queries to improve performance. The query optimizer determines an efficient query plan by considering the spatial predicates, available indexes, and the distribution of data across the cluster.

Spatial queries are executed in a distributed manner using Apache Spark's computational capabilities. The query execution engine distributes the query workload across the cluster, with each node processing a portion of the data. Intermediate results are combined to produce the final result set. Since spatial objects are very complex with many coordinates, Apache Sedona implements a custom serializer for efficiently moving spatial data throughout the cluster.

After query execution, the results are aggregated and presented to the user; they can be further processed or visualized using Sedona's integration with other geospatial tools, libraries, and visualization frameworks such as Kepler.gl.

Apache Sedona leverages various optimization techniques to improve query performance. These optimizations include predicate pushdown, which pushes spatial predicates down to the index or file storage layer, reducing the amount of data to be processed. Sedona also supports indexing strategies like indexing on multiple attributes or using advanced indexing structures for specific query patterns.

Apache Sedona enables efficient spatial query processing through spatial indexing, distributed query execution, query optimization, and spatial partitioning. By leveraging these techniques, Sedona provides scalable and high-performance geospatial data processing capabilities, allowing users to perform complex spatial queries and analysis on large-scale datasets.

We've mentioned several times now that Apache Sedona leverages Apache Spark as a distributed compute layer. Understanding a bit about Spark can be helpful when working with Apache Sedona.

Apache Spark Overview

Apache Spark is an analytical engine designed for processing large-scale data. One of the most significant advantages is its unified architecture, which enables the use of batch processing, stream processing, and machine learning algorithms through the same DataFrame API across multiple languages, including Java, Scala, Python, SQL, and more.

You can run an Apache Spark application in local mode, which is particularly useful during application development or on an Apache Spark cluster. In local mode, your processor threads act as Apache Spark executors; there is no new implementation of the data processing algorithms in local mode when you are using the cluster. We focus on the Apache Spark cluster architecture in this section.

The Apache Spark application runs an independent set of tasks on a cluster (Figure 1-1). It is coordinated by the driver program, where the SparkContext/Spark Session lives. The driver program communicates with the cluster manager (Spark standalone, Kubernetes, Yarn) to allocate specific resources on the cluster of executors. Once you've got all the resources needed, SparkContext is responsible for sending the code to the executors (jar files and Python code) and for sending tasks to the executors.

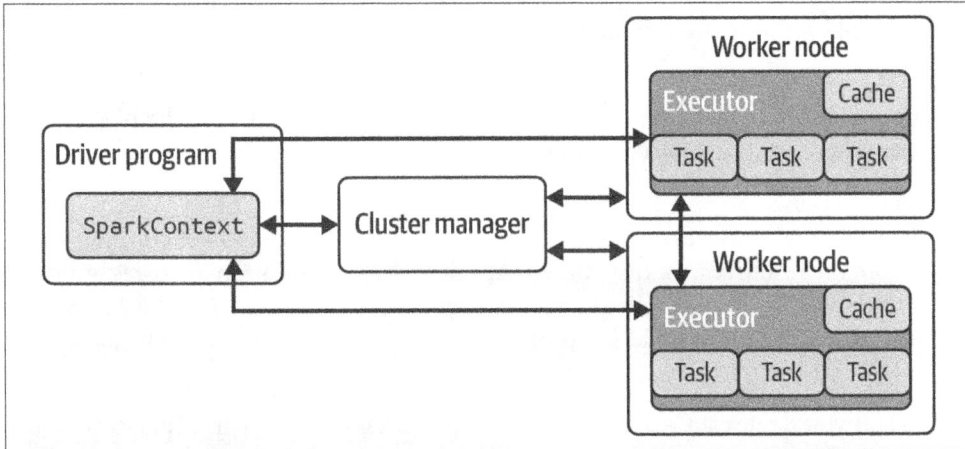

Figure 1-1. Apache Spark cluster architecture

> The driver node is the place where you keep all the data loaded to pandas DataFrames or any other Python objects in your Apache Spark application. Despite the multiple node architecture in Apache Spark, using collect() on an Apache Spark DataFrame or toPandas() will transfer all the data to the driver, which might cause your application to crash if the data is too large to be handled in the driver node. When you run Apache Sedona inside the Jupyter Notebook environment, the driver node is running in the same process as Jupyter Notebook.

Let's explain some of the Apache Spark concepts we will use in the book:

Application jar
    Contains the application logic packaged into a Java jar file. If your application requires additional dependencies, you must either provide them in each cluster node or create a *fat jar file* (a jar with packed dependencies in it, not only your application code) that includes all dependencies. This does not include the Apache Hadoop jar files, as they are already provisioned at runtime; it's better to exclude them to avoid conflicts during the application runtime.

Data caching

Apache Spark computes everything in memory, but without persisting the data on disk or in memory directly, it will be recalculated each time you call an action on your data processing pipeline. For example, when you perform a spatial join and use the resulting DataFrame in multiple places, or when working with the data in the Jupyter Notebook environment, it might be helpful to call `df.cache()` and trigger it with an action like `count` to cache the data. Hence, it's instantly available without any computation.

Apache Spark driver

Responsible for coordinating your distributed application; this is the place where `SparkContext` and `SparkSession` live.

Cluster manager

The external service through which the Apache Spark driver communicates to obtain resources. A distributed Apache Spark application requires multiple worker nodes to parallelize your application. You can run Apache Spark distributed applications on k8s clusters, YARN clusters, or standalone clusters.

Deploy mode

When you deploy an Apache Spark job on the cluster, you can decide where the application driver is. If you would like to run it inside the cluster, then select *cluster* mode; when you want to run it externally outside the cluster, choose *client* mode.

Worker node

This is the part of the Apache Spark cluster where you can run your application.

Partitioning

The process of splitting data into smaller chunks is called partitioning. Each executor takes one partition at a time and processes it.

Executor

An executor is the process created for the application on the worker node. Each application has its executors. Each executor can have one or multiple CPU cores to use.

Task

A unit of work to schedule on one executor. For instance, validating whether the polygons intersect with points for one of the partitions is a task.

Job

Parallel computation in Apache Spark consists of multiple stages. It's invoked by calling an Apache Spark action, so, for example, a spatial join operation might be a job.

Shuffling

Distributed analytical applications need to distribute the data across the worker nodes properly so that each executor can process the corresponding partitions. Comparing data partitions for shops and roads across different locations always yields an empty result. To resolve this, you need to shuffle your data, which involves distributing it so that shops in California are in the same partition as roads in California, allowing for proper comparison. Shuffling is a costly operation, so when it is not needed, it is better to avoid it.

Narrow operation

An operation that doesn't require reshuffling your data beforehand. Shuffling is a costly operation that is better avoided. In Chapter 10, we give you examples of how you can transform your Apache Sedona code to follow narrow operations instead of wide. Mapping is a narrow operation, for example, changing column A based on some condition. Broadcast join is a narrow operation, as it copies one dataset entirely to each executor and shifts the operation to mapping.

Wide operation

A wide operation requires shuffling before operating. Nonbroadcast spatial join is an example of a wide operation, or the grouping of data by some key.

Data skew

A negative situation when some workers are assigned more complex computations than others, resulting in longer processing times for some workers, which negatively impacts your application's performance. It can lead to slower processing times and application crashes due to insufficient memory resources, as the overwhelmed worker might have too much data to process. In Chapter 10, we prepared some examples of how to reduce the risk of skewed spatial joins.

Adaptive Query Execution

Adaptive Query Execution (AQE) is a runtime optimization in Apache Spark that dynamically optimizes query plans based on actual data statistics gathered during execution. It's the process that can redistribute the skew partition to multiple executors to speed up your processing.

Apache Spark exposes two APIs, Resilient Distributed Dataset (RDD) and DataFrame. RDD is a low-level API in Apache Spark. You will rarely need to operate on the RDD API, if ever. We recommend using the DataFrame API or the Dataset API, which are high-level, optimized wrappers on top of the RDD.

A DataFrame is a Dataset of the type Row, which is an Apache Spark internal type, not statically typed. In the Dataset API, you can use your types for better data integrity and type safety. Instead of operating on SQL fields and functions, you write your own algorithms and data transformations. The Dataset API is only available in Scala and Java. We mostly focus on the Python language, which is why we use DataFrame in this book.

To get more information about Apache Spark, follow the official documentation (*https://oreil.ly/i8PoJ*).

Understanding Apache Sedona's Architecture and Components

Now that we understand some fundamental components of Apache Spark, let's see how Apache Sedona extends them to enable spatial functionality while leveraging Spark's distributed compute framework.

Apache Sedona Data Structures

Apache Sedona extends Spark's RDD and DataFrame data structures with *spatial RDDs* and *spatial DataFrames* by adding support for spatial data types (point, polygon, linestring, etc.), spatial operations, and spatial indexing. We will work extensively with these data structures throughout the book, with a focus on spatial DataFrames, beginning in Chapter 2.

Spatial SQL

Apache Sedona's spatial DataFrames support spatial SQL, an extension of SQL with over two hundred spatial-specific functions that enable manipulating and processing both vector and raster spatial data, in addition to the functionality of Spark SQL.

Spatial Query Optimizations

Apache Sedona implements optimizations for distributed spatial queries for large-scale spatial data. These queries interface with Spark's query optimizer and ensure the use of Sedona's custom spatial indexes and data types to enable performance and scalability.

Some of the types of spatial queries supported by Apache Sedona include:

Spatial range query
> Also known as a spatial window query or a bounding box query, the spatial range query retrieves all spatial objects within a specified region.

Spatial range join query
> Similar to a spatial range query, the spatial range join query combines two datasets based on their spatial relationships within a specified range by retrieving pairs of spatial objects from two datasets that overlap within the specified region. The spatial relationship can vary depending on the use case but can include intersection, containment, or overlap of the geometries.

Spatial distance join query
> This query combines two datasets based on their spatial proximity. It identifies pairs of geometries from different datasets that are within a specified distance of each other. The result of a spatial distance join query is a set of matching pairs of geometries that satisfy the distance condition.

Spatial kNN
> The spatial k-nearest neighbors query finds the k nearest neighbors to a given point or geometry in a spatial dataset, where k is a user-defined parameter.

Support for Spatial File Formats

Apache Sedona supports dataset readers and writers for many spatial file types, including GeoJSON, GeoParquet, Apache Parquet and Iceberg with spatial features, shapefiles, GeoTIFF, ArcGrid, NetCDF/HDF, and support for reading directly from databases such as PostGIS. We will cover working with spatial files in depth in Chapter 3.

Visualization

Apache Sedona offers integrations with Kepler.gl and deck.gl. These visualization options allow for creating interactive geospatial visualizations using GPU-accelerated rendering. Both visualization options offer custom styling and rich visualization options including point data, complex geometries, heatmaps, choropleths, and 3D extrusions.

Other options for visualization with Apache Sedona include integration with the Python data ecosystem using tools such as Matplotlib and GeoPandas.

Integration with PyData Ecosystem

Apache Sedona seamlessly integrates with many Python data libraries and tools for working with geospatial data including:

Jupyter

The Jupyter Notebook–based development environment is the most common way to develop using Apache Sedona and will be the predominant interface used in this book. Jupyter provides an integrated environment for data exploration and analysis by integrating code, visualizations, and documentation in a single interface. By integrating Apache Sedona into a Jupyter Notebook, users can write code in Python, Scala, or SQL using Apache Sedona's geospatial functions, perform data processing, and visualize the results in the same notebook.

GeoPandas

GeoPandas is a popular Python library for working with geospatial data. The integration with Apache Sedona enables users to manipulate geospatial data using GeoPandas data structures and operations, while leveraging Apache Sedona's spatial indexing and analytical functions. GeoPandas also integrates well with popular visualization libraries in the Python ecosystem. Users can seamlessly switch between GeoPandas for data manipulation and Apache Sedona for geospatial analytics without the need for extensive data conversions or complex integration steps.

Rasterio

Rasterio is a popular Python library for reading, writing, and manipulating raster data. Apache Sedona provides a wide range of spatial operations that can be applied to raster data and the integration with Rasterio further extends the raster processing functionality available to Apache Sedona users.

Shapely

Shapely is a widely used Python library for geometric operations and manipulations. By integrating Shapely with Apache Sedona, users can leverage Shapely's extensive geometry manipulation capabilities to create, modify, and analyze geometric objects, thereby enhancing Apache Sedona's processing capabilities.

Benefits of Apache Sedona

Apache Sedona is a spatial-first framework for working with large-scale data that leverages the scalability of distributed compute frameworks. What then are the benefits of using Apache Sedona over other tools in the geospatial data analytics ecosystem?

Scalability

Apache Sedona is designed to handle large-scale geospatial datasets. Leveraging the distributed compute infrastructure of Apache Spark enables parallel processing, allowing query execution to scale horizontally across multiple machines.

High performance

Making use of geospatial-specific indexing structures such as R-trees and quadtrees, optimizing query planning, and an efficient data partitioning and custom serialization method purpose-built for geospatial data results in efficient data retrieval, which minimizes data transfer and maximizes query parallelism.

Reduced cost

Somewhat related to high performance is the benefit of reduced costs when running large-scale data processing operations in a large cluster. The improved performance of Apache Sedona results in less time spent running the expensive compute resources for a large cluster.

Rich spatial operations

Apache Sedona provides a comprehensive set of spatial operations, including point-in-polygon, distance calculation, spatial joins, spatial aggregations, raster data functionality, and more. These operations are optimized for performance and integrated with Apache Spark's DataFrame and SQL APIs, making it easy to perform complex geospatial analytics tasks.

Integration with the Apache Spark ecosystem

Apache Sedona seamlessly integrates with the Spark ecosystem, enabling users to leverage its powerful data processing capabilities. Apache Sedona can be used alongside other Spark libraries and tools to perform end-to-end data analysis workflows, combining geospatial data processing with machine learning.

Community support and active development

Apache Sedona benefits from an active and growing community of contributors and users. The community provides support, shares best practices, and contributes to the development and enhancement of the Apache Sedona project, ensuring ongoing improvements, bug fixes, and the availability of new features.

Open standards and interoperability

Apache Sedona adheres to open geospatial standards such as Open Geospatial Consortium (OGC) standards for spatial SQL, supporting the GeoParquet specification, and the ability to read and write many common geospatial data formats like shapefiles and GeoJSON, enabling data exchange and integration with existing geospatial workflows.

Seamless integration with the PyData ecosystem

Apache Sedona seamlessly integrates with common Python geospatial libraries such as GeoPandas, Shapely, and Rasterio. Through the use of user-defined functions (UDFs), these libraries can be leveraged to define custom logic, which can then leverage the scalability of Apache Sedona's parallel execution.

The Developer Experience

The developer experience of Apache Sedona is designed to be user-friendly and accessible, leveraging the familiarity, capabilities, and principles of Apache Spark. This includes APIs and language support that align with Apache Spark, including support for Scala, Java, Python, and R, allowing developers to choose their preferred programming language, as well as Jupyter Notebook compatibility, enabling interactive data exploration and easy sharing of geospatial analyses.

Apache Sedona's support for Spatial SQL allows developers to express geospatial operations and queries using familiar SQL syntax. This feature simplifies the development process for developers who are already proficient in SQL and reduces the learning curve for working with Apache Sedona.

> The focus of this book will be on using Apache Sedona using Python and spatial SQL, mostly within a Jupyter Notebook environment. While we will touch on other approaches to interacting with Apache Sedona, these tools will be our focus.

Who Uses Apache Sedona

While Apache Sedona is used by many different types of data practitioners, there are a few common types of users and use cases that emerge.

Data scientists working with large-scale geospatial data use Sedona to perform advanced geospatial analysis on large geospatial datasets to gain insights and make data-driven decisions. By integrating with machine learning frameworks, Apache Sedona allows data scientists to incorporate geospatial features into their predictive models. This integration enables the development of geospatial machine learning algorithms and predictive analytics on spatial data.

Data engineers use Apache Sedona to process and transform geospatial data at scale, leveraging the distributed processing power of Apache Spark and Sedona's unique focus on extensive geospatial operations and manipulation capabilities to transform geospatial data into desired formats. By leveraging the connectors and utilities provided by Sedona to ingest geospatial data from various sources, data engineers can efficiently integrate geospatial data into their data pipelines, perform ETL operations, and prepare the data for downstream analytics.

Data analysts performing ad-hoc analysis use Apache Sedona to explore and visualize geospatial data. They can apply spatial queries, aggregations, and visualizations to understand patterns, relationships, and trends in the data. Apache Sedona's capabilities enable data analysts to answer location-based questions and generate meaningful geospatial insights.

Common Apache Sedona Use Cases

So what exactly are users doing with Apache Sedona? Here are some common examples of what users are doing with Apache Sedona:

- Creating custom weather, climate, and environmental quality assessment reports at a national scale by combining vector parcel data with environmental raster data products

- Generating planetary scale GeoParquet files for public dissemination via cloud storage by combining, cleaning, and indexing multiple public datasets

- Converting billions of daily point telemetry observations into routes traveled by vehicles

- Enriching parcel-level data with demographic and environmental data at a national level to feed into a real estate investment suitability analysis

Many of these use cases can be described as *geospatial ETL* operations. ETL (extract, transform, load) is a data integration process that involves retrieving data from various sources, transforming and combining these datasets, then loading the transformed data into a target system or format for reporting or further analysis. Geospatial ETL shares many of the same challenges and requirements of traditional ETL processes with the additional complexities of managing the geospatial component of the data, as discussed earlier in the chapter: working with geospatial data sources and formats, spatial data types and transformations, and the scalability and performance considerations required for spatial operations such as joins based on spatial relationships.

You can also use Apache Sedona with ELT (extract, load, and transform) processes. ELT stands for extract, load, and transform. The main difference between the typical ETL process is that we start by loading the data into the warehouse directly and then perform the transformation part. In Chapter 6, we will show you how you can integrate Apache Sedona Spark with dbt.

Community Adoption

Apache Sedona has gained significant community adoption and has become a popular geospatial analytics library within the Apache Spark ecosystem. As an Apache Software Foundation (ASF) project, Apache Sedona's governance, licensing, and community participation align with ASF principles.

Apache Sedona has an active and growing developer community, with contributors from a number of different organizations and over 100 individuals interested in geospatial analytics and distributed computing. At the time of writing, Sedona has now reached 61 million downloads, with a rate of 2.4 million downloads per month, and usage is growing at a rate of 150% year over year.

Organizations in industries including transportation, urban planning, environment monitoring, logistics, insurance and risk analysis, and more have adopted Apache Sedona. They leverage Apache Sedona's capabilities to perform large-scale geospatial analysis, extract insights from geospatial data, and build geospatial analytical applications at scale. The industry adoption of Apache Sedona showcases its practical relevance and real-world use cases.

Apache Sedona has been featured in conferences, workshops, and research publications related to geospatial analytics, distributed computing, and big data processing. These presentations and publications contribute to the awareness, visibility, and adoption both within the enterprise and within the research and academic communities.

The Future of the Project

Apache Sedona is dynamically evolving to help solve geospatial data problems. There are plenty of features on which the project will focus:

- Native support for Parquet and Iceberg geospatial features
- Simplifying the transition for GeoPandas users to Apache Sedona with the Geopandas API. You write the code as you would in GeoPandas, but under the hood, you are running Apache Sedona.
- Efficient processing of the small and medium-sized geospatial data with Apache SedonaDB, which is a DataFusion-based framework written to process geospatial data efficiently on a single node. The entire database has been written in Rust, but it also has ports to the Python language.

- Improving the Apache Sedona Python API with more GeoArrow internals. Currently, Apache Sedona supports transforming a Sedona Spatial DataFrame from GeoPandas or to GeoPandas using GeoArrow. Additionally, support for vectorized UDFs is presently limited, but this limitation will be addressed over time.

- A geography data model with vast ST (spatial type) functions coverage for the data type.

- The addition of more ST and RS (raster spatial) functions as well as geospatial data type saving and loading. Support for predicate pushdown wherever it's possible for data formats.

Resources

Throughout this book we will refer to specific documentation and resources relevant to the topics covered in each section. However, there are some important resources that will be useful throughout your journey working with Apache Sedona:

- Apache Sedona documentation (*https://sedona.apache.org/latest*)
- Community Discord server (*https://sedona.apache.org/latest/community/contact*)
- Community forums (*https://discord.com/invite/EzW28RRj6x*)
- Apache Sedona on GitHub (*https://github.com/apache/sedona*)
- Book repository, with all examples used (*https://github.com/wherobots/apache-sedona-book*)

Summary

In this chapter we introduced Apache Sedona and the cloud native geospatial data ecosystem. We discussed how Apache Sedona evolved out of the need for a scalable geospatial-focused analytics framework and how Apache Sedona is architected to take advantage of distributed computation for processing large-scale geospatial data. We also reviewed the architecture of Apache Sedona and discussed the APIs for working with data in Apache Sedona.

Now that we have an understanding of what Apache Sedona is and what it is used for, in the next chapter we're ready to get hands on with Apache Sedona as we get started using Apache Sedona and spatial SQL.

## CHAPTER 2

Getting Started with Apache Sedona

In this chapter, you will learn how to do the following:

- Run, test, and deploy an Apache Sedona Python program.
- Get started with Apache Sedona using Docker.
- Use the spatial DataFrame data structure to work with data in Apache Sedona.
- Use spatial SQL to query and manipulate geospatial data.
- Visualize spatial data using SedonaKepler.

Throughout the book, we focus on the Apache Sedona OSS version. We primarily focus on the Jupyter Notebook environment, with some code also written as an Apache Sedona program that can be deployed and run on the cluster. We prepared many examples for the book, which you can find in the repository (*https://github.com/wherobots/apache-sedona-book*). Please follow the README file to run the examples properly. For convenience, we prepared docker-compose and CLI tools, which can be used interchangeably to run the examples for each chapter or subchapter. Most of the examples are in Python and SQL, but we also provide some Scala examples throughout the book. In Chapter 9, we also provide examples of how to use Apache Sedona with various cloud providers, such as AWS, GCP, or Azure.

How to Run the Apache Sedona Python Program

Apache Sedona is available on PyPI repositories (*https://oreil.ly/psbjI*) and conda (*https://oreil.ly/WuKy8*). You can install it using popular Python package managers like pip, uv, conda, or poetry. In this section, we will use uv, which is a powerful and fast Python package and project manager, written in Rust. Please follow the official documentation (*https://oreil.ly/LLDM0*) on how to install uv on your system.

To add Apache Sedona, simply use the following command:

```
uv add "apache-sedona[spark]"
```

Apache Sedona provides geospatial functionality to many systems, like Apache Spark, Apache Flink, and Snowflake. When we pass [spark] after the package name, we say that we want to include PySpark dependencies in our application.

Now we will create a simple application that only makes a geometry object from a well-known text (WKT) string (a geometry text representation). First and foremost, the goal is to create an Apache Sedona context:

```
from sedona.spark import SedonaContext

additional_packages = [
    "org.apache.sedona:sedona-spark-3.5_2.12:1.8.0",
    "org.datasyslab:geotools-wrapper:1.8.0-33.1"
]

config = SedonaContext.builder() \
    .config("spark.jars.packages", ",".join(additional_packages))

sedona = SedonaContext.create(config.getOrCreate())
```

Apache Sedona requires additional jars to function properly; you can provision them by adding the spark.jars.packages option to your Apache Sedona config, or copy jars to your existing Apache Spark cluster (*https://oreil.ly/lTmoA*) ($SPARK_HOME/jars).

Now we can provide the logic to create a geometry object from a WKT string:

```
wkt = "POINT(1 1)"

sedona.sql(
    f"SELECT ST_GeomFromWKT('{wkt}') AS geom"
).show()
```

To run the application, you can run a uv command in the root directory of the Apache Sedona Python project as follows:

```
uv run src/simple-app.py
```

This will produce the following DataFrame:

```
+-----------+
|       geom|
+-----------+
|POINT (1 1)|
+-----------+
```

Now, we will complicate the example a little bit. We will load data from a CSV file in an S3-compatible MinIO bucket, create a spatial DataFrame, perform a spatial join with some data wrangling, and save the data in Parquet format, also on MinIO. To ensure our application works as intended, we will write tests using the pytest framework. Finally, we will deploy the application to the Apache Spark cluster.

First, we start by loading the data from a CSV file. We will have additional discussion on possible data sources you can load in Apache Sedona in Chapter 3. We create a separate function to simplify the possibility of testing the code later:

```python
def load_places(sedona: SparkSession, location: str) -> DataFrame:
    places = sedona \
        .read \
        .format("csv") \
        .option("delimiter", "\t") \
        .load(location) \
        .selectExpr(
            "_c0 AS id",
            "_c1 AS category_code",
            "_c2 AS category_name",
            "_c3 AS name",
            "_c4 AS wkt",
        )

    return places
```

Our file has no header, and the column separator is tab (so our file is more like tab-separated values, or TSV). We perform simple column renaming and return the resulting DataFrame object. Then we need to filter our data to ATMs and restaurants. We will use those two place types to find the number of restaurants within a 500-meter radius of the ATMs. Again, we create an additional function:

```python
def get_places_by_category(places: DataFrame, category: str) -> DataFrame:
    return places \
        .filter(f"category_name = '{category}'") \
        .selectExpr(
            "id",
            """ST_Transform(
              ST_GeomFromWKT(wkt),
              'EPSG:4326',
              'EPSG:2180'
            ) AS geometry"""
        )
```

We reuse the same places DataFrame, which we loaded in the load_places function. As an additional parameter, we use the category in the filter expression to select only those records whose category matches. The last step is to convert the WKT string to the Sedona internal geometry object. We use the ST_GeomFromWKT function to achieve this; additionally, we transform the data to the EPSG:2180 coordinate reference system (CRS) (more on CRS in Chapter 4), which enables the use of metric-based coordinates, simplifying the spatial join condition.

Our final transformation involves saving the data to an Apache Parquet file, followed by spatially joining ATMs and restaurants within a 500-meter radius to determine the number of restaurants for each ATM within this radius:

```
def get_atm_within_distance_to_restaurant(
        sedona: SparkSession,
        atms: DataFrame,
        restaurants: DataFrame
) -> DataFrame:
    atms.createOrReplaceTempView("atms")

    restaurants.createOrReplaceTempView("restaurants")

    sedona.sql("Spatial Join SQL") \
        .createOrReplaceTempView("nearby_atms_and_restaurants")

    return sedona.sql("aggregate SQL")
```

We take three arguments: the Sedona context and the atms and restaurants Data-Frames. We create the temporary views based on DataFrames to use them inside the SQL queries. The spatial join is as follows:

```
SELECT
    a.id AS atm_id,
    r.id AS restaurant_id,
    a.geometry AS geometry
FROM atms a
JOIN restaurants r ON ST_DWithin(a.geometry, r.geometry, 500)
```

We take the atms table view and join it with the restaurants table view based on the ST_DWithin condition, which matches within a 500-meter radius. You will learn more about spatial relations in Chapter 4. We had to transform the data to metric to use a simple planar distance function. ST_DWithin allows you to join based on the distance on a spheroid, but it's slower. We will show more examples in Chapter 10, where you will learn about optimizations in Apache Sedona.

Before storing the data in Apache Parquet, we need to aggregate it by atm_id. We take the first geometry and count the number of restaurant_ids:

```
SELECT
    atm_id,
    FIRST (geometry) AS geometry,
    COUNT (restaurant_id) AS number_of_restaurants
FROM nearby_atms_and_restaurants
GROUP BY atm_id
```

The last step is to store the result in the Parquet format:

```
number_of_restaurants.write \
    .format("parquet") \
    .mode("overwrite") \
    .save(output_path)
```

If you want to see the whole application, please go to the official repository. We added arguments to the Python application to enable easy switching of input and output paths:

```
uv run src/app.py --places_location path --output_path path
```

Now let's write a simple test and run it. We will write tests for each function, but here we only show tests for `get_atm_within_distance_to_restaurant`; you can find all of them in the repository prepared for this book. In the function signature, we have the Sedona context, `atms` DataFrame, and the `restaurants` DataFrame.

The test signature takes one argument, the Sedona context, which will be provided via the pytest fixtures (*https://oreil.ly/I1c8K*):

```
def test_get_atm_within_distance_to_restaurant(
        sedona_session: SparkSession
)
```

The pytest fixture definition is as follows:

```
@pytest.fixture
def sedona_session() -> SparkSession:
    # create and return Sedona context here
    return sedona
```

To create a spatial DataFrame using a function, you can use Shapely objects, so our `atms` DataFrame in tests looks as follows:

```
from shapely.geometry import Point
from sedona.spark.sql.st_functions import ST_Transform
from pyspark.sql.functions import col, lit

atms = sedona.createDataFrame(
    [
        (1, "ATM A", Point(19.003, 50.003)),
        (2, "ATM B", Point(19.8, 50.1)),
        (3, "ATM C", Point(19.7, 50.2))
    ],
    ["id", "name", "geometry"]
).select(
```

```
        "id",
        "name",
        ST_Transform(
            col("geometry"),
            lit("EPSG:4326"),
            lit("EPSG:2180")
        ).alias("geometry")
    )
```

We use the Sedona context and call the `createDataFrame` method, passing a list of Python tuples as the argument. Each tuple element represents a value in a specific row. We also pass the column names. We pass the point geometries, using world coordinates. We would like to cast them to the metric CRS system used in the application code. We similarly create the `restaurants` DataFrame. Next in the tests, we call the test function by passing the essential arguments:

```
result = get_atm_within_distance_to_restaurant(
    sedona=sedona_session,
    atms=atms,
    restaurants=restaurants
)
```

The last step in the tests is to write some assertions to make sure that the result is what we expect:

```
values = result.collect()

assert len(values) == 1
assert values[0].atm_id == 1
assert values[0].number_of_restaurants == 3
assert round(values[0].geometry.x, 3) == 500214.923
assert round(values[0].geometry.y, 3) == 237301.911
```

To run the tests, type the following command:

```
uv run pytest -s tests
```

This means we run the pytest framework inside the tests directory and use the -s flag to display the output sent to standard output.

The last step is to deploy our application on the existing Apache Spark cluster. We will use an Apache Spark local cluster using Docker containers. To run the application, we can run the `spark-submit` command (*https://oreil.ly/lTmoA*):

```
./spark-submit \
    --packages YOUR_MAVEN_PACKAGES_HERE \
    --conf CONFIGURATION_KEY=CONFIGURATION_VALUE \
    --conf CONFIGURATION_KEY=CONFIGURATION_VALUE \
    app.py --places_location s3a://sedona/points \
        --output_path s3a://sedona/output
```

To add Apache Sedona to your cluster, you can either provide the jars in the cluster or use the `--packages` flag to provision them from Maven coordinates. More on the installation of Apache Sedona in different providers can be found in Chapter 9. The `--packages` flag might look as follows for your Apache Sedona application:

```
SEDONA_SPARK=org.apache.sedona:sedona-spark-3.5_2.12:1.8.0

GEOTOOLS=org.datasyslab:geotools-wrapper:1.8.0-33.1

--packages $SEDONA_SPARK,$GEOTOOLS
```

You can add Sedona-specific configuration properties like `sedona.join.autoBroad castJoinThreshold` to your application. More on optimizing Apache Sedona applications can be found in Chapter 10.

Finally, we pass the name of the Python script we want to submit. Our script also takes two additional parameters, so we pass them just after the script. For a complete example, please follow the official examples prepared for the book. That's it, you have submitted your first Apache Sedona application.

The Apache Sedona Docker Image

Although manual installation of Apache Sedona may seem complicated, you can simplify the process by running the provided Apache Sedona Docker image. If you're not familiar with Docker, it's an open source tool designed to automate the deployment, scaling, and management of applications by "containerizing" applications and their dependencies into lightweight and portable "containers" that can run consistently across operating systems and environments.

Docker images are read-only templates used to create containers. They contain the application and its dependencies and are built from a set of instructions written in a Dockerfile. You can learn more about Docker, including installation instructions, at the official website (*https://docker.com*).

The maintainers of Apache Sedona publish an official Apache Sedona Docker image that bundles Apache Sedona, Apache Spark, Jupyter, Python, and other dependencies of Sedona. The benefits of using the official Apache Sedona Docker image include:

Ease of setup
The image comes pre-configured with all necessary dependencies, reducing the complexity of setting up a Sedona environment manually.

Consistency
The Docker image ensures a consistent environment across different environments, minimizing the risk of configuration issues on different machines.

Isolation

   Docker containers provide isolation from the host system and other containers, ensuring Sedona runs in a clean environment without conflicts.

Portability

   The Docker image can run on any system that supports Docker, including local machines, on-premises servers, and cloud platforms, facilitating easy deployment.

The official Apache Sedona Docker image is a convenient way to get started with Apache Sedona and is suitable for development and testing on a single machine, but it is not designed to take advantage of the highly scalable benefits of running spatial operations across a distributed cluster of machines. To leverage the distributed benefits of Sedona, we will take advantage of cloud services such as Wherobots Cloud, AWS EMR, and Microsoft Fabric.

To get started with the Apache Sedona Docker image, first pull the image from DockerHub using the `docker pull` command, optionally specifying a version. This will download the Docker images from the DockerHub remote repository to the local machine.

For example, to pull the latest image use the `latest` tag:

```
docker pull apache/sedona:latest
```

As of the time of writing, version 1.8.0 is the latest Apache Sedona release so we will use this version by specifying it in the `docker pull` command:

```
docker pull apache/sedona:1.8.0
```

Next, to run the Docker image we use the `docker run` command, specifying configuration options for binding ports from the local machine to the container as well as memory allocation:

```
docker run -e DRIVER_MEM=6g -e EXECUTOR_MEM=8g \
-p 8888:8888 -p 8080:8080 -p 8081:8081 \
-p 4040:4040 apache/sedona:1.8.0
```

Let's break down this command to see what each piece is doing:

`docker run`

   This is the Docker command used to create and start a new container from a specified image.

`-e DRIVER_MEM=6g`

   This flag sets an environment variable inside the container that specifies the amount of memory allocated to the driver process.

`-e EXECUTOR_MEM=8g`

   This flag indicates the executor process should use 8 gigabytes of memory.

`-p 8888:8888`
> This flag maps port 8888 on the host machine to port 8888 on the container. This is used to expose the Jupyter Notebook environment running in the container to the host machine.

`-p 4040:4040`
> This flag maps port 4040 on the host to port 4040 on the container, which exposes Spark UI, a web-based interface for monitoring and managing Spark applications.

`apache/sedona:1.8.0`
> This is the image name and tag.

After starting the Docker container, open a browser window and navigate to *http://localhost:8888*. This will open the Jupyter Notebook environment, which will be our main development interface for Apache Sedona.

Overview of the Notebook Environment

Apache Sedona Docker provides a Jupyter Notebook environment, ideal for experimenting with the tool and conducting exploratory analysis using Apache Sedona and the Python ecosystem.

Jupyter Notebook is an open source web application that enables users to create and share documents that can contain code, visualizations, narrative text, and interactive elements. It is widely used in data science, scientific computing, and machine learning environments for its ability to mix code execution with explanatory text. Notebooks can be checked into version control such as Git and published to the web to be shared with others.

Jupyter notebooks serve as a powerful development interface for Apache Sedona, enabling data practitioners to interactively develop, execute, and visualize spatial data processing workflows.

Within the Jupyter notebook we can work with Apache Sedona using either Python or Scala. Python is our language of choice used throughout this book. Using Python allows us to take advantage of Sedona's integration with Python tooling both in the geospatial realm and the general Python data ecosystem.

Let's take a hands-on approach to introduce some of the basic steps for getting started when working with Sedona. If you haven't already, follow the steps in "The Apache Sedona Docker Image" on page 27 to launch the official Sedona Docker container. Then open a web browser and navigate to *http://localhost:8888*.

First, create a new Python notebook in Jupyter and add the following code in the first cell to initialize your Sedona environment:

```
from sedona.spark import *

config = SedonaContext \
    .builder() \
    .master("spark://localhost:7077") \
    .getOrCreate()

sedona = SedonaContext.create(config)
```

This will initialize the Sedona cluster. Other common configuration options at this step include configuring access to cloud object storage such as AWS S3. We'll see how this works in the next chapter when we cover working with files.

In the previous chapter we introduced the concept of the spatial DataFrame. Let's take a deeper look at this important data structure.

The Spatial DataFrame

While there are a few different data structures available for working with Sedona, the most performant and robust is the spatial DataFrame, which is a two-dimensional tabular data structure that organizes data into rows and columns similar to a table in a relational database. Spatial DataFrames are distributed data structures, meaning the underlying data is distributed across machines in the cluster, enabling operations on massive datasets. The spatial DataFrame is an extension of the standard DataFrame you may be familiar with but adds additional functionality for working with spatial data, notably support for spatial data types and spatial operations.

Spatial DataFrames support both *spatial SQL*–based operations for querying and manipulating data and a more imperative interface known as the *DataFrame API*.

Typically we construct spatial DataFrames by loading data from the storage layer, but let's create a simple example to familiarize ourselves with the basic concepts. In the next chapter we'll introduce how to load data from files.

Now we are ready to create a new DataFrame, `cities_df`, which will contain a city name and its longitude and latitude:

```
cities_df = sedona \
    .createDataFrame(
        [
            ("San Francisco", -122.4191, 37.7749),
            ("New York", -74.0060, 40.7128),
            ("Austin", -97.7431, 30.2672)
        ],
        ["city", "longitude", "latitude"]
    )
```

```
cities_df.show()
+-------------+---------+--------+
|         city|longitude|latitude|
+-------------+---------+--------+
|San Francisco|-122.4191| 37.7749|
|     New York|  -74.006| 40.7128|
|       Austin| -97.7431| 30.2672|
+-------------+---------+--------+
```

We can view the schema of this DataFrame with the `printSchema()` method:

```
cities_df.printSchema()
root
 |-- city: string (nullable = true)
 |-- longitude: double (nullable = true)
 |-- latitude: double (nullable = true)
```

Note that the `Longitude` and `Latitude` types are doubles, not a geometry or "point" type. To take advantage of Sedona's functionality for working with spatial data we'll make use of a *spatial SQL* function to add a new column to the DataFrame, leveraging Sedona's geometry type.

There are two APIs for working with data in a spatial DataFrame: using *spatial SQL* and using the *DataFrame API*. In this chapter we will explore both options for working with data in Sedona's spatial DataFrame, first using spatial SQL.

Introduction to Spatial SQL

Spatial SQL is a set of extensions to the Structured Query Language (SQL) that allows for the processing and analysis of spatial data within a table-based data environment, such as an RDBMS.[1]

Spatial SQL builds upon the core SQL language by introducing new data types, functions, and operators to handle the unique requirements of spatial data. This enables data practitioners and applications to perform a wide range of spatial queries, spatial joins, spatial aggregations, and spatial analyses with a familiar SQL syntax and environment.

Since spatial SQL implementations are based on the same standard, applications leveraging spatial SQL are portable and minimal updates are needed to migrate from one system to another. The spatial SQL standard was first published in 1999. It has since matured with multiple updates and has been adopted by a number of implementations, including PostGIS and Apache Sedona. The spatial SQL standard consistently uses the

---

1 The official specification for spatial SQL is known as ISO/IEC 13249-3 SQL/MM Part 3: Spatial and was originally derived from the Open Geospatial Consortium Simple Features Specification for SQL.

prefix ST_ for all function names. This prefix originally stood for "Spatial Type" as the early version of the standard intended to cover spatiotemporal functionality as well; however, this was dropped in favor of the SQL/Temporal standard.

Unfortunately, the scope of the spatial SQL standard does not include raster data. Apache Sedona spatial SQL functions use the prefix convention RS_ for functions that use raster data, a convention that may not be shared with other systems.

Spatial SQL functions can be grouped as belonging to one of the following four categories:

Constructors
Convert between geometries and external data formats. For example, ST_Geom FromWKT(string) to construct a geometry from a well-known text (WKT) string.

Functions
Retrieve properties or measures from a geometry or compare two geometries with respect to their spatial relationship. For example, ST_Distance(A, B) to compute the distance between two geometries *A* and *B*.

Aggregations
Returns the aggregated value on the given column. For example, ST_Union_Aggr(A) returns the union of all polygons in column *A*.

Predicates
Returns *true* or *false* after evaluating a logic judgment based on spatial relationships. For example, ST_Contains(A, B) to check if geometry *A* fully contains geometry *B*. Spatial predicate functions are often used in spatial joins or spatial range queries.

To execute a spatial SQL statement that references cities_df, we will first create a temporary view of the DataFrame:

```
cities_df.createOrReplaceTempView("cities")
```

This will allow us to reference cities_df as a view in our SQL queries. To run a spatial SQL query we use the sedona.sql method, passing in our query. A new spatial DataFrame will be returned.

As noted previously, so far our cities_df DataFrame is using double types to represent longitude and latitude. To take advantage of the spatial functionality of this data we want the location information of each row to be represented as a *geometry* type. Our first spatial SQL statement will use the ST_Point function to create point geometries from the latitude and longitude representations:

```
cities_df = sedona \
    .sql("""
        SELECT
            *,
            ST_Point(longitude, latitude) AS geometry
        FROM cities
    """)

cities_df.show(truncate=False)
+-------------+---------+--------+-------------------------+
|city         |longitude|latitude|geometry                 |
+-------------+---------+--------+-------------------------+
|San Francisco|-122.4191|37.7749 |POINT (-122.4191 37.7749)|
|New York     |-74.006  |40.7128 |POINT (-74.006 40.7128)  |
|Austin       |-97.7431 |30.2672 |POINT (-97.7431 30.2672) |
+-------------+---------+--------+-------------------------+
```

Note that this query returns a new DataFrame and that we've overwritten our previous `cities_df` variable. Now, if we inspect the schema of our new DataFrame we can see that the `geometry` column is of type `geometry`. The `geometry` type supports point, linestring, polygon, and multi versions of each, as well as mixed geometry types. Spatial DataFrames can support multiple geometry typed columns.

We can view the schema of the new `cities_df` DataFrame, which will now include the `geometry` column:

```
cities_df.printSchema()
root
 |-- city: string (nullable = true)
 |-- longitude: double (nullable = true)
 |-- latitude: double (nullable = true)
 |-- geometry: geometry (nullable = true)
```

So far we've used the `ST_Point` constructor spatial SQL function to create a point geometry type column. Let's explore other ways to use spatial SQL to manipulate and create new geometries. We've seen the point geometry type, but we can also work with more complex geometries like polygons.

The `ST_Buffer` function will return a polygon where all points of the polygon are at least a given distance from all points of the input geometry, creating a buffer around the input geometry. Using the city point geometries as inputs, we'll use the `ST_Buffer` function to create buffers around each point with a radius of 1 km. For the third parameter to the `ST_Buffer` function, we pass as true, indicating that we are using the spheroid to calculate distances in meters—more on the spatial reference system and geography model in Chapter 4.

First, because we modified the `cities_df` DataFrame, we'll need to replace the temporary view `cities` that we defined earlier:

```
cities_df.createOrReplaceTempView("cities")
```

Now we create a new DataFrame that will contain the name of each city and a polygon geometry that represents the buffer:

```
buffer_df = sedona \
    .sql("""
        SELECT
            city,
            ST_Buffer(geometry, 1000, true) AS geometry
        FROM cities
    """)

buffer_df.show()
+-------------+--------------------+
|         city|            geometry|
+-------------+--------------------+
|San Francisco|POLYGON ((-122.40...|
|     New York|POLYGON ((-73.994...|
|       Austin|POLYGON ((-97.732...|
+-------------+--------------------+
```

Working with the DataFrame API

In addition to the SQL API, we can work with spatial DataFrames using a programmatic API known as the DataFrame API. Both methods allow us to manipulate and analyze data, but the DataFrame API can be more intuitive for developers familiar with programming languages like Python. The DataFrame API supports chaining multiple operations together in a more readable manner and supports many built-in functions. The DataFrame API may have a steeper learning curve for users not familiar with functional programming paradigms and writing complex queries can become cumbersome when compared to SQL.

Let's explore using the DataFrame API to create a linestring geometry connecting each city, such as a flight or train route between the cities. In SQL this statement would look like the following, making use of the ST_MakeLine function and the col lect_list SQL function, which creates an array of the individual point geometries from each row in the cities view:

```
SELECT
    ST_MakeLine(collect_list(geometry)) AS geometry
FROM cities
```

Now let's see how this would be accomplished using the programmatic DataFrame API. When using the DataFrame API, we first import the necessary Spark functions from the pyspark.sql.functions module and any spatial SQL functions from the sedona.sql.st_functions module. Then we can chain together these functions:

```
from sedona.sql.st_functions import ST_MakeLine
from pyspark.sql.functions import collect_list, col

route_df = cities_df.select(
    ST_MakeLine(collect_list(col("geometry"))).alias("geometry")
)

route_df.show(truncate=False)
+-----------------------------------------------------------------+
|geometry                                                         |
+-----------------------------------------------------------------+
|LINESTRING (-122.4191 37.7749, -74.006 40.7128, -97.7431 30.2672)|
+-----------------------------------------------------------------+
```

As the preceding example demonstrates, we can accomplish the same spatial operations with both spatial SQL and the DataFrame API. While choosing which form to use can sometimes be a personal preference, there are advantages and disadvantages to each approach.

Visualizing Data

When working with spatial data it can be important to visualize the data to help us interpret the results of our analysis or as a quality control to verify our data. There are several options for visualizing spatial data with Sedona, including many of the Python-based tools such as Matplotlib or Leafmap. We will explore some of these options later on in the book; however, the first spatial visualization tool we'll make use of is SedonaKepler.

SedonaKepler is an integration with the Kepler.gl visualization library and Apache Sedona that enables visualizing vector geospatial data overlaid over a basemap in an interactive map. We cover visualization in depth in Chapter 6.

Summary

In this chapter we took a deeper hands-on look at two important pieces of Apache Sedona: spatial SQL and the spatial DataFrame. Spatial SQL allows us to create, manipulate, and analyze spatial data using Sedona's spatial DataFrame. The spatial DataFrame is a distributed data structure that supports spatial data types and working with massive datasets. We also saw how to get started with Sedona using both the Apache Sedona Docker image and local installation. Docker is great to quickly start with Apache Sedona, but a standalone installation helps you develop an application and maintain it inside the Git repository.

We showed how you can create a simple Apache Sedona Python application, write tests for it, and ship it to an Apache Spark cluster.

So far we've limited our usage of Sedona to manually created small, trivial-sized examples, but in real-world analysis we typically encounter data in many different formats and sources. In the next chapter we'll see how to use Sedona to load, manipulate and analyze spatial data in many different formats including CSV, GeoJSON, shapefile, and Parquet. We'll also learn about the benefits of cloud native geospatial file formats like GeoParquet, Apache Parquet, and Apache Iceberg, and see how to use Sedona to create and query spatial datasets using GeoParquet. Following is some additional documentation to expand on the concepts discussed in this chapter:

- Spatial SQL function documentation (*https://oreil.ly/Hrejq*)
- SedonaKepler documentation (*https://oreil.ly/6ClNq*)
- Sedona Docker documentation (*https://oreil.ly/CfSI4*)

## CHAPTER 3

Loading Geospatial Data into Apache Sedona

For many years the shapefile was the primary geospatial file format. It worked well for smaller datasets and when people analyzed data on local machines. Because modern technology changes rapidly and data proliferates, shapefiles are no longer sufficient due to the lack of support for complex data types like arrays, hard-to-maintain files, scaling issues, column name limits, and much more. People tried to fix the bottlenecks of shapefiles by introducing new data formats such as GeoJSON and GeoPackage. These are suitable data formats in some instances, but also have limitations. In recent years, we have seen the rise of GeoParquet as a standard for storing geospatial analytical data. This helped unlock the native geospatial support in Apache Parquet and Apache Iceberg formats.

Any mature analytical system must allow users to load data from the most common data formats, and Sedona provides this capability. However, some of the data formats mentioned here are not well designed for distributed systems.

In this chapter, we will discuss the foundations of geospatial data formats, such as data serialization techniques like well-known binary and well-known text. We will also discuss which formats to use when processing data efficiently in a distributed fashion.

In the first part of this chapter, we will discuss challenges related to storing tabular vector data formats. Then, we will review vector data serialization techniques and discuss how Apache Sedona does that for the internal data model. Finally, we will look step by step at how to load popular vector data formats into spatial DataFrames.

The second part focuses on the raster data format and how to load GeoTIFF files to Apache Sedona. The last example of that section shows how you can easily combine raster and vector data in Apache Sedona.

Reading data from databases is a frequent task in the data engineering space, and that's what the third part covers. In the last section of this chapter, we will put our knowledge into practice and prepare analytics code for the New York Taxi dataset.

Loading Vector Data Formats

Storing geospatial data is challenging, but concisely describing geospatial data is even more challenging. When considering that we might analyze billions of records in a DataFrame, we need to ensure that we can write data relatively quickly and possibly reduce the space required to transfer data over the network and data storage on the disk. We can distinguish a few complexities when storing geospatial data:

- The number of points that giant polygons or linestrings might have.
- Storing data with multiple dimensions.
- In complex geometry shapes, polygons might have many holes, which we need to encode.
- Many different geometry types: point, polygon, linestring, circle, triangle.
- Coordinate reference systems (CRSs) (we can't compare data from different CRSs).

Before beginning a step-by-step explanation on how to load data into a geospatial DataFrame, we will introduce commonly used geospatial serialization methods and how Apache Sedona is suited to those techniques. It's important to understand common methods as they might help you later when dealing with data sources that you are not familiar with and that Sedona doesn't support.

> *Loading* and *reading* are used interchangeably in this book.

Vector Data Serialization

Vector data serialization is a process of transforming geospatial objects into a byte array. Two well-known ways of storing geospatial data are *well-known text (WKT)* and *well-known binary (WKB)*. The Open Geospatial Consortium (OGC) initially defined and described the formats in their Simple Feature Access. The current standard definition is in the ISO/IEC 13249-3:2016 standard.

WKT uses strings to represent geometry in a concise way that is easy for humans to read. It can describe objects like polygons, multiline strings, or points in two, three, or four dimensions.

An example WKT string looks like this:

```
LINESTRING (
  20.9972017 52.1696936,
  20.9971687 52.1696659,
  20.997156 52.169644,
  20.9971487 52.1696213
)
```

Due to margin limitations, we had to split the WKT string into multiple lines; most libraries should be able to parse it, but not all.

WKB represents geospatial data in a binary format and helps reduce the size of stored and transferred data. It supports various shapes, such as polygons, linestrings, points, circles, curves, and many more. WKB can also store information about the CRS, and similarly to WKT, it has E as a prefix, which stands for extended (EWKB, EWKT).

Let's try to encode a linestring to WKB:

```
LINESTRING (
  20.9972017 52.1696936,
  20.9971687 52.1696659,
  20.997156 52.169644,
  20.9971487 52.1696213
)

01 ❶
02 00 00 00 ❷
04 00 00 00 ❸
FF 03 51 9C 48 FF 34 40 96 2B 17 85 B8 15 4A 40  ❹
47 18 AB 72 46 FF 34 40 8A DF B9 9C B7 15 4A 40
9B 02 99 9D 45 FF 34 40 37 FB 03 E5 B6 15 4A 40
B9 BF 1F 23 45 FF 34 40 3E 1A 98 26 B6 15 4A 40
```

❶ The first-byte stores information about byte order: 00 is big-endian, and 01 is little-endian.

❷ The next four bytes encode the geometry type, which is, in our case, LINESTRING.

❸ The next four bytes represent the number of points for a linestring.

❹ Four pairs with 16 bytes each (x, y coordinates of 8 bytes for each double value).

FF 03 51 9C 48 FF 34 40 96 2B 17 85 B8 15 4A 40 corresponds to the pair (20.9972017, 52.1696936), which you can see in our linestring.

Apache Sedona Serialization

Apache Sedona uses a custom serialization method to convert geometry data into a byte array. Natively, Apache Sedona supports (multi)points, (multi)linestrings, (multi)polygons, and geometry collection. We can store 2D and 3D objects and measure the value for each geometry.

Serializing data starts by combining the geometry type, dimension type (XY, XYZ, XYZM, XYM), and information about whether the geometry spatial reference identifier (SRID) has been specified using efficient byte shift operations. That's the first byte. Next, if we have the SRID specified, we put 3 bytes for the SRID and then the number of coordinates as the next 4 bytes. Then, based on geometry type, we encode coordinates, internal rings, etc. Let's try understanding it based on a linestring with two dimensions and 4326 SRID. We'll use the same example as previously:

```
LINESTRING (
  20.9972017 52.1696936,
  20.9971687 52.1696659,
  20.997156 52.169644,
  20.9971487 52.1696213
)

23 ❶
00 10 E6  ❷
04 00 00 00 ❸
FF 03 51 9C 48 FF 34 40 96 2B 17 85 B8 15 4A 40 ❹
47 18 AB 72 46 FF 34 40 8A DF B9 9C B7 15 4A 40
9B 02 99 9D 45 FF 34 40 37 FB 03 E5 B6 15 4A 40
B9 BF 1F 23 45 FF 34 40 3E 1A 98 26 B6 15 4A 40
```

❶ Combination of geometry type (linestring), coordinate type (XY), and information if the SRID is present

❷ Encoded SRID

❸ Number of coordinates

❹ Pairs of x,y coordinates

Differences Between Vector Data Formats

Massive geospatial analytics is not very different from analyzing other types of data. The most popular and efficient formats for that purpose are distributed columnar files, which can help you quickly select the desired set of columns and analyze them in a distributed way. The most popular data formats that meet those criteria are Apache Parquet with native geospatial support and GeoParquet—we will cover them in more detail in Chapter 8. We also expect that GeoParquet will be less and less used due to the recent changes in the Apache Parquet specs.

The specifications for both Iceberg and Parquet are merged, but they are not yet fully integrated. Once they are integrated, we will update the code examples in the repository (*https://github.com/wherobots/apache-sedona-book*). Because this transformation is not quite complete, we do not include spatial Parquet or Iceberg in this section.

GeoParquet is a new concept that arises from the need to process vast amounts of geospatial data efficiently for analytics. It has become a de facto standard in geospatial processing, but there are still many data sources in different data formats. When you want to integrate them with your spatial data lakehouse, you need a framework that exposes multiple APIs to load data from the most popular data formats. With Apache Sedona, you can load data directly from:

- Shapefiles
- GeoPackage
- GeoParquet
- GeoJSON
- WKB
- Flat files with WKT (CSV, TSV)
- OpenStreetMap (OSM) Protobuf files

Using third-party libraries, you can also load:

- XML

One project that made geospatial data more accessible is the OpenStreetMap (OSM) project (*https://www.openstreetmap.org*). It's developed and maintained by volunteers who collect data from satellite images and surveys or import from open data sources. You can find data in OSM like buildings, POIs, rivers, roads, and more. On top of the open data, multiple other projects exist, like open routing or even the Overture Maps Foundation. The OSM project shares the data via various formats, like XML, but one of the most popular is OSM pbf, which is lighter than XML. Throughout the book, we will often use the OpenStreetMap project data.

Distributed Versus Nondistributed Files

Let's try to understand the difference between distributed and nondistributed files. Imagine you are storing geospatial data in GeoJSON and creating one file on your hard disk. That makes it less efficient when you want to distribute your data across many machines, as initially you need to split the data into chunks on the driver node (your driver node needs to be bigger) or copy all the data to worker nodes (which requires additional space). That's why distributed computing engines like Apache Spark mostly rely on files like Apache Parquet or ORC to store compressed data in smaller sizes, usually 128 MB up to 1 GB.

When using Apache Sedona to process and analyze mid-sized to massive datasets, it is highly recommended that you use distributed formats such as Parquet or a tabular format like Apache Iceberg.

Normally, when you load single files, you see in your directory:

```
geometry
    └── gis_osm_roads_free_1.json
```

You would rather have something like this when you want to optimize your data for parallel data processing:

```
geometry
    └─distributed
          ├─part-00000-8cd272bd-a8bb-4163-9fbb-9a2b2834a422-c000.snappy.parquet
          ├─part-00001-8cd272bd-a8bb-4163-9fbb-9a2b2834a422-c000.snappy.parquet
          ├─part-00002-8cd272bd-a8bb-4163-9fbb-9a2b2834a422-c000.snappy.parquet
          └─part-00003-8cd272bd-a8bb-4163-9fbb-9a2b2834a422-c000.snappy.parquet
```

Reading Flat Files

There are at least a few ways of storing geospatial data in flat files like CSV or TSV files, which are easy to use because you can store longitude and latitude as separate columns. However, things get tricky for more complex geometries like polygons or linestrings. To safely store data (CSV parsing as a pair of points might be separated by commas), it is better to use the WKT format and quote the geometries so that data will not be corrupted for data consumers. Another method is using tab-separated files, which do not collide with how the WKT format is described.

> Flat files can be easily distributed for workloads, but they are schemaless, so if you don't know the exact schema, Apache Spark needs to waste cycles inferring it. Another drawback is the vast size occupied on the disk. You can try gzip compression, but using columnar formats like GeoParquet is still better.

Now, let's try to read the CSV file using the WKT column. Our file content looks like the following:

```
"osm_id","wkt"
"4326379","LINESTRING (21.01921 52.171363, 21.0190588 52.1713167)"
"4326702","LINESTRING (20.9883374 52.197691, 20.9882718 52.1975611)"
"4308966","LINESTRING (20.9975912 52.1851127, 20.9975981 52.1848)"
```

We use a CSV file prepared in the Docker image. Please follow the README file prepared for this chapter:

```
import sedona.sql.functions as sf

sedona.read \
    .format("csv") \
    .option("header", "true") \
    .option("quote", '"') \
    .load(path) \
    .withColumn("wkt", sf.ST_GeomFromText("wkt")) \
    .show()
```

As a result, we get a spatial DataFrame with a corresponding schema:

```
+----------+----------------------+
| osm_id   |                   wkt|
+----------+----------------------+
| 4326379  | LINESTRING (21.01...)|
| 4326702  | LINESTRING (20.98...)|
| 4308966  | LINESTRING (20.99...)|
| 4311409  | LINESTRING (21.00...)|
| 4315349  | LINESTRING (21.00...)|
| 4317242  | LINESTRING (20.98...)|
+----------+----------------------+

root
 |-- osm_id: string (nullable = true)
 |-- wkt: geometry (nullable = true)
```

Reading Shapefiles

Shapefiles, an open format created by ESRI, are still the most popular geospatial data format. It's a vector data format that can store primitive data types like points, lines, and polygons but cannot store topological information. It contains a set of files, some of which are mandatory and some of which are optional (see Table 3-1).

Table 3-1. Contents of a shapefile[a]

File extension	Description	Mandatory or optional
.shp	The spatial data itself (vector data)	Mandatory
.shx	The shape index format	Mandatory
.dbf	Other nongeometry attributes related to the shape	Mandatory
.prj	Information about the projection	Optional

[a] For a better understanding of each file extension, please refer to the official ESRI documentation (*https://oreil.ly/xnorC*).

Shapefiles are not recommended for storing geospatial data for analytics, especially when analyzing vast amounts of data. It has many drawbacks, like its relatively large size compared to the Parquet format, its limitation on column names, and its inability to store nested columns.

With Apache Sedona, you can quickly load your shapefile from a folder or a single file on your local machine or any cloud object storage like S3:

```
sedona.read \
    .format("shapefile") \
    .load(path) \
    .select("osm_id", "geometry") \
    .show(5)

+-------+--------------------+
| osm_id|            geometry|
+-------+--------------------+
|4307220|LINESTRING (21.01...|
|4307329|LINESTRING (20.99...|
|4307330|LINESTRING (20.99...|
|4308966|LINESTRING (20.99...|
|4308968|LINESTRING (21.01...|
+-------+--------------------+
```

Reading GeoJSON

JSON is a popular data exchange format with various uses, from configuration files to data serialization. It is easy for humans to read, but it comes with the cost of a relatively large amount of disk space needed to store it. By its nature, JSON is not distributed, and it lacks a schema, which is a significant drawback for distributed analytics and data loading.

GeoJSON is a spatial extension of the JSON data format that supports polygon, point, and linestring geometries and their multi-equivalents. It encodes geospatial and nongeospatial data in three major fields: properties, geometry, and type.[1]

---

1 For the full specification, refer to *https://geojson.org*.

A point feature described in GeoJSON looks like this:

```
{
  "type": "Feature",
  "geometry": {
    "type": "Point",
    "coordinates": [-111.763382, 34.872260]
  },
  "properties": {
    "name": "Apache Sedona",
    "type": "Distributed Geospatial Data processing engine"
  }
}
```

You are more likely to find more complex examples like the following, where you can see more than one feature gathered in the `FeatureCollection` type:

```
{
    "type": "FeatureCollection",
    "features": [
    {
        "type": "Feature",
        "geometry": {
            "type": "Point",
            "coordinates": [102.0, 0.5]
        },
        "properties": {
            "prop0": "value0"
        }
    },
    {
        "type": "Feature",
        "geometry": {
            "type": "Point",
            "coordinates": [102.0, 0.5]
        },
        "properties": {
            "prop0": "value0"
        }
    }]
}
```

You can use the following code to load a GeoJSON file in Apache Sedona:

```
sedona.read \
    .format("geojson") \
    .option("multiLine", "true") \
    .load(path) \
    .show(5)
```

```
+--------------------+--------------------+-------------+----------------+
|                 crs|            features|         name|            type|
+--------------------+--------------------+-------------+----------------+
|{{urn:ogc:def:crs...|[{MULTILINESTRING...|masovia_roads|FeatureCollection|
+--------------------+--------------------+-------------+----------------+
```

From this, we get access only to the top level of the GeoJSON file. To get the actual data, we need to "melt" feature data into new rows, so the final code might look as follows:

```
sedona.read \
    .format("geojson") \
    .option("multiLine", "true") \
    .load(path) \
    .selectExpr("explode(features) as features") \
    .select("features.geometry", "features.properties.osm_id") \
    .show(5)
```

This is the resulting DataFrame:

```
+--------------------+-------+
|            geometry| osm_id|
+--------------------+-------+
|MULTILINESTRING (...|4307220|
|MULTILINESTRING (...|4307329|
|MULTILINESTRING (...|4307330|
|MULTILINESTRING (...|4308966|
|MULTILINESTRING (...|4308968|
+--------------------+-------+
```

> GeoJSON is not a distributed file format. When loading a large file, you might encounter heap memory issues from the Apache Spark driver node. To overcome that, you can increase spark.driver.memory to a much larger value, like 2 GB. Please refer to Spark's official docs to find other possible configuration options.

Loading GeoJSON from a single file is not an optimal option because you load all the data on the driver node and then split it using the explode function to worker nodes. The explode function returns a new row for each element in an array or map data. What can you do to improve that? One way is to use the distributed GeoJSON format, which takes the top feature rows and stores each row as JSON in a new line:

```
{ "type": "Feature", "properties": { "osm_id": "4311413", "fclass": ...}
{ "type": "Feature", "properties": { "osm_id": "4315349", "fclass": ...}

sedona.read \
    .format("geojson") \
    .load(path) \
    .selectExpr("geometry", "properties.*") \
    .show(5)
```

```
+--------------------+-------+
|            geometry| osm_id|
+--------------------+-------+
|MULTILINESTRING (...|4311413|
|MULTILINESTRING (...|4315349|
|MULTILINESTRING (...|4307220|
|MULTILINESTRING (...|4307329|
|MULTILINESTRING (...|4307330|
+--------------------+-------+
```

Reading GeoPackage

GeoPackage is the standard for encoding geospatial data in SQLite file format. It gains the advantages of the SQLite file format, such as updating your data in place. GeoPackage also allows filtering your data based on the boundary box (or *bbox* for short), which is the rectangle area between two points, in most cases the bottom left corner and the top right corner. This significantly reduces the processing time. The GeoPackage specification allows the storage of vector and raster data. In this section, we will discuss vector data.

GeoPackage encodes vector data in an object containing the header and geometry. The header keeps metadata information like SRS information and the geometry boundary. Keeping the header separate from the WKB-encoded geometry object allows us to filter data before deserializing it and loading it into the internal data model. Let's look at the signature:

```
StandardGeoPackageBinary {
  GeoPackageBinaryHeader header;
  WKBGeometry geometry;
}
```

The GeoPackage file format was an idea to replace shapefile as the primary geospatial data format. It works well for single-machine data processing, e.g., GeoPandas, or any UI-based tool like ArcGIS or QGIS. However, it is not the recommended exchange data format for distributed frameworks and vast amounts of data, such as your ETL pipelines and analytics workloads.

Apache Sedona has implemented DataSourceV2 for GeoPackage, so you can easily access metadata and load your vector data.

You can write the following Sedona code to see precisely what tables the GeoPackage file contains. The GeoPackage file may contain multiple tables; with the following code you can see which tables can be read. It's suitable for files with unknown content:

```
sedona.read \
    .format("geopackage") \
    .option("showMetadata", "true") \
    .load(path) \
    .select("table_name", "data_type", "srs_id") \
    .show(5)

+--------------------+---------+------+
|          table_name|data_type|srs_id|
+--------------------+---------+------+
|gis_osm_roads_free_1| features|  4326|
+--------------------+---------+------+
```

Now that we know what the GeoPackage file contains, we can load and process it:

```
sedona.read \
    .format("geopackage") \
    .option("tableName", "gis_osm_roads_free_1") \
    .load(path) \
    .select("osm_id", "geom") \
    .show(5)

+-------+--------------------+
| osm_id|                geom|
+-------+--------------------+
|4307220|MULTILINESTRING (...|
|4307329|MULTILINESTRING (...|
|4307330|MULTILINESTRING (...|
|4308966|MULTILINESTRING (...|
|4308968|MULTILINESTRING (...|
+-------+--------------------+
```

Reading GeoParquet

GeoParquet is a columnar data format that extends Apache Parquet, allowing the storage of spatial vector data like points, lines, and polygons. It is a fully distributed file format that is digestible by Apache Spark. GeoParquet is the de facto standard for storing spatial analytics data and will be described in more detail in Chapter 8. Apache Sedona was one of the initial frameworks with native support for GeoParquet.

To load the GeoParquet data format, simply write the following code:[2]

```
sedona \
    .read \
    .format("geoparquet") \
    .load(path) \
    .show(5)
```

---

2 The GeoParquet standard has now been incorporated into the core Parquet format, meaning Sedona's Parquet and GeoParquet implementations will soon be fully equivalent.

```
+-------+--------------------+
| osm_id|            geometry|
+-------+--------------------+
|4307220|LINESTRING (21.01...|
|4307329|LINESTRING (20.99...|
|4307330|LINESTRING (20.99...|
|4308966|LINESTRING (20.99...|
|4308968|LINESTRING (21.01...|
+-------+--------------------+
```

The advantage of GeoParquet is predicate pushdown, which can help you skip some data files and drastically improve your query performance. Geoparquet encodes a bbox of the data inside the file in metadata. Then, when you read the data, Apache Sedona skips the files outside the specified filters. It's recommended that you sort geospatial data by its Geohash and keep geometries close to each other in the same file. With a random data split, you might end up with bboxes of the same size and place.

> For even more performant queries, consider using a covering field for your geospatial data. To understand this better, please refer to Chapter 8, which discusses the GeoParquet data format.

In the following example, let's download and prepare an Overture places dataset. You can download the dataset for this exercise using the Overture Maps command-line tool (*https://overturemaps.org*). In the example notebooks, the command line is already installed:

```
overturemaps download --bbox=left,bottom,right,top \
   -f geoparquet --type=place -o places.geoparquet
```

Let's store the dataset using predicate pushdown to reduce the number of files read. In our example, you will store data in GeoParquet format and order by Geohash (an indexing technique that will be covered in more detail in the next chapter):

```
sedona \
    .read \
    .format("geoparquet") \
    .load(path) \
    .withColumn("geohash", f.expr("ST_GeoHash(geometry, 2)")) \
    .orderBy("geohash") \
    .write \
    .format("geoparquet") \
    .save("target_path")
```

Now, let's visualize the boundary boxes of each of the files (Figure 3-1).

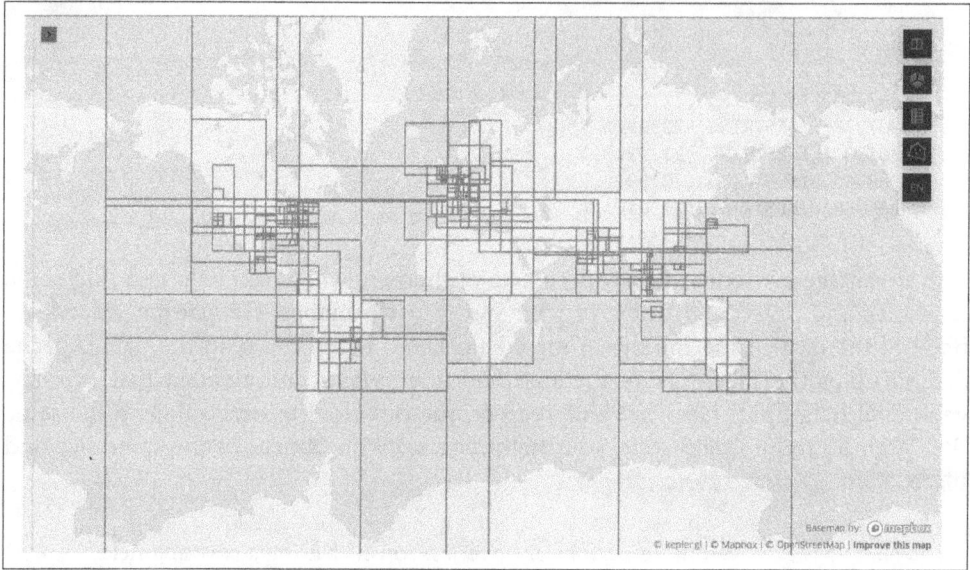

Figure 3-1. The boundary boxes for each of the files in `overture_places_sorted`

Loading all the data when you already know that you don't need everything is a waste of computer resources. You saved your data from Overture places for faster analytics later based on the boxes. Now let's test that in practice. We will try to load data for California, marked by the rectangle on Figure 3-2.

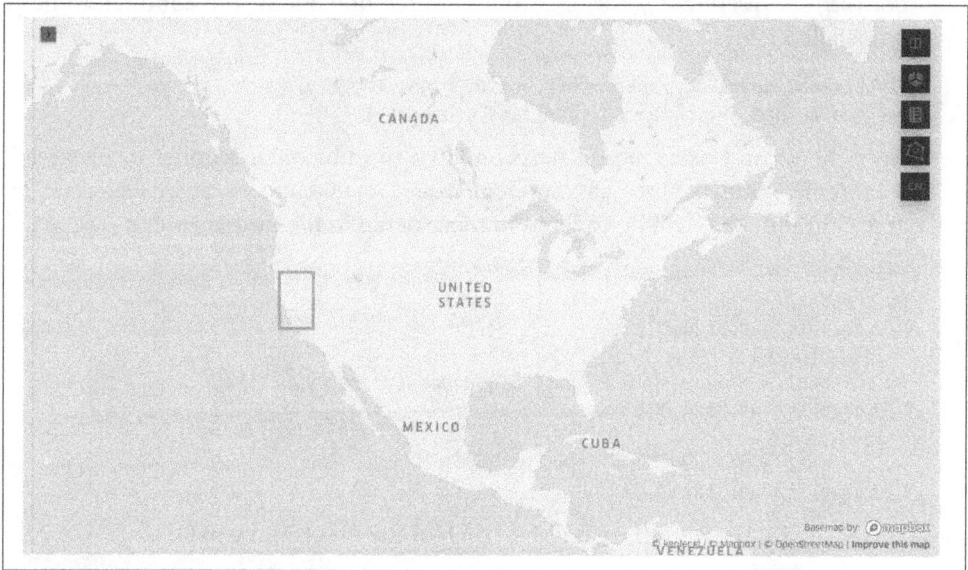

Figure 3-2. California filter range query polygon

The reduction of loaded files is significant, from 200 files to 7. Instead of loading all 200 files into memory, we read the bbox information from file metadata for each one of them and skip files whose bbox is outside the filter predicate (from version 1.1.0 GeoParquet spec, the bbox field is inside the covering field: more details in Chapter 8). Reading metadata is quick. Now let's follow the Apache Sedona code for a better understanding of the concept:

```
envelope_str = "-123.425407, 35.749839, -118.763583, 41.806623"

df = sedona \
    .read \
    .format("geoparquet") \
    .load(path) \
    .where(f"ST_Within(geometry, ST_PolygonFromEnvelope({envelope_str}))") \
    .selectExpr("brand.names.primary as name") \
    .groupBy("name") \
    .count()
```

In the example, we read the data from the GeoParquet location on the S3 bucket. Then we use the where statement to filter based on the predicate ST_Within (*it looks as if the geometry data is inside the second geometry*). To create a geometry from the envelope, we use the ST_PolygonFromEnvelope function. The last step is to select the names of the brands and calculate the count for data grouped by name.

We can examine if the predicate pushdown filter was properly applied by reading the Apache Spark physical plan (Apache Spark uses a tree structure to show all the transformations). To read the Spark physical plan, we need to run the explain method on the DataFrame created from GeoParquet files:

```
df.explain()

== Physical Plan ==
AdaptiveSparkPlan isFinalPlan=false
+- HashAggregate(keys=[name#12369], functions=[count(1)])
   +- Exchange hashpartitioning(name#12369, 200),
      ENSURE_REQUIREMENTS, [plan_id=4948]
      +- HashAggregate(keys=[name#12369], functions=[partial_count(1)])
         +- Project [brand#12350.names.primary AS name#12369]
            +- Filter (isnotnull(geometry#12339) AND
               **org.apache.spark.sql.sedona_sql.expressions.ST_Within** )
               +- FileScan geoparquet [geometry#12339...
                  DataFilters: [isnotnull(geometry#12339),
                  **org.apache.spark.sql.sedona_sql.expressions.ST_Within** ],
                  Format: GeoParquet with spatial filter
                  [geometry INTERSECTS POLYGON ((-123.425407 35.749839,
                  -123.425407 ...)],
                  Location: InMemoryFileIndex(1 paths)
                  [file:..cloud-geospatial/chapter3/d...,
                  PartitionFilters: [], PushedFilters: [IsNotNull(geometry)],
                  ReadSchema: struct<geometry:binary,
                  brand:struct<names:struct<primary:string>>>
```

The important line to us is `Format: GeoParquet with spatial filter` as it indicates that the spatial filter was applied when reading the GeoParquet file. The full line containing that text is bolded in the code.

We skip GeoParquet files based on the boundary box placed in the file. To see that in the Spark UI, you need to run the `show` method or any other that takes an action on the DataFrame. You can look at the mentioned UI in Figure 3-3. Apache Spark runs code using a technique called lazy evaluation, meaning it won't do any calculation until you invoke any action method on your DataFrame, like `show` or `count`. An exception to the rule is the `groupBy` method, as the count after it is not considered an action.

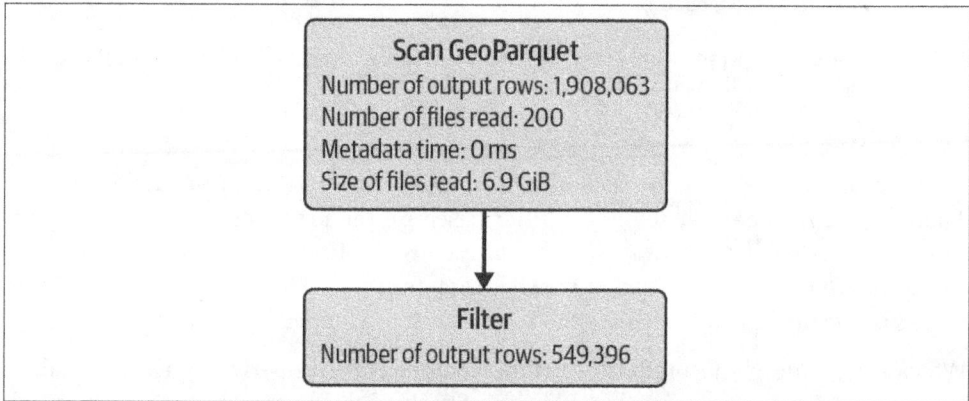

Figure 3-3. Spark processing graph showing GeoParquet predicate pushdown

Introduction to Raster Data Formats (GeoTIFF)

As discussed in Chapter 1, the raster data format represents spatial data using a matrix with columns and rows. The smallest part is a cell called a pixel. A raster might contain *n* matrices with the data, and each of the matrices is called a band. The definition might also suit a picture you can take using your phone, but there is a considerable difference when discussing spatial images called rasters; we add a spatial reference to them, meaning we can tell where they lay in our coordinate reference system. So, when we take a satellite or aerial image as an example, we can precisely say where each pixel lies on the Earth's surface. Thanks to that property, we can combine them with vector data to perform even more advanced analytics. So while a photo taken on your phone will only contain three bands, blue, green, and red (BGR), satellite images may contain many more, such as a thermal band.

In Figure 3-4, you can see a small piece of a satellite raster and one selected band. The raster is represented as a 2D array, and the smallest unit is a pixel defined by an array cell. Each pixel has its own value, and the figure is colored based on those values.

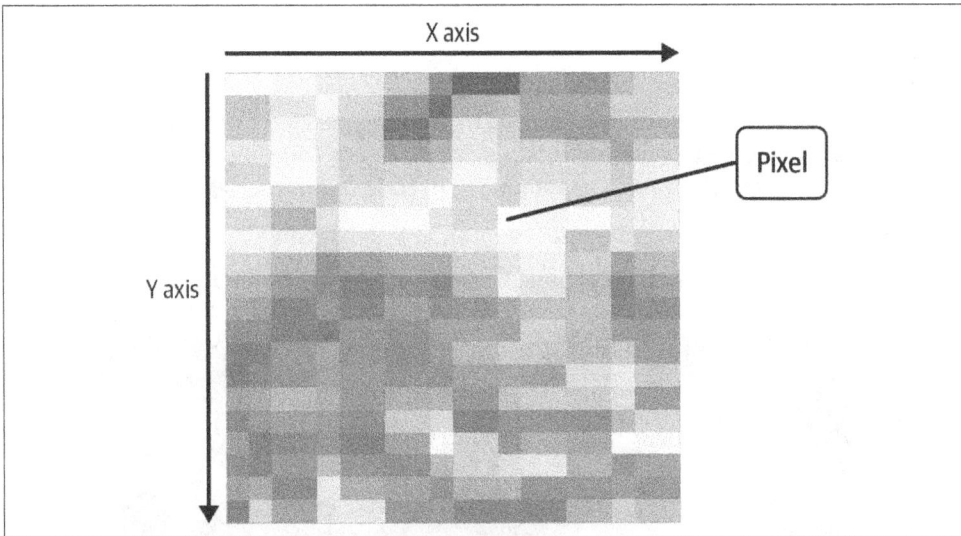

Figure 3-4. Small part of a raster showing pixels

A commonly used data format for storing geospatial raster data is GeoTIFF. GeoTIFF is an open metadata extension to the TIFF image format. It adds a geospatial reference to it, allowing the image to be located on the Earth's surface.

How Sedona Processes Rasters

For each of the DataFrame cells, Apache Sedona keeps one raster file in a cell. To keep data processing smoothly, we recommend either using a number for smaller GeoTIFF files or the RS_Tile function to split your huge image into smaller ones.

Let's load a GeoTIFF Landsat satellite image representing Japan and create simple map algebra statistics using Sedona for a specific vector area. We need to load the satellite image into a spatial DataFrame. We start by loading the raster file into a raw binary DataFrame:

```
geotiff_df = sedona \
    .read \
    .format("binaryFile") \
    .load(path)
```

Since it's a GeoTIFF file format, we can use the RS_FromGeoTiff function to load it into a spatial DataFrame:

```
geotiff_df \
    .selectExpr("RS_FromGeoTiff(content) AS raster") \
    .createOrReplaceTempView("japan")
```

We use the b02, b03, and b04 bands, the BGR (blue, green, red) channels from the Landsat satellite image. It is around 60 MB in size. If we try to process it directly, we end up with a Java heap space error message (all data is in one DataFrame cell, which is inefficient). To avoid that, we need to use the previously mentioned RS_Tile function. Another benefit of using it is the possibility of splitting our processing and doing it more efficiently. We can use simple SQL code to do that:

```
SELECT EXPLODE(RS_Tile(raster, 50, 50)) AS tile FROM japan
```

Now, we can do map algebra on terrain checked by a polygon (Figure 3-5).

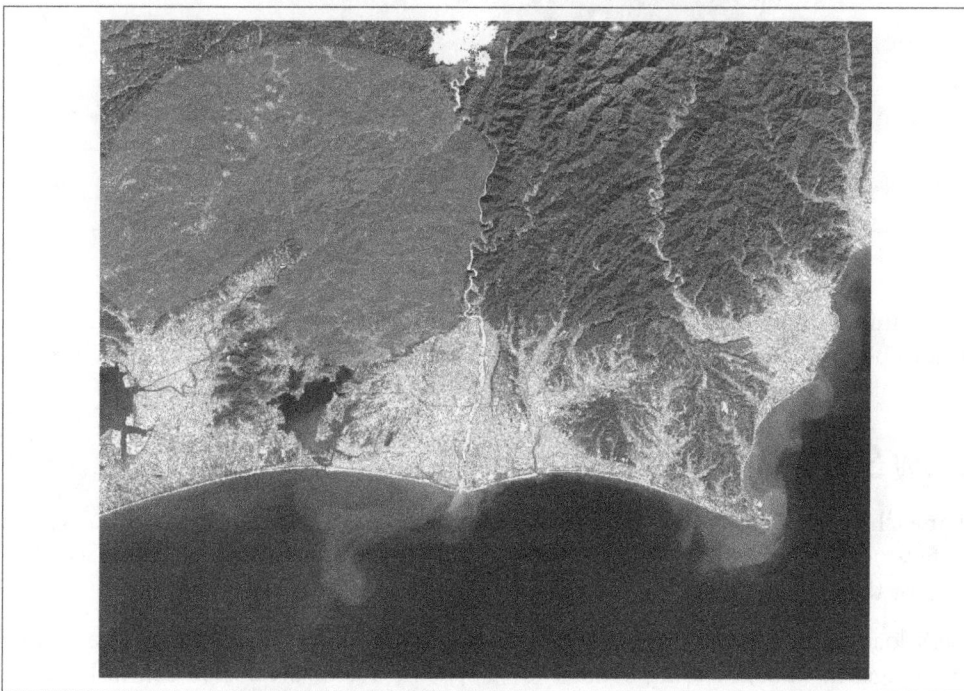

Figure 3-5. Landsat raster for Shizuoka Prefecture, Japan (source: ESA)

Don't worry if you don't understand the following code. We'll cover it in more detail in Chapters 4 and 5. The example aims to show you how quickly you can load raster data and transform it, even with a combination of vector data. That's the power of Apache Sedona—a simple SQL query is enough to analyze and transform combined raster and vector data:

```
WITH algebra_result AS (
    SELECT
        RS_MapAlgebra(
            tile,
            'D',
            'out = (rast[1] - rast[0]) / (rast[1] + rast[0]);'
```

```
        ) AS raster,
        ST_SetSRID(ST_GeomFromText('{wkt}'), 32653) AS geom
    FROM tiles
),
clipped AS (
    SELECT
        RS_Clip(raster, 1, geom) AS raster
    FROM algebra_result
    WHERE RS_Intersects(geom, raster)
)
SELECT raster
FROM clipped
```

You can see how easy it is to load the data from GeoTIFF into Apache Sedona and how quickly you can start to analyze the data and create data transformations.

In this example, the index has no specific meaning. In Chapter 5, we will look in more depth how to use Sedona to calculate popular indexes like NDVI used in raster analysis.

In this example, we are using the RS_MapAlgebra function to perform calculations on pixel values. We add a column with polygon data, which will be later used in another part of CTE. At the end, we clip the raster to the geometry of the polygon.

Loading Data from Databases

It's common for engineering roles in the data space to load data from various sources to move them to a data lake, warehouse, or lakehouse. Many companies have created digital products, and lots of their data is stored in databases, yet they are not well suited for analytics. To unblock its full potential and save it on your data platform of choice, first you need a way to read it.

PostGIS, for a long time, was the most mature platform for geospatial data storage and analytics, thus there is a lot of data sitting there that can be moved to the GeoParquet format for analysis by Apache Sedona in a more performant way. In this section, we'll walk through the process of reading geospatial data from PostgreSQL, MySQL, and MongoDB. These examples will use both RDBMS and NoSQL databases.

Relational database management systems (RDBMS) are a way of storing data in a system mainly based on entity relations. Data is written to tables, which contain rows and columns with strictly defined data types. Popular relational databases include PostgreSQL and MySQL.

NoSQL stands for Not Only SQL, a database group that mainly does not use relations or tables to store data. The databases were created with scalability in mind. Most of them sacrifice the ACID properties for better scalability and throughput. Popular NoSQL databases include MongoDB, CouchBase, and Amazon DynamoDB.

Apache Sedona and Apache Spark internals are written mainly in Java and Scala, so when you need to read data from the database, you'll use the JDBC driver. JDBC (Java Database Connectivity) is an API that allows Java clients to talk with databases using the previously defined interfaces.

Reading from PostgreSQL (PostGIS)

PostgreSQL with the PostGIS extension is one of the most mature geospatial processing systems. It supports various SpatialSQL functions, indices, and optimization techniques for geospatial pipelines. PostGIS encodes geometry into the *extended well-known binary (EWKB)* format. One significant difference from WKB is that EWKB adds SRID encoding to the binary data (coordinate reference systems will be explained in more detail in Chapter 4).

Example of an EWKT string:

```
SRID=4326;POINT(-52.3 21)
```

Now, let's try to load data from PostgreSQL to a spatial DataFrame. We need a PostgreSQL driver to exchange data. Similarly to any jar package, we can add it to the Sedona session configuration using the `spark.jars` property:

```
config = SedonaContext \
    .builder() \
    .config("spark.jars.packages", 'org.postgresql:postgresql:42.7.4') \
    .getOrCreate()

sedona = SedonaContext.create(config)

postgresql_url = "jdbc:postgresql://localhost:5432/sedona"
```

Loading external packages to the Sedona application may take some time, depending on the package size and internet connection. When the dependencies are downloaded and the Apache Sedona session is ready, we can load and transform them into a spatial DataFrame:

```
table_name = "points"

df = sedona \
    .read \
    .format("jdbc") \
    .option("url", postgresql_url) \
    .option("user", "sedona") \
    .option("password", "sedona") \
    .option("dbtable", "points") \
    .option("driver", "org.postgresql.Driver") \
    .load()

df.show()
```

```
+-------+-------------------+
|  name|           location|
+-------+-------------------+
|Point A|0101000020E610000...|
|Point B|0101000020E610000...|
|Point C|0101000020E610000...|
+-------+-------------------+
```

Our data still needs to be cast to Sedona's internal type called geometry. We can achieve this by calling the ST_GeomFromEWKB function:

```
df.selectExpr(
    "name",
    "ST_GeomFromEWKB(location) AS geom"
).show()
```

```
+-------+-------------+
|  name|         geom|
+-------+-------------+
|Point A|POINT (10 20)|
|Point B|POINT (30 40)|
|Point C|POINT (50 60)|
+-------+-------------+
```

Reading from MySQL

MySQL encodes geometry using serialized SRID numbers and follows WKB. It supports (multi)point, (multi)polygon, (multi)linestring, and geometry collection. To read it, you can use the ST_GeomFromMySQL function, which translates MySQL geometry binaries into Geometry objects in Sedona.

You need a JDBC driver jar package. Similar to the PostgreSQL example, you can use the spark.jars option and load the connection driver for MySQL mysql:mysql-connector-java:8.0.33.

To load the spatial data from a MySQL table, you can use a code snippet like the following:

```
mysql_url = f"jdbc:mysql://localhost:3306/{database_name}"

df = sedona \
    .read \
    .format("jdbc") \
    .option("url", mysql_url) \
    .option("user", user_name) \
    .option("password", password) \
    .option("dbtable", "points") \
    .option("driver", "com.mysql.cj.jdbc.Driver") \
    .load()

df.show()
```

```
+-------+--------------------+
|  name|            location|
+-------+--------------------+
|Point A|[E6 10 00 00 01 0...|
|Point B|[E6 10 00 00 01 0...|
|Point C|[E6 10 00 00 01 0...|
+-------+--------------------+
```

As you can see, the data is in a binary format, and to cast it to the Sedona internal format, you can apply the ST_GeomFromMySQL function on the location column and alias it as geom:

```
df.selectExpr(
    "name",
    "ST_GeomFromMySQL(location) AS geom"
).show(3, False)
```

```
+-------+-------------+
|  name|         geom|
+-------+-------------+
|Point A|POINT (10 20)|
|Point B|POINT (30 40)|
|Point C|POINT (50 60)|
+-------+-------------+
```

Reading from MongoDB

MongoDB is a NoSQL database that uses GeoJSON to represent geometry objects. We need the Mongo Spark connector available in our Sedona session to load data to the geospatial DataFrame. We can achieve that by adding the jar to the session:

```
'org.mongodb.spark:mongo-spark-connector_2.12:10.4.0'
```

Once we have the connector, we must write simple code like the following to read the data from MongoDB. MongoDB uses collections to keep the data; think about it as a table that has no strict schema:

```
df = sedona \
    .read \
    .option("database", "sedona") \
    .option("collection", "points") \
    .format("mongodb") \
    .load()
```

```
+----------------------------+
|location                    |
+----------------------------+
|{Point, [-74.006, 40.7128]} |
|{Point, [-118.2437, 34.0522]}|
+----------------------------+
```

MongoDB uses GeoJSON to store geospatial data. To load columns from GeoJSON to the internal Sedona model, you need to apply the ST_GeomFromGeoJSON function. Initially, when we do that, we get an exception as the function requires a string as input; however, the connector to MongoDB parses it by default as an object, which you can see on the following schema:

```
root
 |-- _id: string (nullable = true)
 |-- location: struct (nullable = true)
 |    |-- type: string (nullable = true)
 |    |-- coordinates: array (nullable = true)
 |    |     |-- element: double (containsNull = true)
 |-- name: string (nullable = true)
```

We can fix that by using the to_json function, and our working example looks like this:

```
import pyspark.sql.functions as f

df.withColumn("location", f.to_json(f.col("location"))) \
    .selectExpr("name", "ST_GeomFromGeoJSON(location) AS geom") \
    .show(2, False)
```

Data Synchronization

When creating geospatial analytics pipelines using Apache Sedona, your data source may be an external database used by a transactional system. Setting up a read replica for your primary database is an excellent way to avoid downgrading the database's performance and, in the worst case, disturbing business processes.

Database replication is a process of copying the existing database to different instances so you can use it for analytics purposes without worrying about downtime on the primary database. How does database replication work? It strongly relies on the change data capture (CDC) mechanism, which constantly monitors changes in the database based on the write-ahead log (WAL) file, whether it is record addition, update, or removal. The only downside of this approach is that data freshness might be slightly delayed and there may be minimal impact on database performance. All writes also need to be materialized in a database replica. Most databases in the cloud, like CloudSQL on GCP or Aurora on AWS, support replication out of the box.

Debezium is a popular CDC library that helps replicate changes. It uses Apache Kafka as an intermediate step to store messages from the database log file. You can combine Debezium with Kafka Connect to easily replicate your data between the database log and different databases (it doesn't have to be the same database system).

We can leverage Debezium with PostGIS to load geospatial data to Sedona and save it to a GeoParquet file, which might be a way to move the data from external systems to a data lake. I'll guide you through how you can do that, but before that, let's introduce yet another important topic for creating data pipelines, idempotency.

When writing an ETL pipeline and loading data from sources, it is vital to make it idempotent so that any consecutive runs will produce the same output. Hence, the data engineering team has no worries about repeating a failed process.

Most transactional tables have audit columns like `created_at` and `updated_at`, which can be incorporated to have predictable data chunks each time. Another benefit of using this approach is being able to load smaller chunks of data and reduce network traffic. To do that, we can use the query parameter in loading options. Let's create a simple application that reads from a PostGIS dataset based on date ranges. When reading data from PostgreSQL using the Apache Spark JDBC connector, you can place the query in the *query* option. Recalling the previous example with loading data from PostgreSQL, the only change you have to make is replacing `.option("dbtable", "points")` with `.option("query", query)` where the query variable is the following SQL query:

```
SELECT *
FROM polygons
WHERE COALESCE(UPDATED_AT, CREATED_AT)
    BETWEEN '2020-01-01 00:00:00' AND '2024-01-01 00:00:00'
```

CDC with PostgreSQL to GeoParquet Source

The previous example makes our pipeline idempotent. However, it requires a read replica of the PostgreSQL database and prior knowledge of when we must run our batch jobs to include all the data. Another drawback is that audit columns might not exist, and in that case, we are forced to load all the data each time we need to refresh. We can use the CDC mechanism, which detects changes (CREATE, DELETE, UPDATE) on a table and sends the data to an external sink, to load our geospatial data from PostGIS tables to mitigate this issue (Figure 3-6). For that purpose, we'll incorporate Debezium to read the data from WAL files from the PostgreSQL database.

The process starts from the PostGIS table named *points,* followed by the integration of Debezium with the WAL files produced by PostgreSQL. Debezium automatically pushes the data into an Apache Kafka topic called *sedona-debezium.public.points.* We use Apache Sedona to load the data from Kafka in batch mode. Once the data is loaded by Apache Sedona to a spatial DataFrame, we store that on an S3 bucket in a GeoParquet data format. You can see the whole process in Figure 3-6.

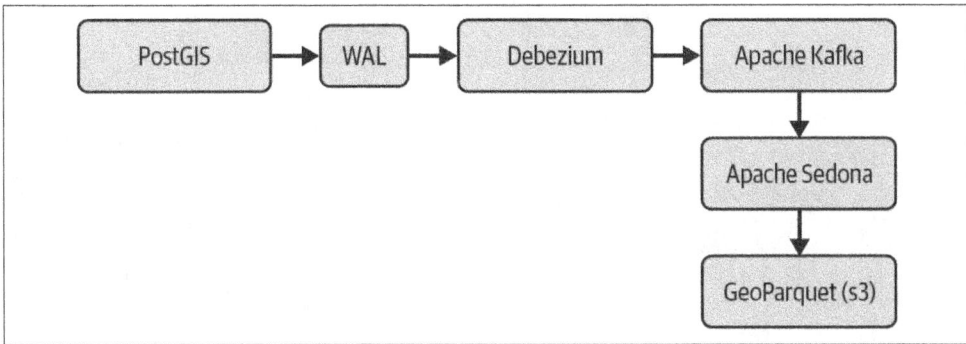

Figure 3-6. Reading from PostgreSQL CDC

We can consider two ways of loading the data: batch and streaming. In this section, we focus on loading and saving using the batch approach.

We need to read our data from Apache Kafka as Debezium reads the WAL file and puts messages on the Kafka topic. To do so, we need the Spark SQL Kafka connector:

```
org.apache.spark:spark-sql-kafka-0-10_2.12:3.5.1
```

To load data from the Kafka topic, we can use the following code:

```
df = sedona \
    .read \
    .format("kafka") \
    .option("kafka.bootstrap.servers", "localhost:9092") \
    .option("subscribe", "sedona-debezium.public.points") \
    .load()
```

Debezium pushes JSON messages on a Kafka topic with a schema similar to this:

```
{
  "schema": {
    "type": "struct",
    "fields": [
      {
        "type": "string",
        "optional": true,
        "field": "name"
      },
      ...
    ]
  },
  "payload": {
    "before": null,
    "after": {
      "name": "Point A",
      ...
    },
    "source": {
```

```
        "version": "2.3.4.Final",
        "connector": "postgresql",
        "name": "sedona-debezium",
        ...
        "table": "points"
      }
    }
  }
```

To read the data, we need to provide a Spark schema:

```
import pyspark.sql.types as t

data = t.StructType([
    t.StructField("name", t.StringType(), True),
    t.StructField("location", t.StructType([
        t.StructField("srid", t.IntegerType()),
        t.StructField("wkb", t.BinaryType())])
    )
])

before = t.StructField("before", data, True)
after = t.StructField("after", data, True)

payload = t.StructField("payload", t.StructType([before, after]) )

schema = t.StructType([payload])
```

Now that we have the schema, we can load changes to the spatial DataFrame:

```
import pyspark.sql.functions as f

geometry_df = df \
    .select(
        f.from_json(f.expr("CAST(value AS STRING)"), schema).alias("data")
    ) \
    .selectExpr(
        "data.payload.after.name as name",
        "data.payload.after.location.wkb as wkb",
        "data.payload.after.location.srid AS srid"
    ) \
    .selectExpr("name", "ST_SetSRID(ST_GeomFromWKB(wkb), srid) AS geom")
```

Finally, we can save data to the S3 bucket in GeoParquet format:

```
geometry_df \
    .withColumn("geohash", f.expr("ST_GeoHash(geom, 5)")) \
    .orderBy("geohash") \
    .write \
    .mode("overwrite") \
    .format("geoparquet") \
    .save("s3a://<your-bucket>/postgis-cdc-batch")
```

Hands-On Use Case: New York Taxi Data Analysis

The New York Taxi dataset contains information gathered by the Taxi and Limousine Commission (TLC) about trips completed by yellow and green cabs and for-hire vehicles (Uber and Lyft). It's a free and public dataset.

Let's analyze the yellow cab data from 2015 to 2016. We want to try to find the answer to the following questions:

- What are the most popular areas for pickups?
- What are the 10 most popular routes?

Let's start by loading data into a DataFrame. Then, we can explore it and try to clean it before we start any analytics:

```
path = "s3a://apache-sedona-book/source_data/nyc_yellow"

nyx_taxi = sedona \
    .read \
    .format("parquet") \
    .load(path)
```

For our analysis, we need:

- `pickup_longitude`
- `pickup_latitude`
- `dropoff_longitude`
- `dropoff_latitude`
- `total_amount`

Data comes from an external data source, which might have some errors and incorrect values; it's important to track and filter outliers. Data quality is a significant factor in any analytics process. Before answering the questions we asked at the beginning, we need to clean our dataset so it is reliable and ready to use. We can start by creating a plot with sample pickup locations.

Figure 3-7 shows that some points are far from New York so we need to filter them out.

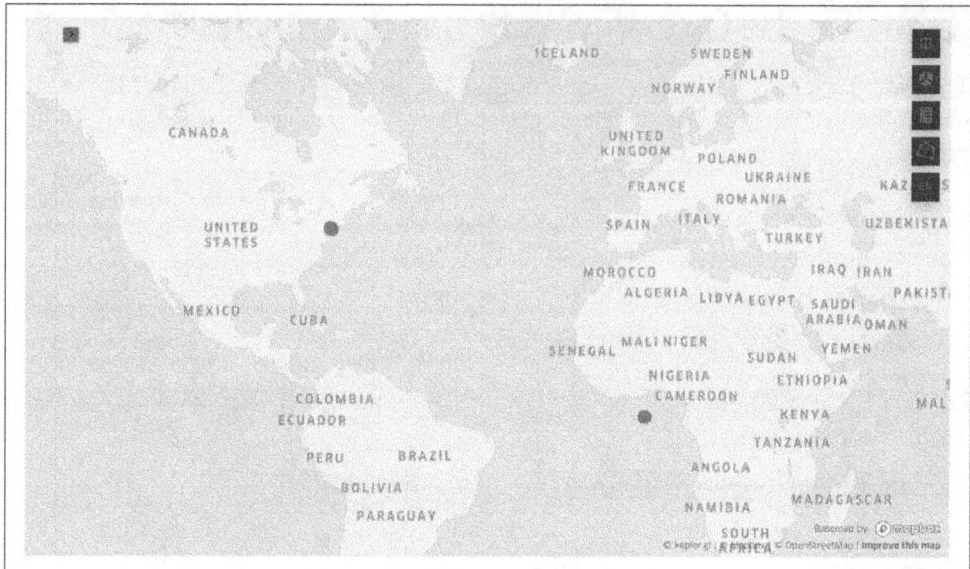

Figure 3-7. Outlier observations that need to be filtered out

We can filter our area based on a polygon for dropoff and pickup points. You can easily do this by using the Sedona `ST_Within` function to filter the points. In this step, we can also remove all amounts with values below zero by using the filter `total_amount > 0` (Figure 3-8).

```
SELECT
    *
FROM taxi
WHERE ST_Within(dropoff_geom, ST_GeomFromText('{polygon_wkt}'))
  AND ST_Within(pickup_geom, ST_GeomFromText('{polygon_wkt}'))
  AND total_amount > 0
```

where `polygon_wkt` is

```
POLYGON (
  (-74.11902 40.83533,
  -74.22186 40.64965,
  -73.75749 40.60368,
  -73.73730 40.69323,
  -73.89882 40.90133,
  -74.12557 40.91424,
  -74.11780 40.83556,
  -74.11902 40.83533)
)
```

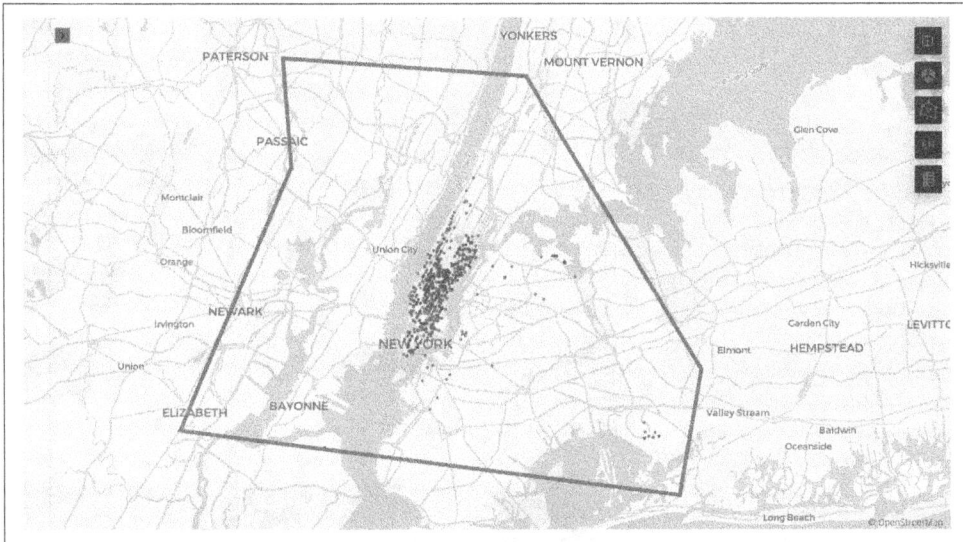

Figure 3-8. Area used for the analysis

Now, you are ready to answer the first question.

The Most Popular Areas for Pickups and Dropoffs

To aggregate our data into smaller areas, we use the H3 index, which is a technique for dividing the globe into smaller hexagon grids. We'll cover indexing in geospatial data in the next chapter. Stay tuned! The solution has some drawbacks including points lying close to the borders of hexagon grids distorting results. However, for the simplicity of this example, we will stick to this methodology.

We start by finding the H3 cell for each of the pickup points. Then, we aggregate by the first index from the resulting array (for each point, we get only one H3 grid) and get the count and geometry from the H3 indexes for visualization purposes:

```
WITH h3_index AS (
    SELECT
        ST_H3CellIDs(dropoff_geom, 8, true)[0] AS h3_id
    FROM taxi_cleaned
)
SELECT
    h3_id,
    count(h3_id) AS cnt,
    ST_H3ToGeom(array(h3_id))[0] AS geom
FROM h3_index
GROUP BY h3_id
ORDER BY count(h3_id) DESC
```

The answer to our question can be seen in Figure 3-9, with the darkest hexagons representing the most popular pickup areas. Incidentally, the majority of the areas are found in Manhattan.

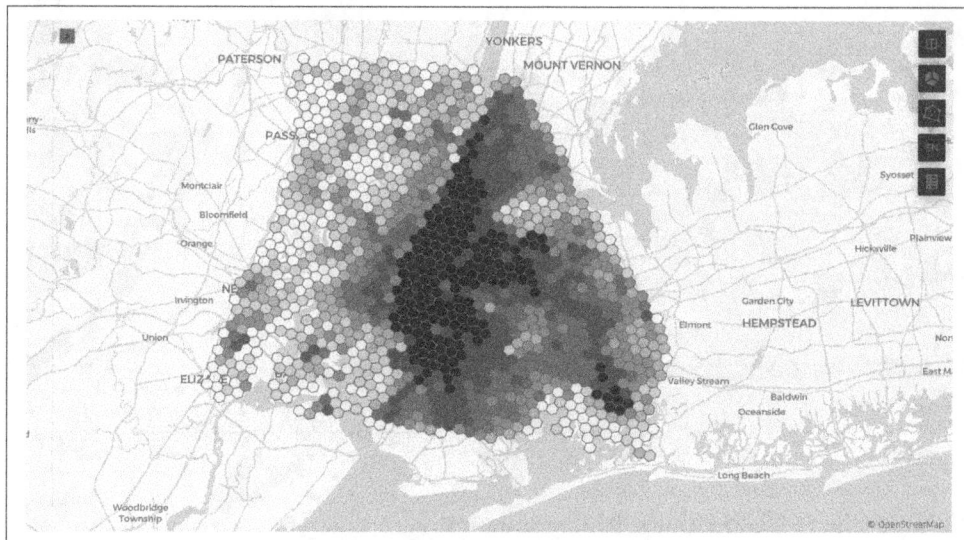

Figure 3-9. Hexagon density map showing the most popular pickup areas

Now let's find the answer to the next question.

The 10 Most Popular Routes

We start by finding the H3 cells for each pickup and dropoff point. Let's name the result of that query h3_indexes:

```
SELECT
    ST_H3CellIDs(pickup_geom, 8, true)[0] AS h3_pickup_id,
    ST_H3CellIDs(dropoff_geom, 8, true)[0] AS h3_dropoff_id
FROM taxi_cleaned
```

Then, we concatenate the H3 indexes in order to aggregate A → B and B → A as the same route. The result lands in the view indexed:

```
SELECT
    CASE
        WHEN h3_pickup_id > h3_dropoff_id
            THEN CONCAT(h3_dropoff_id, ' ', h3_pickup_id)
            ELSE CONCAT(h3_pickup_id, ' ', h3_dropoff_id)
    END AS id,
    h3_pickup_id,
    h3_dropoff_id
FROM h3_indexes
```

We need to aggregate the results and order them by count (grouped view):

```
SELECT
    id,
    count(id) AS cnt,
    first(h3_pickup_id) AS h3_pickup_id,
    first(h3_dropoff_id) AS h3_dropoff_id
FROM indexed
GROUP BY id
```

The last step is to produce a line from the starting H3 cell to the ending H3 cell. We can use the ST_MakeLine function combined with the ST_Centroid function:

```
SELECT
    h3_pickup_id,
    h3_dropoff_id,
    ST_MakeLine(
        ST_Centroid(ST_H3ToGeom(array(h3_pickup_id))[0]),
        ST_Centroid(ST_H3ToGeom(array(h3_dropoff_id))[0])
    ) AS geom,
    cnt
FROM grouped
ORDER BY cnt DESC
LIMIT 20
```

The top 10 popular routes are shown in Figure 3-10.

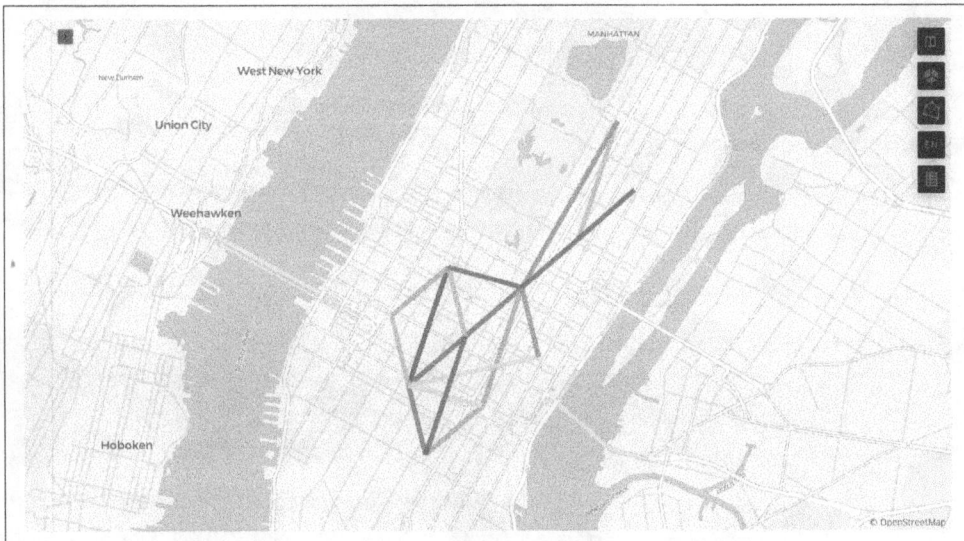

Figure 3-10. Most popular routes based on the New York Taxi dataset

Summary

Apache Sedona is a mature geospatial framework that helps you load data from various sources and the most popular geospatial data formats. Using only one tool, you can combine your analytics with vector and raster data and scale it from small to enormously large datasets.

In this chapter, you learned how to load vector data from popular data formats like GeoParquet, GeoJSON, and shapefiles. You also learned why some formats (e.g., GeoParquet) are better suited for distributed data processing. Now, you can load and process raster data from GeoTIFF using many functions from the Sedona catalog. A deep understanding of how databases encode geospatial data will help users load formats that we didn't cover in this book, such as Oracle and Redis. Lastly, we covered using Sedona in real examples to analyze New York Taxi data.

## CHAPTER 4

Points, Lines, and Polygons: Vector Data Analysis with Spatial SQL

Vector data is the most commonly used data type in spatial data analysis; it simplifies how we describe surrounding objects. You can tell the location of hops, road intersections, and earthquake epicenters using a set of coordinates called points. To describe road networks or rivers, you can use linestrings, and for buildings or prohibited areas or parks in cities, polygons. Long story short, vector primitives are the foundation of any geospatial framework, the key ingredients you can't ignore.

MapReduce, a distributed execution framework introduced by Google, allowed analyzing an amount of data unimaginable before for vast masses. Then, Apache Hive simplified how we communicate with MapReduce by introducing an SQL wrapper on top of it. While this made analytics even more straightforward to execute, Apache Spark then did something even more remarkable by making processing and transforming the data more concise and significantly faster. The early era of big data frameworks tried to eliminate SQL, but SQL is one of the finest ways to express data transformations. The more people try to bury SQL, the more prominent it becomes.

The complexity of vector data analysis increases not only with the number of records you have in a DataFrame but also with how large your single vector observations are and how they are located relative to each other. Big data tools such as Apache Spark work well for large-scale data processing but are not optimized for geospatial data. To give you some context, trying to process large amounts of geospatial data with a framework not adapted for this purpose might take days or years, or even never finish at all.

Apache Sedona combines the strengths of Apache Spark and optimized geospatial algorithms to provide an intuitive platform for quickly processing small, medium, and even unimaginable amounts of data, all while using well-known SQL.

Vector data, also known as geometry and geography, is a way to describe spatial objects using a set of pair coordinates. Using a finite number of points helps to simplify the calculus and improve the overall performance of queries. *Finite* is a crucial word here but knowing when your geometry shapes are too complex is even more critical. It's like vitamins; not only is the lack of them harmful, but higher levels are toxic, too. If your geometries represent the object with accepted precision, then it's better not to add more vertices to them.

Just as atoms are building blocks for the entire Earth, so too are geometries for spatial analytics. Knowledge of singular atoms is an exciting topic, but their relations, connections, and influence on each other help us understand the universe. The same is true for the geometries and spatial relationships in spatial analytics. Spatial relationships are what give you insights from geospatial data. Where is the closest shop, which areas are at flood risk, or what are the most used parts of the city for taxi drivers? Those are some of the examples that incorporate spatial relations to spatial vector data.

Apache Sedona was created to simplify geospatial data processing and analytics and make it available to as many people as possible, processing small, moderate, and vast amounts of vector data and spatial queries using one framework.

Vector Data Model and Spatial Relationship

We have already used the geometry terms in the previous chapter but now let's dive into them in depth. Apache Sedona defines a generic abstraction with the Geometry type, which might be (multi)polygon, (multi)point, (multi)linestring, or a geometry collection. Apache Sedona follows the guides from the OGC Simple Feature specification (*https://oreil.ly/Elhoz*):

Point
> The simplest geometry type. It might be a pair of 2D coordinates XY or 3D XYZ. Apache Sedona also allows you to keep an additional value, called the M value (it's any measure you can add if it's numeric, like a timestamp), for both 2D and 3D points, XYM and XYZM. All the Google places you see on the map are points.

Linestring
> A finite set of points connected together, composing a geometry with nonzero length but with 0 area. It might be a straight line or a curve. Real-world examples include rivers, roads, and paths.

Polygon
> A set of points where the first point is the same as the last. It has both a length and an area greater than 0. Polygons can have holes, which must be considered when dealing with them. The hole is the interior boundary or boundaries that are not overlapping with each other inside the polygon. The area created by those boundaries is excluded from the polygon area.

To reduce the amount of space needed to save the geometry data for each one of the preceding, there is a multi equivalent. So, you can define a multipoint, multilinestring, or multipolygon. For example, you can reference storing parts of a building as one multipolygon, and then all the nongeospatial fields can be put in one row to reduce the space needed to process it.

Geometry collection
> A container for other geometries, such as (multi)points, (multi)lines, and (multi)polygons. It's useful for storing different geometries related to the same entity, such as building shapes and their centroids (geometric center) and boundaries.

Spatial Relationships

Imagine solving a jigsaw puzzle. It is all in pieces when you first open the box. To solve it, you need to find the patterns and matching pieces to complete the puzzle. The same idea can be used to describe the spatial data model and spatial relationships: geometries are the puzzle pieces you are trying to match, and the spatial relationship is the matching process. To understand your geospatial data better, you need to solve the spatial relationships between your geometries. For example, to find restaurants 1km from your location, you need to create a buffer and find all the restaurants that intersect with the polygon you created. Most geospatial systems already have built-in functions to search for relations inside your data, such as intersects, contains, touches, etc.

Before we discuss the common spatial relationships, it's important to understand the three essential components of the vector model:

Boundary
> The edge of a geometric shape

Exterior
> The space outside the boundary

Interior
> The space inside the boundary

For a polygon, this is intuitive: the exterior is all the space outside the polygon (including holes), the boundary is the line composing the polygon, and everything (else) is the interior. For a linestring, it gets tricky. The exterior is all the space outside the linestring, the interior is the linestring shape, and the boundaries are the linestring start and end points (Figure 4-1). The definition of a point is even more complex: the interior is the point itself, the boundary is an empty set, and the exterior is everything else.

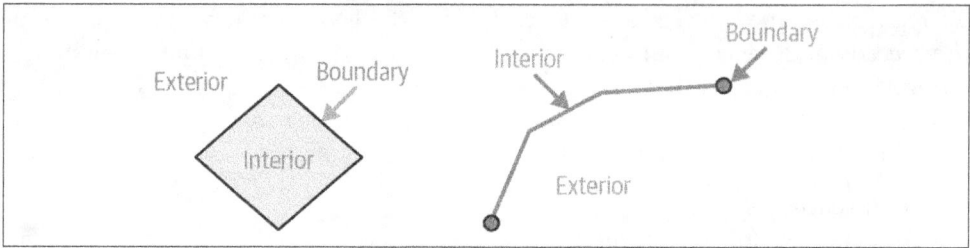

Figure 4-1. Exterior, boundary, and interior definition for polygon and linestring

That will be useful knowledge for common geometry relation types and the DE-9IM model that you will learn later in this chapter. Now, we can switch to the most commonly used geometry relationships:

ST_Intersects

When you identify if geometry A has any common point with geometry B, you are trying to determine if geometry A intersects geometry B. The relation is transitive, so when A intersects geometry B, B also intersects geometry A (Figure 4-2).

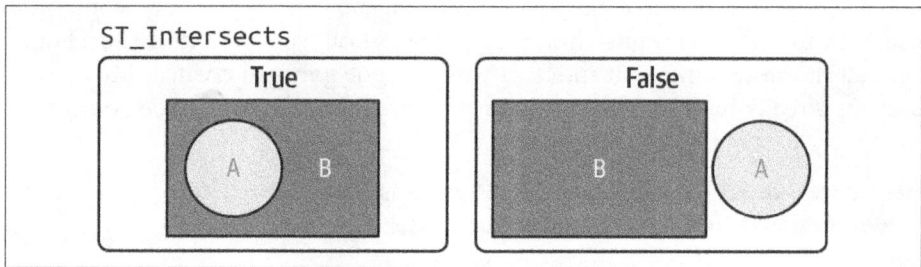

Figure 4-2. ST_Intersects spatial relationship

ST_Contains (A: Geometry, B: Geometry)

The contains predicate returns true only if geometry B is inside geometry A. If the geometry is partially outside, the function returns false (Figure 4-3a). In other words, no points of B lie in the exterior of A and the interiors of A and B have at least one point in common.

ST_Crosses (A: Geometry, B: Geometry)

Geometry A crosses geometry B only when both geometries share the same interior points, but not all of them (Figure 4-3b). Their intersection geometry must be one dimension lower than the maximum dimension of both geometries. For example, two polygons can't cross, as the only possible way for intersection geometry to be a line is when two polygons share their border, which is not their interior. Points can't cross the polygon, but multipoints can, as some points might lie outside.

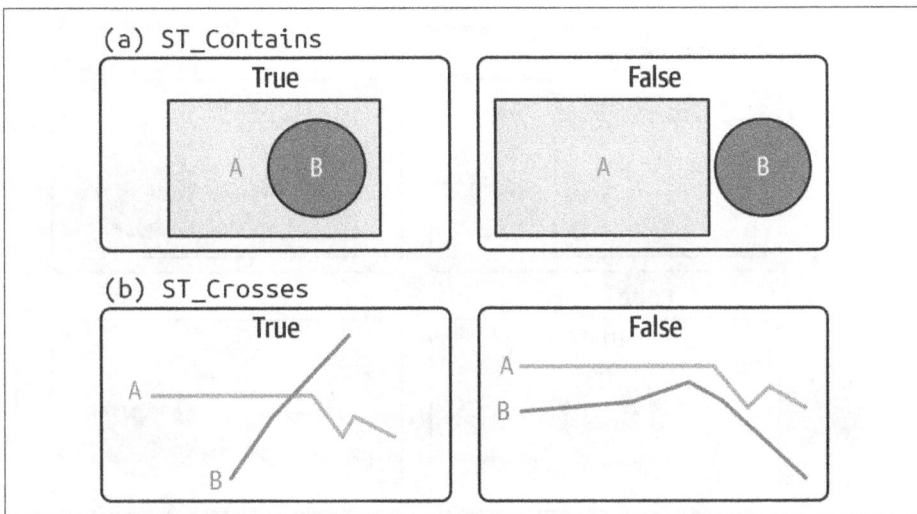

Figure 4-3. (a) ST_Contains, (b) ST_Crosses spatial relationships

ST_Disjoint (A: Geometry, B: Geometry)

If geometry A has no common points with geometry B, we say they are disjointed. It's the opposite operation of the intersects function (Figure 4-4a).

ST_Equals (A: Geometry, B: Geometry)

Only two geometries with the same points in the same order are equal; point A is equal to point B only if the two coordinates of A and B are equal. Linestrings and polygons have to share the same points in the same order and with the same number (Figure 4-4b).

ST_Overlaps (A: Geometry, B: Geometry)

Geometry A overlaps with geometry B only when they meet the following criteria: their interiors intersect and each has at least one point inside the other. The geometries can't be equal, and geometry A can't be entirely inside geometry B to meet the preceding criteria (Figure 4-4c).

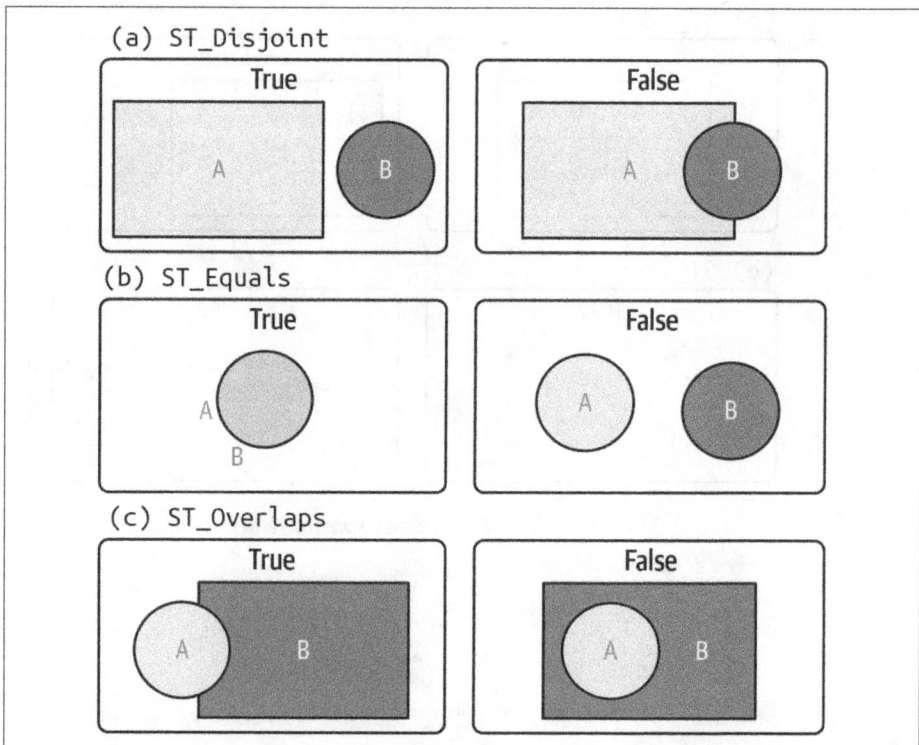

Figure 4-4. (a) ST_Disjoint, (b) ST_Equals, (c) ST_Overlaps spatial relationships

ST_Touches (A: Geometry, B: Geometry)

This is true when geometry A has a common border with geometry B. For example, two polygons share the same edge, vertex, or linestring, sharing line segments (Figure 4-5a).

ST_Within (A: Geometry, B: Geometry)

This is the opposite of the ST_Contains, as it's true when no points of A lie in the exterior of B and the interiors of A and B have at least one point in common. So even if polygon B has a hole, geometry A must lie outside that hole and inside polygon B. Also, the function returns false when the point lies on the boundary (Figure 4-5b). It's always TRUE that ST_Contains(A, B) == ST_Within(B, A).

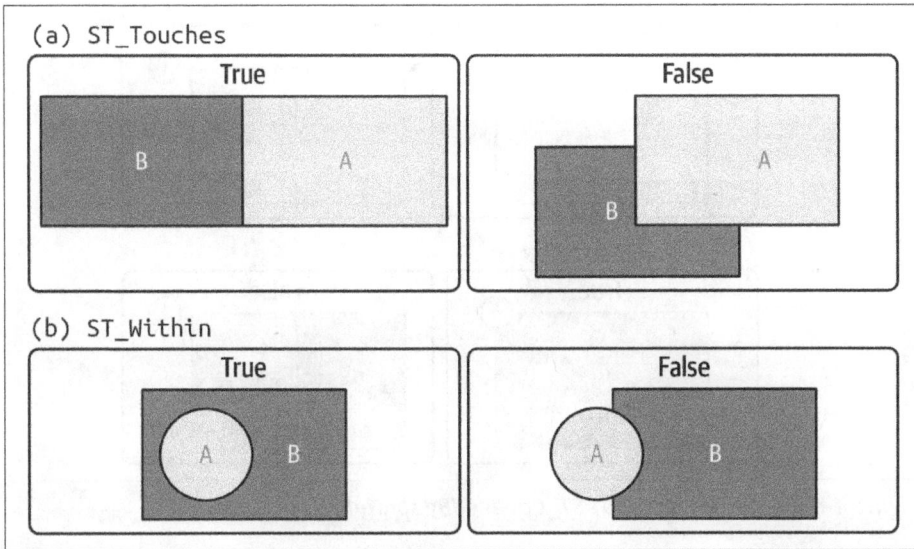

Figure 4-5. (a) *ST_Touches*, (b) *ST_Within* spatial relationships

`ST_Covers (A: Geometry, B: Geometry)`
> Verifies if all elements of geometry B lie inside geometry A (intersecting with the boundary included). So, geometry A covers all of the geometry of B, which can be translated to the opposite, so no points in B are outside geometry (in the exterior of) A (Figure 4-6a).

`ST_CoveredBy (A: Geometry, B: Geometry)`
> The opposite of `ST_Covers`, as it indicates if all points of geometry A are inside geometry B, including the boundary (Figure 4-6b). It is always true that `ST_Cover edBy(A, B) == ST_Covers(B, A)`.

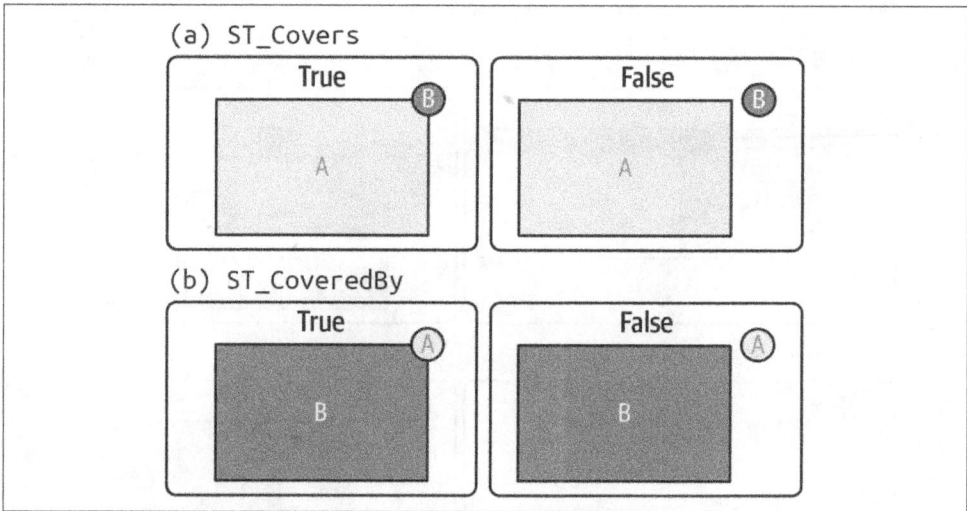

Figure 4-6. (a) `ST_Covers`, (b) `ST_CoveredBy` spatial relationships

> Apache Sedona uses the `ST_` prefix, which stands for spatiotemporal, which PostGIS introduced to geospatial functions. As of the publication of this book, Apache Sedona supports nearly 200 spatial functions for vector data and 100 for processing raster data. Currently, the Simple Features Specification doesn't require adding prefixes.

Dimensionally Extended 9-Intersection Model (DE-9IM)

The examples we have discussed so far do not end with spatial relationships. If your analysis requires a more convoluted function than the ones explained earlier, you can use the Dimensionally Extended 9-Intersection Model (DE-9IM). Let's imagine you need to examine the electrical cables that need to point to the building polygon only at one point, which is on the boundary of the polygon. `ST_Touches`, for instance, will return true where more than one point lies in the geometry. `ST_Intersects` will not work because we need to have cable outside the building polygon. We can use the DE-9IM model to define the conditions, like:

- A cable boundary can relate to the polygon only by one point.
- None of the points from the cable can be in the interior of the polygon.

The DE-9IM is a way to model how geometric objects relate. Every spatial object has the same three components we are familiar with:

- Boundary
- Exterior
- Interior

It can be challenging to grasp how DE-9IM might be used, so let's walk through an example and review it step by step. Let's describe the relation between geometries using the DE-9IM table for the polygon and line, as shown in the top left corner of Figure 4-7. We will try to find the DE-9IM result, and how the line relates to the polygon. In Figure 4-7, the DE-9IM table has rows representing parts of the linestring (interior, boundary, exterior) and columns representing the polygon.

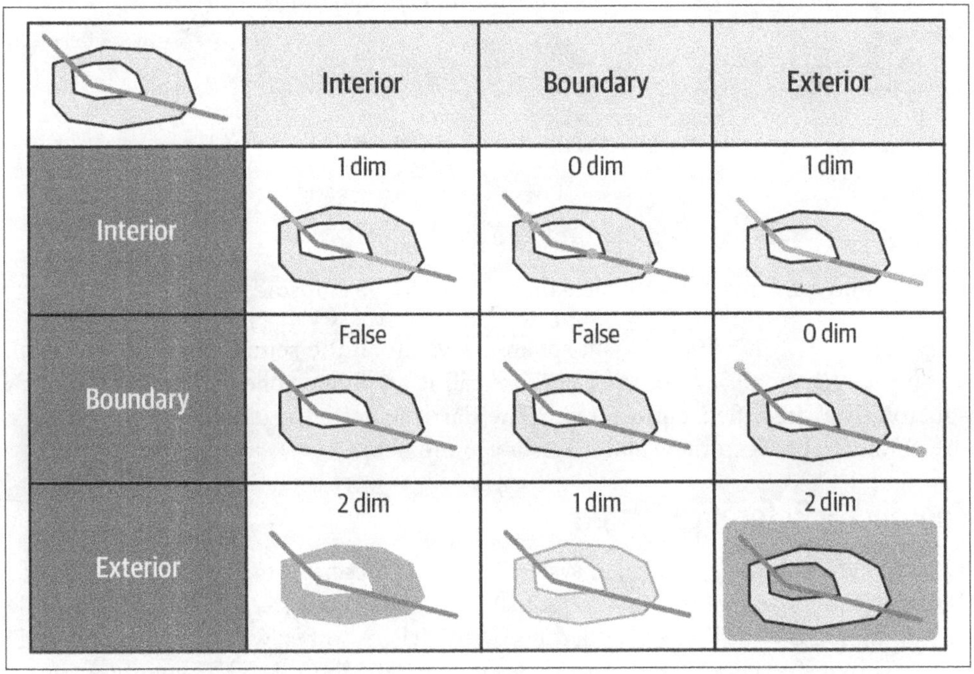

Figure 4-7. Using this table, we calculate the DE-9IM for the linestring and polygon

For the interior and interior relation, we can see that common points formulate the one-dimensional geometry, two linestrings. We can see the set of points for the boundary and the interior, so the dimension is 0. When the two geometries share the points that create the polygon, the result is two dimensions, like the interior and exterior in the example. When there is no common point, we note that it is false, like for the interior and boundary.

We can combine the result into a string: 101FF0212, going row by row and for each row, for all the columns (from left to right). You can use the `ST_Relate(A: Geometry, B: Geometry)` function from the Apache Sedona SQL function catalog to get the same result.

Spatial Reference System and the Geography Model

The Earth's shape is described by gravity, not topography. Its true shape is called a *geoid*, which is the theoretical shape of the Earth, made from the surface at the average sea and ocean level and prolonged below the land. The closest mathematical figure to the geoid is the *ellipsoid*.

The ellipsoid is a 3D geometry where all plane cross-sections are either circles or ellipses. Mathematically, we can describe it using an equation:

$$\frac{x^2}{a^2} + \frac{y^2}{b^2} + \frac{z^2}{c^2} = 1$$

where

- a, b, and c are semi-principal axes of the ellipsoid
- x, y, and z are given coordinates that are inside the ellipsoid

A special case of the ellipsoid is a sphere in which all the semi-principals are equal, $a = b = c$. When two are equal, $a = c$, we call it an oblate spheroid or a *spheroid*. A spheroid is a simplified Earth model. The Earth's rotation causes the different sizes; the difference between the a and b axes is around 20km.

Coordinate Reference System

We use the coordinate reference system (CRS) to describe the location of either a 2D or 3D point on the Earth's surface. A 2D model uses (X, Y) coordinates while the additional Z coordinate is added in 3D models. Another way of expressing a 3D model is by using curvilinear coordinates φ (geodetic latitude), λ (longitude), and h (ellipsoidal height).

Most GIS systems use (X, Y) (map projections onto 2D space) coordinates or (X, Y, Z). In the geography model, you will most likely see (φ, λ) while h is omitted as, in most cases, we don't focus on the exact value of h operating under the assumption that the Earth's surface is smooth.[1] The CRS on the ellipsoid model is shown in Figure 4-8. To place a point in space, we need a coordinate system, as well as a point where that coordinate system starts the datum.

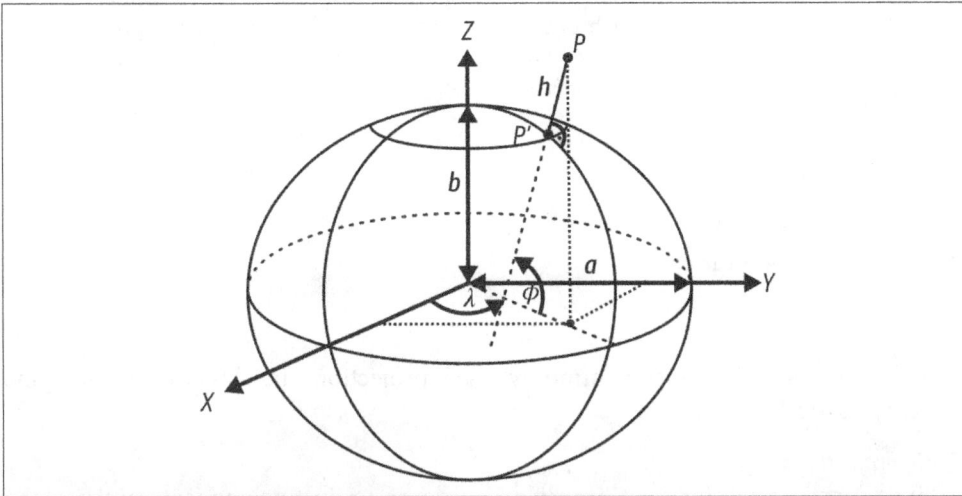

Figure 4-8. Ellipsoid model showing curvilinear coordinate (φ, λ, h) (in most GIS problems, h is omitted as it's the distance from the ellipsoid center, and in most analytics problems, we use h = earth surface)

Datum

To correctly place the coordinate system (ellipsoid) in space, we need the orientation of the CRS and origin point at a specific time (epoch). That's the definition of the datum. The most recognized datum are:

- WGS84

- NAD27 and NAD83

- ED50 and ETRS89

WGS84 is the most commonly used ellipsoid model in spatial analytics. The World Geodetic System, based on the WGS84 ellipsoid, was primarily designed for the US Defense Mapping Agency and is the nominal datum for GPS.

---

1 See this explanation (*https://oreil.ly/QlGmE*) for further details.

Map Projections

Map projection is the process of transforming the Earth's shape into a flat surface called a map. There are many map projection types, and depending on the use case, you might choose one over another.

> Mathematician Carl Friedrich Gauss proved that it is impossible to project the Earth onto a flat map without distortion. Each projection may preserve valid values for one feature but will distort others. The main properties of maps are:
>
> - Area
> - Shape
> - Direction
> - Bearing
> - Distance

Now, let's discuss the most commonly used projections in classical cartography: conic, cylindrical, and planar:

Conic projections
>   The most straightforward example is a conic projection tangent to the globe along a line of latitude (standard parallel). The meridians are projected onto the conical surface, intersecting at the conic's apex. The lowest distortion is inside the standard parallel line, growing farther away from it. Conic projections are mostly found representing midlatitude zones that are east-to-west oriented.
>
>   Examples:
>
>   - Albers equal-area conic
>   - Equidistant conic
>   - Lambert conformal conic

Cylindrical projections
>   Cylinder projections use cylinders to transform the 3D Earth's shape into a map. We can change the rotation of the cylinder to get less distortion on the line of tangency. The most well-known normal cylindrical projection is the Mercator, where the line of tangency is Earth's equator. Meridians are geometrically projected onto the surface of the cylinder, and for parallels, we use mathematical formulas to project them and get 90-degree angles. The distance between each meridian is the same, but for parallels, the further we get from the equator, the larger the distance between them. This projection works well for navigation purposes as it is conformal and keeps the directions along straight lines.

Examples:

- Mercator
- Transverse Mercator

Planar projections

As the name suggests, planar projections involve projecting the Earth onto a map using a plane. The plane may touch the Earth at one point or many (secant). Sometimes, the planar projection is called an azimuthal projection or a zenithal projection. The touching point might be between the North and South Poles and is identified by central longitude and latitude. Planar projections can have three aspects: polar, equatorial, and oblique.

When working with geospatial data, you might encounter many projections. Transformation is the process of calculating coordinate values for another projection based on different projections.

Transformation

Transformation is the process of translating coordinates from one CRS to another. The transformation between CRSes with different datums also changes the underlying ellipsoid for new coordinates. Depending on the method selected for the transformation, the accuracy can range from centimeters to meters. There are a few techniques that you might use, like the 3-parameter transformation or the 7-parameter Helmert transformation.

The most effortless transformation is the 3-parameter transformation, which moves the origin point to a different datum. We must use the same ellipsoid model and orientation. The formula is as follows:

$$X_{targ} = \Delta X + X_{source}$$

$$Y_{targ} = \Delta Y + Y_{source}$$

$$Z_{targ} = \Delta Z + Z_{source}$$

Unfortunately, in most cases, we need a 7-parameter formula called the Helmert transformation, which considers the following parameters:

R_x, R_y, R_z
  Rotations around the X, Y, and Z axes

T_x, T_y, T_z
  Movement of coordinates (translation)

D

Rescale factor

$$\begin{bmatrix} X \\ Y \\ Z \end{bmatrix}_{(T)} = \begin{bmatrix} X \\ Y \\ Z \end{bmatrix}_{(S)} + \begin{bmatrix} T_X \\ T_Y \\ T_Z \end{bmatrix} + \begin{bmatrix} 0 & -R_Z & R_Y \\ R_Z & 0 & -R_X \\ -R_Y & R_X & 0 \end{bmatrix} \begin{bmatrix} X \\ Y \\ Z \end{bmatrix}_{(S)} + D \begin{bmatrix} X \\ Y \\ Z \end{bmatrix}_{(S)}$$

Spatial SQL and Vector Data Manipulation

Spatial SQL is a way to express geospatial data transformation using well-known and loved SQL. For the SQL examples in this chapter, we assume you have created an Apache Sedona session and invoked all the code using sedona.sql("SQL HERE").

At the time of writing, Apache Sedona supports (multi)point, (multi)linestring, (multi)polygon, and geometry collection. You can create geometry types using various constructor functions like ST_GeomFromText *(Wkt: String)*, which parses the WKT string and transforms it to Sedona's internal geometry representation. You can also write simple SQL code:

```
SELECT ST_GeomFromText('POINT (151.241012 -33.843705)') AS geom
```

When you ask for the schema of the result DataFrame, you can spot that no matter which geometry type you have in the data (point, polygon, etc.), the printSchema() command always returns geometry:

```
root
|-- geom: geometry (nullable = true)
```

This is because Sedona uses a generic object to handle geometry. To determine the precise geometry type of the geometry column in the DataFrame, you can use the ST_GeometryType(A: Geometry) function. From now on, we will simplify our example, assuming that the result of the previous query is now stored in the view called points, which has a geometry column named geom.

```
SELECT
    ST_GeometryType(geom) AS geom_type
FROM points
```

The result of the query shows that we are dealing with a point type:

```
+-----------+
| geom_type |
+-----------+
| ST_Point  |
+-----------+
```

Anyone who works in the GIS field knows how painful it is to deal with different CRSes. To overcome this particular issue, the idea of unifying those codes was developed. One entity that did that is the European Petroleum Survey Group, or EPSG for short.

> SRID and CRS are close in meaning. SRID is an identifier for a specific CRS that some standardization organizations, such as EPSG, maintain.

We talked before about CRS and how it is vital for geospatial data; it's impossible to get accurate results when you compare data from different CRSes. You can verify the code of the CRS of the data you are loading using the ST_SRID function. It returns the EPSG code:

```
SELECT
        ST_SRID(geom) AS srid
    FROM points
```

That gives us:

```
+-----+
|srid |
+-----+
| 0   |
+-----+
```

That's not what we expected. If you don't provide an SRID when creating the spatial DataFrame, Apache Sedona can't infer it automatically (for many formats like GeoParquet, GeoPackage, and Shapefile, SRID is inferred automatically; for binary data with SRID inside like EWKB, the SRID will also be propagated properly). To manipulate the geometry SRID, you can use two spatial functions: ST_SetSRID and ST_Transform.

There is a significant difference between ST_SetSRID and ST_Transform. In the case of the former, we don't change the coordinates data in all situations. We only assign the SRID code to it. On the other hand, ST_Transform modifies coordinates if we shift the SRID. We've already talked about transformation techniques in the "Transformation" section. Our example is a point in Sydney, Australia, and its longitude and latitude coordinates from EPSG:4326 SRID. Let's assign the SRID and transform it to EPSG:3857, a pseudo-Mercator projection:

```
SELECT
        ST_Transform(ST_SetSRID(geom, 4326), 'EPSG:3857') AS geom
    FROM points
```

The corresponding data:

```
+------------------------------------------------+
| geom                                           |
+------------------------------------------------+
| POINT (16836072.44 -4007834.68)                |
+------------------------------------------------+
```

> Apache Sedona infers the CRS from the file for most geospatial data formats.

When calculating the distance between two points on the Earth's surface, you must consider its curvature. The great circle distance (geodesic distance) is the shortest path between two points on the Earth's surface. To perform this calculation, we assume the Earth is perfectly spherical, so the computation is simplified. Assuming that the Earth is more of an ellipsoid than a sphere, we call the distance between two points the spheroid distance.

When your analytics considers larger areas on the Earth's surface, consider using the distance functions, which allow for calculating geography distances (spheroid, sphere) in Apache Sedona instead of in the local coordinate reference system. Your geometry objects have to be in the WGS84 system, then use the ST_DistanceSphere or ST_DistanceSpheroid functions. In spatial joins, for instance, the ST_DWithin function has an additional parameter, usespheroid, that uses geography-based distance.

CRS is crucial for distance measurement. By default, when you use the ST_Distance function, which measures the distance between the two geometries, it returns the value in the unit of measure for a given CRS of the geometries. In our example of transformation to EPSG:3857, we would get the distance in meters. Sedona offers several distance functions. Let's explore some of them and learn when to use each one (Table 4-1).

Table 4-1. Distance functions available in Apache Sedona

Function name	Description
ST_Distance(a: geom, b: geom)	The Euclidean distance between two geometries. Apache Sedona does not transform coordinates. The result is in the same units as the input coordinates. For example, if you use longitude and latitude coordinates, the distance will be in degrees. Note: if you calculate the distance between two geometries where one of them is a nonpoint one, then the distance is between the two closest points of those geometries; if the geometries share any common point, then the distance will be 0.

Function name	Description
ST_Distance Sphere(a: geom, b: geom)	The Haversine/great circle distance. It returns a result in meters. The calculation is faster than ST_DistanceSpheroid, at the cost of less accurate results. It's beneficial when calculating the distance between points across different continents. It's more complex than ST_Distance as it uses trigonometry formulas instead of Pythagoras's formula. For nonpoint geometries, ST_DistanceSphere uses the centroids of the left and right geometries.
ST_Distance Spheroid(a: geom, b: geom)	Geodesic distance between geometries using the WGS84 spheroid. This is more accurate than ST_DistanceSphere but it is slower. The primary use case is for data spread across large areas. For nonpoint geometries, ST_DistanceSpheroid uses the centroids of the left and right geometries.

Remember when we mentioned that the more points a geometry has, the more complex the queries are? This is because the algorithms used for spatial relationship exploration highly depend on the number of points in each geometry.

Let's start by finding out if two points intersect. To get the result, you only need to compare two coordinates.

What if we validate if the point intersects with the linestring? We need to go to every line segment, and if we encounter the point, that resolves the line-segment formula. In this case, we need to look at all the points. It might get even trickier for points in polygon verification. We can use the raycasting algorithm, which is described in the following two steps:

1. Draw an infinite line from the point in any direction
2. Calculate the number of times the line intersects the polygon's edges

If the number of the intersecting points is odd, the point is inside the polygon. Otherwise, it's outside. As you can imagine, the more points your polygon has, the larger the number of comparisons. You can simplify this by verifying first by the boundary box and later by the exact polygon.

Let's continue exploring Apache Sedona SQL functions. Imagine you've created the catchment areas based on the travel time from all the train stations in your city. The polygons you have are pretty complex. To simplify your polygons for faster data processing, you can use the ST_Simplify(geom: Geometry, tolerance: Double) function to reduce the number of points in your polygons. The tolerance is the distance in the units of measure of a given CRS. The result of the function is shown in Figure 4-9.

```
SELECT ST_Simplify(geom, 0.01)
```

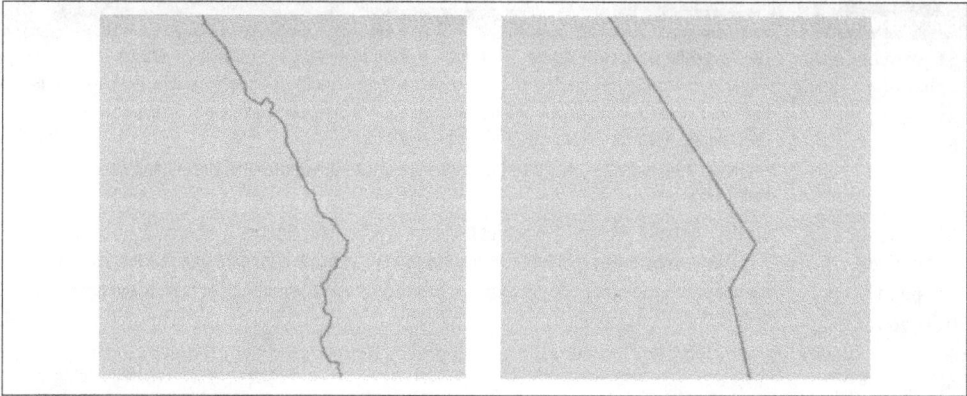

Figure 4-9. Result of the ST_Simplify function on the linestring geometry: on the left is an input geometry, and on the right is the output

Our next stop is the functions ST_StartPoint and ST_EndPoint. We use the road dataset from the OSM project to find the start and end points of a given road. The data sample looks as follows:

```
+--------+-----------------+------------+-------------------+
| osm_id|             name|      fclass|           geometry|
+--------+-----------------+------------+-------------------+
|9566542|      Cầu Thê Húc|     footway|LINESTRING (105.8...|
|9656653|      Phố Mã Mây|residential|LINESTRING (105.8...|
|9656730|  Cầu Chương Dương|     primary|LINESTRING (105.8...|
|9963509|     Phố Hàng Cót|    tertiary|LINESTRING (105.8...|
|9964440| Phố Quốc Tử Giám|residential|LINESTRING (105.8...|
+--------+-----------------+------------+-------------------+
```

The output of our simple query might later be used to create a DataFrame with a road network graph, which might then be used to solve routing problems. Our input is a table named roads with an ID field called osm_id and a geometry (linestring) named geometry:

```
SELECT
    osm_id as id,
    ST_StartPoint(geometry) AS geom
FROM roads
UNION ALL
SELECT
    osm_id AS id,
    ST_EndPoint(geometry) AS geom
FROM roads
```

We can divide the query into three parts: the first and the second are the starting and ending points, while the third is the glue holding them together using the UNION ALL clause, which appends the first query result with the second one.

We can continue exploring Sedona's spatial functions. As an exercise we will prepare an area where the roads will be blocked for the marathon in Hanoi. You have a road dataset and have been given the names of the streets where the race takes place. Let's try to do that using Apache Sedona. We will continue using the same DataFrame as in the previous example:

```
SELECT
    ST_ConvexHull(ST_Union_Aggr(geometry))
FROM roads
WHERE (name = 'Phố Giảng Võ' OR name = 'Phố Kim Mã') AND fclass = 'primary'
```

> A convex hull is the smallest convex set that contains a geometry. A convex set, on the other hand, is a set of points fulfilling a requirement. We can draw a line between any pair of points inside the set of points so that the line is not outside the polygon created by that set of points.

To find the area, we need a couple of things:

- We start by filtering the data to the given road names Phố Giảng Võ and Phố Kim Mã. We only need primary roads, and that ends our filter predicate.
- ST_Union_Aggr is an aggregation function that takes all the geometries from rows and merges them into one.
- ST_ConvexHull finds the convex hull of the given geometry.

Our next task is to find an area 500m from the initial location and list all the roads that need to be closed. For simplicity, let's assume that we saved our previously created area in a table called convex_hull:

```
SELECT DISTINCT name
FROM roads
WHERE ST_Intersects(geometry, (
    SELECT
        ST_Transform(
            ST_Buffer(
                ST_Transform(geom, 'EPSG:3405'),
                500
            ),
            'EPSG:4326'
        ) AS geom
    FROM convex_hull
))
```

Our data uses EPSG:4326 for the coordinates, which is a degree coordinate system, so the result is in degrees rather than meters. To overcome this, we must transform it into metric CRS and find the buffer geometry. The epsg.io website allows us to discover CRSes for any country. We are not using the previously mentioned EPSG:3857 as the error for measuring distance increases drastically when moving from the equator, so for Vietnam, the error is not negligible. The next step is to find the buffer for that geometry and transform it again into the initial CRS, our subquery geometry.

ST_Intersects represents predicates, which might be used to filter our data in a where clause. We can also use them in an optimized way with join statements. We'll discuss that in the next part of this chapter, "Spatial Queries." ST_Intersects, as we discussed at the beginning of that chapter, verifies if two geometries have a common point.

The last step in the query is to take the distinct names of the roads we must close off. Your result DataFrame should look similar to the following (only the top five rows are shown):

```
+--------------------+
|                name|
+--------------------+
|      Ngõ 152 Hào Nam|
|        Ngõ Quan Thổ 1|
|    Ngõ 20 Thành Công|
| Ngõ 8B Phố Vũ Thạnh|
|Ngõ 156 Mai Anh Tuấn|
+--------------------+
```

We can simplify the query using the ST_DWithin function and the spheroid argument. Unfortunately, this solution isn't the fastest; you can see why in Chapter 10, which describes the optimization of the Apache Sedona program:

```
SELECT
    DISTINCT name
FROM roads
WHERE ST_DWithin(geometry, (SELECT geom FROM convex_hull), 500, true)
```

For the predicate clause, we use the ST_DWithin function, which searches a given radius from geometry A and validates whether the second argument, geometry B, is inside the radius. We passed the distance in meters as the third parameter because, as a fourth parameter, we passed true to use the spheroid distance in meters. We went through a couple of the geospatial functions available in Apache Sedona. For more information, refer to the official Apache Sedona documentation (*https://oreil.ly/LV2Ua*).

Spatial Queries

The main goal of any spatial query is to investigate spatial relations between geometries. We previously discussed the types of relations between geometries. We can filter GPS coordinates based on the road polygon (intersects). If our relation is more complicated, we can use the ST_Relate function. We discussed many spatial SQL functions and how to apply them to the data loaded from commonly used data sources. However, we have yet to cover how to combine multiple tables to answer location-based questions. Before doing that, you must first understand the JOIN operation in SQL, what types of JOIN operations can be found in Spark SQL, and how each one works. If you are already a Spark user, you can skip that part.

Spark Distributed Joins

Before we explore how Apache Spark performs the joins under the hood, let's examine the relevant key concepts.

Shuffling is a process of redistributing data across many nodes to perform operations. It mostly happens before aggregations or join operations, where specific data needs to be adequately reorganized to achieve a performant final result. Shuffling is costly, so the less we need to do it, the better the overall performance of your Spark application.

Narrow operation is a process of applying some function to a Spark row or column that does not require the reorganization of data (shuffling). It's easy to distribute narrow operations to your distributed cluster. *Wide operation* is an operation that requires data reorganization (shuffling) before taking an action.

In computer science, a *hash table* is a data structure that uses hash operations to store and locate elements in memory for fast lookups. It usually needs $O(1)$ to access an element based on a given key, but it occupies $O(n)$ space.

Hash join is the join type when for one of the datasets, we create a map and use the join key as the key for the map. Then, we map the other dataset and get the value from the created map ($O(1)$ operation).

A *broadcast join* is a type of join in Apache Spark in which one side of the join (the smaller) is copied to the nodes before the join. By default, it's turned on, and the limit on the dataset size is 10 MB. You can turn this option off by setting spark.sql.autoBroadcastJoinThreshold to −1, and you can increase/decrease the size threshold by manipulating that property.

Using the `hint` method, you can force Apache Spark to use a specific join strategy. For example, with books and authors:

```
spark \
    .table("authors") \
    .join(
        spark.table("books").hint("broadcast"),
        "author_id"
    )
```

And for SQL:

```
SELECT /*+ BROADCAST(b) */ *
FROM authors a
JOIN books b ON a.id = b.author_id
```

A *broadcast hash join* is a type of join where we copy the data from a smaller dataset to all the nodes, after which Apache Spark performs a hash map join against the split data from a larger dataset. You can see how it works in Figure 4-10.

Broadcast join can significantly improve your query performance by copying the data to the nodes of your cluster instead of shuffling both sides of your join. On the left of the figure, you can see a large table on the left side of the join and a small one on the right side. In broadcast join instead of shuffling the left side we chunk it only, and we copy the right side to all the nodes (of course it can be reversed, so right is large and left is small).

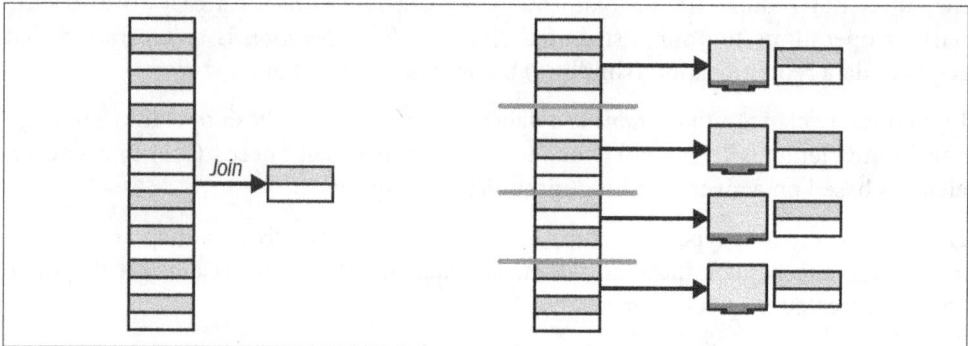

Figure 4-10. A broadcast hash join

In a *shuffle hash join,* the idea is to split your data based on a range (both datasets, left and right) and send it across the network to specific nodes. Then, based on chunks of the data, you create a hash map using the join key as a key and all other values as values for a hash map. Data corresponding to specific keys lands on the same machines.

Creating the hash table might be expensive, especially when your hashed dataset is large, which can lead to Java heap space errors on your worker nodes and job failures. A hash join is a good way to join a massive dataset on the left and a relatively small dataset on the right side (but larger than the broadcast limit). Hash map joins can only be used for equity comparisons (as we search the map to get a value, and any other searches make no sense). The simplified visualization of the hash map join is shown in Figure 4-11.

In Figure 4-11 we assume we already did the data shuffling and we have matching partitions. The hash map join has map joins row by row in the left partition and checks if for a given key there is an entry in the right partition (converted to a map). In table joins we need to also take the specific columns after join, so the simplified code for the row with id = 5 in the left partition would be `dict.get(5).get("name")`.

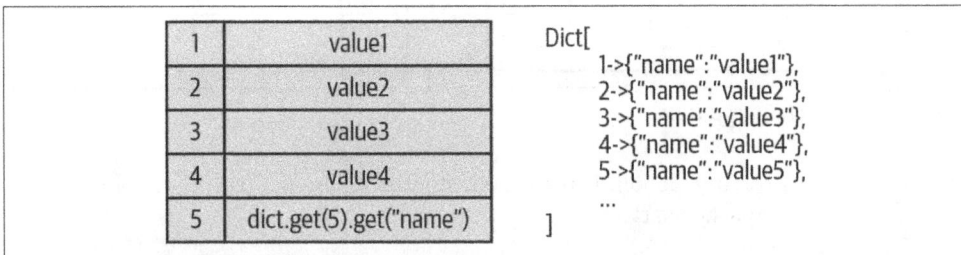

1	value1
2	value2
3	value3
4	value4
5	dict.get(5).get("name")

```
Dict[
    1->{"name":"value1"},
    2->{"name":"value2"},
    3->{"name":"value3"},
    4->{"name":"value4"},
    5->{"name":"value5"},
    ...
]
```

Figure 4-11. Hash map join

In a sort-merge join (Figure 4-12) for each shuffle split, we sort the data from the left dataset and from the right based on the merge keys. Then, we move the pointer to where the smaller value is (either left or right) when we hit the predicate, and then we merge the tuples to produce a row that meets the criteria (inner join). The mechanism is slightly different when we use other joins as we need to include not only matched rows.

In Figure 4-12 again, similarly to the hash join, we assume we have properly shuffled the data. And we analyze the partitions, left and right. The sort-merge join algorithm needs sorting of both partitions before starting the algorithm. In the figure, you can see four steps of the join, where we put the pointer and move it until we get a match.

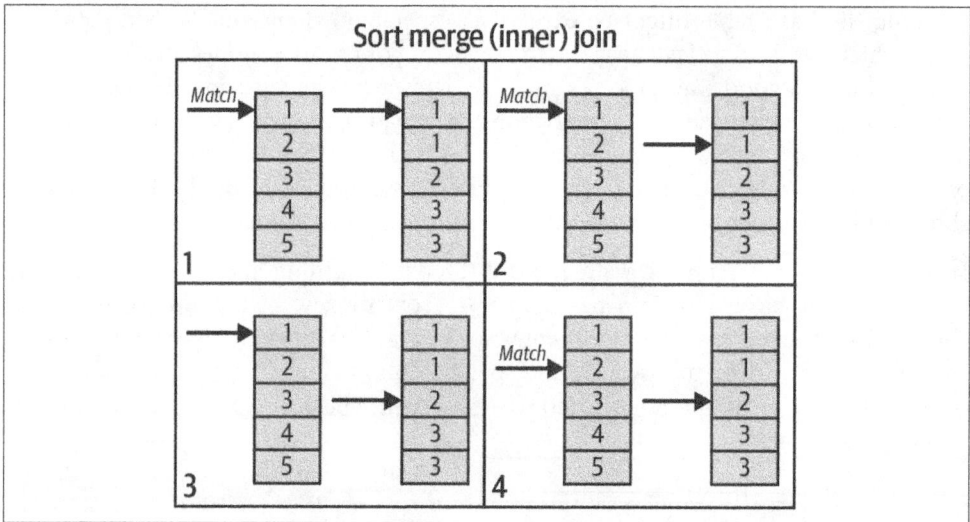

Figure 4-12. Sort-merge join

> A sort-merge join is the default strategy when you perform a join in Apache Spark.

A *broadcast nested loop join* is a mechanism where we copy the broadcasted side of the join to all the nodes. The difference is how we join inside the node compared to the hash join. In the nested loop join, as the names suggest, we loop over the left tuple, and inside the loop, we loop over the right dataset. The complexity is O($m*n$), where m is the size of the left dataset, and n is the size of the right dataset. Using simple Python code, we can write the following:

```
result = []
for l in left:
    for r in right:
        if not match(l, r):
            continue

    result.append((l, r))
```

It might be used when the smaller part of the join is small enough that the effort of creating a hashmap is greater than just looping the elements (dozens of records at most).

When performing the Cartesian product join (shuffle-and-replicate nested loop join), we must shuffle our data before using the nested loop join inside the node. It's the least performant way of joining the data in Apache Spark. You may encounter this type of join when Apache Spark can't find any optimization to speed up the joining process. We can cause this kind of join when applying our own join function:

```python
import pyspark.sql.types as t
import pyspark.sql.functions as f

intersects = f.udf(lambda left, right: left.intersects(right), t.BooleanType())

result = points \
    .alias("p") \
    .join(
        lines.alias("l"),
        intersects(f.col("p.geom"), f.col("l.geom"))
    )
```

For the points and lines tables, we create the UDF function, which verifies whether two geometries intersect. When you run the explain method (result.explain()) for the resulting DataFrame, you will see the following physical plan:

```
== Physical Plan ==
*(3) Project [id#44L, geom#45, id#52L, geom#53]
+- *(3) Filter pythonUDF0#75: boolean
   +- BatchEvalPython [<lambda>(geom#45, geom#53)#66], [pythonUDF0#75]
      +- CartesianProduct
         :- *(1) Project [_1#40L AS id#44L, _2#41 AS geom#45]
         :  +- *(1) Scan ExistingRDD[_1#40L,_2#41]
         +- *(2) Project [_1#48L AS id#52L, _2#49 AS geom#53]
            +- *(2) Scan ExistingRDD[_1#48L,_2#49]
```

We can see the Cartesian product, which is a nested loop join. The advantage of using Apache Sedona is that it gives you the necessary optimizations for common geospatial transformations like spatial join, the KNN query, or KNN join. We will discuss the significant optimization provided for vector data by Apache Sedona for you later in this chapter. Now let's try to understand what a spatial join is and how it is different from other join types mentioned to this point in this chapter (hash join, loop join, sort-merge join).

Spatial Joins

A *spatial join* is an operation used to merge two datasets based on spatial relations, which we went through at the beginning of this chapter. We can combine our data if they intersect with each other, if they share a common boundary, etc. How different is a spatial join from joining data based on equality? While dealing with points, comparing geometry data does not seem complex. However, once you start handling polygons with hundreds or even tens of thousands of points each, the complexity grows considerably. Imagine how much time and resources would be needed when not having access to any optimization technique and needing to use a nested loop join to compare each polygon! We can write the spatial join query using the following SQL syntax:

```
SELECT
    s.name,
    c.name
FROM city AS c
JOIN superhero AS s ON ST_Contains(c.geom, s.geom)
```

We abstract the complex spatial join into a simple SQL query, which can be scaled starting from smaller datasets up to large ones. Either we have a couple of heroes for whom we want to find the cities, or we have billions of them and all the cities and villages in the world. The key is the optimizations, which we can simplify to make this possible.

One of the optimizations that we can start with is comparing rectangles created based on extreme points in the polygon data. How does this help? We will only use four points for comparison, making filtering out data that does not meet the criteria easier. Still, we need to loop over all the records on the left and right, so the more data we have, the more challenging it becomes to get the result. Like nonspatial data, one of the optimization techniques is indexing to create data locality and reduce the number of comparisons of complex geometry objects. In the next section, we will go through the most commonly used indexing techniques.

Spatial Indexes

Joining spatial data without optimization techniques might never finish, as many spatial objects have complex geometries with enormous numbers of points. The more observations we have in a spatial data frame, the more time is needed to compare more geometries. A few techniques can be incorporated to optimize spatial join operations:

Minimal boundary rectangle (MBR)
   The smallest rectangle that can be built on top of a geometry shape. We can pre-eliminate geospatial objects that do not meet the criteria by using MBR. For example, it's not worth comparing the shape of London with POIs (points of interest) from Seoul.

Tree data structure
   A data structure in computer science that consists of nodes, sometimes called leaves, connected in hierarchical order. Dividing the data into smaller units might help reduce the number of queries and reduce the algorithm's time complexity. The top element in the tree is called the root, and leaves connected below the node are called children.

Binary tree
   A tree data structure that divides elements into two for each node so that every child of the node on the left is less than the node, and the child on the right is greater than or equal to the node.

R-tree

A tree structure that uses MBRs to order spatial data hierarchically. It reduces the number of queries needed to ask spatial questions. R-tree works well for intersection queries. Instead of asking for all the elements in the dataset, we can reduce the number of comparison elements to just the neighborhood.

R-tree is a commonly used data structure in a spatial world. To construct it, we start by constructing an MBR for each geometry object (Figure 4-13). Then, we combine close MBRs with larger MBRs up to the root (A).

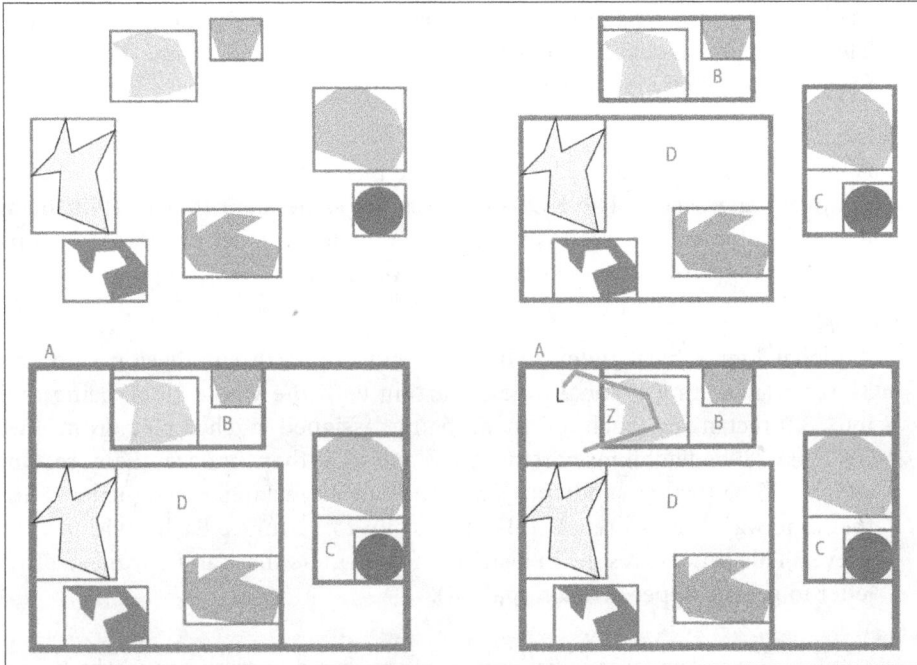

Figure 4-13. Steps to produce and query R-tree

Then, when we try to find the geometries that intersect with Line L, we only ask if the geometry of L intersects with larger rectangles A; if so, then we continue with D, C, and B, then with smaller rectangles within the rectangle B. Finally, only Polygon Z can intersect with the L geometry, so we use the intersection algorithm to prove our candidate and return the result.

Two main benefits of using R-tree are fewer comparisons and reduced complexity of comparisons.

KD-tree

A type of binary tree used in many geospatial problems, like nearest-neighbor searches. The idea is to split the area into two subareas using a perpendicular plane and continue until we reach a predefined level of depth. The maximum number of steps depends on the final criteria: the max tree depth or the number of points in a given subarea. Assuming that we have a 2D KD-tree, then the process is as follows. We start by splitting the x-axis into two subareas. We chose an x split point based on the criteria x-min < x-split < x-max, in most cases, which is a median of the set of x points to keep the splits even. With all the data left from the split, we move to the left part of the tree, greater than or equal to the x-split, and move to the right. Then we split two subareas based on the y-axis and use the same criteria to select the y-split and the side of the tree.

KDB-tree

A mixture of KD-tree and B-tree, which is a tree data structure that helps optimize data access. The KDB-tree uses the same algorithm to split the space into two subareas, but each is not its node. Instead, nodes are placed into pages, and the tree references the pointer to the root page.

Geohash

A global hierarchical index that uses recursive earth subdivision into smaller 32 rectangles. It's a gradual index. Starting with the whole globe being divided into 32 rectangles, each of them being assigned a character from the list "0123456789bcdefghjkmnpqrstuvwxyz", we can then choose these rectangles, which will be further subdivided into another 32 rectangles assigned a character the same way. We can repeat this process up to 12 times. Each division is called a level. This process results in a string of characters that can be truncated by one letter to get the upper division (parent).

> The more initial characters are shared between two Geohash indexes, the more spatially close they are to each other. This is not always true in reverse, as two cells might be close to each other but share no prefix at all.

S2Cell

Based on a hierarchy of cells created on top of the Earth sphere model. Similar to Geohash and H3, the concept of level is introduced. The top level is made from the six faces of a cube onto the unit sphere. The following consecutive levels are based on the recursive process of subdividing space into four children.

You can see curves when dividing because the Earth is not flat. We can divide it into four children up to level 30, approximately 1cm × 1cm in size. Each cell has a unique 64-bit identifier called s2cellId, and we order them to maximize the locality of reference.

H3

A global hierarchical index that uses hexagonal grids to divide the Earth's surface into smaller chunks. It was invented at Uber and shared publicly, and since then, it has gained a lot of traction. We assign an ID, which is unique globally, to each grid. H3 is an excellent index for range queries, nearby searches, finding the shortest path, and more. The considerable advantage of H3 is the equal distance between all six neighbors, which is invalid for other indexes like square-based ones (Geohash or S2).

Sedona implements many H3 functions such as ST_H3CellDistance, ST_H3Cell IDs, ST_H3KRing, and ST_H3ToGeom.

> An H3 cell cannot divide into six equal cells; it is an approximation done by rotating lower-level grids. This makes it possible to truncate the index length to get a parent. It is also possible to get all the children of the parent index. Geographically, the index is an approximation, but logically, it's exact. Thanks to these properties, implementation is fast because it uses primarily bit operations.

Optimized Spatial Joins

In most spatial databases like PostGIS, you may encounter spatial indexes like R-tree, which is well suited for intersections and proximity searches. You can optimize the spatial join, which previously was a nested loop join, by leveraging the following steps:

1. Create an index on one of the sides of the join.
2. Loop over the side of the join, which has no index created.
3. For each observation query, search the index to find possible candidates fulfilling the criteria.
4. For returned observations from the index, filter them using your predicate.

We can use simplified Python code to find spatial join results with R-tree. Assume we have left and right datasets and an R-tree index called r_index. You can see the visualization of the R-tree indexing using the following code in Figure 4-14:

```
result_index = []

for r in right:
    candidates = r_index.intersection(get_bounds(r))
    candidates_filtered = [[c, r] for c in candidates if predicate(c, r)]
    result_index.extend(candidates_filtered)
```

In Figure 4-14, for each point, we ask only for the largest rectangle and then three smaller ones (I–III), and only for points inside of rectangle III do we need to verify with a more complex geometry than a rectangle. Other points do not intersect any of the rectangles I–III. It's even more visible for larger datasets as the number of comparisons is reduced from thousands or millions to a few.

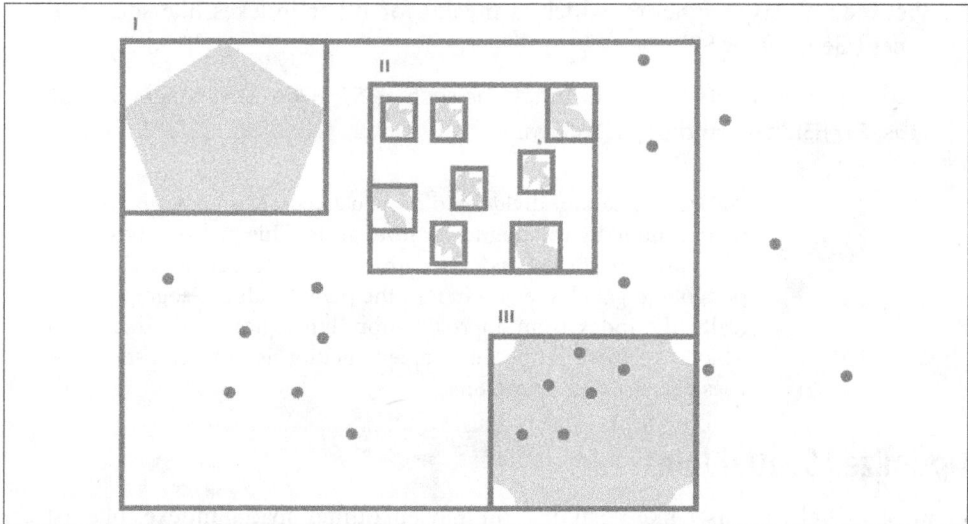

Figure 4-14. Visualization of R-tree indexing

With indexing and proper data storage, we can get decent query performance until we hit the floor, which is the dataset size. The more data we have, the longer it takes one machine to finish a query. Then, we end up with a long query that may not finish or fail due to memory issues. We can quickly reach that point using PostgreSQL, and it's a matter of GB, not even TB of data. But how can we improve the approach to handle more data? Apache Sedona and its optimization techniques allow you to scale geospatial data processing to a global scale with optimized clusters to process in mere minutes instead of days.

To better understand the whole mechanism under Sedona spatial join optimization, we need to understand spatial partitioning and the kind of problem it solves.

Spatial Partitioning

One key challenge of parallelizing geospatial computation is distributing the work-load on many machines. How can we avoid common pitfalls like data skew or spending enormous time reshuffling data? The answer is *spatial partitioning*.

Spatial partitioning assigns observations from a geospatial DataFrame to the proper partition. We can do that in many ways, starting by using an equal grid and dividing the whole spatial DataFrame MBR into smaller grids. Let's take buildings from the OSM project for Egypt to understand the concept better. First, we find minX, minY, maxX, and maxY for the spatial DataFrame.

We split the data into multiple partitions, but over half of them have almost no data. Equal grid partitioning is not the best approach for unevenly distributed geospatial data. You can see how it splits the data for non-evenly distributed geometries, such as those in Egypt, in Figure 4-15.

Figure 4-15. Spatial partitioning using the equal grid method for Egyptian buildings

We can try using different mechanisms (KDB-tree) to partition buildings and see if we can achieve more even partitions. This will reduce hot spots and data skew during shuffle operations such as aggregation and joining. In Figure 4-16, you can see that for areas where there are fewer geometries, the partitions are larger; for cities like Cairo, there are way more partitions.

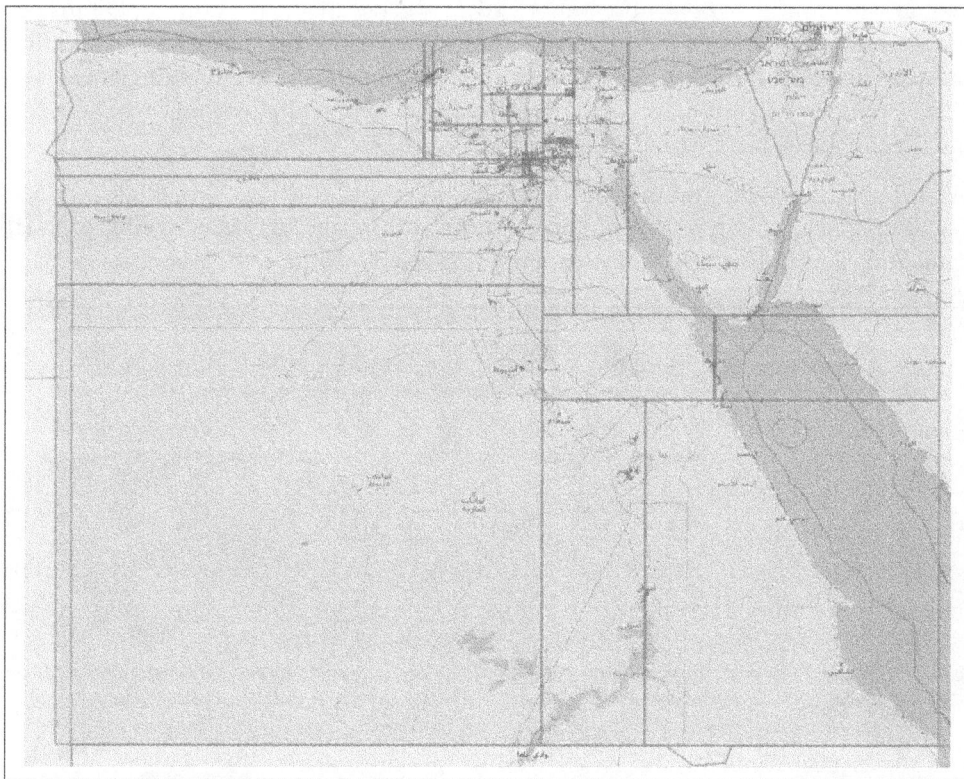

Figure 4-16. Spatial partitioning using a KDB-tree for Egypt buildings

As you can see, the data distribution in the partitions looks better. Now, with all the machinery (spatial partitioning, spatial join, spatial indexing), we can move forward to distributed spatial joins, the origin, and heart, of Apache Sedona.

Distributed Spatial Joins

Initially, we used nested loop joins for spatial joins, which was far from perfect. Then, we looked into the optimized version, which uses R-tree to reduce queries and increase overall performance. Before going through the whole process, let's understand which spatial join queries are optimized with Apache Sedona and when.

Sedona autodetects the broadcasted side for the broadcast join and optimizes the spatial join. To bump the value, you can use the `sedona.join.autoBroadcastJoinThreshold` config property. The join is detected following these rules:

Inner
> Either side prefers to broadcast left if both sides have the hint.

Left semi
> Broadcast right.

Left anti
> Broadcast right.

Left outer
> Broadcast right.

Right outer
> Broadcast left.

The Spark physical plan for a spatial join with broadcast optimization looks like the following:

```
== Physical Plan ==
BroadcastIndexJoin pointshape#52: geometry, BuildRight, BuildRight, false
ST_Contains(polygonshape#30, pointshape#52)
```

Apache Sedona is using *distance join* optimization for queries that use distance comparison. So, asking for points of interest 100m from roads is optimized. Apache Sedona out of the box provides you with optimization for not only Euclidean distances like `ST_HausdorffDistance` and `ST_FrechetDistance` but also `ST_DistanceSpheroid` and `ST_DistanceSphere`. When you want to limit geometries to lay inside the given distance to geometry, then use the < or > symbols, or add = to get <= and >=, which are less than or equal to or greater than or equal to, accordingly. When you join two DataFrames based on laying fully within a 100m distance on a spheroid, the query might look like the following:

```
SELECT
    df1.*
FROM df1, df2
WHERE ST_DistanceSpheroid(df1.geom, df2.geom) < 100
```

Or, using the `JOIN` keyword:

```
SELECT
    df1.*
FROM df1
JOIN df2 ON  ST_DistanceSpheroid(df1.geom, df2.geom) < 100
```

To ensure your spatial join is optimized, look for `DistanceJoin` in the Spark physical plan:

```
== Physical Plan ==
DistanceJoin df1#12: geom, df2#33: geom, 100.0, true
```

Range join is an optimization in Apache Sedona for spatial join operations related to spatial predicate functions such as `ST_Contains`, `ST_Intersects`, `ST_Within`, and `ST_DWithin`. To examine if the query uses an optimized version after running, explain the search method for `RangeJoin` text in the Spark physical plan, as shown:

```
== Physical Plan ==
RangeJoin df1#20: geom, df2#43: geom, false…
```

An example of the query looks like the following:

```
SELECT
    df1.*
FROM df1, df2
WHERE ST_DWithin(df1.geom, df2.geom, 10.0)
```

Or, using the `JOIN` keyword:

```
SELECT
    df1.*
FROM df1
JOIN df2 ON ST_DWithin(df1.geom, df2.geom, 10.0)
```

Now, we can connect all the pieces and explain step-by-step Apache Sedona optimization for spatial joins:

> You can change the value of the `sedona.global.index` property to turn off the global index for partitions.

Let's analyze how Apache Sedona is parsing the query (range query optimization):

```
SELECT
    left.*
FROM points AS p
JOIN polygons AS pl ON ST_INTERSECTS(p.geom, pl.geom)
```

First, Apache Sedona examines the left and right datasets to determine whether they can be broadcast. If yes, one of the datasets is copied to other machines and used to build an index. This operation is similar to how we wrote a spatial join using R-tree.

Things become more interesting when both datasets are larger than the broadcast threshold. The first question is how to distribute the data on the nodes so that the result always returns the same result. The answer is spatial partitioning. Sedona initially gathers statistics about your dataset to partition your data and distribute it evenly based on the configuration value chosen for the spatial partitioning (KDB-tree, equalgrid). When the `global.index` configuration value is enabled, Sedona creates an additional R-tree index for faster lookups for the partition geometries (it might be helpful when the number of partitions is enormous), then, we assign an MBR for each geometry. We use the created rectangle to assign the partition. That might cause the geometry to split into more than one partition, but with a larger scale, comparing simpler geometries is more performant. Ultimately, our result dataset will still not contain such invalid pairs, as they will be filtered out later either in the deduplication process or by comparing the exact geometries.

The left and right Resilient Distributed Datasets (RDDs) are partitioned based on spatial partitioning. We zip them together and loop over pairs of corresponding spatial partitions. For the left side (can be configured using the `sedona.join.indexbuild side`), we create the index, and for the right, we loop over the records, query the index, and filter based on a given predicate. We can assign multiple partitions for polygon and linestring data, and we might end up with duplicates to fix the issue. Sedona deduplicates the data at the end. We can sum up the process in the following steps:

1. Create spatial partitioning geometries based on the data subset
2. Assign spatial partitions for the left and right datasets based on MBR geometries
3. Zip left RDD and right RDD
4. Loop over zipped pairs
5. Create an index on the left side
6. Use an index to get a list of candidates for the predicate
7. Filter candidates
8. Append to the result
9. Deduplicate

Finding nearest neighbors in a distributed fashion is not easy. For a long time, Apache Sedona supported only finding k-nearest neighbors (KNN) for one geometry at a time. Recently, Wherobots' contribution introduced a KNN query for two datasets to Apache Sedona.

Distributed KNN Joins

Imagine you are on the highway driving home, but the low fuel light turns on, so you ask your navigation system to find the closest petrol stations on your route. The underlying algorithm in your app is the KNN search query, which stands for *k-nearest neighbors* problem. When you buy a new home, the appraiser most likely chooses the *k*-closest properties similar to your desired apartment when assessing its value. KNN helps you understand the surroundings and how they impact the data you observe.

As an example, let's examine the dataset with houses where we have a location (longitude, latitude), property assessed value, and its identifier. We aim to find the five closest properties (excluding the target property) and calculate the median price.

Let's start with 10 observations only. With so few observations, we can start with the most straightforward solution, the beloved brute force. We need to loop over our data, sort it in ascending order, copy it, and slice it into *k* elements. Python code might look like this:

```python
import math
import statistics

k = 3

result = []
for identifier, lon, lat, value in properties:
    sorted_by_distance = sorted(
        properties,
        key=lambda row: calculate_distance(lon, lat, row[1], row[2])
    )

    median_value = statistics.median([
        row[3] for row in sorted_by_distance
    ][1:k+1])

    result.append(median_value)
```

That works for 10 elements, and we can quickly develop a solution. What if we have 10,000 observations? Which indexing method would work best for the real estate example? If you thought of R-tree, you are correct. The idea is to think about that particular problem using the range queries. The simplified version of the algorithm looks as follows:

1. We start by guessing the range distance, D.

2. If the query returns at least *k* elements, we do the next step. Otherwise, we increase the range and come back to step 2.

3. We sort the returned elements and return *k* of them.

This is a process that is not optimized, so we could do it better.

Let's complicate the example even further by dramatically increasing the number of points to 1,000,000,000. How can we perform the KNN algorithm in a distributed fashion? There is no straightforward solution.

Using the same technique as in spatial join usually results in incorrect values. Points close to the spatial partitioning boundaries might not have sufficient observations to select from. As you can see, the trickiest part is correctly partitioning the data.

One of the proposed solutions by Dong Xie et al.,[2] implemented in Apache Sedona, starts from partitioning data using a modified *quadtree version*. That data structure helps to keep the spatial locality and to make partitions balanced. Initially, we create the quadtree based on the data sample. Then, we create a global R-tree index (T) based on the same sample as for the quadtree. We must take only a subset dataset to preserve the data patterns and not overwhelm the driver node. For each partition of the quadtree, we find the centroid; for that centroid, we look for the k-nearest neighbors using the global R-tree mentioned before. The kth neighbor (furthest in case of the distance) is selected to calculate the buffer that will be used to extend the quadtree boundaries. The formula for the buffer is as follows:

$$\gamma_i = 2u_i + |cr_i, s_k|$$

where $2u_i$ is twice the distance from the centroid to the furthest point in the partition and $|cr_i, s_k|$ is the distance between the centroid of the partition and the kth nearest neighbor. We extend each partition based on the calculated distance γ_i, creating the buffer. Then, for each partition, we intersect with other partitions to find intersecting partition boundaries. Those combinations will be used to perform the KNN query. The process of creating the spatial partitions in the KNN query in Apache Sedona has been visualized in Figure 4-17.

The last step is to zip each extended partition with the right side (initial quadtree partitioning) and calculate the KNN for each one locally using the same approach as for smaller datasets, including the R-tree.

---

2 Dong Xie et al., "Simba: Efficient In-Memory Spatial Analytics" (*https://oreil.ly/LfjwP*), in *Proceedings of the 2016 International Conference on Management of Data (SIGMOD '16)* (Association for Computing Machinery, New York, NY, 2016), 1071–1085.

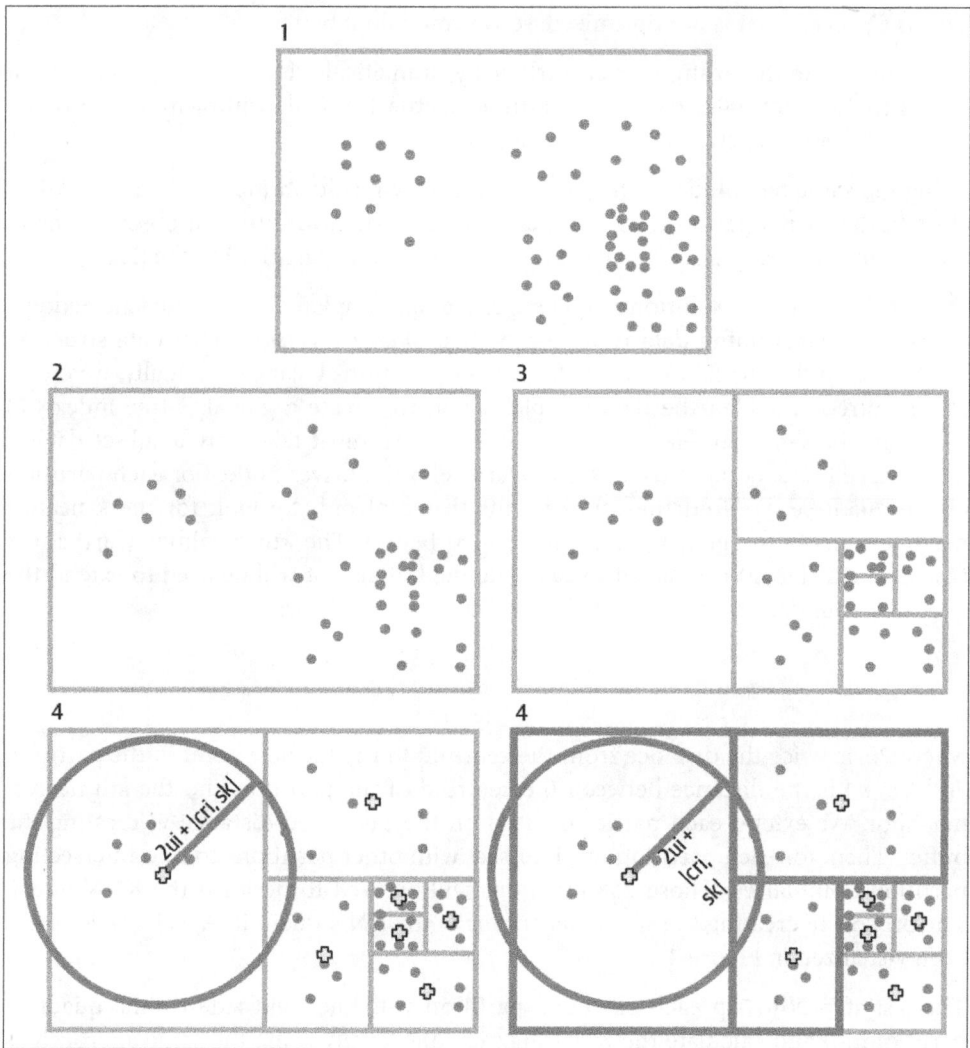

Figure 4-17. KNN query: (1) initial dataset, (2) sampling data, (3) quadtree partitioning, (4) creating a buffer using formula, (5) quadtree extended boundaries

In Apache Sedona, you can use Sedona SQL to find *k*-nearest neighbors in a distributed way. The function signature is as follows:

```
ST_KNN(R: Table, S: Table, k: Integer, use_spheroid: Boolean)
```

Here R and S are spatial DataFrames, k is the number of neighbors to find, and use_spheroid is a Boolean argument indicating whether we want to use the geography model to find neighbors.

Let's look at the following query as an example of a KNN join query. We look for the three closest neighbors for each query row from the `queries` table. We look for them in the `objects` table. We use spheroid distance:

```
SELECT
    QUERIES.ID,
    OBJECTS.ID
FROM QUERIES
JOIN OBJECTS ON ST_KNN(QUERIES.GEOM, OBJECTS.GEOM, 3, false)
```

When you run the `explain` method on the resulting DataFrame, you should expect part of the Spark physical plan to look like the following:

```
== Physical Plan ==
AdaptiveSparkPlan isFinalPlan=false
+- Project [ID#34, ID#79]
   +- KNNJoin GEOM#40: geometry, GEOM#85: geometry, Inner, 3, false,
      **org.apache.spark.sql.sedona_sql.expressions.ST_KNN**
```

> When you want to include your filters after the KNN operation, not before (predicate pushdown), you can use the barrier function:
>
> ```
> SELECT
>     Q.ID,
>     O.ID
> FROM
>     QUERIES AS Q
> JOIN
>     OBJECTS AS O ON ST_KNN(Q.GEOM, O.GEOM, 3, false)
> WHERE
>     barrier(
>         'RATE > 8.0 AND PRICE <= 200',
>         'RATE',
>         O.RATE,
>         'PRICE',
>         O.PRICE
>     )
> ```
>
> You can achieve the same effect by caching the DataFrame before applying the filter:
>
> ```
> knn_query_df.cache()
> ```
>
> ```
> knn_query_df.where(...)
> ```

Hands-On Use Case: Real Estate Analysis

When you buy a house there are three significant factors to consider: the first is location, the second is location, and the final one is location. The distance to work, access to public transportation, concentration of traffic jams, and nearby shops and restaurants are a few of the factors you might consider when looking for a new place to live. In this section, you will use the planetary scale building dataset from Overture Maps and the POIs dataset by Foursquare to calculate features that might be useful for property selection.

We start by loading the data in the Jupyter notebook (you can find all the examples in the official repository for the book). Our dataset is already available using an S3 bucket. For the simplicity of this exercise, we'll use already created tables in the Jupyter notebook environment.

Your goal is to create a feature set that might be used as an input for a machine learning model predicting the price or as a data source for a web application that helps people buy the home of their dreams.

We aim to enrich *residential* buildings with a set of features:

- Distance to the closest road or railway
- Number of grocery stores within a 500m radius
- Most common POI types in the neighborhood

For that purpose, we use the Overture building, Overture transportation, and Foursquare POI datasets. Let's explore the datasets' schemas and decide what columns might be helpful to calculate the three features.

The Overture building dataset has many columns, but for our analysis, we need the ID, which is the unique identifier of the building; the geometry field, which is of type `geometry`; and the last class, which filters buildings to residential only.

We use the Overture transportation dataset to calculate the distance to the closest road or railway. We use class and subclass to properly select railways and roads that might be noisy. The last column we will need is the `geometry` column, which is the `geometry` data type.

To get the "number of grocery stores within a 500m radius" and "most common POI types in the neighborhood," we need to load the Foursquare POI dataset. The Foursquare dataset has two tables: `categories` and `places`. The former stores information about the categories that might be used for the places dataset; the latter stores, for example, category IDs and the POIs' location.

First, you need to load the data. We will consider only residential buildings in the selected area of Chicago:

```
area_of_analysis = """POLYGON(
        (-87.9401 41.6445,
        -87.9401 42.0230,
        -87.5237 42.0230,
        -87.5237 41.6445,
        -87.9401 41.6445)
```

```
    )"""

buildings = sedona \
    .read \
    .format("geoparquet") \
    .load(f"s3a://apache-sedona-book/buildings") \
    .where(f"ST_Intersects(geometry, ST_GeomFromText('{area_of_analysis}'))") \
    .where("class='residential'")
```

Then, we need to filter the transportation dataset to include roads that might cause
noise: motorways, trunk roads, primary, secondary, and tertiary roads. We will also
include all railways, assuming that they are noisy by default. The output of the query
is in the `noisy_roads` table view:

```
roads = sedona \
    .read \
    .format("geoparquet") \
    .load(f"s3a://apache-sedona-book/source_data/us_roads_repartitioned") \
    .where(f"ST_Intersects(geometry, ST_GeomFromText('{area_of_analysis}'))")

noisy_road_classes = [
    "motorway",
    "trunk",
    "primary",
    "secondary",
    "tertiary"
]

noisy_roads = roads.where(
    (
        (
            (f.col("class").isin(noisy_road_classes)) &
            (f.col("subtype") == "road")
        ) |
        (
            (f.col("subtype") == "rail") &
            (f.expr("class IS NULL"))
        )
    )
)

noisy_roads.createOrReplaceTempView("noisy_roads")
```

The last step is to prepare a POI dataset that includes grocery stores:

```
places = sedona \
    .read \
    .format("geoparquet") \
    .load(f"s3a://apache-sedona-book/source_data/us_places") \
    .where(f"ST_Intersects(geom, ST_GeomFromText('{area_of_analysis}'))")

categories_raw = sedona \
    .sql("""
```

```
        SELECT
            category_id
        FROM categories
        WHERE category_name = 'Grocery Store'
    """
    ).collect()

categories = [c[0] for c in categories_raw]

places \
    .where(f.arrays_overlap("fsq_category_ids", f.lit(categories))) \
    .select("fsq_place_id", "geom") \
    .createOrReplaceTempView("grocery_stores")
```

You now need to filter the categories table to `category_name` equal to `'Grocery Store'`. As it might produce more than one `category_id`, we will store it in the list of `category_ids`. Each POI can have many categories assigned; to filter them to category IDs, you can use the `arrays_overlap` function, which returns true when two arrays have at least one element in common. The result is stored in the `grocery_stores` view.

Now that you have finished the prerequisites, you can enrich the building dataset with three features.

You will start with the closest road or railway problem; it might be translated to a KNN query with one nearest neighbor. As input, we need the `buildings` and `noisy_roads` tables. Both tables are in EPSG:4326 CRS; we can either transform the coordinates to a common meter-based CRS or use the geography model to get the distance in meters. In this example, we use the geography model and `ST_Distance Spheroid`, which returns results in meters for two pairs of long and lat. The SQL query is saved to the `closest_road_or_railway` view:

```
SELECT
    b.id,
    ST_DistanceSpheroid(b.geometry, n.geometry)
FROM buildings AS b
JOIN noisy_roads as n ON ST_KNN(b.geometry, n.geometry, 1)
```

To get the second feature, we must spatially join *buildings* and the previously created `grocery_stores` view. Similarly to the KNN query, we use the spheroid distance for the `ST_DWithin` function; we pass true as the fourth parameter to get the distance in meters. Lastly, we aggregate the result by adding an ID to count the number of grocery stores nearby. We store the SQL query in the `grocery_stores_nearby` view:

```
WITH grocery_stores_nearby AS (
    SELECT
        b.id AS building_id,
        g.fsq_place_id AS g_id
    FROM buildings AS b
    JOIN grocery_stores AS g ON ST_DWithin(g.geom, b.geometry, 500, true)
)
SELECT
    building_id AS id,
    count(g_id) AS number_of_grocery_stores
FROM grocery_stores_nearby
GROUP BY id
```

To get the top three most popular POI categories within 300 meters, we will write spatial SQL code. We will split the SQL for readability. First, we start from the spatial join; we can use ST_DWithin and use the geography data type to find POIs in a 300m radius. The result lands in the view pois_intersected:

```
SELECT
    b.id AS building_id,
    p.fsq_place_id AS poi_id,
    p.fsq_category_ids
FROM buildings AS b
JOIN places AS p ON ST_DWithin(p.geom, b.geometry, 300, true)
```

Then we create an additional row for each element in the fsq_category_ids column in the places table, and we store the result in the pois_with_categories view:

```
SELECT
    building_id,
    poi_id,
    explode(fsq_category_ids) AS category_id
FROM pois_intersected
```

After the spatial join, you need to aggregate the data by two dimensions, building_id and category_id:

```
SELECT
    building_id AS id,
    count(poi_id) AS number_of_pois,
    category_id
FROM pois_with_categories
GROUP BY id, category_id
```

Window Functions

Window functions operate on the group of data called a *window*, and for each of the rows in the group, we return the value based on that group's values.[3] Let's explore the example used in the unique POIs category count:

```
row_number() OVER (PARTITION BY id ORDER BY number_of_pois DESC) as rank
```

As an input, let's assume we have a DataFrame with the following data:

```
+---+--------------+-----------+
|id |number_of_pois|category_id|
+---+--------------+-----------+
|1  |13            |1          |
|1  |8             |2          |
|1  |7             |3          |
|2  |1             |4          |
|2  |5             |5          |
|2  |5             |1          |
+---+--------------+-----------+
```

PARTITION BY creates a group of rows based on the ID column; in the POIs case, you can see two groups (for ID 1 and ID 2). For each group, we order the rows based on the `number_of_pois` column in descending order. The `row_number` function assigns an increasing natural number for each row, unique in the group (window). For ties, it doesn't assign the same value but the following natural number. Our example after applying the function looks like the following:

```
+---+--------------+-----------+----+
|id |number_of_pois|category_id|rank|
+---+--------------+-----------+----+
|1  |13            |1          |1   |
|1  |8             |2          |2   |
|1  |7             |3          |3   |
|2  |5             |1          |1   |
|2  |5             |5          |2   |
|2  |1             |4          |3   |
+---+--------------+-----------+----+
```

To rank the result based on the number of POIs in each category, we can use the window function ROW_NUMBER:

```
SELECT
    id,
    row_number() OVER (
        PARTITION BY id ORDER BY number_of_pois DESC
    ) as rank,
```

---

[3] "Window Functions" (*https://oreil.ly/xMtW5*). In *Spark 3.5.1 Documentation*.

```
        category_id
FROM pois_cnt
```

We can filter the view based on the rank column using the `rank <= 3` predicate:

```
SELECT
    id,
    category_id
FROM pois_ranked
WHERE rank <= 3
```

We use `category_id` for that analysis, but to better understand what we got, we have to join the data with the `categories` table. We do that almost at the end, as the number of buildings after filtering is smaller than the number of POIs. It's a good habit to join as late as possible when you filter or aggregate your data, as moving data over the network is a costly operation.

The remaining part aggregates the data into a list and moves `category_name` to a list for each key; in our case, we can use `collect_list` to build `id`:

```
SELECT
    id,
    collect_list(category_name) AS category_names
FROM pois_with_categories_resolved
GROUP BY id
```

Now that we have all the desired features, let's do the final join to get the result table:

```
SELECT
    b.id,
    b.geometry,
    pc.category_names,
    gs.number_of_grocery_stores AS number_of_gs,
    cr.distance_to_road_or_railway AS dist_to_rr
FROM buildings AS b
LEFT JOIN poi_categories_nearby AS pc ON pc.id = b.id
LEFT JOIN grocery_stores_agg AS gs ON gs.id = b.id
LEFT JOIN closest_road_or_railway AS cr ON cr.id = b.id
```

And the result table:

```
+--------+-------------------+-------------------+------------+------------+
|     id|           geometry|     category_names|number_of_gs|  dist_to_rr|
+--------+-------------------+-------------------+------------+------------+
|08b26...|POLYGON ((-86.565...|               NULL|        NULL|      614.18|
|08b26...|POLYGON ((-85.256...|[Dining and Drink...|          1|      107.23|
|08b26...|POLYGON ((-85.202...|               NULL|        NULL|      581.34|
|08b27...|POLYGON ((-88.022...|[Community and Go...|        NULL|      346.49|
|08b27...|POLYGON ((-88.023...|[Community and Go...|        NULL|      349.34|
|08b2a...|POLYGON ((-74.018...|[Travel and Trans...|          1|      159.26|
|08b2a...|POLYGON ((-74.019...|[Business and Pro...|          2|       90.22|
|08b2a...|POLYGON ((-78.921...|[Community and Go...|          1|      109.28|
+--------+-------------------+-------------------+------------+------------+
```

Summary

This chapter was quite intense, but we covered a lot regarding vector data processing in Apache Sedona. We started from a vector data model and relationship, which is significant for processing data consciously with Apache Sedona. The geography model is key to understanding the implication of the selected CRS, why you need a geography data type, and why we have so many different EPSG codes. Spatial queries and joins are the most potent tools in Apache Sedona. That's why Sedona was created in the first place. You might feel overwhelmed by the amount of knowledge, but this will help you write better Sedona code and understand why calculations sometimes take longer when not properly optimized.

In the last section of this chapter, we used an open source dataset to create an analytics pipeline for the real estate sector.

## CHAPTER 5

Raster Data Analysis

In many modern OLAP and OLTP databases and data processing engines, you can use some of the geospatial vector functions, but raster processing is, in most cases, missing. Combining them in one library is a rare thing. Apache Sedona provides the capability to analyze and process both vector and raster data types. Raster data is semi-structured data collected by aerial and satellite imagery. To get the information from it, we need sophisticated functions, which Apache Sedona provides for you. In this chapter, we will explain the raster data model used in Apache Sedona and then proceed to discuss loading and writing to raster data. Processing raster data includes operations on pixels in one band and multiple bands. We will cover different raster spatial functions, as well as the zonal statistics and map algebra operations. Spatial join in Apache Sedona is optimized not only for vector data but also for raster data. We will conclude the chapter with an insurance risk modeling use case that combines vector and raster data.

The Raster Data Model

A raster is a spatial data model that defines space as an array of cells called pixels arranged into rows and columns. It is a discrete representation of the space. The simplest raster consists of a single 2D array with values (Figure 5-1). Each raster consists of rows and cells, and the numbering starts from the top left corner and ends at the bottom right. Each coordinate refers to the centroid of the pixel. The numbering and the pixel location depend on the system or library. In Apache Sedona, the centroid of the pixel is used as the anchor. In access functions like RS_Value, Apache Sedona uses the column-row order, as shown in the figure.

To represent the color raster, we need representations of the three primary colors: red, green, and blue. Rasters might be more complex than three colors; for example, Sentinel-3 Mission images (*https://oreil.ly/zZ5Vc*) have 21 bands with different purposes, such as assessing vegetation or measuring water vapor absorption. A raster containing multiple arrays with values is called a multiple-band raster; a single array in such a raster is named a band. Raster data might contain missing values, where the actual value is unknown; we refer to such areas as NoData values. There is no strict value assigned to it, such as NULL; for NoData values, you will see integer values like –99999.

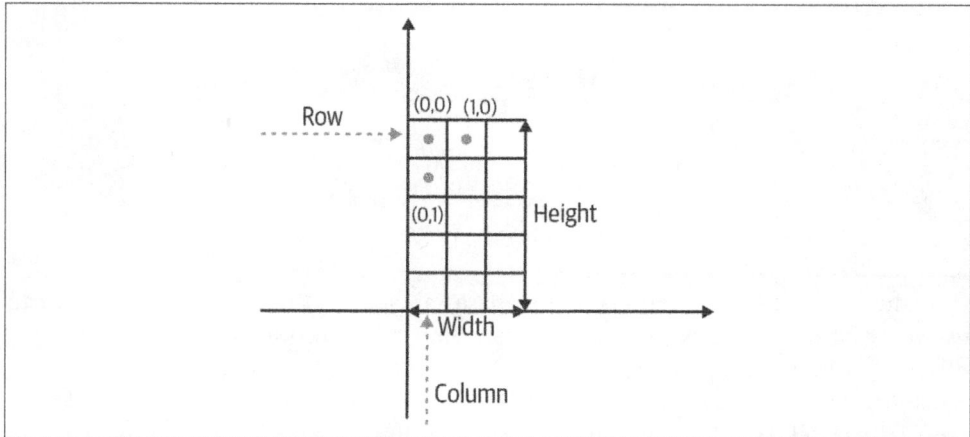

Figure 5-1. The simplified raster definition

With the column-row order, we can only use equally spaced coordinates, such as (1, 0), (2, 0), and (3, 0). We can only provide the column and row coordinates, which are very limited. We can't define the rotation of the raster, the scale of the pixel, or the translation in space. The missing component in our current definition is the mathematical transformation function, which calculates real-world coordinates based on row and column coordinates. The process of finding parameters for the function is called *georeferencing*. The transformation functions, in order of increasing complexity, are:

- Affine transformation (first-order polynomial)
- Polynomial transformations (higher order)
- Spline transformations
- Projective transformation

Another challenging aspect of handling raster data is the coordinate reference system (CRS) assigned to it. When you work with only one, the complexity arises when you want to display it on a map, as you need a transformation function to convert the raster coordinates into real-world ones. The complexity occurs when combining two rasters with different CRSes, as transforming one raster to the second CRS may result in a different origin, orientation, or scale than initially. When we process two rasters, we need to have two arrays where a pixel from raster A in the array with index *i,j* corresponds to the same *i,j* in the array in the second raster. So the pixel value for the transformed raster might end up in a different place. That's why we need to estimate the value of the pixel for the *i,j* index after transformation; there are many methods to resample the pixel value like nearest neighbor, bilinear, or cubic.[1]

Apache Sedona utilizes the geotools library object `GridGeometry2D` and affine transformation as mathematical transformations to convert pixel coordinates into real-world coordinates. Affine transformation is a geometric transformation that preserves lines and parallelism but not necessarily Euclidean distances and angles. For a raster application, we can represent the affine transformation as a 3×3 matrix:

$$\begin{bmatrix} \text{ScaleX} & \text{SkewX} & \text{TranslationX} \\ \text{SkewY} & \text{ScaleY} & \text{TranslationY} \\ 0 & 0 & 1 \end{bmatrix}$$

- *ScaleX* and *ScaleY* are scaling factors for the x-axis and y-axis, respectively.
- *SkewX* and *SkewY* are the skew factors for the x and y axes.
- *TranslationX* and *TranslationY* are translation parameters for the x and y axes.

There are multiple types of affine transformations based on the transformation matrix values. Before we list them, let's show an example of what the calculus looks like. Our transformation matrix looks as follows:

$$\begin{bmatrix} 2.5 & 0 & 1 \\ 0 & 1.5 & 1 \\ 0 & 0 & 1 \end{bmatrix}$$

In the example, we transform the raster from Figure 5-1. We will start by transforming a single pixel, and then we will utilize Python code to automate the process. We will take the second row and third column as an example (1, 2 as we numerate from 0). We will use an affine matrix with the following transformation:

- Translation in both the x-axis and the y-axis by 1
- Scale of the x and y coordinates

---

1 See this guide (*https://oreil.ly/mL0ck*) for more information on geometric operations with rasters.

The vector used in the matrix multiplication is:

- [2]: column number
- [1]: row number
- [1]: constant value

The formula to get the transformed coordinates is:

$$\begin{bmatrix} x_w \\ y_w \\ 1 \end{bmatrix} = \begin{bmatrix} 2.5 & 0 & 1 \\ 0 & 1.5 & 1 \\ 0 & 0 & 1 \end{bmatrix} \cdot \begin{bmatrix} 2 \\ 1 \\ 1 \end{bmatrix}$$

where x_w and y_w are the world coordinates in the given CRS:

$$x_w = 2.5 \times 2 + 0 \times 1 + 1 \times 1 = 5 + 1 = 6.0$$

$$y_w = 0 \times 2 + 1.5 \times 1 + 1 \times 1 = 1.5 + 1 = 2.5$$

To accelerate the calculation, we can use the `affine` library in Python. The library uses the arguments a, b, c, d, e, and f in the matrix, which correspond to *ScaleX*, *SkewX*, *TranslationX*, *SkewY*, *ScaleY*, and *TranslationY*, respectively:

$$\begin{bmatrix} a & b & c \\ d & e & f \\ 0 & 0 & 1 \end{bmatrix}$$

We need to define the affine transformation object:

```
from affine import Affine

at = Affine(a=2.5, b=0, c=1, d=0, e=1.5, f=1)

def transform(a: Affine, row: int, col: int) -> tuple[float, float]:
    return a * (col, row)
```

We use the `Affine` object for the transformation function, which has the `__mul__` method implemented. In Python, the `__mul__` method is a dunder method that overloads the * operation for the class instance.[2] We can then multiply it by the tuple of column and row numbers in the raster. Now we can utilize the `transform` function to find the real-world coordinates from the four envelope coordinates:

---

2 See the Python data model documentation (*https://oreil.ly/NnOWU*) for more information.

```
>> transform(at, row=0, col=0)
(1.0, 1.0)

>> transform(at, row=0, col=2)
(6.0, 1.0)

>> transform(at, row=4, col=2)
(6.0, 7.0)

>> transform(at, row=4, col=0)
(1.0, 7.0)
```

There are a few types of affine transformations:

- *Translation* shifts the coordinates for either x, y, or both. To translate x by five and y by six, the matrix looks as follows:

$$\begin{bmatrix} 1 & 0 & 5 \\ 0 & 1 & 6 \\ 0 & 0 & 1 \end{bmatrix}$$

- *Scaling* uses the diagonal parameters of the affine matrix to scale down or scale up the size of the pixel values. Scaling can be done by the same factor (uniform) or by different factors (nonuniform). To scale x by 0.5 and y by 1.5, we can use the matrix:

$$\begin{bmatrix} 0.5 & 0 & 0 \\ 0 & 1.5 & 0 \\ 0 & 0 & 1 \end{bmatrix}$$

- *Rotation* is used to rotate the raster by the given angle. It can be done by using the combinations of *ScaleX*, *ScaleY*, *SkewX*, and *SkewY*, where these parameters are derived from the cosine and sine of the rotation angle. To rotate the raster by 60 degrees, we can use the following matrix:

$$\begin{bmatrix} 0.5 & -\dfrac{\sqrt{3}}{2} & 0 \\ \dfrac{\sqrt{3}}{2} & 0.5 & 0 \\ 0 & 0 & 1 \end{bmatrix}$$

- *Shearing* keeps the parallel lines from the raster, but it doesn't hold the perpendicular properties. We have to manipulate the *SkewX* and *SkewY* parameters to provide the shearing for the raster. We can use the following affine matrix to skew x by a factor of 2 and y by a factor of 3:

$$\begin{bmatrix} 1 & 2 & 0 \\ 3 & 1 & 0 \\ 0 & 0 & 1 \end{bmatrix}$$

- *Reflection* flips the object over a specified axis, which can be achieved by combining scaling and rotation. In the example, we use -1 to reflect on the y-axis:

$$\begin{bmatrix} -1 & 0 & 0 \\ 0 & 1 & 0 \\ 0 & 0 & 1 \end{bmatrix}$$

Raster SQL and Raster Data Manipulation

One advantage of using Apache Sedona is its unified support for geometry and raster data processing through SQL functions. You are already familiar with the ST functions designed to transform the geometry types from Chapter 4.

> Apache Sedona uses the RS prefix for raster functions, which helps distinguish them from vector functions. On the other hand, PostGIS prefixes all spatial functions with ST, regardless of the input data type.

We can categorize raster functions into several distinct types.

Raster Loader

Apache Sedona exposes raster spatial functions to convert the binary object into the internal Apache Sedona raster object. Typically, you start by reading the binary file:

```
df = sedona \
    .read \
    .format("binaryFile") \
    .load("/some/path/*.asc")
```

And then use `RS_FromGeoTiff` (to load GeoTIFF data), `RS_FromArcInfoAsciiGrid` (load AsciiGrid), and `RS_FromNetCDF` (load from NetCDF) to transform binary content to the raster datatype.

To create the raster object from scratch, you can combine the RS_MakeEmptyRaster and RS_MakeRaster functions. Here is the function definition for RS_MakeEmptyRaster:

```
RS_MakeEmptyRaster(
    numBands: Integer,
    bandDataType: String = 'D',
    width: Integer,
    height: Integer,
    upperleftX: Double,
    upperleftY: Double,
    scaleX: Double,
    scaleY: Double,
    skewX: Double,
    skewY: Double,
    srid: Integer
)
```

RS_MakeEmptyRaster creates an empty raster with no data filled in. You pass arguments like:

numBands

With a value greater than one, RS_MakeRaster requires passing the second band after the first one.

bandDataType

Data type of pixel value, such as 'D', which is double.

width, height

The parameters to specify the size of the raster.

upperleftX, upperleftY

Parameters that indicate where the raster starts; you can think of them as the translation parameters from the affine matrix.

scaleX, scaleY, skewX, skewY

The other four parameters from the affine matrix we explained in "The Raster Data Model" on page 115.

srid

The CRS ID for the raster.

RS_MakeRaster fills the empty raster with actual values:

```
RS_MakeRaster(refRaster: Raster, bandDataType: String, data: ARRAY[Double])
```

It takes the following three arguments:

refRaster
> The raster column.

bandDataType
> Data type of pixel value

data
> An array with the value for each pixel. You pass it starting from (0, 0) and going column-wise, row-wise, and band-wise.

To create a raster with one band, we use scaleX=1, scaleY=1, starting at point (0, 0), with a 5×5 shape, zero skewX and skewY, with double pixel data type and the 4326 CRS. You can use the following Python code:

```python
import itertools

input_raster = [
    [1, 1, 16, 2, 6],
    [2, 3, 12, 16, 17],
    [8, 17, 5, 20, 7],
    [14, 8, 15, 4, 11],
    [10, 13, 19, 6, 9]
]

flatten = list(itertools.chain.from_iterable(input_raster))
array_input = ", ".join([str(number) for number in flatten])

raster_df = sedona \
    .sql(
        f"""
        WITH empty_raster AS (
            SELECT
                RS_MakeEmptyRaster(
                    1, 5, 5, 0.0, 0.0, 1.0, 1.0, 0.0, 0.0, 4326
                ) AS rast
        )
        SELECT
            RS_MakeRaster(rast, 'D', ARRAY({array_input})) AS rast
        FROM empty_raster
        """
    )
```

We start by defining a two-dimensional list in Python, as it is easier to read it this way instead of keeping everything in one list. Then, we flatten the input_raster list of lists into a single list using the itertools.chain from_iterable function. We need to use string concatenation with the join function to pass it as an SQL argument. We will use input_raster in later examples. raster_df is stored in the temporary view called raster. We will also use this raster in the following examples.

Writing to Raster Formats

Apache Sedona supports converting a raster column to popular raster formats, including ArcGrid, GeoTIFF, and PNG. We can use the following raster spatial functions for this purpose:

```
SELECT
    RS_AsArcGrid(rast)
FROM raster

SELECT
    RS_AsGeoTiff(rast)
FROM raster

SELECT
    RS_AsPNG(rast)
FROM raster
```

Each function converts the raster column into a binary column with a binary representation of the particular format. If you use the RS_AsGeoTiff function, the raster column will now be a binary column with a GeoTIFF binary. The previously mentioned functions don't store data in any file. The binary file format in Apache Spark does not support writing to files. To save the data to a file, you can use the foreach method on the converted DataFrame and save the data for each row. In the following example, we will save the result of the RS_AsGeoTiff function to the GeoTIFF file:

```
import uuid
import os

def save_to_file(data: bytearray, path: str):
    file_name = str(uuid.uuid4())
    with open(os.path.join(path, f"{file_name}.tif"), "wb") as f:
        f.write(data)

geotiff_binary = sedona.sql(
    """
    SELECT
        RS_AsGeoTiff(r.tile)
    FROM raster
    LATERAL VIEW RS_TileExplode(rast, 2, 2) r
    """
)

geotiff_binary.foreach(
    lambda x: save_to_file(x[0], "data/sql_functions/writing")
)
```

We use a UUID ID for each file, as we don't have the rows in order. Then, on each row, we run the function on the first element, as the input for the `foreach` function is the row. It works when we run Apache Sedona locally; it will also work in the cluster, but it will store the data locally on the machine where it is running. If you want to store data in a distributed file system, such as HDFS, or object storage, like S3, you must incorporate the specific client and save the data using it. For instance, to store data on S3, you might need to use the `boto3` library. You can reuse the function to store the data locally, where your notebook instance is. Then, instead of using a `foreach` loop, you can use the `collect` method to retrieve all the data in your Jupyter Notebook environment and use Python for the loop to save the data. An important consideration is that your DataFrame might be too large and may not fit on the Jupyter Notebook hosting machine.

Pixel Functions

The purpose of pixel functions is to help convert raster data into geometry objects. If you want to convert the raster pixel centroids into points, you can use `RS_PixelAs Centroids`, which takes two arguments: the raster column and the band number. The function returns the list of points; you can combine it with the `Explode` function and `LATERAL VIEW` command to create a spatial DataFrame with a row for each pixel:

```
SELECT
    pixels.col.*
FROM raster
LATERAL VIEW EXPLODE(RS_PixelAsCentroids(rast, 1)) pixels
```

This will give you the following results:

```
+----------------+-----+---+---+
|            geom|value|  x|  y|
+----------------+-----+---+---+
|POINT (0.5 4.5)|  1.0|  1|  1|
|POINT (1.5 4.5)|  1.0|  2|  1|
|POINT (2.5 4.5)| 16.0|  3|  1|
|POINT (3.5 4.5)|  2.0|  4|  1|
|POINT (4.5 4.5)|  6.0|  5|  1|
+----------------+-----+---+---+
```

One common use case is to convert raster data into a polygon geometry. To achieve this, you can use the `RS_PixelAsPolygons` function, which returns each pixel's polygons list. We can combine `RS_PixelAsPolygons` with `ST_Union_Aggr` to merge the pixels into larger polygons based on the pixel values:

```
WITH pixelized AS (
    SELECT
        RS_PixelAsPolygons(rast, 1) AS pixels
    FROM raster
)
```

```
SELECT
    ST_Union_Aggr(pixel.geom) AS geom
FROM pixelized
LATERAL VIEW explode(pixels) AS pixel
WHERE pixel.value > 2 and pixel.value < 14
```

In this example, we convert each raster pixel to a polygon, then use the
ST_Union_Aggr function to merge the pixel geometry with pixel values between 2
and 14 into the polygon:

```
+-----------------------------------------------------------------------+
|geom                                                                   |
+-----------------------------------------------------------------------+
|MULTIPOLYGON (((3 0, 3 1, 3 2, 4 2, 4 3, 5 3, 5 2, 5 1, 5 0, 4 0, 3 0)),...)|
+-----------------------------------------------------------------------+
```

Geometry Functions

The functions in this section aim to create geometry objects based on the raster
metadata. One of them is RS_Envelope, which returns the envelope geometry of the
raster:

```
SELECT
    RS_Envelope(rast) as geom
FROM raster
```

```
+----------------------------------+
|geom                              |
+----------------------------------+
|POLYGON ((0 0, 0 5, 5 5, 5 0, 0 0))|
+----------------------------------+
```

If the raster is not skewed, the result of the RS_Envelope function is the same as
RS_ConvexHull. However, if there is skew, the results of those functions diverge.
skew_raster contains the exact pixel values, but in RS_MakeEmptyRaster, we passed
1.0 as the skewX value:

```
SELECT
    RS_ConvexHull(skew_raster) as convex_hull_geom,
    RS_Envelope(skew_raster) as envelope_geom
FROM raster
```

```
+-------------------------------------+-------------------------------------+
|convex_hull_geom                     |envelope_geom                        |
+-------------------------------------+-------------------------------------+
|POLYGON ((0 5, 5 5, 10 0, 5 0, 0 5))|POLYGON ((0 0, 0 5, 10 5, 10 0, 0 0))|
+-------------------------------------+-------------------------------------+
```

Raster Accessors

The raster accessor functions can help you retrieve metadata about the raster, such as skewX, skewY, width, and height:

```
SELECT
    RS_Height(rast) as height,
    RS_Rotation(rast) as rotation,
    RS_ScaleX(rast) as scale_x,
    RS_SkewX(rast) as skew_x
FROM raster

+------+--------+-------+------+
|height|rotation|scale_x|skew_x|
+------+--------+-------+------+
|     5|     0.0|    1.0|   0.0|
+------+--------+-------+------+
```

Raster Band Accessors

In the raster band accessors, you will find functions like RS_Count, which calculates the number of pixels in a specific band. The common ground is that you operate on a single band in the raster band accessor functions:

```
SELECT
    RS_Count(rast) as count
FROM raster

+-----+
|count|
+-----+
|   25|
+-----+
```

The following example uses RS_SummaryStatsAll, which calculates statistics for the entire raster band. We use a subquery and the * operator to retrieve each attribute of the struct column and map it to the top-level column in the resulting DataFrame:

```
SELECT r.stats.*
FROM (
  SELECT
      RS_SummaryStatsAll(rast, 1) AS stats
  FROM raster
) AS r

+-----+-----+----+------------------+---+----+
|count|  sum|mean|            stddev|min| max|
+-----+-----+----+------------------+---+----+
| 25.0|242.0|9.68|5.842739083683268|1.0|20.0|
+-----+-----+----+------------------+---+----+
```

RS_ZonalStats is also a raster band accessor function, but we will cover it in detail in the "Zonal Statistics" on page 132.

Raster Predicates

Apache Sedona supports three raster predicates: RS_Contains, RS_Intersects, and RS_Within. These predicates enable validating the spatial relationship between raster and vector/raster data. "Joining Raster Data" on page 143 provides more information on raster predicates.

Raster-Based Operators

This group of functions helps you modify the existing raster by adding a new band, clipping the raster, combining multiple rasters, and more. We can use RS_AddBand to add the new band from rast_add to the rast column. By default, it adds a new band at the end of the raster and takes the first band from the second raster. To prove that the raster was appended, we call the RS_NumBands function to observe the total number of bands in the raster. The rasters must have the same width and height:

```
SELECT
   RS_NumBands(RS_AddBand(rast, rast_add)) AS num_bands
FROM raster

+---------+
|num_bands|
+---------+
|        2|
+---------+
```

When working with image data for any machine learning model, you may want to clip the raster data based on the geometry shapes to use only the area from the geometries. To do that, you can use the RS_Clip function in Apache Sedona. We pass the raster column as the first argument, the band we want to clip as the second, and the clip geometry polygon as the third:

```
SELECT
    RS_Envelope(RS_Clip(
        rast,
        1,
        ST_GeomFromText('POLYGON((1 1, 1 2, 2 2, 2 1, 1 1))')
    )) AS envelope
FROM raster

+-----------------------------------+
|envelope                           |
+-----------------------------------+
|POLYGON ((1 1, 1 2, 2 2, 2 1, 1 1))|
+-----------------------------------+
```

Sometimes, the raster data is noisy, and you need to interpolate the values after removing clouds from a satellite image. Or the camera from the drone or plane has a fabric flaw. You can use the Apache Sedona RS_Interpolate function to fill the missing values. The function performs interpolation on a raster using the inverse distance weighted (IDW) method. The function takes the following arguments as input:

raster
 The raster used in the function.

band
 The band number used for the interpolation, default: 1.

power
 Used in inverse distance, it's a real number. So if we take the power = 2, then the partial formula for one cell is $1/(dist(i))^2$, default: 2.

mode
 Interpolation mode, either "Variable" or "Fixed".

The other two arguments, numPointsOrRadius and maxRadiusOrMinPoints, are dependent on the selected mode:

In "Variable" mode:

numPointsOrRadius
 Number of nearest input points to be used for interpolation.

maxRadiusOrMinPoints
 Max search radius distance, default: diagonal length of the raster.

In "Fixed" mode:

numPointsOrRadius
 Distance radius is used to find the neighbor pixels; the default is the diagonal length of the raster.

maxRadiusOrMinPoints
 The minimal number of pixels used for the interpolation, default: 0.

Let's analyze the interpolation result from Figure 5-2. We look at a pixel with raster coordinates (0, 2). With a distance of 1.5, the neighbors of the pixel are (0, 1) = 1, (0, 3) = 2, (1, 1) = 3, (1, 2) = nan, (1, 3) = 16. The nan value has no data, so we need to skip it. So the valid neighbors are (0, 1) = 1, (0, 3) = 2, (1, 1) = 3, (1, 3) = 16.

1.0	1.0	nan	2.0	6.0
2.0	3.0	nan	16.0	17.0
8.0	nan	5.0	20.0	7.0
14.0	8.0	15.0	4.0	11.0
nan	13.0	nan	6.0	9.0

1.00	1.00	4.17	2.00	6.00
2.00	3.00	7.89	16.00	17.00
8.00	7.18	5.00	20.00	7.00
14.00	8.00	15.00	4.00	11.00
12.40	13.00	10.00	6.00	9.00

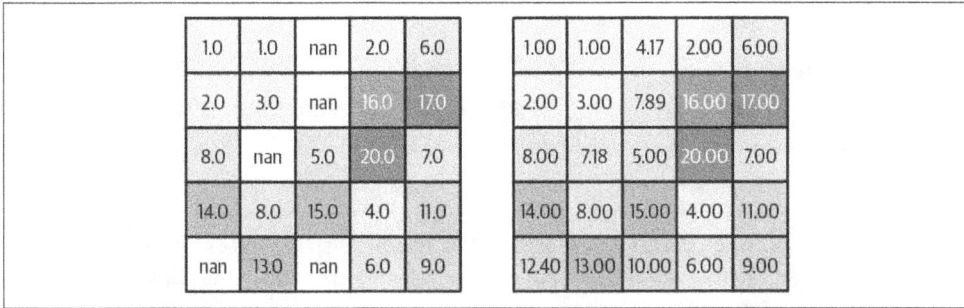

*Figure 5-2. Interpolation of the left raster and the resulting raster on the right side
(pow=2, mode='Fixed', numPointsOrRadius=1.5)*

The formula for the IDW is the weighted sum:

$$\frac{\sum_{i=1}^{n} w_i(x) \times u_i}{\sum_{i=1}^{n} w_i(x)}$$

where u_i is the pixel value of the ith neighbor, and $w_i(x)$ is the ith neighbor weight.

We calculate the weight for each neighbor pixel using the following formula:

$$w_i(x) = \frac{1}{d(x, x_i)^p}$$

where d is the distance between the pixel with a missing value and the neighbor pixel, and p is the power.

For example, the weight for the pixel with coordinates (1, 3) is:

$$\frac{1}{\sqrt{(1-0)^2 + (3-2)^2}^2} = \frac{1}{\sqrt{2}^2} = \frac{1}{2} = 0.5$$

Using a weight dependent on the inverse distance and raised to the power of 2, we magnify the importance of pixels close to the missing value and decrease their significance with increasing distance. For the pixel with coordinates (0, 3), the distance is 1, and the weight is also 1. So to get the interpolated value for the pixel with coordinates (0, 2):

$$\frac{1 \times 1 + 2 \times 1 + 3 \times 0.5 + 16 \times 0.5}{1 + 1 + 0.5 + 0.5} = \frac{1 + 2 + 1.5 + 8}{3} = \frac{12.5}{3} = 4.17$$

Raster Tiles

When the raster you are processing is large and you want to distribute the work-load as much as possible, you can use raster tile functions like RS_Tile and RS_TileExplode.

> A large raster might be stiff to process using tile functions. The splitting process might lead to the Java heap space errors. For large single-file rasters exceeding 1 GB, we recommend splitting the raster using Rasterio or a similar library and storing the resulting files in a directory with multiple raster files.

To split the 5×5 raster into many rasters with dimensions less than or equal to 2x2, we can use the following code:

```
SELECT
    rast.*
FROM raster
LATERAL VIEW RS_TileExplode(rast, 2, 2) rast

+---+---+--------------------+
|  x|  y|                tile|
+---+---+--------------------+
|  0|  0|GridCoverage2D["g...|
|  1|  0|GridCoverage2D["g...|
|  2|  0|GridCoverage2D["g...|
|  0|  1|GridCoverage2D["g...|
|  1|  1|GridCoverage2D["g...|
|  2|  1|GridCoverage2D["g...|
|  0|  2|GridCoverage2D["g...|
|  1|  2|GridCoverage2D["g...|
|  2|  2|GridCoverage2D["g...|
+---+---+--------------------+
```

The difference between RS_Tile and RS_TileExplode is that RS_TileExplode returns one row per tile directly (like explode), while RS_Tile returns an array of tiles:

```
RS_TileExplode(rast, 2, 2) = EXPLODE(RS_Tile(rast, 2, 2))
```

Map Algebra Functions

Many GIS applications require calculations on multiple bands for each pixel. The operation combining band or multiple band pixel values is called map algebra. We'll cover this in detail later in the "Map Algebra" section.

Raster Visualization

It's convenient to see what your data represents in the space to validate the result, during the exploratory analysis, or to show the result. In Apache Sedona, you have a few ways to visualize the data:

- Save as binary using the RS_AsBase64 function
- Save as HTML using the img tag with RS_AsImage. In the notebook environment, you can combine this with the display_image function from the SedonaUtils class:

```
from sedona.raster_utils.SedonaUtils import SedonaUtils

htmlDF = sedona.sql(
    """
    SELECT
        RS_AsImage(rast, 300)
    FROM raster
    """
)

SedonaUtils.display_image(htmlDF)
```

The RS_AsImage function takes two arguments: the raster object and the image width.

If you need the NumPy-like display, use the RS_AsMatrix function, which takes the raster column and returns a DataFrame with a string column:

```
matrix = sedona \
    .sql("SELECT RS_AsMatrix(rast) FROM raster") \
    .head()[0]

print(matrix)

| 1.0   1.0  16.0   2.0   6.0|
| 2.0   3.0  12.0  16.0  17.0|
| 8.0  17.0   5.0  20.0   7.0|
|14.0   8.0  15.0   4.0  11.0|
|10.0  13.0  19.0   6.0   9.0|
```

Zonal Statistics

Zonal statistics is the process of calculating statistics for a given zone, where the zone is vector data. Currently, Apache Sedona has two functions implemented to provide statistics:

- RS_ZonalStats
- RS_ZonalStatsAll

RS_ZonalStats can calculate only one statistic (like pixel count or sum of pixel values); on the other hand, RS_ZonalStatsAll returns a struct with all the statistics.

In Figure 5-3, you can see the 2D raster data on the left with dimensions of 5×5 pixels. On the right side of the figure, you can see the same raster and geometry polygon. Imagine that we have a spatial view named density, with fields rast of RasterType and geom of GeometryType. Our raster data has only one band, and one of the rows contains the data shown in Figure 5-3. Now let's run the following code:

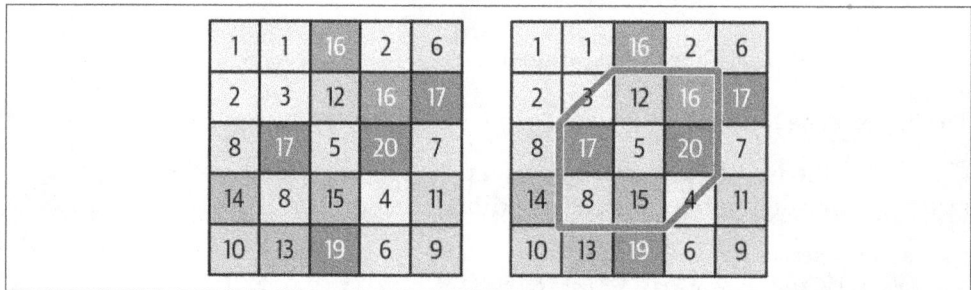

Figure 5-3. Zonal statistics of the 5×5 raster

```
SELECT RS_ZonalStats(rast, geom, "sum") FROM density
```

The output is the sum of all pixel values intersecting with the geometry. In our example, the sum is 100.

There are multiple implementations of the RS_ZonalStats; please follow the Apache Sedona official documentation to familiarize yourself with them. You can also refer to the book's official Jupyter Notebook examples for this chapter to view all versions with visualizations. RS_ZonalStats has four additional parameters that may change the output of the function:

band *(int)*

>   The band number of the raster; if not passed, it defaults to 1.

allTouched *(Boolean)*

>   A parameter indicating if we include intersected raster pixels, even if they intersect only by one point. The default value is false, and in this scenario, the function only considers pixels whose centroids intersect with the geometry.

excludeNoData *(Boolean)*

>   A parameter indicating if the function will exclude the no data values from calculations. The default value is true.

lenient *(Boolean)*

>   Validates if the raster intersects with the geometry. If the value is false and geometries don't intersect, an `IllegalArgumentException` is raised. The default value is true and in this case the null value is returned.

> When you pass the function raster and geometry columns with different CRSes, this function automatically transforms the geometry CRS to the raster CRS.

`RS_ZonalStats` supports multiple statistics: the number of pixels (count), the sum of pixel values (sum), the mean value (mean|average|avg), the middle value (median), the most common value (mode), the standard deviation (stddev|sd), the variance (variance), the minimum value (min), and the maximum value (max). Note that the pipe used in some of the statistics means that there are alternative names that hold the exact calculus definition, so if you choose mean or average, you get the same value.

When you run `RS_ZonalStatsAll` on the raster column, you get the Apache Spark struct type with all statistics. Let's run the `RS_ZonalStatsAll` function on the raster and geometry polygon from Figure 5-3:

```
SELECT RS_ZonalStatsAll(rast, geom) FROM density

+-------------------------------------------------------------+
|all_stats                                                    |
+-------------------------------------------------------------+
|{9.0, 100.0, 11.11…, 12.0, 20.0, 6.29…, 39.61…, 3.0, 20.0}   |
+-------------------------------------------------------------+
```

When you look into this structure, it's hard to understand which column is for which statistic. You can print the schema and select the fields individually, but you can also use the * accessor for the struct field:

```
WITH zonal_all AS (
    SELECT
        RS_ZonalStatsAll(rast, geom) AS stats
    FROM density
)
SELECT stats.* FROM zonal_all
```

The result table looks as follows:

```
+-----+-----+-----+------+----+------+--------+---+----+
|count|  sum| mean|median|mode|stddev|variance|min| max|
+-----+-----+-----+------+----+------+--------+---+----+
|  9.0|100.0|11.11|  12.0|20.0|  6.29|   39.61|3.0|20.0|
+-----+-----+-----+------+----+------+--------+---+----+
```

Finally, let's look at a zonal statistics real-world example. When you buy or rent a house or flat, one critical factor is the noise level in your neighborhood. We can use zonal statistics to calculate the minimum and maximum noise. Another promising statistic we can use is *stddev*, which can help us understand how much the noise level differs from the average value. Let's explain what steps we need.

- We will use Redfin listings (*http://www.redfin.com*); you can easily download the data from the website. We also placed the data in the S3 bucket created for the book.
- We will analyze the New York City data for properties sold.
- We will create a 20, 50, and 100m buffer for each property.
- We will calculate three zonal statistics for each buffer: min, max, and stddev.
- We will use the raster initial CRS, ESRI:102039, which uses meters as the unit of measure.

We start from the already prepared prerequisites, like those Apache Sedona installed, and two tables with the data:

- Properties, spatial table with points (id: int, geom: geometry)
- Noise, spatial table with raster data (rast: raster)

We start to filter the raster and geometry data to the extent shown in Figure 5-4. For the noise data raster, we will use the RS_Clip function, which takes as arguments the raster data, band number, and the polygon we use to clip the raster data in. For properties, we use the filter clause, and as the predicate, we use the ST_Intersects function. That helps us reduce the places we take into account in our analysis.

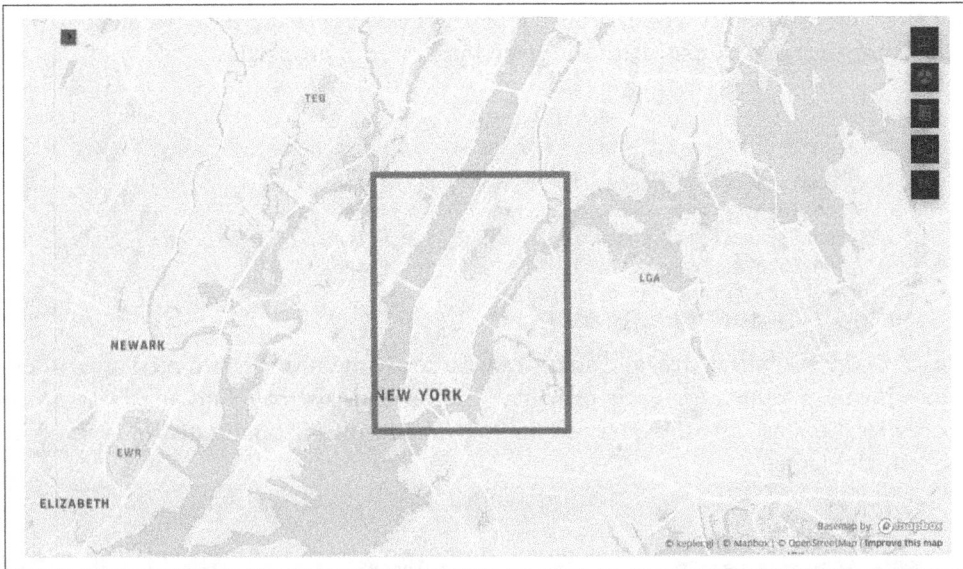

Figure 5-4. The extent used to calculate the noise statistics for the properties neighbor-hood

Next, we need the buffers from the properties we include in the analysis. We will use the ST_Buffer function to calculate at each 20, 50, and 100m radius. So, for one radius, we would use the following SQL query:

```
SELECT
    id,
    ST_Buffer(geom, 20) AS geom,
    "20" AS buffer
FROM properties
UNION ALL
SELECT
    id,
    ST_Buffer(geom, 50) AS geom,
    "50" AS buffer
FROM properties
UNION ALL
SELECT
    id,
    ST_Buffer(geom, 100) AS geom,
    "100" AS buffer
FROM properties
```

We store the result of this query in the `properties_buffers` view. The next step is calculating the zonal statistics for the given buffers from properties:

```
SELECT
    p.id,
    buffer,
    RS_ZonalStats(rast, geom, 1, "median") AS median_value,
    RS_ZonalStats(rast, geom, 1, "stddev") AS stddev_value,
    RS_ZonalStats(rast, geom, 1, "min") AS min_value,
    RS_ZonalStats(rast, geom, 1, "max") AS max_value
FROM properties_buffers AS p, noise
WHERE RS_Intersects(rast, geom)
```

We select the ID, buffer size, and statistics we already mentioned, and median, stddev, min, and max values for each property. In the end, we can find the least noisy properties. Let's use an SQL query to do that. The result of zonal statistics is saved in the statistics table:

```
SELECT *
FROM statistics
ORDER BY min_value ASC NULLS LAST, stddev_value ASC
```

Here are the five top-level records:

```
+----------+------+------------+------------+---------+---------+
|        id|buffer|median_value|stddev_value|min_value|max_value|
+----------+------+------------+------------+---------+---------+
|1687435128|   100|       49.86|        6.05|    45.06|    63.68|
|-219883926|    50|       50.32|         3.4|    45.44|    53.35|
|-219883926|   100|       50.32|         4.1|    45.44|    58.51|
|-219883926|    20|       48.55|        2.49|    46.79|    50.32|
|1687435128|    50|       55.98|        5.95|    47.16|    63.68|
+----------+------+------------+------------+---------+---------+
```

Map Algebra

Map algebra is a calculus based on raster pixel values and a combination of mathematical expressions across one or more raster bands. It gives you the flexibility to transform the raster data using rich expressions. In Apache Sedona, you can perform the map algebra operations in two ways:

- Using the `RS_MapAlgebra` function
- Using more specialized functions like `RS_Add`, `RS_Multiply`, `RS_Subtract`, etc.

The `RS_MapAlgebra` function is more flexible and helps you perform all the operations from the second point. In this part of the chapter, we will focus on this function. In the official repository for the chapter, you will find examples with other functions to perform the map algebra operations. Now, let's move on to the `RS_MapAlgebra` function signature:

```
RS_MapAlgebra(rast: Raster, pixelType: String,
    script: String, noDataValue: Optional[Double])
```

where:

- rast is the raster data.
- pixelType is the type of the output pixel (D (double), F (float), I (integer), S (short), US (unsigned short), or B (byte)). When you pass NULL as the pixelType argument, the source data type will be used in the output.
- The script is the map algebra expression that will be applied to the raster data.
- noDataValue is the no-data value to be used in the output raster.

We will start with simple examples and progress to more complex ones. Ultimately, we will focus on the real-world applications of map algebra, such as calculating a Normalized Burn Ratio (NBR) index. We will use a raster with three bands and 5×5 pixels each (Figure 5-5), which makes the explanations clearer. Our column with raster data is named rast, and we store it in an SQL view named ma, which is the short name for map algebra.

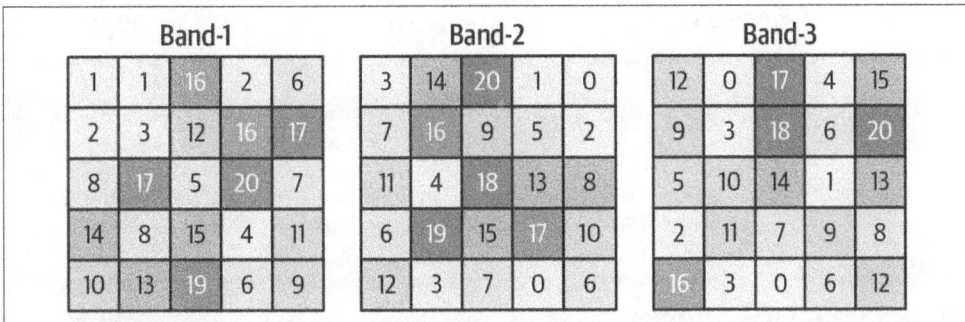

Band-1

1	1	16	2	6
2	3	12	16	17
8	17	5	20	7
14	8	15	4	11
10	13	19	6	9

Band-2

3	14	20	1	0
7	16	9	5	2
11	4	18	13	8
6	19	15	17	10
12	3	7	0	6

Band-3

12	0	17	4	15
9	3	18	6	20
5	10	14	1	13
2	11	7	9	8
16	3	0	6	12

Figure 5-5. Three-band raster used in the examples

The Jiffle language (*https://oreil.ly/hzJMV*) is used for the expressions in the Apache Sedona RS_MapAlgebra function and supports many features like:

- Defining variables
- Arithmetic and logical operators
- Ternary expression
- Conditional expressions
- Loops
- Built-in functions

We can use an access pattern similar to Python's, such as accessing an element in the list to access a specific band in the expression. If you want to create a new raster from the first band, you can simply use this SQL:

```
SELECT
    RS_MapAlgebra(rast, NULL, 'out = rast[0];') AS rast
FROM ma
```

We pass NULL as the second argument, so we do not have to cast our input raster cells. For the expression, we use out = rast[0];, which takes the first band from our raster. The result must be assigned to the variable named out, and we must end it using a semicolon. The result converted to the NumPy array looks identical to Band-1 in Figure 5-5:

```
[[ 1.  1. 16.  2.  6.]
 [ 2.  3. 12. 16. 17.]
 [ 8. 17.  5. 20.  7.]
 [14.  8. 15.  4. 11.]
 [10. 13. 19.  6.  9.]]
```

When working with rasters, you often combine multiple bands into one to calculate an index; this index could be a health of vegetation index or an index to monitor wetlands. In the following example we will use the access pattern to calculate the mean value from all three bands:

```
SELECT
    RS_MapAlgebra(
        rast,
        NULL,
        'out = (rast[0] + rast[1] + rast[2])/3;'
    ) AS rast
FROM ma
```

The result is a NumPy array:

```
[[ 5.3  5.  17.7  2.3  7. ]
 [ 6.   7.3 13.   9.  13. ]
 [ 8.  10.3 12.3 11.3  9.3]
 [ 7.3 12.7 12.3 13.3  9.7]
 [12.7  6.3  8.7  4.   9. ]]
```

We will extend the previous mean example with a conditional expression. We will filter values less than 8 and greater than 15 and assign no data to them (−1):

```
mean_value = (rast[0] + rast[1] + rast[2])/3;

out = (mean_value > 15 || mean_value < 8) ? -1 : mean_value;
```

In the script, mean_value represents the value we calculated in the previous example. We use the ternary expression to assign -1 when the value is greater than 15 or less than 8. Otherwise, we assign the original value. In the SQL query, we also assign the −1 value as a no data value as the fourth parameter in the RS_MapAlgebra function:

```
SELECT
    RS_MapAlgebra(rast, NULL, '{script}', -1) AS rast
FROM ma
```

The SQL query collected for Python NumPy looks as follows:

```
[[ nan  nan  nan  nan  nan]
 [ nan  nan 13.   9.  13. ]
 [ 8.  10.3 12.3 11.3  9.3]
 [ nan 12.7 12.3 13.3  9.7]
 [12.7  nan  8.7  nan  9. ]]
```

We passed the NULL value as the second argument in the previous examples to keep the input data type. In the following example, instead of filling the values with no data, we will assign one if the mean raster value is inside the range <8,15> and zero otherwise. With the output raster, we will create a geometry object based on the pixel values with one.

We need to slightly modify the script used in the previous example. We assign it true or false instead of returning -1 or the source value:

```
out = (mean_value > 15 || mean_value < 8) ? false : true;
```

And as the second argument, we must pass 'B' as the return datatype, which is a Boolean:

```
SELECT
    RS_MapAlgebra(rast, 'B', '{script}') AS rast
FROM ma
```

When we collect the query in Python, we get the following NumPy array:

```
[[0. 0. 0. 0. 0.]
 [0. 0. 1. 1. 1.]
 [1. 1. 1. 1. 1.]
 [0. 1. 1. 1. 1.]
 [1. 0. 1. 0. 1.]]
```

To transform the 1.0 values from the output raster, we will combine the RS_PixelAs Polygons and ST_Union_Aggr functions:

```
WITH pixelized AS (
    SELECT
        RS_PixelAsPolygons(
            RS_MapAlgebra(rast, 'B', '{script}'),
            1
        ) AS pixels
    FROM ma
)
SELECT
    ST_Union_Aggr(pixel.geom) AS geom
FROM pixelized
LATERAL VIEW explode(pixels) AS pixel
WHERE pixel.value = 1.0
```

We start by converting the map algebra output raster to pixels using the `RS_PixelAs Polygons` function. As the second argument, we pass the band number we want to use. As a result, we get a DataFrame with an array instead of the raster data. Each element in the array contains the pixel's geom, value, and x and y coordinates:

```
root
 |-- pixels: array (nullable = true)
 |    |-- element: struct (containsNull = true)
 |    |    |-- geom: geometry (nullable = true)
 |    |    |-- value: double (nullable = true)
 |    |    |-- x: integer (nullable = true)
 |    |    |-- y: integer (nullable = true)
```

In the second part of the query, we use `LATERAL VIEW` to melt the array into multiple rows in the Apache Sedona spatial DataFrame. The resulting DataFrame of the query is presented here:

```
+-----------------------------------+-----+---+---+
|geom                               |value|x  |y  |
+-----------------------------------+-----+---+---+
|POLYGON ((0 5, 1 5, 1 4, 0 4, 0 5))|0.0  |1  |1  |
|POLYGON ((1 5, 2 5, 2 4, 1 4, 1 5))|0.0  |2  |1  |
|POLYGON ((2 5, 3 5, 3 4, 2 4, 2 5))|0.0  |3  |1  |
|POLYGON ((3 5, 4 5, 4 4, 3 4, 3 5))|0.0  |4  |1  |
|POLYGON ((4 5, 5 5, 5 4, 4 4, 4 5))|0.0  |5  |1  |
+-----------------------------------+-----+---+---+
```

With that table, we can filter the pixel to a value of 1 and use the `ST_Union_Aggr` function to create a single polygon from multiple polygons (Figure 5-6).

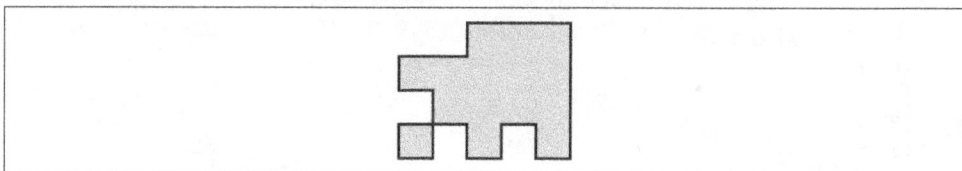

Figure 5-6. Polygon created based on the conditional expression on the raster

As the last example, we will calculate the average using a 3×3 pixel mask, which is a smaller sliding matrix (3×3) that we treat as the neighborhood for the calculations (Figure 5-7). We take into account the eight neighboring pixels plus the current pixel value, sum them, and divide by the number of pixels (nine). For the edges, we keep the source values.

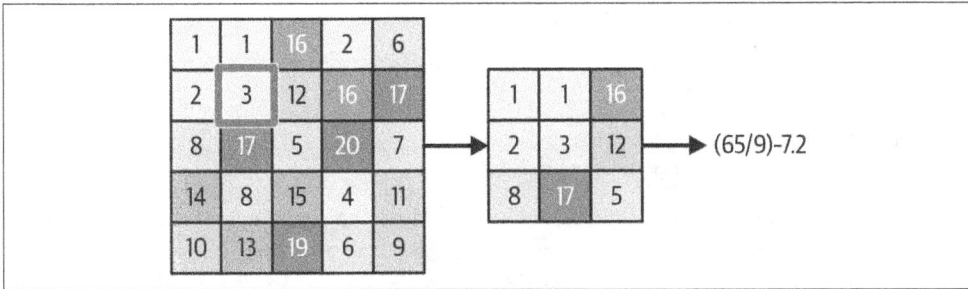

Figure 5-7. Calculating the average pixel value in the neighborhood using a mask of 3×3 pixels

First, we define the script:

```
out = rast[0];
x = x();
y = y();
isWithinYRange = (y > 0 && y < height()-1);
isWithinXRange = (x > 0 && x < width()-1);


if (isWithinXRange && isWithinYRange) {
    delta = [-1, 0, 1];
    n = 0;
    foreach (dy in delta) {
        foreach (dx in delta) {
            n += rast[0][dx, dy];
        }
    }
    out = n/9;
}
```

We start by assigning the default value to the output, so we assign the input value to all the cells on the edges. Then, we create two values, x and y, based on pixel values and function accessors. To make the code more readable, we also create temporary variables, isWithinYRange and isWithinXRange. This verifies whether or not x and y are lying on the edges. Then, we use a foreach loop to loop over the neighbor pixels. We also add the pixel value to the temporary sum variable called n. The last step is to divide the value by 9. We return the numeric value to use 'D' as the output type in the following SQL query:

```
SELECT
    RS_MapAlgebra(rast, 'D', '{script}') AS rast
FROM ma
```

The resulting raster, as a NumPy array, looks as follows:

```
[[ 1.    1.   16.    2.    6. ]
 [ 2.    7.2 10.2 11.2 17. ]
 [ 8.    9.3 11.1 11.9  7. ]
 [14.   12.1 11.9 10.7 11. ]
 [10.   13.   19.    6.    9. ]]
```

Common use cases for map algebra include calculating indices based on satellite or photogrammetry images. In the following example, we will calculate the Normalized Burn Ratio (NBR) (*https://oreil.ly/Cg4Pb*), an index designed to highlight burnt areas in large fire zones. The equation to calculate the NBR takes near infrared (NIR) and short wavelength infrared (SWIR) channels.

In this example, we use data from the Sentinel-2 mission (*https://oreil.ly/_jDh_*). We have already preprocessed band 11 (SWIR) to a 10m resolution. We have two directories, *b11_tiles* and *b08_tiles*, containing files. Each file in both directories follows the same naming convention: *tile_{row}_{column}.tif* (e.g., *tile_2_0.tif*). The corresponding files have the same boundary, so we can safely use map algebra on the corresponding files. They have the same boundary and the same number and size of pixels. We start by loading both raster tiles directories, and we retrieve the two columns, rast (raster data type) and directory (*file_path*). Loading SWIR tiles looks as follows (for nir, we change only the directory we load from):

```
from pyspark.sql.functions import input_file_name

swir_channel = sedona \
    .read \
    .format("binaryFile") \
    .load("data/map-algebra/b11_tiles/") \
    .withColumn("file_name", input_file_name()) \
    .selectExpr("RS_FromGeoTiff(content) AS rast", "file_path") \
    .createOrReplaceTempView("swir_raw")
```

Then we need to split file_path to obtain file_name, which we can use to join the two channels:

```
SELECT
    rast,
    element_at(split(file_path, "/"), -1) AS file_name
FROM swir_raw
```

We register a new view based on the query result to the swir view and for the corresponding nir_raw to the nir view. Then we can use join and map algebra implementation, which allows us to use two raster files as the first two arguments:

```
SELECT
    RS_MapAlgebra(
        n.rast,
        s.rast,
        'D',
```

```
        'out = (rast0-rast1)/(rast0+rast1);',
        -9999
    ) AS rast
FROM swir AS s
JOIN nir AS n ON s.file_name = n.file_name
```

We join two raster DataFrames based on the filename. The script for map algebra out = (rast0-rast1)/(rast0+rast1); isn't complex.

Joining Raster Data

In Chapter 4 we covered how spatial joins work for vector data in depth and discussed how Apache Sedona performs distributed spatial joins. We also covered the optimization techniques used in Apache Sedona to make the joins efficient and fast. There are several similarities in the process of joining raster data with a raster of geometry data compared to joining geometry and geometry data. We will cover the whole process, show the similarities, and discuss the differences.

There are three raster predicates at your disposal: RS_Contains, RS_Intersects, and RS_Within. The logic is the same as the ST equivalents:

- RS_Contains checks if the raster boundary contains the geometry or boundary of the second raster.
- RS_Intersects checks if the raster boundary intersects with the geometry or boundary of the second raster.
- RS_Within checks if the raster boundary is within the geometry object or the boundary of the second raster.

You can swap the argument order for all the preceding predicates, and the join will still be optimized. So, RS_Contains(rast, geom) and RS_Contains(geom, rast) will be optimized. However, the processing time may vary due to differences in table sizes for geometry and raster objects.

Apache Sedona provides interoperability for raster data types and geometry or raster types in the following scenarios:

- Spatial range query
- Spatial join query (RangeJoin optimization)

For both the range query and the join query, Apache Sedona supports three previously mentioned spatial predicates and the three mentioned type pairs. The range query does not require any additional data reshuffling; we can filter the data and verify whether the boundary of the raster meets the criteria from the predicate.

For raster with raster or raster and geometry join, the left and right sides of the join will be transformed to the WGS84 CRS, regardless of whether the join sides' CRS match.

An example of a range query between a raster and a geometry looks as follows:

```
SELECT r.rast
FROM raster_data AS r
WHERE RS_Intersects(
    r.rast,
    ST_GeomFromWKT('POLYGON((3 4, 3 12, 8 12, 8 4, 3 4))')
)
```

`RS_Intersects` and other raster predicates are overloaded, so they will work when you switch the parameter order or pass two rasters as parameters. All the overloaded function definitions for `RS_Intersects` look as follows. Other predicates, `RS_Contains` and `RS_Within`, also follow this pattern:

```
RS_Intersects(raster: Raster, geom: Geometry)
RS_Intersects(geom: Geometry, raster: Raster)
RS_Intersects(raster0: Raster, raster1: Raster)
```

Apache Sedona implements optimized joins for rasters in the following scenarios (left means the left side of the join, and right means the right side of the join):

- Left: raster, right: geometry
- Left: geometry, right: raster
- Left: raster, right: raster

When you run the `explain()` method on the spatial DataFrame, look for the `Range Join` keyword; this indicates that optimization is turned on. When one side of the join is small enough, the `BroadcastIndexJoin` optimization will be performed:

```
SELECT r1.rast
FROM rast1 as r1
JOIN rast2 as r2 ON RS_Intersects(r1.rast, r2.rast)
```

The top of the physical plan after running the `explain` method on the result DataFrame for the spatial join between two raster DataFrames looks like this:

```
== Physical Plan ==
*(1) Project [rast#39]
+- RangeJoin rast#39: raster, rast#85: raster, INTERSECTS,
**org.apache.spark.sql.sedona_sql.expressions.raster.RS_Intersects**
```

Similar to the raster-to-raster join, the same optimization is available when running the raster-to-geom join:

```
SELECT r.*
FROM raster as r
JOIN geometries as g ON RS_Intersects(r.rast, g.geom)
```

When your query that joins raster data with geometry or raster data using the three predicates we mentioned before is optimized with the `RangeJoin`, Apache Sedona performs the following steps:

1. Implicitly convert the left side and right side of the join to the WGS84 CRS, regardless of the data type.

2. Get the raster's envelope. For nonempty CRS and non-WGS84 rasters and Data-Frames, Apache Sedona expands the envelope by 10% in all four directions. The implicit conversion from non-WGS84 to WGS84 may introduce an additional error, impacting the join result pairs.

3. If the vector geometry or raster envelope crosses the antimeridian, it's split into two halves.

4. Apply spatial partitioning.

5. Apply indexes if they are turned on.

6. Apply the filter predicate on the spatial join pairs (left and right).

Steps 1 to 3 differ from joining the geometry and geometry data. When we unified the raster data with the geometry (using the envelope), steps 4 to 6 are identical to those in a vector-to-vector join.

In the following examples, we will calculate the sum of the population threatened by the wildfires. For this purpose, we will use the Joint Research Centre (JRC) raster data (*https://oreil.ly/6vHm0*). The JSR raster data we will use contains the Forest Fire Danger Index (FFDI) from August 2024, an index that helps assess the fire risk in the area. It uses the five-level class scale, as shown in Table 5-1.

Table 5-1. FFDI index scale with class

FFDI value	FFDI class
0 - 5	low
5-12	moderate
12-25	high
25-50	very high
> 50	extreme

Another raster dataset we will use is the world population density GeoTIFF file (*https://oreil.ly/UKobp*). The shape of the raster is width: 43200 and height: 21600. The output table consists of the FFDI class and its corresponding population. Now we will cover each step to transform input DataFrames into a table with a population sum.

We start from loading the data to temporary views, FFDI and population. To further distribute the processing of the data, we split the FFDI view into smaller chunks. We can safely use the Apache Sedona `RS_TileExplode` function, as the raster size is not large, and we can fit the input raster in a single cell. Another advantage of this approach is that it allows for more partitions, which can be calculated separately. We will explain this in a later example:

```
SELECT
    raster.tile as rast,
    raster.x,
    raster.y
FROM ffdi
LATERAL VIEW RS_TileExplode(rast, 100, 100) raster
```

We use a 100x100 pixel resolution in the exploded raster. We also keep the x and y, which we will use in the `GROUP BY` statement to speed up the merging of the pixel polygons later.

In the notebooks example for this subsection, we use a Common Table Expression (CTE) to calculate the result table. For better readability, we will split it into multiple SQL queries. First, we need to convert the pixels into geometry polygons:

```
SELECT
    RS_PixelAsPolygons(rast, 1) AS pixels,
    x,
    y
FROM ffdi_tiles
```

We retain the x and y coordinates, and we utilize the first band from the `ffdi_tiles` view when using the `RS_PixelAsPolygons` function. The result of the previous query is stored in the view called `pixelized`.

Next, we use the `explode` function in the lateral view to prolong the table based on the pixel polygons. We filter pixels to the (0–255) range to exclude outliers. We also reclassify the pixel values based on the FFDI class table mapping (Table 5-1). The result lands in the `classified` view:

```
SELECT
    pixel.geom,
    x,
    y,
    CASE
        WHEN pixel.value > 50 THEN 'extreme'
        WHEN pixel.value > 25 THEN 'very high'
```

```
        WHEN pixel.value > 12 THEN 'high'
        WHEN pixel.value > 5 THEN 'moderate'
        WHEN pixel.value > 0 THEN 'low'
    END AS fire_danger_class
FROM pixelized
LATERAL VIEW explode(pixels) AS pixel
WHERE pixel.value > 0 AND pixel.value < 255
```

We will utilize the x, y, and fire_danger_class columns in the GROUP BY statement to enhance our processing parallelism. To merge the pixel values, we use the ST_Union_Aggr function. We keep the result in the fire_danger view:

```
SELECT
    ST_Union_Aggr(geom) AS geom,
    fire_danger_class
FROM classified
GROUP BY fire_danger_class, x, y
```

```
+-------------------+-----------------+
|               geom|fire_danger_class|
+-------------------+-----------------+
|MULTIPOLYGON (((-...|             high|
|MULTIPOLYGON (((7...|              low|
|MULTIPOLYGON (((3...|         moderate|
|MULTIPOLYGON (((7...|         moderate|
|MULTIPOLYGON (((-...|             high|
+-------------------+-----------------+
```

Now we will use the fire_danger table as the zones for the RS_ZonalStats function. Now is the time to combine the population DataFrame with the fire_danger DataFrame. We will use a raster with a vector spatial join (RangeJoin):

```
SELECT
    rast,
    ST_Buffer(
        ST_Intersection(RS_Envelope(rast), geom),
        -0.0001
    ) AS geom,
    fire_danger_class
FROM population AS p
JOIN fire_danger AS f ON RS_Intersects(p.rast, f.geom)
```

> Raster spatial joins can also use the broadcast join optimization (BroadcastIndexJoin). If the data is small enough, optimization is automatically enabled. To disable it, set the Apache Spark config spark.sql.autoBroadcastJoinThreshold to –1.

We use the RS_Intersects function to include any pixel touching the zones. We use the ST_Intersection(RS_Envelope(rast), geom) expression to get the common area between the raster and geometry. The ST_Buffer function is used with a negative buffer because it shrinks geometry slightly to avoid boundary-touching errors during overlay. It doesn't guarantee containment, it only reduces topology conflicts. This geometry will be used later in the zonal statistics function. We refer to the result of the query as the intersection. We can safely use the zonal statistics function with 'sum' as the fourth parameter. We keep it in the zonal_stats table view:

```
SELECT
    RS_ZonalStats(rast, geom, 1, 'sum') AS population_sum,
    fire_danger_class
FROM intersection
```

The last step is to aggregate the results by fire_danger_class:

```
SELECT
    fire_danger_class,
    CAST(sum(population_sum) AS DECIMAL(38, 0)) AS population_sum
FROM zonal_stats
GROUP BY fire_danger_class
```

```
+------------------+--------------+
|fire_danger_class|population_sum|
+------------------+--------------+
|              low|    4380648415|
|         moderate|    1724886324|
|             high|     905684324|
|        very high|     339913259|
|          extreme|       7835287|
+------------------+--------------+
```

Our estimated calculation shows that as many as 7.8 million people might be endangered by the extreme fire hazard.

Hands-On Use Case: Insurance Risk Modeling

A crucial part of this book is focused on providing real-world use cases where you can combine the flexibility and scalability to answer spatial questions. In this example, we will use multiple spatial data sources to provide the insurance risk index for European buildings. We will combine raster and vector data using the concepts you learned in this chapter. We highly recommend analyzing the code from the book and following the notebook code. We left plenty of visualization, which might help you understand the data.

Climate change is causing many natural disasters to intensify in Europe, and we can think of the two that resonate the most:

- Floods
- Wildfires

We will use the forest fire raster data from Copernicus (*https://oreil.ly/01490*). The data has three layers based on the risk of the fire:

- High
- Intermediate
- Low

We will use all three to assess the potential fire risk nearby. We need to assign different weights based on risk. The high risk has the most significant weight value, and the low risk has the lowest. The pixel size is around 10km × 10km.

Climate change is causing real harm; it changes our neighborhoods and is causing natural disasters like wildfires. The JRC (Joint Research Centre) is the European Commission's science and knowledge service, providing independent scientific advice, for example, on the impact of climate change and potential risks to the economy and society:

> The unprecedented wildfires sweeping Europe over the last four years show the undeniable effects of climate change on wildfire regimes. Climate change is not only increasing the size of the areas affected by wildfires, but also making individual fires more intense, prolonging the fire season beyond the traditional summer period, and causing fires to happen in areas that were not usually affected by them. The latest JRC report on Forest Fires in Europe, the Middle East and North Africa 2023 shows that last year was one of the worst five years for wildfires in EMEA since 2000. Wildfires affected over 500,000 hectares of natural lands, roughly half the size of the island of Cyprus.[3]

Floods cause significant harm in Europe despite flood embankments and retention tanks. As seen in the recent events in 2024 in Valencia, Spain, and Central and Eastern Europe, high water can devastate a neighborhood. The Joint Research Centre provides open, detailed raster data (pixel size 100m × 100m) for Europe. The data consists of different levels based on the occurrence of high water (rp, return period).[4] Each pixel value is a modeled value for the water depth in meters. The analysis focuses on frequent floods with a return period of either 10 or 20 years.

Emergency services are crucial in an emergency, as they provide aid and prevent complete devastation of the surroundings. Our analysis includes the closest fire hydrant, fire department, and police department. We incorporate the KNN analysis based on the Overture Maps Foundation infrastructure and the place datasets.

---

3 Joint Research Centre, "2023 Among the Five Worst Years for Wildfires in Europe, but 2024 Provides Some Relief" (*https://oreil.ly/0hC1U*), Joint Research Centre: EU Science Hub, 2024.

4 Calum Baugh et al., "Modelled Flood Inundation for Different Return Period Scenarios at the Global Scale" [Dataset], European Commission, Joint Research Centre (JRC), 2024.

With many electronic devices in a concentrated space, we increase the risk of an unwanted fire. There are many examples of battery fires from electric vehicles and scooters. As the next risk factor, we consider the neighborhood's population: the higher the population, the more probable the danger event. For this use case, we use the same population data as in "Joining Raster Data" on page 143. The higher the population in the neighborhood, the higher the risk of accidents, such as fire and theft.

The denser the population and the greater the concentration of buildings, the greater the chance of a harmful event and the spread of a damaging event like fire. As the last parameter, we will calculate the number of buildings within a 500m radius. We will use the building dataset from the Overture Maps Foundation; we will only use the residential buildings.

The idea is to calculate all the factors and normalize them to the <0,1> interval using the following formula:

$$normalized = \frac{value - minValue}{maxValue - minValue}$$

We will apply the weights and create an index for each normalized factor. Based on the building indices, we will visualize using Kepler.gl.

Now let's go through each of the components; each feature with a higher value causes a higher likelihood of damage to the property:

- Population density
- Flood risk
- Fire risk
- Closest police department
- Closest fire department
- Closest fire hydrant
- Residential building density

Population Density (building_population)

We use building geometries for the population and join the population raster using the RS_Intersects function. We also use the ST_Intersection function to find the geometry inside the envelope of the raster tiles. We use the negative ST_Buffer to avoid topology errors to ensure the building geometry is inside the raster envelope.

This is crucial to the next step, which is the calculation of zonal statistics. We store the partial result in the `population_data` view:

```
SELECT
    b.id,
    ST_Buffer(
        ST_Intersection(b.geometry, RS_Envelope(rast)),
        -0.00001
    ) AS geometry,
    rast
FROM buildings AS b
JOIN population AS p ON RS_Intersects(geometry, rast)
```

Based on the intersection result in the `population_data`, we can run the `RS_Zonal Stats` function. We look for the population sum, so we take the sum as the third argument in `RS_ZonalStats`. Each building can have many tiles matched to it, so we need to group the results by ID and take the sum of the zonal statistic function:

```
SELECT
    id,
    SUM(RS_ZonalStats(rast, geometry, "sum")) AS population
FROM population_data
GROUP BY id
```

Flood Risk (flood_stats)

The flood risk data is in the EPSG:3035 CRS (*https://epsg.io/3035*). We need to transform the building data to the common CRS; we don't have to for the join, as the data is automatically transformed to the common CRS in raster joins. The temporary result is stored in the `flood_data` view:

```
SELECT
    b.id,
    ST_Buffer(ST_Intersection(
        ST_Transform(b.geometry, 'epsg:4326', 'epsg:3035'),
        RS_Envelope(rast)
    ), -0.00001) AS geom,
    rast,
    rp
FROM buildings AS b
JOIN flood AS p ON RS_Intersects(geometry, rast)
```

We will calculate two zonal statistics for the flood data: the minimum and maximum values for the flood height in meters. We also filter the min and max values to not be equal to `'NaN'`. Similar to the population data, we group by ID and add the RP column to the `GROUP BY` clause (return period). We can safely call the MIN and MAX functions on `RS_ZonalStats` to get the min value for each group (`id`, `rp`). We must pivot the longer format to the wide format, where we remove the `rp` dimension (10 or 20 years) to create additional columns for the corresponding values. For example, for id=1 and rp=20, we create columns min_20 and max_20, and we put in the values 1 and 2, respectively. The transformation process is illustrated in Figure 5-8.

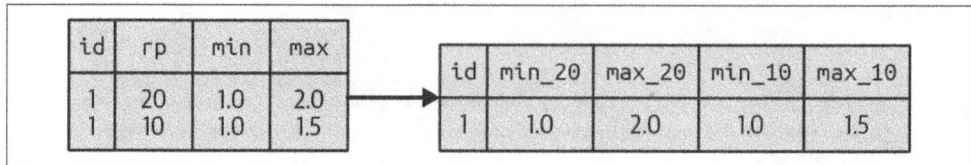

Figure 5-8. Transforming data from the long to the wide form using the pivot function

```
WITH flood_risk AS (
    SELECT
        id,
        rp,
        Min(RS_ZonalStats(rast, geom, "min")) AS min_value,
        Max(RS_ZonalStats(rast, geom, "max")) AS max_value
    FROM flood_data
    GROUP BY id, rp
    HAVING min_value <> 'NaN' AND max_value <> 'NaN'
)
SELECT * FROM flood_risk
PIVOT (
    FIRST(min_value) AS min,
    FIRST(max_value) AS max
    FOR rp IN (
        '10' AS flood_10,
        '20' AS flood_20
    )
)
```

Fire Risk (fire_risk_stats)

The spatial SQL code for fire risk looks similar to the flood data, but the common ground CRS is 3857. The partial result is stored in the fire_risk_data view:

```
SELECT b.id,
    ST_Buffer(
        ST_Intersection(
            ST_Transform(b.geometry, 'epsg:4326', 'epsg:3857'),
            RS_Envelope(rast)
        ),
        -0.00001
    ) AS geom,
    rast,
    risk
FROM buildings AS b
JOIN fire_risk AS p ON RS_Intersects(geometry, rast)
```

The code for the zonal statistics is almost the same as for the flood raster, with the distinction that we have different pivot groups: high, intermediate, and low:

```
WITH fire_risk AS (
    SELECT
        id,
        risk,
        Min(RS_ZonalStats(rast, geom, "min")) AS min_value,
        Max(RS_ZonalStats(rast, geom, "max")) AS max_value
    FROM fire_risk_data
    GROUP BY id, risk
    HAVING min_value <> 'NaN' AND max_value <> 'NaN'
)
SELECT * FROM fire_risk
PIVOT (
    FIRST(min_value) AS min,
    FIRST(max_value) AS max
    FOR risk IN (
        'high' AS fire_risk_high,
        'intermediate' AS fire_risk_intermediate,
        'low' AS fire_risk_low
    )
)
```

Closest Police and Fire Departments

To get the closest police department, fire department, and fire hydrant, we use a KNN join. We use the ST_DistanceSpheroid function to obtain the result in metric units, which provides the distance.

Closest police department (closest_police_department):

```
SELECT
    b.id,
    ST_DistanceSpheroid(b.geometry, p.geometry) AS distance
FROM buildings AS b
JOIN police_department AS p ON ST_KNN(b.geometry, p.geometry, 1)
```

Closest fire department (closest_fire_department):

```
SELECT
    b.id,
    ST_DistanceSpheroid(b.geometry, f.geometry) AS distance
FROM buildings AS b
JOIN fire_departments AS f ON ST_KNN(b.geometry, f.geometry, 1)
```

Closest fire hydrant (closest_fire_hydrants):

```
SELECT
    b.id,
    ST_DistanceSpheroid(b.geometry, f.geometry) AS distance
FROM buildings AS b
JOIN fire_hydrants AS f ON ST_KNN(b.geometry, f.geometry, 1)
```

Residential Building Density (building_density)

To get the building density, we use the `ST_DWithin` function. As the fourth parameter, we pass true to use spheroid distance, as we want to use a 500m radius. Then we aggregate the result using the `COUNT` aggregation function:

```
WITH nearby_buildings AS (
    SELECT
        b1.id AS b1_id,
        b2.id AS b2_id
    FROM buildings AS b1
    JOIN buildings AS b2 ON ST_DWithin(b1.geometry, b2.geometry, 500, true)
)
SELECT
    b1_id AS id,
    count(*) AS density
FROM nearby_buildings
GROUP BY b1_id
```

We then combine the results, and then we need to normalize them:

```
SELECT
    b.id,
    bp.population,
    f.flood_10_min,
    f.flood_10_max,
    f.flood_20_min,
    f.flood_20_max,
    fr.fire_risk_high_min,
    fr.fire_risk_high_max,
    fr.fire_risk_intermediate_min,
    fr.fire_risk_intermediate_max,
    fr.fire_risk_low_min,
    fr.fire_risk_low_max,
    bd.density,
    cf.distance AS closest_fire_department_distance,
    cp.distance AS closest_police_department_distance,
    ch.distance AS closest_fire_hydrants_distance
FROM buildings AS b
LEFT JOIN building_population AS bp ON bp.id = b.id
LEFT JOIN flood_stats AS f ON f.id = b.id
LEFT JOIN fire_risk_stats AS fr ON fr.id = b.id
LEFT JOIN building_density AS bd ON bd.id = b.id
LEFT JOIN closest_fire_department AS cf ON cf.id = b.id
LEFT JOIN closest_police_department AS cp ON cp.id = b.id
LEFT JOIN closest_fire_hydrants AS ch ON ch.id = b.id
```

Each of the factors of the index is normalized and multiplied by the weights:

```
"population": 0.05,
"flood_10_min": 0.1,
"flood_10_max": 0.12,
"flood_20_min": 0.1,
```

```
"flood_20_max": 0.05,

"fire_risk_high_min": 0.1,
"fire_risk_high_max": 0.2,
"fire_risk_intermediate_min": 0.03,
"fire_risk_intermediate_max": 0.03,
"fire_risk_low_min": 0.01,
"fire_risk_low_max": 0.01,

"density": 0.05,

"closest_fire_department_distance": 0.05,
"closest_police_department_distance": 0.05,
"closest_fire_hydrants_distance": 0.05,
```

We use the decimal weights to sum them to one, so we don't have to divide the sum of values. We present the result on the map using the SedonaKepler extension; you can see it in Figure 5-9. The lower the index value, the lower the possibility of an accident that might cause damage to the building. We can observe higher values where the building concentration is denser and closer to the Vistula River.

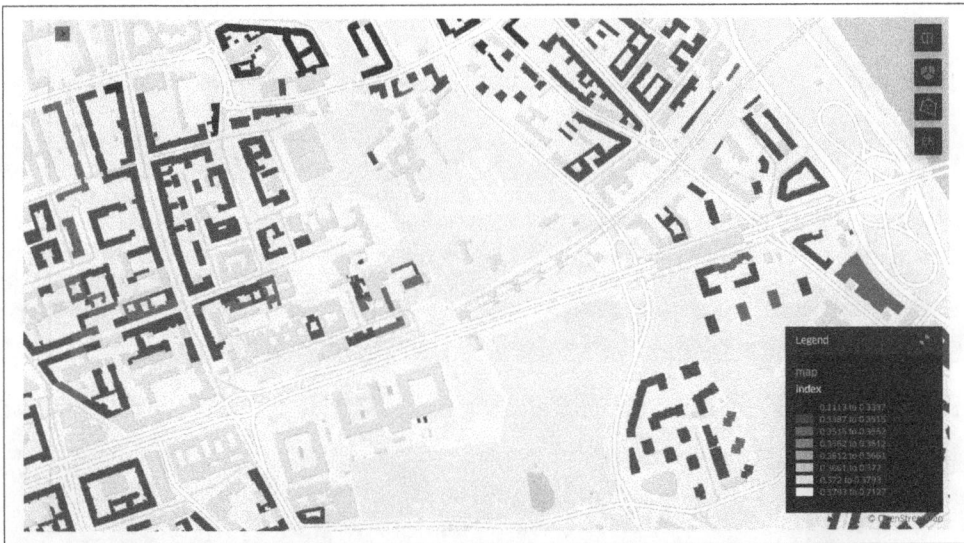

Figure 5-9. Visualization of the buildings using the calculated insurance risk score

Summary

Initially, Apache Sedona supported vector data; raster data was added in recent years, and the number of features and functions is improving with each release. As we went through the raster model, we covered many challenges when processing raster data, including handling multiple CRS, multiple bands, large arrays, and transforming array coordinates to real-world coordinates. Each row with raster data has a complex internal structure that requires proper handling. Apache Sedona simplifies it with readily available RS functions. You can use map algebra functions and zonal statistics, but the most value comes from the easy integration of vector and raster data in one library. In this chapter, we focused on the typical raster data transformations. In Chapter 7, we will cover how to combine machine learning with raster data.

In the hands-on section, we utilized raster and vector data to create an insurance risk model incorporating various features, such as flood and fire risk maps. We used vector data, such as fire station locations, to calculate the distance to the closest one.

In Chapter 6, we will cover the Python ecosystem and how you can integrate Apache Sedona with Python libraries, like GeoPandas, Rasterio, Airflow, and dbt.

## CHAPTER 6

Apache Sedona and the PyData Ecosystem

Python is an all-purpose, interpreted language with high-level abstractions. It is known for its simplicity and readability to the extent that perfectly clean code written in Python has been nicknamed Pythonic. Fast prototyping, ease of use, and a rich set of community-driven frameworks and libraries made Python very popular among those working in data. Initially, in the Hadoop era, data engineers used Java and Scala to process large amounts of data, while data scientists mainly used R to create machine learning models. However, Python was so convenient to use that, in both areas, it has become great for both data engineering and data science. Despite the native slowness of Python and compute-heavy resource utilization, the Python community created integrations with low-level fast languages like C, Fortran, Java, and recently, Rust.

Up to 2019, Apache Sedona only exposed its API for Scala, Java, and SQL. Thanks to a community-driven initiative, Apache Sedona got initial support for the DataFrame API in Python. In early 2020, the missing spatial RDD operations were also included, and the library was officially published in the PyPI repositories, making it publicly available and easy to install. The Apache Sedona team initially anticipated thousands of downloads per month, but expectations were exceeded, and today, the project is standing at over 1.5 million monthly downloads.

The complexity of geospatial problems requires using different tools and libraries to create the final output. Apache Sedona integrates with popular Python libraries to handle geospatial data like GeoPandas, Shapely, Rasterio, Kepler.gl, PyDeck, and more.

Manipulating Geospatial Vector Data

One of the advantages of Apache Sedona is its integration with popular Python vector libraries like GeoPandas or Shapely. You can quickly call the `toPandas` method on your Sedona spatial DataFrame to convert it to the GeoPandas GeoDataFrame. However, that transformation is not without consequences; data has to be synced to the driver node due to GeoPandas's nondistributed nature. Usually, when you work with Apache Sedona, your data is massive. Be cognizant that calling `collect()` on an Apache Sedona Python spatial DataFrame might be destructive to the application due to possible colossal memory usage. Before we plunge into the details of using Geo-Pandas and Shapely together with Apache Sedona, we'll outline how Apache Sedona Python communicates with the native Apache Sedona Java/Scala implementation.

Working with GeoPandas and Shapely

Apache Sedona Python implements two generic data types to work with geospatial data: `GeometryType` for vector data and `RasterType` for raster data.

When you instantiate an Apache Sedona session, you also provision the connection to a JVM machine via the Py4J library. This gateway is kept as long as your Apache Spark session is alive, and all inter-language communication between Python and Java is facilitated.

> Apache Sedona Python supports both the spatial RDD API and spatial DataFrame API. Still, it's highly recommended to use the spatial DataFrame API as it has many functions available and is easier to work with.

While Python is often seen as a slow language, the implementation of algorithms and libraries uses faster, more efficient languages like C, Fortran, Rust, or Java. The Apache Sedona Python API, which is dependent on the core Apache Sedona implementation, is just a wrapper for the Scala/Java version of Sedona Spark spatial DataFrames. The API communicates via the JVM gateway. As long as you don't synchronize the data to Python, you won't encounter performance degradation. Let's consider the following spatial DataFrame as an example:

```
+---+-------------+
| id|         geom|
+---+-------------+
|  1|POINT (21 52)|
|  2|POINT (21 45)|
+---+-------------+
```

As long as you manipulate the DataFrame with operations like the following, you still get the same speed as in Scala/Java, with faster prototyping:

- Spatial SQL functions
  - `spatial_df.selectExpr("ST_X(geom)")`
- Python function wrappers
  - `spatial_df.select(f.ST_X("geom")).show()`
- Spatial joins and spatial aggregations

Be mindful of three scenarios that impact performance:

`DataFrame.collect()`
> In the collect operation, Apache Spark transfers all the data from the nodes to the driver node and deserializes it. The result is a list of PySpark Rows:

```
> spatial_df.collect()

> [Row(id=1, geom=<POINT (21 52)>), Row(id=2, geom=<POINT (21
45)>)]
```

`DataFrame.toPandas()`
> Equivalent to the collect operation, data is transferred to the driver node. The instantaneously deserialized data is transformed into a pandas DataFrame:

```
> result = spatial_df.toPandas()
> type(result)
> pandas.core.frame.DataFrame
```

User-defined functions
> When you apply a user-defined function (UDF) in PySpark, the objects must be deserialized to Python. Due to performance degradation, applying user-defined functions should be considered a last resort when writing your geospatial ETL pipeline.

The three operations mentioned require transforming internal Apache Sedona geospatial data types (vector or raster) to Python, which is costly.

Let us deconstruct the process after calling collect on your spatial DataFrame. As you already know, Apache Sedona natively uses a tailored way of serializing geometry vector data. When the `collect` method is invoked, each record in your spatial DataFrame is serialized to the internal Sedona binary format and then deserialized to Python Shapely objects using efficient Sedona custom C serialization (Figure 6-1).

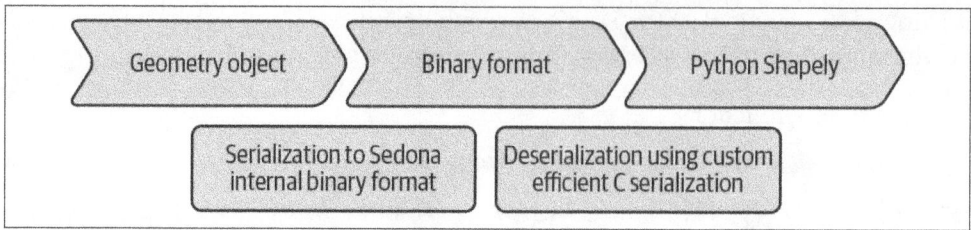

Figure 6-1. Process of converting the Sedona internal geometry object into a Python Shapely geometry object

> Running `toPandas()` or `collect()` could pose a risk to your spatial pipeline when the amount of data in the spatial DataFrame is larger than the memory defined for your driver node. It could result in an application failure due to memory overflow.

Calling `toPandas()` on a spatial DataFrame also triggers this mechanism; instead of being returned as a list, the data is returned as a pandas DataFrame. To transform into a GeoPandas GeoDataFrame, run the following code:

```
import geopandas as gpd

gpd.GeoDataFrame(df.toPandas(), geometry="geom")
```

Transferring geospatial data between the Java virtual machine and Python might take a lot of time. We can do better by leveraging Apache Arrow and its geospatial extension, GeoArrow.

Apache Arrow (*https://oreil.ly/xWx_d*) is an in-memory columnar data format used in Spark to sync the data between the JVM and Python processes. Users who transform data between pandas/NumPy and Spark benefit the most. If you work with geospatial data and the Python ecosystem, you often use GeoPandas (pandas) for vector data processing and Rasterio (NumPy) to transform raster data. Both scenarios are great candidates for Arrow and GeoArrow.

> By default, conversion to or from a pandas DataFrame does not use Arrow. To turn it on, you need to set the Spark configuration parameter `spark.sql.execution.arrow.pyspark.enabled`. If an exception occurs during the conversion, Apache Spark automatically falls back to non-Arrow conversion. You can turn it off by setting config `spark.sql.execution.arrow.pyspark.fall back.enabled=false`. When you use the `dataframe_to_arrow` function, you don't have to mind setting the Spark config mentioned previously; the transformation uses efficient GeoArrow conversion.

Simply write the following code to load the Sedona spatial DataFrame to GeoPandas using GeoArrow:

```
from sedona.spark import dataframe_to_arrow
import geopandas as gpd

gpd.GeoDataFrame.from_arrow(dataframe_to_arrow(df))
```

We already loaded the data using Sedona to a spatial DataFrame, and we called it the df variable and then converted it using GeoArrow. The time needed for the whole process dropped from 7 seconds to 3 seconds when using GeoArrow conversion compared to not using it. Chapter 10 provides more on optimization techniques and benchmarks.

Despite the proactive Apache Sedona community, you may encounter data formats that are not available to load natively using the DataFrame API, or you may already have existing code that is using Shapely. To convert a Python list of lists containing Shapely geometries to a spatial DataFrame, simply type:

```
from shapely.geometry import Point
import sedona.sql.types as st
import pyspark.sql.types as t

schema = t.StructType(
    [
        t.StructField("id", t.IntegerType()),
        t.StructField("geom", st.GeometryType()),
    ]
)

sedona.createDataFrame([
    [1, Point(21, 52)],
    [2, Point(21, 45)]
], schema=schema)
```

As you can see, alongside the geometries, we have another element in the list, an integer type called id. We need to provide a schema to properly name columns. You can also simplify it by using a list of Python dictionaries. The process of transforming Shapely objects into Apache Sedona internal geometries has been visualized in Figure 6-2:

```
sedona.createDataFrame([
    {"id": 1, "geom": Point(21, 52)},
    {"id": 2, "geom": Point(21, 45)}
])
```

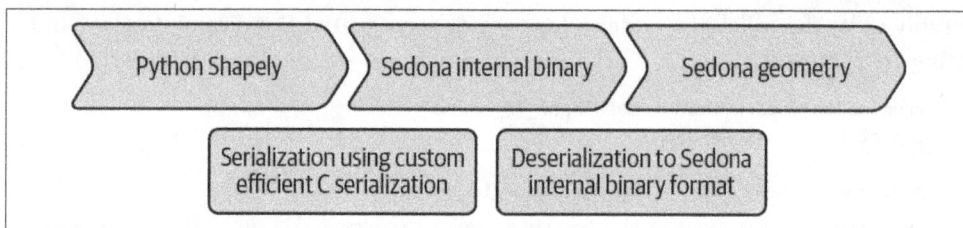

Figure 6-2. Process of transforming Shapely objects to the Apache Sedona internal geometry model

To transform a GeoPandas GeoDataFrame to an Apache Sedona spatial DataFrame, simply use the Apache `SparkSession` `createDataFrame` method:

```
sedona.createDataFrame(gdf)
```

This method does not use Arrow optimization to serialize GeoPandas objects into a Sedona spatial DataFrame. However, you can use `create_spatial_dataframe(spark: SparkSession, gdf: gpd.GeoDataFrame)` to leverage this optimization:

```
from sedona.utils.geoarrow import create_spatial_dataframe
```

```
create_spatial_dataframe(spark, gdf)
```

Using the same dataset we used to convert Sedona to GeoPandas, we can decrease the conversion time from 5 seconds to around 1 second.

> If you are experienced with GeoPandas and want to leverage Apache Sedona's scalability, you can utilize the recently introduced Apache Sedona GeoPandas API. You are using the GeoPandas code, but underneath, you are utilizing the powerful Apache Sedona library. Just change your import from
>
> ```
> import geopandas as gpd
> ```
> to
> ```
> import sedona.spark.geopandas as gpd
> ```

What do you do when no function suits your use case? You have at least two options available. First, you can create an issue on the official repository or volunteer to write it yourself. Secondly, you can implement a user-defined function (UDF) independently. However, UDFs are not an efficient method. If possible, using the existing functions is recommended. Why is that? When you apply a UDF, you must perform costly serialization to Python from the internal Spark data model.

Now, assume you can't use existing functions to solve your problem. To create a custom function to be applied to the DataFrame column, you can use the Apache Spark UDF feature. At the time of writing, PySpark supports nonvectorized and vectorized UDFs. They differ in how Apache Spark processes the data. A nonvectorized UDF is applied to each row one by one, which incurs a huge penalty for serializing and deserializing objects from Python to JVM and from JVM to Python.

On the other hand, vectorized UDFs, also known as pandas UDFs because pandas is used to process the data on each worker, use Apache Arrow, which is language-agnostic and can be transferred and interpreted quickly by many languages. For vectorized UDFs, Apache Spark uses batch data instead of row by row.

A nonvectorized UDF is applied to each row, one by one. When we transform Sedona geometry objects to Python, we convert them to Shapely objects. Every function in Shapely is available to you.

We will cover both UDF types, vectorized and nonvectorized. Imagine you must write a function calculating the symmetrical difference between smaller and larger buffers created from the geometry. Buffer a has a smaller radius, and buffer b has a larger one. We visualize that in Figure 6-3. If we consider the point as the geometry, the function returns a "donut" shape, the shape between the end of the smaller and larger radius. We will call the registered UDF function ST_BufferDistanceNonVector ized for the nonvectorized UDF, and for vectorized, we will name it vectorized_sym metrical_buffer_distance_udf, and we will call it using the Apache Spark Python API instead of the SQL API.

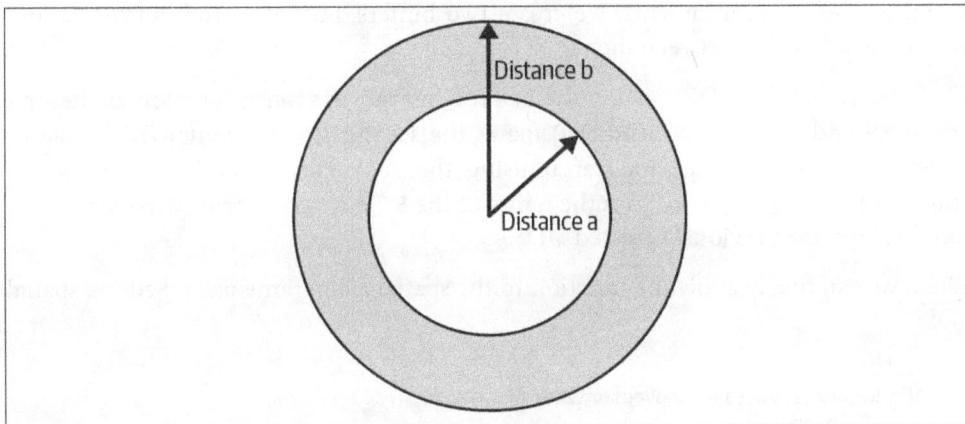

Figure 6-3. The result of the ST_BufferDistance function

We will start with nonvectorized. Let's analyze the following code:

```python
import pyspark.sql.functions as f
import sedona.sql.types as st
import shapely.geometry.base as b

def create_buffer_distance(
    s: b.BaseGeometry,
    distance_from: float,
    distance_to: float
) -> b.BaseGeometry:
    buffer_a = s.buffer(distance_from)
    buffer_b = s.buffer(distance_to)
    return buffer_b.difference(buffer_a)

buffer_distance_udf = f.udf(create_buffer_distance, GeometryType())

sedona.udf.register(
    "ST_BufferDistanceNonVectorized",
    buffer_distance_udf
)
```

The `create_buffer_distance` function takes three arguments:

- `s: shapely.BaseGeometry`
- `distance_from: float`
- `distance_to: float`

Based on the input arguments, we create two buffers, `buffer_a` and `buffer_b`, and return the difference between them.

Then, we create the UDF, passing the `create_buffer_distance` function as the first argument and the Sedona `GeometryType` as the second. To make our UDF available in Sedona SQL, we must register it using the `register` method on the Sedona context method; we need to pass the name of the `ST_BufferDistanceNonVectorized` function and the previously created UDF.

Then, we can finally apply the function to the spatial DataFrame using Sedona spatial SQL:

```sql
SELECT
    ST_BufferDistanceNonVectorized(
        geometry,
        CAST(0.0001 AS FLOAT),
        CAST(0.0002 AS FLOAT)
    ) AS geometry
FROM roads
```

Nonvectorized UDFs are a last resort for transforming your spatial data, and you can fare better by using vectorized UDFs, also known as pandas UDFs. Based on our benchmarks, vectorized UDFs can give you two times faster execution time and smaller memory consumption in your Apache Sedona application.

To use the optimized vectorized version of the UDF, we must use the `sedona_vector ized_udf` Python decorator. We don't have to change the existing `create_buffer_dis tance` function; we can reuse it and apply the decorator. In the decorator params, we pass the `GeometryType()` return type because we return a new geometry object. As the argument in the `vectorized_symmetrical_buffer_distance_udf` function, we take a Shapely geometry object and return a Shapely geometry object. Inside the function, we call the previously created `create_buffer_distance` function:

```
@sedona_vectorized_udf(return_type=GeometryType())
def vectorized_symmetrical_buffer_distance_udf(
        geom: b.BaseGeometry
) -> b.BaseGeometry:
    return create_buffer_distance(geom, 0.0001, 0.0002)
```

The last step is to apply the function on the spatial DataFrame column:

```
df.select(
    vectorized_symmetrical_buffer_distance_udf(f.col("geometry"))
).show(10)
```

Raster Data Tools

One of the significant advantages of using Apache Sedona is that it allows for seamless operating on both vector and raster data types. You don't need to use different libraries to process raster and vector data. One framework "to rule them all": vector and raster data. If you find that you still need Rasterio in your Apache Sedona application, then this chapter section is for you. You can easily integrate Rasterio with Apache Sedona spatial DataFrames, and the following section shows examples of how you can do that.

Similar to the vector data `GeometryType`, Apache Sedona Python implements an additional SQL type to handle raster data named `RasterType`. As of writing the book, converting Apache Sedona's internal raster type to Python is one-directional and you can only deserialize it to Python.

> When you run the `collect` method on the geospatial raster dataframe, be careful because you might easily hit the buffer overflow error. Raster tile size might be larger than the maximum limit for one cell in a spatial DataFrame. You can fix this either by bumping the `spark.kryoserializer.buffer.max` Apache Spark configuration property or using the `RS_TileExplode` function to split your raster data into smaller tiles.

When deserializing a spatial DataFrame to Python, with raster data inside, the internal spatial DataFrame raster data type is translated into an `InDbSedonaRaster` Python object. `InDbSedonaRaster` keeps information about raster width, height, bands metadata, affine transformation, and coordinate reference system. We will describe each of them shortly. There are many libraries for the raster data type, including Xarray, Rasterio, and NumPy. `InDbSedonaRaster` has methods implemented to transform your raster data to the data container of choice, NumPy or Rasterio.

Similar to vector data, when you use the `toPandas()` method, `collect()`, or a UDF on raster data, then the internal Apache Sedona raster model is deserialized to Python `InDbSedonaRaster`. You can see this process in Figure 6-4.

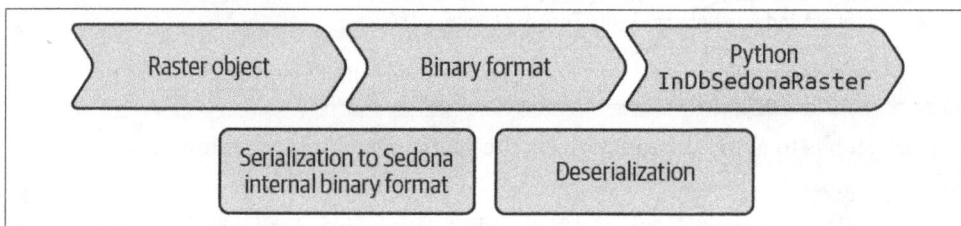

Figure 6-4. Raster data deserialization with Apache Sedona

Now, let's review how this looks in practice. We will load a small part of the global flood hazard map (*https://oreil.ly/Rlv3l*) using Apache Sedona:[1]

```
geotiff_df = sedona \
    .read \
    .format("binaryFile") \
    .load("ID73_S20_W70_RP10_depth.tif") \
    .selectExpr("RS_FromGeoTiff(content) AS rast") \
    .selectExpr("RS_TileExplode(rast, 4096, 4096) AS (x, y, rast)")
```

We use the `RS_TileExplode` function to avoid memory issues and to split the raster into smaller tiles, 4096 by 4096 pixels.

Then, we use the `.head()` method on the spatial DataFrame to take the first element from the spatial DataFrame. We also need to access the `rast` field from the `Row` object to get the raster object:

```
>> row = geotiff_df.head()
>> type(row)
pyspark.sql.types.Row
>> raster = row.rast
>> type(raster)
sedona.spark.raster.sedona_raster.InDbSedonaRaster
```

---

1 Calum Baugh et al., "Global River Flood Hazard Maps" (*https://oreil.ly/4JFgZ*) [Dataset], European Commission, Joint Research Centre (JRC) [Dataset] PID, 2024.

Now, let's look into the fields that we can find in the `InDbSedonaRaster` Python object:

```
>> raster.width
4096
>> raster.height
4096
>> raster.affine_trans.__dict__
{'scale_x': 0.0008333...,
 'skew_y': 0.0,
 'skew_x': 0.0,
 'scale_y': -0.0008333...,
 'ip_x': -70.0095822...,
 'ip_y': -19.9904333...,
 'pixel_anchor': <PixelAnchor.UPPER_LEFT: 2>}

>> print(raster.crs_wkt)
GEOGCS["WGS 84",
  DATUM["World Geodetic System 1984",
    SPHEROID["WGS 84", 6378137.0, 298.257223563, AUTHORITY["EPSG","7030"]],
    AUTHORITY["EPSG","6326"]],
  PRIMEM["Greenwich", 0.0, AUTHORITY["EPSG","8901"]],
  UNIT["degree", 0.017453292519943295],
  AXIS["Geodetic longitude", EAST],
  AXIS["Geodetic latitude", NORTH],
  AUTHORITY["EPSG","4326"]]

>> len(raster.bands_meta)
1
>> band = raster.bands_meta[0]
>> type(band)
sedona.spark.raster.meta.SampleDimension

>> band.__dict__
{
    'description': 'GRAY_INDEX',
    'offset': 1.0,
    'scale': 0.0,
    'nodata': -9999.0
}

>> type(raster.awt_raster)
sedona.spark.raster.awt_raster.AWTRaster
```

Width and height are the dimensions for the raster, which we transformed from an internal Apache Sedona model to Python. The `affine_trans` parameter is the six-parameter affine transformation. Next, the CRS definition is defined in the `crs_wkt` parameter. `bands_meta` is the list of metadata for each of the bands. In our example, we have only one band, so the list consists of only one element. The metadata for the band contains information about the description, offset, scale, and value defined for representing unavailable data. The last parameter `awt_raster` is the data itself.

InDbSedonaRaster gives you two methods to transform your data to popular libraries in Python to process array data, NumPy and Rasterio. To transform it into a NumPy array, simply call:

```
>> raster.to_numpy()
array([[[-9999., -9999., -9999., ..., -9999., -9999., -9999.],
        [-9999., -9999., -9999., ..., -9999., -9999., -9999.],
        [-9999., -9999., -9999., ..., -9999., -9999., -9999.],
        ...,
        [-9999., -9999., -9999., ..., -9999., -9999., -9999.],
        [-9999., -9999., -9999., ..., -9999., -9999., -9999.],
        [-9999., -9999., -9999., ..., -9999., -9999., -9999.]]],
      dtype=float32)
```

As you can see, there are a lot of -9999 values, which indicate there was no data in the input raster. If you want to fill those values with NaN values automatically, you can use as_numpy_masked() on InDbSedonaRaster:

```
>> raster.as_numpy_masked()
array([[[nan, nan, nan, ..., nan, nan, nan],
        [nan, nan, nan, ..., nan, nan, nan],
        [nan, nan, nan, ..., nan, nan, nan],
        ...,
        [nan, nan, nan, ..., nan, nan, nan],
        [nan, nan, nan, ..., nan, nan, nan],
        [nan, nan, nan, ..., nan, nan, nan]]], dtype=float32)
```

When transforming a raster object of type InDbSedonaRaster to a NumPy array, you lose information about the coordinate reference system. Still, when training a machine learning model, you can use Apache Sedona to process your raster data and then put the prepared images into the training of your computer vision PyTorch model—more on geospatial data science and machine learning in Chapter 7.

You can transform the InDbSedonaRaster into Rasterio and not lose the information about the georeference with the following code:

```
>> rasterio_dataset = raster.as_rasterio()
>> type(rasterio_dataset)
rasterio.io.DatasetReader

>> rasterio_dataset.bounds
BoundingBox(
    left=-70.0095822...,
    bottom=-23.4037666...,
    right=-66.5962489...,
    top=-19.9904333...
)
```

The outcome of the one-way serialization (deserialization) in the Apache Sedona Python raster data type is that you can still write UDFs, but only when the return type is a nonraster, serializable type. Apache Sedona can deserialize the internal Apache Sedona raster type (JVM) to Python InDbSedonaRaster but can't do that in reverse.

So if you have a function that takes an InDbSedonaRaster array as an input and returns other serialized data types like string, bool, or Shapely geometry, you can write your UDF to do that. You can do that using the NumPy array or Rasterio dataset. Now that you've seen how you can operate on InDbSedonaRaster, let's use it in practice to define a UDF, which will return the boundary box geometry of the given raster tiles:

```python
import sedona.raster.sedona_raster as sr
import sedona.sql.types as st
import shapely.geometry as g
import shapely.geometry.base as b

def get_bbox(raster: sr.InDbSedonaRaster) -> b.BaseGeometry:
    bounds = raster.as_rasterio().bounds
    return g.box(bounds.left, bounds.bottom, bounds.right, bounds.top)

sedona.udf.register("ST_GetBBox", get_bbox, st.GeometryType())
```

We named our function get_bbox, which takes InDbSedonaRaster as input and produces a Shapely BaseGeometry. In the function body, we translate the raster to the Rasterio dataset and take the bounds' (left, bottom, right, top) coordinates. The last step is to create a Shapely polygon geometry object using a box function. We register the function and call it ST_GetBBox. To call it, you can simply write the SQL query:

```sql
SELECT ST_GetBBox(rast) AS geom FROM geotiff_df
```

This produces the following result:

```
+------------------------------------------------------------------------+
|geom                                                                    |
+------------------------------------------------------------------------+
|POLYGON ((-70 -23.4, -70 -20, -66.6 -20, -66.6 -23.4, -70 -23.4))       |
|POLYGON ((-66.6 -23.4, -66.6 -20, -63.2 -20, -63.2 -23.4, -66.6 -23.4)) |
|POLYGON ((-63.2 -23.4, -63.2 -20, -60 -20, -60 -23.4, -63.2 -23.4))     |
|POLYGON ((-70 -26.8, -70 -23.4, -66.6 -23.4, -66.6 -26.8, -70 -26.8))   |
|POLYGON ((-66.6 -26.8, -66.6 -23.4, -63.2 -23.4, -63.2 -26.8, -66.6 -26.8))|
+------------------------------------------------------------------------+
```

Scheduling Your Geospatial Code

We know how important it is to optimize your time at work. Hence, incorporating a data scheduler into your organization or side project is key to significantly reducing the effort you dedicate to running and monitoring data flow. There are plenty to choose from, including Apache Airflow, Prefect, Dagster, and Luigi, but we will focus on Apache Airflow as it is the most mature and feature-rich tool. For other tools, please refer to the GitHub materials for this chapter, which include examples of scheduling Apache Sedona data pipelines using Prefect.

Apache Airflow is an open source data scheduling tool. It is written in Python and exposes the Python API to define your scheduled data pipelines. The minimal version of the Apache Airflow distribution consists of a *scheduler*, responsible for scheduling the Dags[2] and submitting the tasks to the executor. The *webserver* presents the Dag's definitions graphically, triggers them, and debugs if necessary. A folder of Dag files can be stored in a local filesystem, object storage, or remote storage. A metadata database is used to store the Airflow tasks and Dag state. One nonrequired component to be aware of is a *worker*, which might be used to parallel your Airflow processing by including more entities that can pick up tasks and complete them.

The primary abstraction in Apache Airflow is a Dag, which consists of tasks. A programming instance is created based on the class definition, as a Dag run is a materialized form of a Dag definition in Apache Airflow. Each Dag contains connected *operators*. When the operator is triggered, we name that instance a task. Another important part of Apache Airflow is a sensor, which waits for a specific condition to be fulfilled to schedule downstream tasks. Imagine a spatial data pipeline that needs to wait to get all the scooter locations for the past hour to start batch processing. You can use a sensor that waits until the data is ready.

To schedule the OSS Apache Sedona version, you can use `SparkSubmitOperator` (or `SparkSqlOperator`). Let us now transition the concepts and tools into practice.

We'll craft a simple example to download GeoParquet data for a specific date from the S3 bucket. We will schedule the Dag daily and use the custom sensor to look at possible releases to download. We will skip the processing if the date is unavailable and the processing date is less than or equal to 1 day from the current date. We do that to accommodate any possible late uploads for a given date (we wait an additional 24 hours for the late data). If the release exists for a given date, we load it, transform it, and save it on S3 using Apache Sedona. Input data is in one GeoParquet file. We sort the data by Geohash to preserve locality within the files. Our simplified process is illustrated in Figure 6-5.

---

2 See the Airflow documentation (*https://oreil.ly/6OPbr*) for more detailed information on Dags.

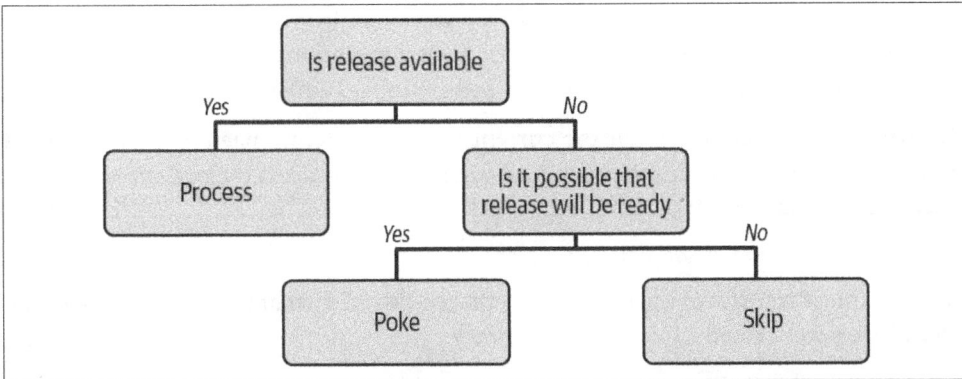

Figure 6-5. Simplified process of ingesting the Overture data from a publicly available S3 bucket

You can find all the code for the Dag in the official repository for this book. We start by creating the custom sensor called `GeoParquetDataReleaseSensor`, which inherits from `BaseSensorOperator`:

```
class GeoParquetDataReleaseSensor(BaseSensorOperator):
    pass
```

We need to implement the `poke` method, which verifies if the condition is met and allows us to proceed with other tasks in the Dag to which the sensor is upstream. The poke method has one parameter besides `self`, which is `context`. `context` is a dict-like object in Apache Airflow that keeps the runtime metadata about the sensor. We will use it to get the execution date later:

```
def poke(self, context):
    pass
```

We will divide the explanation of the poke method implementation into key components, describe them individually, and then compose everything together and explain the full picture.

First, we need to list the available releases on the S3 bucket using the `list_objects_v2` method from the popular Python Boto library to manage AWS cloud resources. The code to list the resources might look as follows:

```
paths = s3.list_objects_v2(
    Bucket="sedona",
    Prefix="transportation/releases/",
    Delimiter="/"
)
```

Then, we must transform the paths to release dates into the format %Y-%m-%d. If you want to analyze the entire code, please follow the book's official repository. This listing method is implemented in the `get_possible_releases` method.

To verify if the release exists for the current Dag run date, we need to get it from the context object passed to the poke function signature. We access the pattern with a key, like in the typical Python dict object:

```
dt = context['execution_date']
```

Then, we must transform the dt object to the %Y-%m-%d format to compare it with the release dates we created using the Boto library:

```
date_formatted = dt.strftime('%Y-%m-%d')
```

Let's follow the conditions we must consider to return a result or raise an exception when necessary. In our scenario, there has to be at least one release on the S3 bucket, so if none exist, we can raise the `AirflowException` to prevent the downstream tasks from continuing to work. If the execution date is already in the listed releases, we can safely return true from the poke function and proceed with further tasks. If the release isn't available today, we can skip it by raising the `AirflowSkipException`. We implement the logic when we skip in the `not_possible_to_have_release` method. The method compares the current and execution dates; if the time diff exceeds one day, we can skip and proceed with the Dag. In all other cases, we return `False` and Apache Airflow triggers the poke in the given interval.

The simplified version of the sensor is as follows. Please follow the book's official repository for a full implementation:

```python
class GeoParquetDataReleaseSensor(BaseSensorOperator):

    def poke(self, context):
        releases = self.get_possible_releases()
        dt = context['execution_date']
        date_formatted = dt.strftime('%Y-%m-%d')

        if not releases:
            raise AirflowException("no releases found.")

        if date_formatted in releases:
            return True

        if self.not_possible_to_have_release(releases, date_formatted):
            raise AirflowSkipException(
                    "skipping this task no release with that date"
            )

        return False
```

Now, let's move to the processing task. We schedule the Apache Sedona code using `SparkSubmitOperator`. Our Airflow instance has to have Apache Spark and Java installed. We first need to add Apache Sedona jar files to our Apache Spark cluster (if we use Apache Spark in client mode, we also need jars in the Apache Airflow instance in the Spark jar directory). We can do this by adding the jar files to our existing Apache Spark cluster or by specifying them in the `SparkSubmitOperator` by passing comma-separated Maven coordinates to the `packages` argument:

```
packages = "org.apache.sedona:sedona-spark-3.5_2.12:1.8.0,package2…"
```

Remember to set up the Sedona session correctly:

```
config = s.SedonaContext \
    .builder() \
    .getOrCreate()

sedona = s.SedonaContext.create(config)
```

`SparkSubmitOperator` is not the only way to run Apache Sedona using Apache Airflow. You can also automate your spatial workloads using the Wherobots Apache Airflow operators.

As of the writing of this book, there are two Wherobots Apache Airflow operators available:

`WherobotsSqlOperator`

Helps you to execute spatial SQL on Wherobots Cloud:

```
WherobotsSqlOperator(
        wherobots_conn_id="connection_id",
        task_id="task_id",
        runtime=Runtime.TINY,
        sql="SELECT * FROM points",
)
```

where `wherobots_conn_id` is the Airflow connection ID created for Wherobots, `runtime` is the size of the machine used to run your spatial SQL and `sql` is your SQL code.

> A Connection in Apache Airflow is a secure saved configuration that stores sensitive information about the connections, such as passwords and API keys, to different entities like databases, cloud accounts, etc. Then, in the code, you reference the connection name only so the possibility of a security breach is much less likely.

WherobotsRunOperator

When your application is more complex than running a single query, the obvious choice is WherobotsRunOperator, which allows you to run Python or Scala applications on the Wherobots Cloud:

```
WherobotsRunOperator(
    name="appName",
    wherobots_conn_id="connection_id",
    task_id="task_id",
    runtime=Runtime.TINY,
    run_python={
        "uri": f"s3://script_location/script.py",
        "args": ["arg1" ...],
    },
    environment={
        "sparkConfigs": {
            "config_key": "value",
        },
    }
)
```

wherobots_conn_id, runtime, and task_id were already covered in the SQL operator, the name is the application name, and run_python is the dict[str, any] with the location of the Python script and possible arguments to use. Last but not least is the environment where you can pass all the Spark configurations you want to apply.

SQL is clean and concise until you have a complex data project with many SQL scripts. In such projects, a lot of code and logic are duplicated. Tests may be nonexistent; people usually test the result manually or, even worse, in production. Managing many SQL scripts may sound like an impossible task, but there is a solution for that: dbt.

Transforming Your Geospatial Data with dbt

Data build tool (dbt) (*https://oreil.ly/Wx4Vn*) is a data transformation tool that helps you manage data projects better by incorporating software engineering principles into the SQL data world. If you are not familiar with dbt, please follow the official documentation (*https://oreil.ly/16cfR*). The tool is rich with features and helps you improve how you manage the data project. Let's look at the key benefits of dbt.

Reusability

dbt follows DRY (don't repeat yourself) programming principles by introducing macros, hooks, and package management.

Maintainability

dbt simplifies managing the project by helping you organize it better, from defining the models to writing and running the tests. A model is an abstraction of how dbt manages and organizes SQL code. Think of it as a smaller subset of your application logic. The model can be materialized as a table or stored as a view. Each model is stored as an SQL file, and you decide by using the proper Jinja template on top of the file if it's a view or table (you can also manage this by project config). The name of the table or view is inherited from the filename. So if you create a file *observations.sql* and you use `SELECT * FROM observations_raw`, then when you run it using `dbt run`, you will get a table or view with the name `observations`.

Extensibility

Write macros and Jinja templates, add community packages to focus on what matters the most to your data application and business logic.

Reliability

Writing unit and data tests (*https://oreil.ly/aRN5i*) for your code and data makes your data trustworthy.

Simplicity

Write SQL or Python code, configure the project using YAML, and specify materialization in Jinja. Don't solve already solved problems.

In this section, we focus on integrating Apache Sedona OSS with dbt.

Writing dbt Applications Using Apache Sedona

There are a few methods and protocols you can use to connect to Apache Sedona OSS from dbt:

- odbc (Open Database Connectivity interface) is used to connect to the Databricks cluster where Apache Sedona is installed (*https://oreil.ly/Xhuh-*).

- `thrift` works best for a local and on-premises installation of Apache Sedona in the cluster. You can also use this connection for Apache Spark hosted in the cloud, such as EMR or Dataproc. Thrift is a lightweight, language-independent software stack for point-to-point RPC implementation.

- `session` is experimental and supports local runs of dbt. It uses the local `SparkSession`, so to run it on an Apache Spark cluster, you need to install dbt in the cluster. Another challenge is the absence of tables during local development, which may necessitate the preparation of test tables for developers to streamline the process.

- `http` is also prepared for the Spark cluster hosted on Databricks. Instead of `odbc`, the `http` protocol is utilized here.

Our demo focuses on the local Apache Spark and Apache Sedona installation. We will use the `thrift` protocol to connect dbt to our Apache Spark cluster.

Now, let's explain the dataset. We will use air quality observations in Europe from the European Environment Agency. We will filter the data to Germany and its neighbors. We will monitor air quality using three indexes: PM1, PM2.5, and PM10. As the internal format to store the geospatial data, we will use GeoParquet. As a result of our application, we will create a density map for each country based on H3 indexes.

> PM10, PM2.5, and PM1 are a mixture of particles in the air with a diameter of less than consecutively 10, 2.5, and 1μm. We measure it by the density in m^3 ($μg/m^3$). For example, the norm for PM10 is 50 $μg/m^3$ per day.

Now, let's explain the dataset we use. We will use one primary dataset called `observations_raw` and one metadata table named `stations_raw`. To create tests, we will also utilize a table with European borders to verify the location of the stations. For each table, we use raw suffixes to mark that the loaded data is unchanged and identical to the source. The transformed tables will be missing those suffixes.

The `observations_raw` table contains the following columns:

`sampling_point_id`
    An identifier of the sampling point. We use this to get the station location data.

`start`
    The beginning of the interval when the observation was gathered. The date-time format is yyyy-mm-dd H:M:S.

`end`
    The end of the interval when the observation was obtained and reported. The date-time format is yyyy-mm-dd H:M:S.

`value`
    The numerical value of the given observation in a given range (`Start` and `End`) and with units (`Unit`)

validity
> Stores the information if the measurement point for the pollutant is valid in a given time frame.[3]

verification
> Stores the information about the verification status of the measurement reported for the pollutant in the given time frame.

The `stations_raw` table contains metadata for the observations:

sampling_id
> An identifier that will help us to combine the data from observations.

iso_code
> The iso code for a country. We will use it to concat with `sampling_id`, which then will be used in the join condition.

longitude
> The longitude in the WGS84 coordinate reference system.

latitude
> The latitude in the WGS84 coordinate reference system.

pollutant
> The index type we take in our analysis, PM1, PM2.5, PM10.[4]

We can keep the `stations_raw` table as a seed (*https://oreil.ly/HOaV1*), which are the CSV files in the *seed* directory of your dbt project. dbt will load the data to the data warehouse using the `dbt seed` command.

We start by filtering the stations to Germany's neighboring countries. We also ensure the data has longitude and latitude filled in by using the predicate `ST_POINT(longitude, latitude) IS NOT NULL`. We also concatenate the `iso_code` with `sampling_id`, which will be later used to join the observations table. To make sure we don't have duplicates, we use the distinct clause on the newly created `sampling_id`:

```
WITH neighbor_stations AS (
    SELECT *
    FROM {{ref('stations_raw')}}
    WHERE country in (
        'Poland',
        'Czechia',
```

---

3 For more information and the categories for validity in the dataset, see the EIONET Data Dictionary (*https://oreil.ly/RDpfH*).

4 For more information and the categories for pollutants in the dataset, see the EIONET Data Dictionary (*https://oreil.ly/qCk1J*).

```
        'Austria',
        'Switzerland',
        'France',
        'Luxembourg',
        'Belgium',
        'Netherlands',
        'Denmark',
        'Germany'
    )
)
SELECT
    DISTINCT lower(concat(iso_code, "/", `sampling_id`)) AS sampling_id,
    country,
    ST_POINT(lon, lat) AS geom,
    air_pollutant AS pollutant
FROM neighbor_stations as s
WHERE ST_POINT(lon, lat) IS NOT NULL
```

`{{ref('stations_raw')}}` is the expression in dbt to use the source table, which we define in the *schema.yaml file*. In our example, we have:

```
sources:
  - name: air_quality
    schema: analytics
    tables:
      - name: observations_raw
      - name: stations_raw
      - name: borders
```

Our database name is `analytics`, and we have three existing tables: `observations_raw`, `stations_raw`, and `borders`. To create `stations_raw`, we used the `dbt seed` command; for the other two, we used external tables. An external table is a table in which files are not managed but only metadata. `dbt seed` is mainly used for smaller tables, so we didn't load observations using the command. You might ask why we don't use `dbt seed` for the borders table. The geometry column fields, using WKT, exceed the limit. It's normal to have a polygon with thousands of characters, especially for complicated country borders.

We store all the geometry tables in the GeoParquet format. You can simply add the header section to your model file:

```
{{ config(materialized='table', file_format='geoparquet') }}
<Your SQL here>
```

To run the model type in the command line:

```
dbt run --select stations
```

For a complete dbt project example, please follow the official repository for the book. Now, let's proceed with the summary and visualization of air pollution on December 3, 2023.

The last step is to prepare a density map based on the H3 cells. We aggregate on a few dimensions: country, h3, pollutant, measurement_date, and measurement_hour. To calculate the measurement_date and measurement_hour, we use the start_time value from the observations table. We take the average of the measures in each grid during the grouping.

The final table that we created for the dbt project looks as follows:

```
+----------------------+------------+-------+-------------------+------------+
|          h3          |    date    | hour  | avg_measurement   | pollutant  |
+----------------------+------------+-------+-------------------+------------+
| 599506708221394943   | 2023-12-01 | 1     | 21.53             | PM10       |
| 599506708221394943   | 2023-12-01 | 13    | 12.68             | PM10       |
| 599506708221394943   | 2023-12-02 | 2     | 11.76             | PM10       |
| 599506708221394943   | 2023-12-02 | 22    | 9.10              | PM10       |
| 599506708221394943   | 2023-12-02 | 23    | 8.65              | PM10       |
+----------------------+------------+-------+-------------------+------------+
```

Testing dbt Applications Using Apache Sedona

Testing the data is as essential as producing it. With suitable quality measures, we can avoid unnecessary costs for fixing data when it is already in production. dbt has a few powerful ways of defining tests, including:

- Plugin extensions
- Macros
- Tests folder

We will define each one to ensure the analysis is accurate and data consumers can safely use it.

One example of plugin extensions is dbt_expectations, which is the port of Great Expectations (*https://oreil.ly/7ZS3u*). We will utilize it to define nonspatial tests in our project. We use macro-defined tests to verify the geospatial columns' correctness. We will create two macro tests to confirm if the stations are in the desired area (Europe) and if the data type is point:

```
{% macro test_within_boundary(model, column_name, boundary) %}
SELECT *
FROM {{ model }}
WHERE NOT ST_Intersects({{ column_name }}, ST_GeomFromText('{{ boundary }}'))
{% endmacro %}

{% macro test_is_point(model, column_name) %}
SELECT *
FROM {{ model }}
WHERE NOT ST_GeometryType({{ column_name }}) = 'ST_Point'
{% endmacro %}
```

Each macro-defined test has two required arguments: `model` and `column_name`. We can extend it by adding as many additional parameters as we want, which gives us a lot of flexibility. For the `test_within_boundary` test, we add a parameter named boundary as a WKT string, which we later use to transform its geometry object using the `ST_GeomFromText` function. The test fails when the query defined produces at least one record. We use the `ST_Intersects` function predicate in our scenario to filter the result to the given polygon. We can use the `ST_Disjoint` otherwise or negate the `ST_Intersects` using the NOT clause, which is what we will do in the example.

To verify the geometry column data type in `test_is_point` we use the `ST_Geometry` `Type` function and compare it to `ST_Point`, and similarly to the previous test, we negate the WHERE clause to make our successful test produce zero records. Now, let's explore the *schema.yaml* file and how to use our geospatial tests on the stations model:

```
models:
  - name: stations
    columns:
      - name: geom
        data_tests:
          - within_boundary:
              boundary: "EUROPE BOUNDARY BOX WKT"
          - is_point
          - not_null
      - name: country
        data_tests:
          - not_null
          - dbt_expectations.expect_column_values_to_be_in_set:
              value_set: [
                "Poland", "Germany", "France", "Belgium", "Switzerland",
                "Luxembourg", "Netherlands", "Austria", "Czechia", "Denmark"
              ]
```

For the geometry column, we defined three tests: `within_boundary`, `is_point`, and `not_null`. We used the `test_` prefix in the macro definition to tell dbt that this is the test macro. In the *schema.yaml* file, we don't need to use the prefix anymore. For the country column, we ensure it is not empty and contains only the countries we want to include in our analysis.

The `dbt_expectations.expect_column_values_to_be_in_set` test is predefined in the `dbt_expectations` package.

We covered two types of tests: plugins and macro-based ones. What if we need to perform more complex tasks considering the whole spatial dataset or many of them? You can define the test in the test directory using as many data models as you want.

To be considered correct, our analysis needs specific coverage in the countries we analyze. There are plenty of ways of doing that. Here, we will use a simplified approach with H3 cells. We will calculate the ratio between the number of H3 cells with at least one station and each country's total number of H3 cells. You can see the example ratio in Figure 6-6.

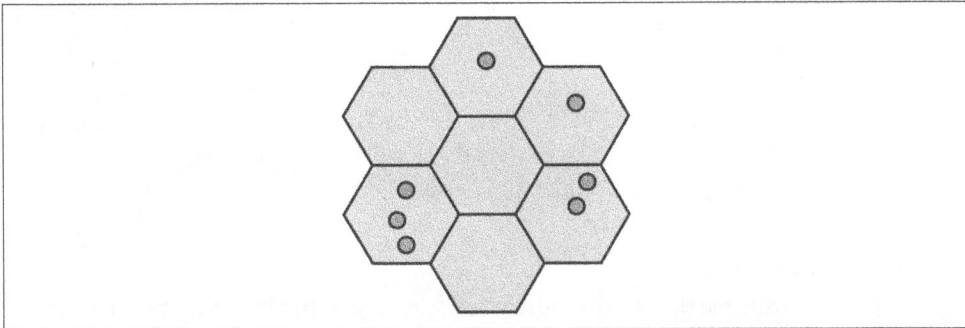

Figure 6-6. The ratio used to verify the input data correctness: 4/7 = 57%

We name our test `test_stations_coverage`. To run it, you can use the `dbt test` command:

```
dbt test --select test_stations_coverage
```

Vector Geospatial Visualization

To analyze the data from a DataFrame, we can use the show method in Spark. We can see the values, but getting the relation for larger datasets is impossible. For geospatial data, even a single row might be hard to imagine as vertices for geometry might be counted in the thousands. People tend to remember images better than words or numbers because our brains process and store visuals more efficiently. Data visualizations play a key role in exploratory analysis or in proving that your output looks valid.

> You can use many techniques to visualize geospatial data. You can create choropleth maps, heat maps, dot density maps, flow maps, hex bin maps, and contour maps. You can find many great articles and books on the topic. We will focus on how you can integrate Sedona spatial DataFrames with popular Python visualization libraries.

Many Python libraries can help you visualize geospatial data. You can create interactive, static, or even 3D visualizations in Python that help you understand the geospatial relations in your data better. Apache Sedona helps you by exposing the built-in Python functions to plot the vector or raster data inside your Jupyter Notebook environment. Before diving into writing any code, let's explain popular geospatial data visualizations:

Geometry/interactive maps
>   These general-purpose maps can be used for any geospatial data for quick analysis or exploration. You can quickly show the roads, buildings, or shapes you want. They might not show the trends or density as well as the following maps, but they are great tools to quickly recognize the patterns in your dataset.

Choropleth map
>   Choropleth maps show geographical divisions, like counties, colored by values assigned to the particular division. They are great for showing population by country or average price in geographic divisions. The visualization uses color progression to show the contrast between the compared geographies. For example, when the population is low in the area, the color might be white, when it is medium, the color might be yellow, and when the population is highly dense, the color could be red.

Scatter maps
>   These maps use raw points (x, y) to represent the occurrence of specific behavior. They do not show the exact density as the points might overlap, but they will show where the phenomenon concentrates. You can use scatter maps to show the location of restaurants in the US or even color them by income.

Heat map
>   This is a map visualization tool that shows the magnitude of the locations in the given dataset. It is helpful to show the density or intensity of the phenomena. A heat map uses color progression to show the difference in density, so where the value is less dense, the color is the beginning of the palette, and for highly dense spaces, the color is taken from the end. We can use it to show crimes committed in the area, traffic congestion, population density, etc.

Now, we will walk you through some popular and valuable libraries you can easily integrate with Apache Sedona.

Kepler.gl

Kepler.gl is an efficient, web-based map application that mainly aims to explore large-scale geolocation data visually. According to official documentation, it can handle millions of points with the possibility to aggregate your data on the fly efficiently. It is highly customizable and can be easily integrated with popular data tools like Jupyter

Notebook or even integrated into a website. In the book, many examples of geospatial visualizations are created using Kepler.gl. We think it's an outstanding solution. You can seamlessly visualize the Apache Sedona spatial DataFrame in Kepler.gl using the Apache Sedona SedonaKepler Python class. Let's follow a quick example:

```
from sedona.maps.SedonaKepler import SedonaKepler
mapview = SedonaKepler.create_map(spatial_df, "Sedona Buildings")
```

In the code snippet, spatial_df is an Apache Sedona spatial DataFrame; the second parameter in the create_map function is the map's name. When you want to add more layers to the map, you can simply add:

```
SedonaKepler.add_df(mapview, another_df, "Sedona roads")
```

In the example, we used Sedona (Arizona) buildings and roads to create a visualization using SedonaKepler (Figure 6-7).

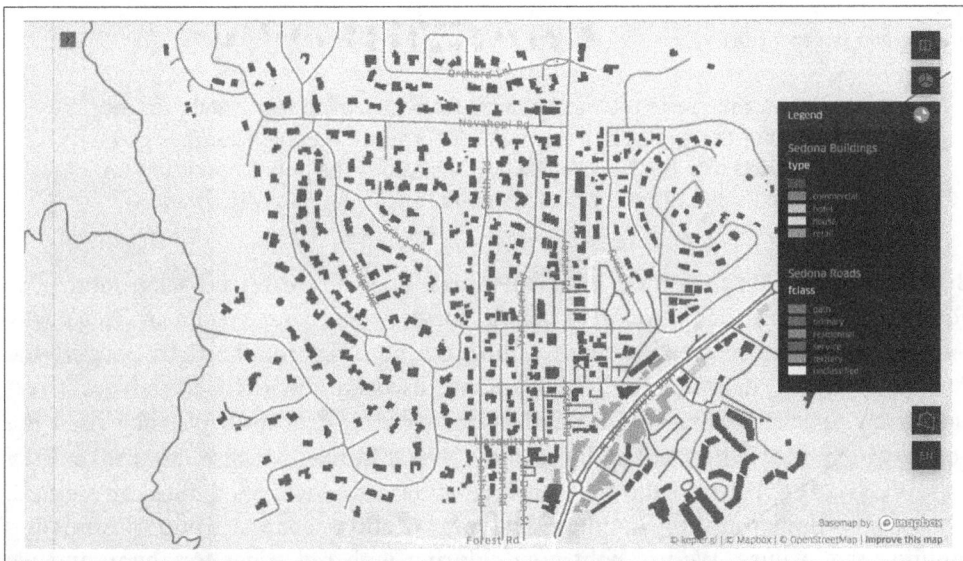

Figure 6-7. Example map visualization of Sedona buildings and roads using OpenStreetMap project data

GeoPandas

GeoPandas helps you to visualize static maps using the plot method on the GeoDataFrame object. It uses Matplotlib for that; it's handy to create maps from the GeoDataFrame in the Jupyter Notebook. We will repeat a similar exercise as with Kepler.gl. We will take buildings from the OSM project for Sedona, Arizona:

```
import geopandas as gpd
import pyspark.sql.functions as f
from sedona.spark import dataframe_to_arrow

gdf = gpd.GeoDataFrame.from_arrow(dataframe_to_arrow(spatial_df))

ax = gdf.to_crs(epsg=3857) \
    .plot(
        column="type", figsize=(10, 10),
        missing_kwds={
            "color": "lightgrey",
            "edgecolor": "red",
            "label": "Missing values"
        },
        legend=True,
        legend_kwds={"title": "Sedona buildings"}
    )

cx.add_basemap(ax)
```

> You can create interactive maps from a GeoPandas GeoDataFrame
> using the explore() method. Underneath, the DataFrame is con-
> verted to a *Folium* visualization. Folium is the popular wrapper on
> the Leaflet JS library that creates powerful mapping visualizations.

By default, the plot method in GeoPandas doesn't create a background. For
geospatial-related visualizations, it's helpful to see where your terrain is. That's why
our example is more complex than calling the gdf.plot method. To convert the
Apache Sedona DataFrame to GeoPandas, we used an efficient GeoArrow conversion from Apache Sedona to GeoPandas (dataframe_to_arrow). We then used the
contextily library with GeoPandas to show the OSM map background. contextily
uses WGS:3857 CRS, so we did the transformation before we called the plot method.
The visualization groups the buildings by type. We add a separate group with missing
building type values. We use light grey coloring with red edges for them, and we
name it "Missing values." We turn on the legend with the title "Sedona buildings."
When you create plots in a Jupyter Notebook, the plot might not be readable. To
avoid zooming in on your web browser, you can pass the size of your figure to the
function. In our example, we enlarged it for better readability; you can see it in
Figure 6-8.

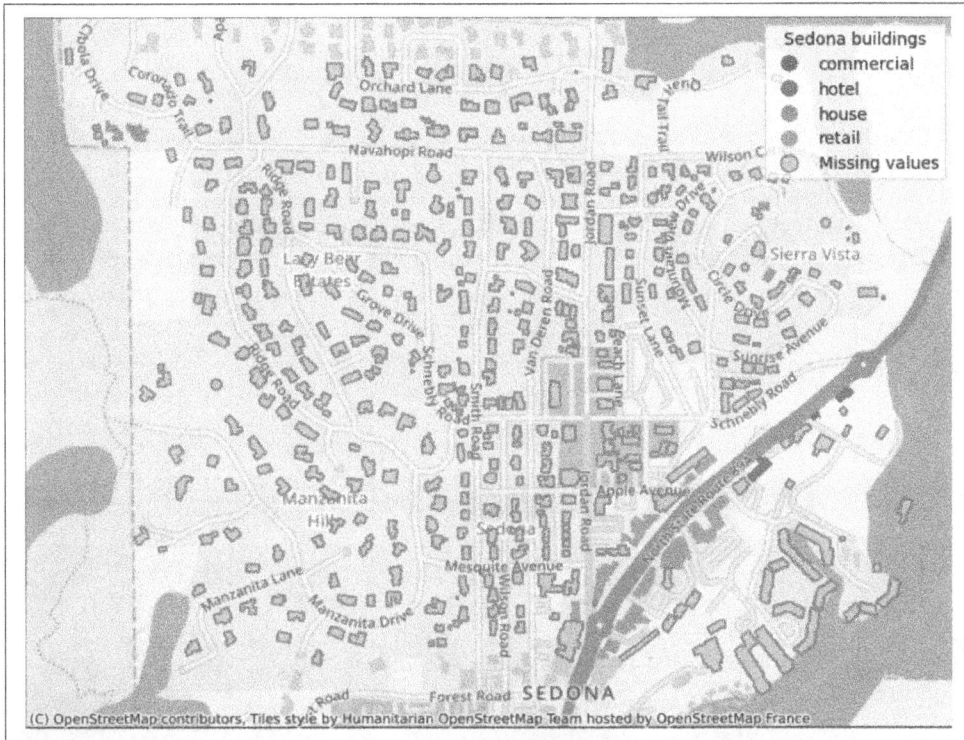

Figure 6-8. Visualization created from a GeoPandas GeoDataFrame

PyDeck

PyDeck is a powerful Python library for high-scale spatial rendering, backed by the powerful deck.gl. deck.gl is a GPU-powered framework for visual exploratory data analysis of large datasets. PyDeck works well in a Jupyter Notebook environment.

To use PyDeck with Apache Sedona, ensure you have installed PyDeck. You can use the `SedonaPyDeck` class (*https://oreil.ly/acyYW*) to create interactive map visualizations, including geometry maps (`create_geometry_map`), choropleth maps (`create_choropleth_map`), scatterplots (`create_scatterplot_map`), and heat maps (`create_heatmap`). In the book, we focus only on one visualization (heat map), but you can find additional examples in the Jupyter Notebook prepared for this chapter. We also highly encourage you to visit the official Apache Sedona and PyDeck documentation.

Now, let's create a heat map using `SedonaPyDeck` to illustrate the crimes in Chicago from 2019. For this purpose, we use the generally available crime dataset from the City of Chicago website (*https://oreil.ly/nQEyN*). The code to create the visualization is simple:

```
from sedona.maps.SedonaPyDeck import SedonaPyDeck

SedonaPyDeck.create_heatmap(
    crimes,
    aggregation="SUM",
    map_style="light"
)
```

To create the heat map, we take the Apache Sedona DataFrame as the first argument. We use the `SUM aggregation` method to show the values when we zoom out of the view. We pass `"light"` as a value to the `map_style` parameter to make the visualization light. You can see the result of the code in Figure 6-9.

Figure 6-9. Crimes heat map visualization using SedonaPyDeck

We covered the vector dataset. Now, let's move forward to the Apache Sedona raster data visualization.

Raster Geospatial Visualization

We covered many examples of visualizing the Apache Sedona vector DataFrame in Python. However, vector data is not the only case for which you can use Apache Sedona. You can use the `SedonaUtils` class to display an Apache Sedona raster DataFrame. In this example, we use the European Copernicus dataset with the Popo-catépetl volcano near Mexico City (Figure 6-10):

```
from sedona.raster_utils.SedonaUtils import SedonaUtils
SedonaUtils.display_image(spatial_df)
```

Figure 6-10. Displaying GeoTIFF raster using Apache Sedona `display_image` function

Summary

Apache Sedona integrates well with the Python ecosystem; you can quickly and efficiently convert the Apache Sedona spatial DataFrame from GeoPandas and to GeoPandas. You can create new ST functions using UDF functions. You can transform the Apache Sedona raster dataset to NumPy or Rasterio. To automate your spatial ETL pipelines or analytics, you can use Apache Airflow with Apache Sedona. If your project involves numerous SQL files, consider using dbt with Apache Sedona and GeoParquet for better management. Finally, Apache Sedona enables effortless geospatial data visualization with popular Python libraries such as Kepler.gl, PyDeck, and Matplotlib.

## CHAPTER 7

Geospatial Data Science and Machine Learning

Geospatial data science is an interdisciplinary field that uses geospatial data (raster and vector data) with machine learning techniques to understand the surrounding world and support decision making in various industries, such as transportation, climate, retail, and real estate.

Many algorithms were invented in the mid-20th century, but due to the lack of efficient and cheap computing power, they were impossible to apply to business-scale problems. With simplified access to efficient computer power in recent years, such as cloud providers, we can solve many previously unsolvable issues. We can apply many machine learning models to improve our daily lives. That is what Apache Sedona is aiming for as well, to make solving complex geospatial problems with the use of statistics and machine learning models easily accessible.

This chapter will teach you how to use Apache Sedona with geospatial statistics algorithms like Moran's I and local outlier detection. We will walk you through applying machine learning models like DBSCAN, KMeans, and XGBoost to solve classification and clustering problems, integrating your Apache Sedona application with MLlib. Raster data is semi-structured data containing a lot of information. One example is combining an image segmentation model to create vector data from raster data in Apache Sedona.

Geospatial Clustering with Apache Sedona (DBSCAN)

Density-based spatial clustering of applications with noise (DBSCAN) is a clustering algorithm that groups points together based on the density in the neighborhood. DBSCAN categorizes the points into three types:

Core points
> If the number of neighbors for the point is greater than the minimum points threshold, then the point is core.

Border points
> Points that are not core but have at least one core point within the ε radius.

Noise points
> Points that are not core and don't have any core points within the ε radius. They might have border points within the ε radius. They are not assigned to any cluster.

The algorithm takes two parameters to create the clusters:[1]

- ϵ (epsilon) is the radius size from which to search for the number of neighbors. Figure 7-1 shows the epsilon value and neighbor points.

- minPts (minimum points) measures the number of points needed in the neighborhood for a point to be considered core. The point from Figure 7-1 is considered a core point as its number of neighbors is greater than minPts (10).

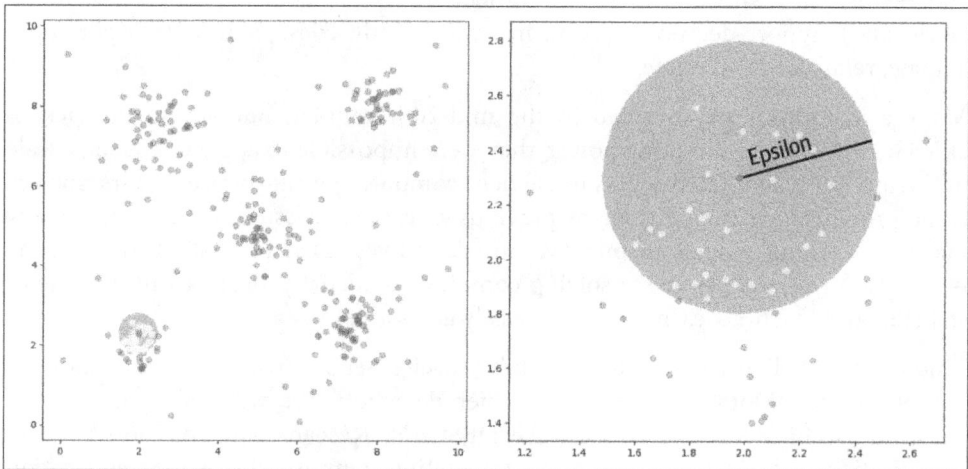

Figure 7-1. Point locations used as input for the DBSCAN algorithm using Apache Sedona

---

1 For more information, see "How to Master the Popular DBSCAN Clustering Algorithm for Machine Learning?" (*https://oreil.ly/7u2Rw*) by Abhishek Sharma.

In the figure, we use ε = 0.5 and the `minPts` = 10. On the left side are point locations, and the selected point is in the bottom left corner with a radius buffer. You can see the zoomed-in image on the right with the same selected point. The selected point is a core point as the number of neighbors, 28, is greater than 10.

The DBSCAN algorithm takes the following steps:

1. Find the number of neighbors for each point within the radius. If the number of neighbors exceeds the minimum point threshold, the point is considered core; otherwise, it is considered a border point.

2. A border point with no core points in the neighborhood is assigned to the noise points.

3. Core points and their neighbors within the ε radius are used to create the graph (*https://oreil.ly/8Rblp*). Based on the graph, the algorithm looks for the connected components in the graph. Each unique subgraph is a cluster.

4. Border points with the core point in their neighborhood are assigned to the cluster of the first core point in their neighborhood.

Apache Sedona uses optimized spatial join to find the neighborhood points for the ε radius and utilizes GraphFrames (*https://oreil.ly/b-6u_*) to find the connected components. The DBSCAN algorithm implemented in Apache Sedona works for all geometry types; for nonpoints, the distance is calculated from the centroid of the geometry (spheroid distance) or between closest points (for nonspheroid distance).

> Apache Sedona uses GraphFrames to solve the graph-connected components query. GraphFrames internally requires the checkpoint directory to be set in the Apache Spark context configuration. You can do this by running the following code:
>
> ```
> sedona.sparkContext.setCheckpointDir("checkpoint")
> ```
>
> The checkpoint is the checkpoint directory.

Let's use the Apache Sedona `dbscan` function to find the clusters for the points' locations in Figure 7-1. As ε, we will take the 0.5 and as a minimum value of points in the neighborhood to be considered core, 10:

```
from sedona.spark.stats.clustering.dbscan import dbscan

dbscan_df = dbscan(
    dataframe=spatial_df,
    epsilon=0.5,
    min_pts=10,
)
```

For the first argument, we pass the spatial DataFrame; the algorithm autodetects the geometry column if there is only one in the DataFrame. Otherwise, it will throw an exception.

The other required parameters are epsilon and `min_pts`. After running the algorithm, the five clusters will appear similar to that shown in Figure 7-2 (we added the convex-like geometries with cluster names for better readability in the book). To play with the algorithm parameters, please follow the official notebook for this section.

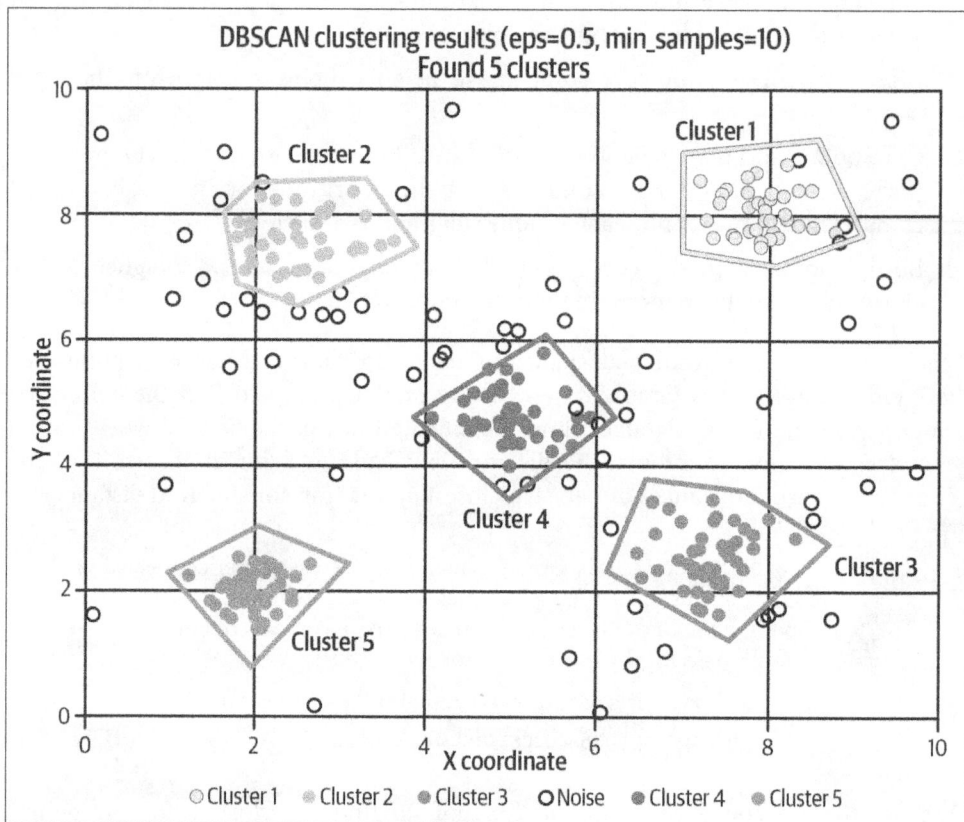

Figure 7-2. DBSCAN result using Apache Sedona for ε = 0.5 and `min_pts` = 10

Outlier Detection (Local Outlier Factor)

Local Outlier Factor (LOF) is an unsupervised[2] machine learning algorithm that detects anomalies based on the local density deviation for points with respect to their neighbors. The algorithm has one argument, k, which is the number of neighbors. The algorithm uses the distances from the k-nearest neighbors to assess and assign a score for each point. The score is the result of comparing the point density and the densities of its neighbors.

The algorithm follows these steps:

- Find the k-nearest neighbors. If we accept ties, there might be more than k nearest neighbors, as neighbors might lie at the same distance for each point.
- Calculate the distance to the point for each of the neighbors. In Apache Sedona, you can choose to use the planar or sphere distance. Then, we take the maximum distance to the neighbors list for each point.
- Get the local reachability density (LRD) ratio. The formula for getting the LRD is as follows:

$$\frac{1}{\sum_{i=1}^{k} \max \left(nkdistance_i, distance(p, n_i) \right) \times \frac{1}{k}}$$

where:

— k is the number of neighbors for the point (if we have ties, there might be more than the initial k).

— $nkdistance_i$ is the maximum distance of the ith neighbor to its neighbors.

— $distance(p, n_i)$ is the distance between the point and the ith neighbor.

So, to simplify the formula, we calculate the inverse of the mean value of each neighbor.

---

2 Unsupervised learning is a type of machine learning where we let an algorithm find patterns without labels; in the case of supervised learning we provide the labels, which helps the algorithm to find a pattern. For example, DBSCAN is an unsupervised machine learning algorithm as we don't provide labels for the training set; the algorithm checks for density and returns the clusters. Examples of supervised learning would be neural networks, where we say that image A, for instance, is a class of cat and image B is a dog. We train the algorithm on these images to say later on that image C is a dog, without providing labels.

- The last step is to compare the average of the LRD of all point neighbors to the LRD of the point:

$$lof = \frac{\frac{1}{k}\Sigma_{i=1}^{k} lrd_{n_i}}{lrd_p}$$

where:

— lrd_n is the LRD of the point neighbors.

— lrd_p is the LRD of the point.

— k is the number of neighbors for the point (if we have ties, there might be more than the initial k).

Now, let's calculate the LOF value for a point location shown in Figure 7-1. We start by calculating the LOF value for one point and then use the Apache Sedona `local_outlier_factor` function to calculate it for the rest of our sample dataset.

Our dataset has point locations, where each one has a unique integer identifier. We start by selecting a point with ID 100. You can see the point with ID 100 in Figure 7-3. We also marked the five closest neighbors. This will be the point at which we will calculate the LOF index value. The point has coordinates $x=2.192$ and $y=5.656$. Then we find the five closest neighbors using the Euclidean distance:

id: 277 $x=1.695$ $y=5.568$
id: 118 $x=2.078$ $y=6.458$
id: 126 $x=2.504$ $y=6.448$
id: 123 $x=2.778$ $y=6.409$
id: 99 $x=1.619$ $y=6.471$

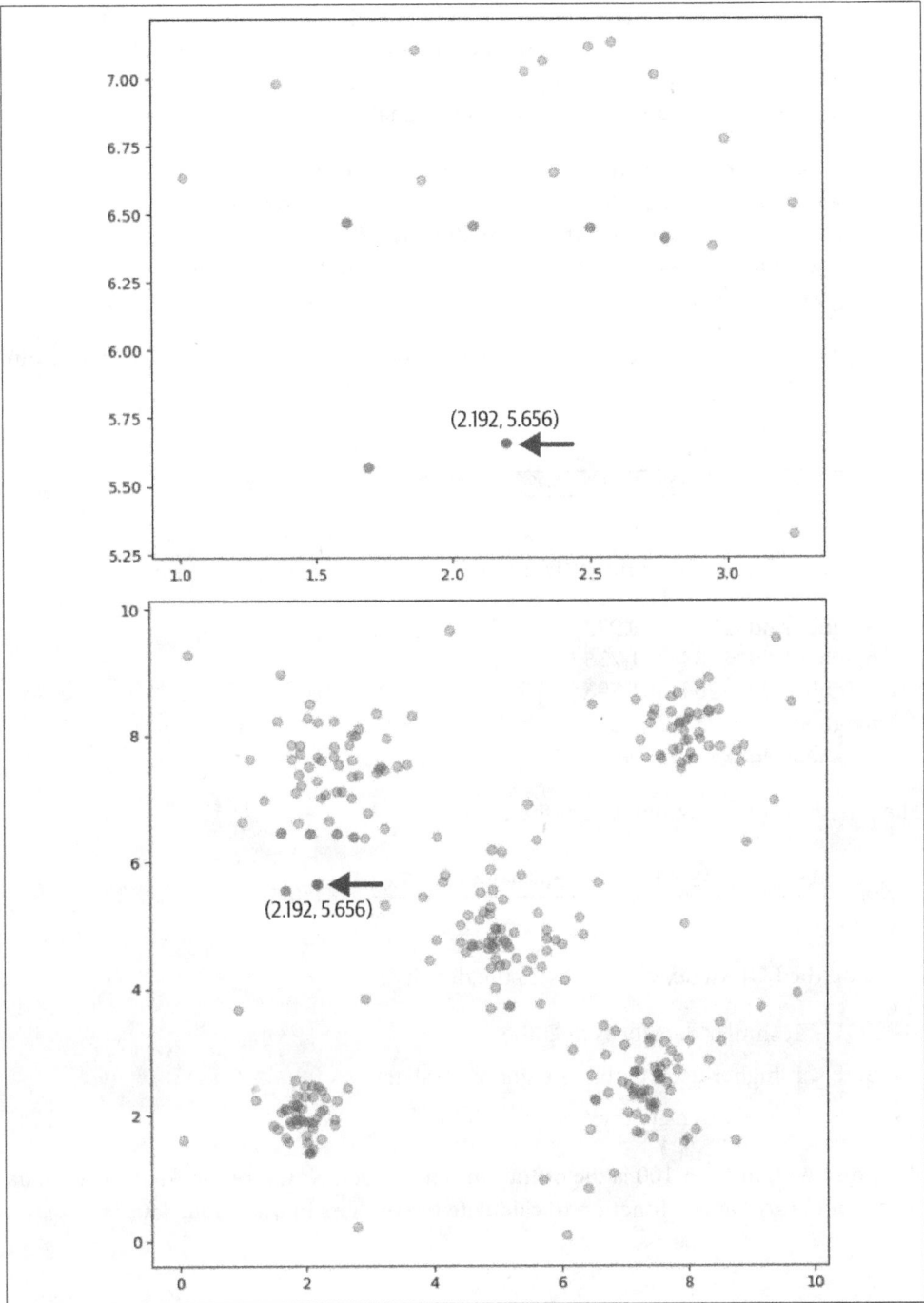

Figure 7-3. Local outlier detection for a point and its five nearest neighbors with point ID 100

Then let's calculate the LRD value for the point with index 100. We need the maximum distance for each neighbor of the point with index 100 to its neighbors and the distance between the point with index 100 and its neighbor. We select the maximum of the two previously mentioned values, the reachability density (rd) value:

neighbor_id=277 max_distance=1.196 distance=0.504 rd=1.196
neighbor_id=118 max_distance=0.595 distance=0.81 rd=0.81
neighbor_id=126 max_distance=0.59 distance=0.852 rd=0.85
neighbor_id=123 max_distance=0.487 distance=0.954 rd=0.954
neighbor_id=99 max_distance=0.68 distance=0.996 rd=0.996

To calculate the LRD value, we must divide 1 by the average value of rd. So in our case, it's the formula:

$$lrd = \frac{1}{\frac{(1.196 + 0.81 + 0.852 + 0.954 + 0.996)}{5}} = \frac{1}{0.962} = 1.04$$

The last step is to calculate the LRD for every neighbor of the point with index 100:

neighbor_id=277 lrd=0.972
neighbor_id=118 lrd=1.736
neighbor_id=126 lrd=1.796
neighbor_id=123 lrd=1.668
neighbor_id=99 lrd=1.444

Then, based on LRD values we get the LOF:

$$lof = \frac{0.972 + 1.736 + 1.796 + 1.668 + 1.444}{5 \times 1.04} = \frac{7.616}{5.20} = 1.465$$

Based on the LOF value, we can assess the density:

- LOF ~ 1, similar density as neighbors
- LOF < 1, higher density than neighbors (inlier)
- LOF > 1, lower density than neighbors (outlier)

The point with index = 100 is the outlier in our dataset. Now let's use Apache Sedona's local_outlier_factor function to calculate the outliers in the whole dataset:

```
import sedona.spark.stats.outlier_detection.local_outlier_factor as lof

lof.local_outlier_factor(
    density_points_sedona_df,
    5
)
```

The `local_outlier_factor` function takes the DataFrame as the first parameter, and the second parameter we pass are the k-nearest neighbors. Other important arguments are `handleTies` (which includes tiebreakers in the KNN join) and `useSphere` (Euclidean distance or sphere). The first five elements in the result DataFrame are shown in the following:

```
+-----+-------------------------------------------------+------------------+
|index|geom                                             |lof               |
+-----+-------------------------------------------------+------------------+
|76   |POINT (7.480335462299658 8.404466746884305)      |1.0927074243981525|
|8    |POINT (2.0275282329606505 1.4037293256197323)    |1.0191584064861596|
|41   |POINT (2.103085486870538 1.4710879533911798)     |1.0371086942776708|
|224  |POINT (4.996987276805067 4.744590013830861)      |0.9561091949623256|
|19   |POINT (1.9959508325786195 1.68268672131323)      |1.2683124973214734|
+-----+-------------------------------------------------+------------------+
```

Hot Spot Analysis (Local Getis–Ord $G_i(*)$)

Local Getis-Ord G_i (*https://oreil.ly/sOZ5E*) is a spatial statistics algorithm that helps identify where the features with high and low values are spatially clustered and statistically significant.

The algorithm has two versions: $G_i(*)$ and G_i. Both are implemented in Apache Sedona; the difference is whether the current element is included in its neighborhood. $G_i(*)$ includes the feature in the neighborhood, and G_i does not. The formula for the $G_i(*)$ is as follows:

$$G_i(*) = \frac{\sum_{j=0}^{n} w_{ij} x_j}{\sum_{j=0}^{n} x_j}$$

where:

- w_{ij} is the weight between the feature and the neighbor.
- x_j is the value for the jth neighbor of the feature.

Apache Sedona implements the local $G_i(*)$ and G_i in the `g_local` function. As the input, the function takes:

dataframe

PySpark DataFrame, which is a spatial DataFrame with the following schema:

```
root
 |-- value: double (nullable = true)
 |-- weights: array (nullable = false)
 |    |-- element: struct (containsNull = false)
 |    |    |-- neighbor: struct (nullable = false)
 |    |    |    |-- value: double (nullable = true)
 |    |    |-- value: double (nullable = false)
```

value

The name of the column used to calculate $G_i(*)$ or G_i; you can modify it by passing it to the x argument of the g_local function.

weights

An array of objects. Each object has a value, which is the weight of the neighbor and the neighbor object. The neighbor object contains the value of the feature.

x

A string value, the name of the column with the value to calculate $G_i(*)$ or G_i

star

A bool value, which says whether we will calculate $G_i(*)$ or G_i

How do you calculate the weights and keep them in the format shown? You can use Apache Sedona's add_distance_band_column or add_binary_distance_band_column functions.

The add_distance_band_column uses the distance function to calculate the weights; the add_distance_binary_column uses constant weights for each neighbor, equal to one. The distance function depends on the selected argument useSpheroid; if it is set to True, then the spheroid distance is selected; otherwise, the planar distance in the unit of the CRS is selected.

To get the $G_i(*)$ index, we can combine the weight function (add_distance_band_column) with the g_local function. We will use point data, the locations of which are shown in Figure 7-4, to calculate the $G_i(*)$ index; the input DataFrame name is hotspot_data:

```
from sedona.spark.stats.weighting import add_distance_band_column

weights_df = add_distance_band_column(
    dataframe=hotspot_data,
    threshold=2.0,
    include_self=True
)
```

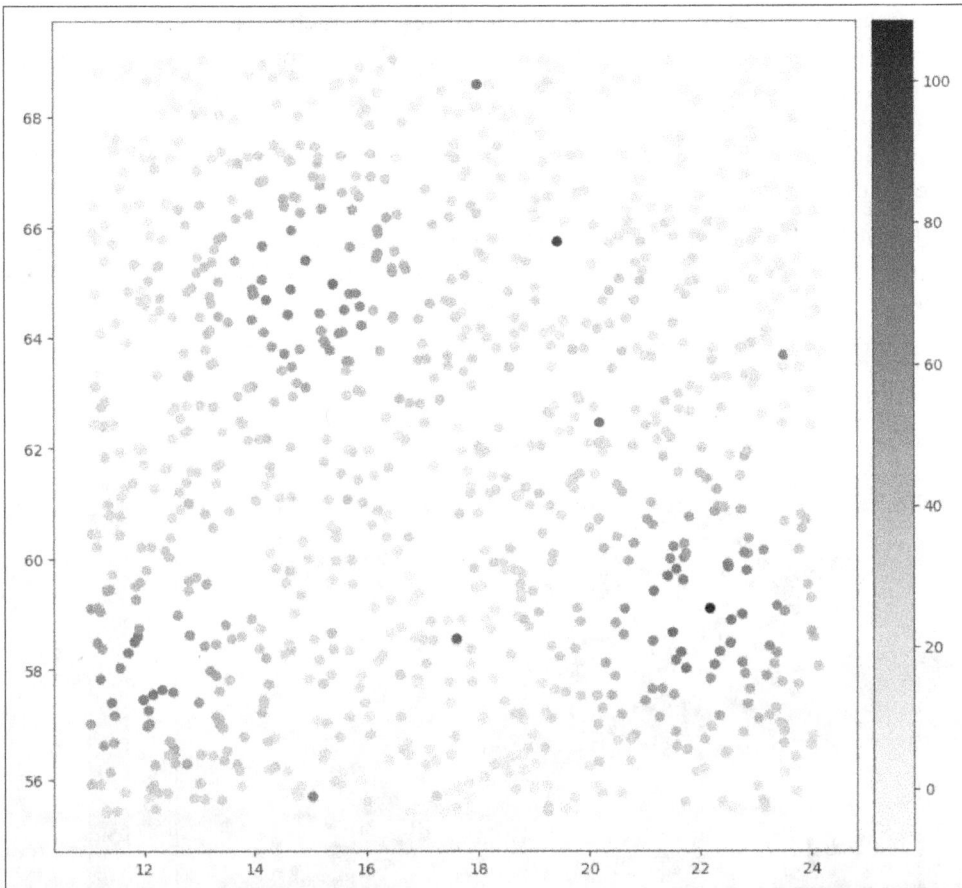

Figure 7-4. Data used in the hot spot algorithm

The threshold is the radius used to search for neighbors. We keep the planar distance, and as the threshold, we pass 2.0. When we calculate the weights, we look into the neighborhood within a certain distance. When we pass `include_self` as `True`, it means that we include the row itself in the neighbor list. This is required to calculate the $G_i(*)$. `weights_df` is the input to the `g_local` function:

```
from sedona.spark.stats.hotspot_detection.getis_ord import g_local

gi_df = g_local(
    dataframe=weights_df,
    x="value",
    star=True
)
```

The intensity value in `hotspot_data` is named `value`, which we pass as the x column. We also pass `star=True` to get the $G_i(*)$ index. The output shows a z-score and p-value. A z-score indicates how far, in terms of standard deviations, a value deviates from the average of its surrounding area. The p-value, on the other hand, quantifies the likelihood that this deviation is due to chance, rather than an actual underlying pattern or phenomenon.

As the last step, we will create a visualization of the z-score. If the value is a low negative, the point is a cold spot. It is considered a hot spot if the value is high and positive. You can see the result of the `g_local` function in Figure 7-5.

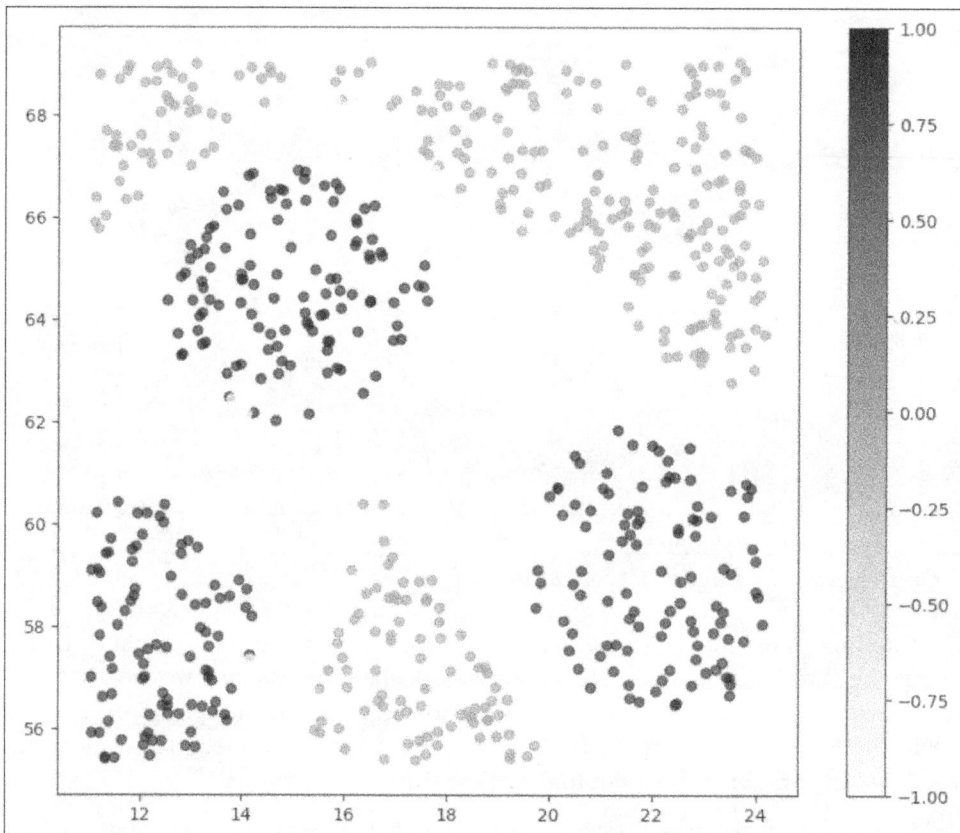

Figure 7-5. Hot spot analysis result: the points with a darker color are the hot spots, and those with a lighter color are the cold spots (x and y axes represent point locations)

Autocorrelation (Moran's I)

Global Moran's I is a spatial autocorrelation measure algorithm (*https://oreil.ly/UfvjV*) that simultaneously uses feature locations and values. Spatial autocorrelation is a measure to assess how spatial features are similar to the nearby values in the space. Positive spatial autocorrelation happens when features with similar values are closer to each other. We talk about negative correlation when closer observations have dissimilar values. A zero value for autocorrelation means there is no spatial correlation, the values are random, and there are no clusters.

The formula to calculate the Global Moran's I autocorrelation is as follows:

$$I = \frac{n}{s_0} \times \frac{\sum_{i=1}^{n} \sum_{j=1}^{n} w_{ij} z_i z_j}{\sum_{i=1}^{n} z_i^2}$$

where:

- w_{ij} is the weight between features i and j (by feature we mean one observation, row, record)
- z_i is the deviation of feature i from its average value ($x_i - X$).
- s_0 is the aggregate of all the spatial weights using the following formula:

$$s_0 = \sum_{i=1}^{n} \sum_{j=1}^{n} w_{ij}$$

Now, let's calculate the spatial autocorrelation for the array on the left side of Figure 7-6. First, we need to get the weight matrix. We will use a simple distance weight matrix, where we will find neighbors within a radius of 1 for each feature.

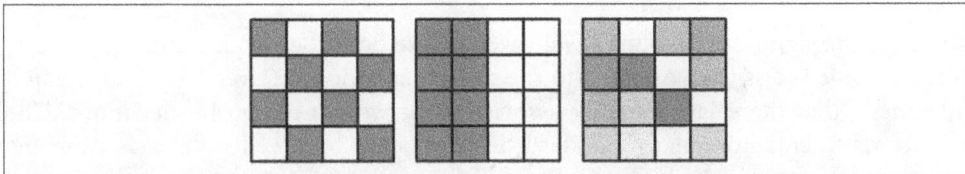

Figure 7-6. Each cell is 1×1, and we use a distance of 1 to find neighbors and calculate the weights: on the left, the autocorrelation value is -1 (negative); in the middle, there is a significant correlation (>0.7); and on the right, there is not significant correlation

Each cell polygon in Figure 7-6 has a size of 1. For example, the cell in the top-left corner has two neighbors, the cell at the center in (0, 1) and (1, 0). Each weight we calculate is divided by the total number of neighbors, so for the top-left corner, the weight for both (1, 0) and (0, 1) is 0.5. The top row weights are as follows:

(x, y) -> $[(x_j, y_j, w_{ij})...]$
$(0, 0)$ -> $[(0, 1, 0.5), (1, 0, 0.5)]$
$(0, 1)$ -> $[(0, 0, 1/3), (1, 1, 1/3), (0, 2, 1/3)]$
$(0, 2)$ -> $[(0, 1, 1/3), (2, 2, 1/3), (0, 3, 1/3)]$
$(0, 3)$ -> $[(0, 2, 0.5), (1, 3, 0.5)]$

Now let's try to calculate each part of the Global Moran's I value. n is the number of observations, so the value is 16. Now let's decompose the s0 value. To get the s0 value, we need to add all the weights for each feature. The sum for the first feature is one, and this is true for every other ith feature. The s0 is 16.

To get the other components of the Moran's I equation, we need to calculate the mean of the values. We have 16 elements, and 8 of them are 1 (dark shading); the average is 0.5. To get the value, we need to subtract the average value from the feature value. We get either -0.5 (for cells with value 0) or 0.5 (for cells with value 1).

Now we have all the pieces to calculate the counter; for the cell with coordinates (0, 0) we get $(0.5 \times (1 - 0.5) \times (0 - 0.5)) + (0.5 \times (1 - 0.5) \times (0 - 0.5)) = 0.5 \times -0.5 \times 0.5 + 0.5 \times -0.5 \times 0.5 = -0.125 - 0.125 = -0.25$. When we sum for each i (each grid cell in the array), we get -4.0.

Next, we need to calculate the z_i^2 before we combine everything together to get the Moran's I value. For each feature, we get a value of 1 or 0; the z is either 0.5 or -0.5. When we square -0.5 or 0.5, we get 0.25. We have 16 cells, so 0.25×16 is 4. Now, let's calculate the Moran's I value:

$$\frac{16}{16} \times \frac{-4}{4} = -1$$

To assess the significance of the result, we analyze both the p-value and the z-score. If the p-value is less than or equal to the chosen significance level, we reject the null hypothesis that there is no spatial association between neighboring locations. The z-score represents how many standard deviations the observed statistic is from the expected value under the null hypothesis. In our case, it helps determine whether a location's feature value is, on average, more similar to those of its neighbors compared to the global average. For a z-score less than -2.58 or greater than $+2.58$, corresponding to a p-value below 0.01, we conclude at the 99% confidence level that there is a significant spatial association for the feature values under study.

In our scenario, the p-value is close to zero, and the z-score is around -5, indicating a minimal chance that a random process created the spatial relationship between neighboring spatial features. This suggests that an underlying process, such as geographic or environmental factors, is more likely to cause the spatial autocorrelation. The negative z-score value indicates strong negative autocorrelation, meaning neighboring locations tend to have very different values.

Now let's use Apache Sedona's Global Moran's I function to calculate the autocorrelation index. We will use the PM10 air quality index from the US Environmental Protection Agency. Our data, after transformation, has three columns:

- Geometry, the location of the station as a point geometry object
- PM10 air quality index (the value is a double type)
- ID as an int, uniquely identifying the station

First, we need to calculate the DataFrame with weights. We will use the distance-based weight function, similar to the previous example, with equal weight for each feature's neighbor. We keep the WGS84 lat lon CRS, and we choose 0.1 of a degree, which is roughly 11km, as a distance:

```
>> from sedona.spark.stats.autocorrelation.moran import Moran
>> moran_i_result = Moran.get_global(weights_df)

MoranResult(
    i=0.93,
    p_norm=0.0,
    z_norm=8.11
)
```

The autocorrelation value is significant, and the p-value and z-score values suggest the autocorrelation result is reliable. Thus, similar values tend to be closer together, which makes sense in the context of air quality data.

Classification, Segmentation, and Object Detection from a Raster

A raster is semi-structured data whose quantity grows rapidly. We use satellites to make an image of Earth. We use planes to gather aerial photos for audit purposes. In Chapter 5, we covered how to use map algebra to provide insights based on raster data. But there is an even bigger challenge and opportunity: using machine learning algorithms to get the vector objects from the images. In the computer vision field, we can select three processes to transform the photos and get the structured data from them: *classification*, *segmentation*, and *object detection*.

Image classification aims to classify the whole picture into one of the unique classes; for example, the raster might be categorized into rural or urban areas.

Image segmentation classifies each pixel into a specific object and class. We can use this process to find the pixels of all buildings in the raster dataset, and then we can create geometry objects based on those pixels, representing specific features.

Object detection takes the raster data and returns the envelope of all class objects. For example, the result might show the envelopes of all planes or buildings from the raster data.

Image segmentation is vital in automating the process of creating geospatial features from raster data. Using image segmentation, we can monitor the Earth's surface and provide valuable insights. In this part, we will use the GeoAI models (*https://oreil.ly/ZyhsI*) to segment the satellite images and create geometry data for spatial features. We initially show how to use the CPU to generate the geometry objects of buildings based on raster data. If you have a GPU on your machine, the code snippet will autodetect this and improve overall performance.

For the predictions, we will use the PyTorch framework. We will use the vectorized UDF in Apache Spark to speed up the process, where the input is a pandas Series object. First, we need to load raster data from the S3 bucket. We store the data in the buildings DataFrame. Let's start by loading the model:

```
import torch
from torchvision.models.detection import maskrcnn_resnet50_fpn

# These parameters ensure consistent normalization

image_mean = [0.485, 0.456, 0.406]
image_std = [0.229, 0.224, 0.225]

device = torch.device("cuda:0" if torch.cuda.is_available() else "cpu")

# Create model with explicit normalization parameters

model = maskrcnn_resnet50_fpn(
    weights=None,
    progress=False,
    num_classes=2,  # Background + object
    weights_backbone=None,
    image_mean=image_mean,
    image_std=image_std,
)

model.to(device)
model_path = "your_model_path"

# Load model weights

state_dict = torch.load(model_path, map_location=device)
model.load_state_dict(state_dict)
model.eval()
```

We will use this model to segment each pixel into a building or not a building. The core of our solution is the vectorized UDF, which allows us to run the code on data chunks and serialize and deserialize the data efficiently:

```
import uuid
from shapely.geometry import GeometryCollection
from utils import sedona_vectorized_udf, SedonaUDFType
from sedona.sql.types import GeometryType
import shapely.geometry.base as b
from sedona.raster.raster_serde import deserialize

@sedona_vectorized_udf(
    udf_type=SedonaUDFType.GEO_SERIES,
    return_type=GeometryType()
)
def extract_buildings(series) -> b.BaseGeometry:
    df = series.apply(lambda x: predict(deserialize(x).as_rasterio()))

    return df
```

The Sedona vectorized UDF allows us to return the same number of elements as the input data; for that reason, we need to return one geometry object. Each Apache Sedona raster object might result in many building instances, so we will return the GeometryCollection object as a result of the predict function:

```
import pyspark.sql.functions as f

buildings_predicted = buildings \
    .selectExpr("RS_FromGeoTiff(content) AS rast") \
    .select(extract_buildings(f.col("rast")).alias("geom"))
```

First, after loading the data, we must cast it to the raster data type using the RS_From GeoTiff function. Then on the raster we call the vectorized UDF extract_buildings

You can transform the DataFrame to get the geometry for each building based on the GeometryCollection object using the Apache Sedona ST_Dump function combined with the Apache Spark explode function:

```
buildings_predicted \
    .selectExpr("EXPLODE(ST_Dump(geom)) AS geometry") \
    .show()

+--------------------+
|            geometry|
+--------------------+
|POLYGON ((586702....|
|POLYGON ((586664....|
|POLYGON ((586683....|
|POLYGON ((586645....|
|POLYGON ((586761....|
+--------------------+
```

The last part is converting the Rasterio object into referenced geometry collection objects:

```python
from shapely.geometry import shape
from shapely.ops import unary_union
from rasterio import features

def predict(img):
    # our data is 4 bands, we need to take only RGB
    np_array = img.read()[:3,::]

    # we need to convert the numpy array to internal tensor model in torch

    img_normalized = torch.from_numpy(np_array).float()

    # if the image maximum value is greater than 1 we need to normalize the
    # image

    if img_normalized.max() > 1:
        img_normalized = img_normalized / 255.0

    # context manager to run the torch models

    with torch.no_grad():
        # we call the model on the tensor representing the input image
        output = model([img_normalized])[0]

        # here we store all unique buildings, then we will use it to create
        # GeometryCollection object

        result_shapes = []

        # we iterate through all unique masks we get from the prediction,
        # each mask represents the detected building

        for m in output["masks"]:
            # the result is a torch tensor, we need to use numpy in the
            # Rasterio raster to vector conversions

            m_numpy = m.numpy()

            # each prediction has probability assigned, we need trustworthy
            # result so we create mask with prediction value greater than 0.7

            mask = m_numpy > 0.7

            # this function for the mask and input array creates the
            # iterator with a polygon representing each pixel; we also pass
            # an affine transformation object to make sure our geometry is
            # properly georeferenced

            shapes = features.shapes(
```

```
        m_numpy,
        mask=mask,
        transform=img.transform
    )

    # here we store all the pixel polygons which we will use to
    # union them together
    polygons = []

    for s in shapes:
        # each s[0] is geojson object, we need to convert it to the
        # shapely base geometry
        polygons.append(shape(s[0]))

        # merging pixels to one polygon/multipolygon geometry
        merged = unary_union(polygons)

        result_shapes.append(unary_union(polygons))

    # we return GeometryCollection object
    return GeometryCollection(result_shapes)
```

Creating Geospatial Machine Learning Models with MLlib

MLlib (*https://oreil.ly/r93Er*) is an Apache Spark machine learning library with the primary goal of providing the tools to create and train machine learning models at scale. It includes:

- Popular ML algorithms
- Feature extraction, selection, and dimension reduction
- Pipelines to automate the process of evaluation and tuning machine learning models
- Storing machine learning models

Apache Sedona extends Apache Spark with spatial functionality, and underneath it uses the Apache Spark DataFrame object. Using MLlib, you can create geospatial data processing pipelines and machine learning models based on spatial data.

In this section, we will focus on how to combine Apache Sedona with MLlib, not how to create the best machine learning models. There are plenty of books that can teach you to do that.[3] We will use the K-means algorithm to cluster similar areas based on the neighborhood. Let's introduce this algorithm before explaining the data sources and methodology.

---

3 Such as *Scaling Machine Learning with Spark* by Adi Polak (O'Reilly, 2023).

K-means is one of the most popular clustering algorithms used in machine learning. It is based on the distance between observations. Although it can be used in dimensions higher than 2D, it will be easier to explain using planar space. Imagine that you have the locations of the points, and each point has two coordinates, X and Y. We want to cluster them together based on the distance.

We start by selecting the number of clusters, the K value. Then, we randomly place k points, the clusters' centroids. Next, we repeat the following steps until we reach convergence. For each point, we look for the nearest centroid; that centroid represents the cluster to which the point is temporarily assigned. Then we loop over the cluster centroids and average the value of all the points temporarily assigned to the cluster; the resulting value is the new cluster centroid coordinates. The stopping condition is when none of the points change their cluster assignment after averaging the point coordinates and electing a new cluster centroid. The K-means algorithm can't use categorical variables, as we average the values of the cluster centroid, and we also use the distance to assign the cluster.

We will use the POI data from the Overture Maps Foundation dataset as our example and create H3 grid cells for the city of Paris. To make our neighborhood clustering more reliable, we will include the 10-minute walk catchments from each centroid of the H3 cell. To do that, we will use an open routing service (*https://oreil.ly/77nUF*) and a UDF to enrich our data with API data.

In each catchment, we will calculate values for the number of POIs with the following primary categories within a 10-minute walking distance:

- Restaurant
- Shopping
- Bakery
- Education
- School
- Pharmacy

- Cafe
- Theatre
- Transportation
- Hospital
- Park

We start by creating the DataFrame with the H3 cells; we use a resolution of 8:

```
paris_polygon_wkt = "POLYGON((2.2241 48.8156, 2.4699 48.8156,...))"

h3_cells = sedona.sql(
    f"""
        WITH h3_cells AS (
            SELECT
                id,
                ST_H3ToGeom(ARRAY(id))[0] AS geom
            LATERAL VIEW EXPLODE(
                ST_H3CellIDs(ST_GeomFromText('{paris_polygon_wkt}'), 8, true)
            ) AS id
```

```
        )
        SELECT
            id,
            geom,
            ST_X(ST_Centroid(geom)) AS lon,
            ST_Y(ST_Centroid(geom)) AS lat
        FROM h3_cells
    """
)
```

We need to get the centroid longitude and latitude coordinates. We need them to calculate the catchment geometries. We will use the Open Route Service (ORS) to get the catchment geometries. We need to call the `/ors/v2/isochrones/foot-walking` endpoint using the POST method. We will create a Python UDF function within which we call the ORS API. We will name the function `ST_GetWalkCatchment`. The function will take three arguments: longitude, latitude, and walk distance in minutes. Let's start by writing a Python function that does that:

```python
import requests
from shapely.geometry import shape, MultiPolygon

OPEN_ROUTING_URL = "http://ors:8082"

def walk_time_polygon(
    lon: float,
    lat: float,
    minutes: int
) -> MultiPolygon | None:
    body = {
        "locations": [[lon, lat]],
        "range": [minutes * 60],
        "range_type": "time"
    }

    response = requests.post(
        url=f"{OPEN_ROUTING_URL}/ors/v2/isochrones/foot-walking",
        json=body
    )

    if response.status_code != 200:
        return None

    response_data = response.json()
    features = response_data["features"]

    shapely_polygons = [
        shape(feature["geometry"]) for feature in features
        if feature["geometry"]["type"] == "Polygon"
    ]

    return MultiPolygon(shapely_polygons)
```

To call the endpoint, we use the Python library requests. The minimum required body we need to pass in the POST requests is locations (we pass one point only) and range, which allows us to pass the possible catchment sizes. We need 10 minute walking catchments, so we need to multiply the *range* field element by 60. We also need to pass the range_type as time. When the response status is different than 200, we return None. For valid responses we take possible polygon features from the JSON response and create the MultiPolygon geometry object, which is the result of our function. We will use the following function to create the SQL UDF in Apache Sedona:

```python
import pyspark.sql.functions as f
import sedona.sql.types as st
import shapely.geometry.base as b

def create_walk_catchment(
    lon: float,
    lat: float,
    minutes: int
) -> b.BaseGeometry | None:
    return walk_time_polygon(lon, lat, minutes)

create_walk_catchment_udf = f.udf(
    create_walk_catchment,
    st.GeometryType()
)

sedona.udf.register(
    "ST_GetWalkCatchment",
    create_walk_catchment_udf
)
```

Before we use the result calculations, we need to filter our places dataset to the desired categories:

```python
categories = [
    "restaurant",
    "shopping",
    "bakery",
    "education",
    "school",
    "pharmacy",
    "cafe",
    "theatre",
    "transportation",
    "hospital",
    "park"
]

paris_places \
    .where(f"categories.primary IN {tuple(categories)}") \
    .selectExpr(
        "categories.primary AS category",
```

```
        "geometry"
    ) \
    .createOrReplaceTempView("selected_categories")
```

Using the SQL query, we can combine the POI-selected categories with the walking catchments from each H3 cell grid:

```
WITH catchments AS (
    SELECT
        id,
        ST_GetWalkCatchment(lon, lat, 10) AS walk_catchment,
        geom
    FROM h3_cells
),
joined AS (
    SELECT
        *,
        c.geom AS grid_geom
    FROM catchments AS c
    JOIN selected_categories AS S ON ST_Intersects(s.geometry, c.walk_catchment)
)
SELECT
    id,
    category,
    count(*) AS count,
    FIRST(grid_geom) AS geom
FROM joined
GROUP BY id, category
```

We use the UDF SQL function ST_GetWalkCatchment to calculate the catchments, then we perform a spatial join to match all selected POIs within the catchment boundaries. We use the ST_Intersects condition to match the POI, catchment pairs. The last step is to group the results by ID of the H3 cell and category. The resulting DataFrame looks as follows:

```
+------------------+--------------+-----+--------------------+
|                id|      category|count|                geom|
+------------------+--------------+-----+--------------------+
|613047287637082111|     education|    4|POLYGON ((2.41381...|
|613047287637082111|          park|    1|POLYGON ((2.41381...|
|613047287637082111|    restaurant|    3|POLYGON ((2.41381...|
|613047287637082111|      shopping|    2|POLYGON ((2.41381...|
|613047287637082111|transportation|    2|POLYGON ((2.41381...|
+------------------+--------------+-----+--------------------+
```

Unfortunately, this DataFrame is unsuitable for MLlib in Apache Spark. We need to pivot it before we run the K-means algorithm:

```
feature_df = sedona \
    .table("catchments_count") \
    .groupBy("id", "geom") \
    .pivot("category", categories) \
    .agg(
```

```
        f.first("count")
    ) \
    .selectExpr(
        "id",
        "geom",
        "COALESCE(restaurant, 0) AS restaurant",
        "COALESCE(shopping, 0) AS shopping",
        "COALESCE(bakery, 0) AS bakery",
        "COALESCE(education, 0) AS education",
        "COALESCE(school, 0) AS school",
        "COALESCE(pharmacy, 0) AS pharmacy",
        "COALESCE(cafe, 0) AS cafe",
        "COALESCE(theatre, 0) AS theatre",
        "COALESCE(transportation, 0) AS transportation",
        "COALESCE(hospital, 0) AS hospital",
        "COALESCE(park, 0) AS park"
    )
```

We will use the `groupBy` statement with the `pivot` function for this, where we pass categories and select the first count for each category. We also want to preserve the geometry column, so we pass it with an ID in the `groupBy` clause. Some of the observations may not have points nearby and have null values, so we use the coalesce function to fill those values with zeros. The DataFrame with a subset of columns looks as follows:

```
+---------+--------------------+-----+---------+--------+----+-------+----+
|       id|                geom|bakery|education|pharmacy|cafe|theatre|park|
+---------+--------------------+-----+---------+--------+----+-------+----+
|61304...|POLYGON ((2.35032...|   52|       50|      25|  42|     53|  12|
|61304...|POLYGON ((2.26893...|    5|        3|       7|   3|      1|   5|
|61304...|POLYGON ((2.36062...|   16|       17|      14|  15|     23|   6|
|61304...|POLYGON ((2.47322...|    0|        1|       0|   0|      0|   0|
|61304...|POLYGON ((2.43537...|    0|        0|       0|   0|      8|   4|
+---------+--------------------+-----+---------+--------+----+-------+----+
```

Apache Spark MLlib requires the DataFrame to have a column with features in the desired format. In our scenario, we will transform our data using the `VectorAssembler` object and then scale it using the `MinMaxScaler` to prevent overrepresented points from defining the cluster:

```
from pyspark.sql import SparkSession
from pyspark.ml.feature import VectorAssembler, StandardScaler, MinMaxScaler
from pyspark.ml.clustering import KMeans

assembler = VectorAssembler(
    inputCols=categories,
    outputCol="features",
)

assembled_df = assembler.transform(feature_df)
```

```
scaler = MinMaxScaler(
    inputCol="features",
    outputCol="scaled_features"
)

scaled_data = scaler.fit(assembled_df).transform(assembled_df)
```

scaled_df looks as follows:

```
+------------------+--------------------+
|                id|      scaled_rounded|
+------------------+--------------------+
|613047304085045247|[1.0, 0.9548, 0.7...|
|613047302585581567|[0.023, 0.0323, 0...|
|613047303986479103|[0.2204, 0.1613, ...|
|613047304168931327|[0.0, 0.0, 0.0, 0...|
|613047304152154111|[0.0066, 0.0, 0.0...|
+------------------+--------------------+
```

The feature column is of type features: vector.

The result of the VectorAssembler.transform function, which is later scaled to the 0 to 1 range, is the input for the K-means algorithm:

```
kmeans = KMeans(k=10, seed=42, featuresCol="scaled_features")
model = kmeans.fit(scaled_data)

predictions = model.transform(scaled_data)
```

We select 10 as the number of desired clusters. To make the result consistent, we consider the random seed number 42. We use the means.fit method to create the model and then model.transform to assign the cluster number for each observation:

```
+------------------+--------------------+----------+
|                id|     scaled_features|prediction|
+------------------+--------------------+----------+
|613047304085045247|[1.0,0.9548387096...|         5|
|613047302585581567|[0.02302631578947...|         0|
|613047303986479103|[0.22039473684210...|         1|
|613047304168931327|(11,[3,4,9],[0.01...|         4|
|613047304152154111|(11,[0,4,7,10],[0...|         0|
+------------------+--------------------+----------+
```

Hands-On Use Case: Analyzing Road Accidents in Germany

Here we focus on analyzing accident data from Germany. We'll incorporate hot spot analysis and create an XGBoost model based on the data to predict the possibility of specific accidents in a given road segment. Creating machine learning models is a convoluted and complex process; we don't aim to make a world-class model, but to show you how you can combine Apache Sedona's built-in functions with powerful machine learning algorithms to enhance your geospatial analytics and help you focus on solving unique problems, not on repeatedly implementing the same spatial algorithms.

In the notebook, we focus on the Bavaria region. Our primary dataset is accident data from the German Accidents Atlas (*https://oreil.ly/0wyDL*). We also use data from Overture to enrich it with causation features, which we will explain later. We also include some synthesized features in the accident dataset and the roads. The accident data contains the following columns, which we will use in the later analysis:

- Point location of the accident
- Accident category
  - Fatal
  - Major injuries
  - Minor injuries
- Lighting conditions
  - Daylight
  - Twilight
  - Darkness
- The alcohol level in the blood of the person who caused the accident is a discrete value (synthesized value) and ranges from 0 to 10.

First, let's analyze the hot spots of the accidents. We will use Apache Sedona's built-in hot spot analysis function. The number of accidents inside the H3 grid cell on level 8 will be the value needed for the weight DataFrame. The output table contains information about the H3 cell ID, the H3 cell geometry, and the number of accidents inside. Based on that, we will create the weight DataFrame, based on a distance of 1000m. We will include each row inside the neighbor list, using the `include_self` parameter:

```
from sedona.stats.weighting import add_distance_band_column

weights_df = add_distance_band_column(
    dataframe=accidents_agg_values,
    threshold=1000.0,
    include_self=True
)
```

```
+------------------+--------------------+-----+--------------------+
|               id|            geometry|value|             weights|
+------------------+--------------------+-----+--------------------+
|608540997026054143|POLYGON ((698663....|    1|[{{60854099702605...|
|608517440992706559|POLYGON ((795894....|    0|[{{60851744099270...|
|608541051753332735|POLYGON ((663010....|    1|[{{60854105175333...|
|608540930001076223|POLYGON ((603397....|    2|[{{60854093000107...|
|608517204182302719|POLYGON ((785863....|    1|[{{60851720418230...|
+------------------+--------------------+-----+--------------------+
```

Then we use the `g_local` function to analyze the hot and cold spots. As we already covered in this chapter, when the z-value is a low negative value, it's a cold spot; when it is a large positive value, it's a hot spot:

```
from sedona.spark.stats.hotspot_detection.getis_ord import g_local

gi_df = g_local(
    dataframe=weights_df,
    x="value",
    star=True
)
```

Figure 7-7 shows that most of the incidents are in cities, with more traffic, crossings, and pedestrians, which is reasonable. Can you prepare a similar analysis, grouping it by accident category (fatal, significant, minor injury)?

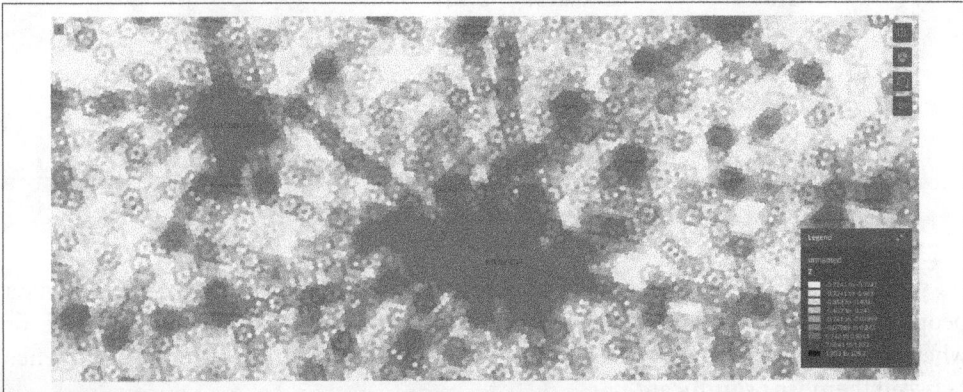

Figure 7-7. Hot spot analysis prepared for the incidents dataset in Germany

Let's dig into the data even more. We will calculate the statistics on how many accidents happen during daylight, twilight, and darkness and group them by accident category:

```
+--------------+------------------+-----+
|      category|lighting_condition|count|
+--------------+------------------+-----+
|         fatal|          Twilight|   34|
|         fatal|          Darkness|  162|
|         fatal|          Daylight|  483|
|major_injuries|          Daylight| 8508|
|major_injuries|          Darkness| 2071|
|major_injuries|          Twilight|  541|
|minor_injuries|          Twilight| 2659|
|minor_injuries|          Darkness| 9751|
|minor_injuries|          Daylight|41201|
+--------------+------------------+-----+
```

At first glance, most accidents happen during the day. There are more cars on the road, so the risk is higher. A critical factor in modeling road safety is traffic congestion. But what is the percentage of each incident category during day, night, and twilight?

```
+--------------+------------------+-------+
|      category|lighting_condition|percent|
+--------------+------------------+-------+
|         fatal|          Darkness|   1.35|
|         fatal|          Twilight|   1.05|
|         fatal|          Daylight|   0.96|
|major_injuries|          Darkness|  17.28|
|major_injuries|          Daylight|  16.95|
|major_injuries|          Twilight|  16.73|
|minor_injuries|          Twilight|  82.22|
|minor_injuries|          Daylight|  82.09|
|minor_injuries|          Darkness|  81.37|
+--------------+------------------+-------+
```

As you can see, the percentage of fatal accidents is highest during darkness—when people tend to drive under the influence of alcohol, or when drivers are tired, or when the light is not good enough to see and react appropriately. But the difference between them isn't significant.

Certain key features that could be used to assess the potential risk of fatal accidents are difficult to get the data for, like overall health, tiredness, and age of the driver, and other factors are also difficult to obtain, like road conditions in real time, distance between drivers, and each car's speed. Our analysis focuses on the data we can get from the Overture roads and infrastructure dataset. We synthesized two additional variables for the learning purpose of this chapter. The two synthesized variables are the previously mentioned alcohol level in the blood and the road quality (using a scale from 0 to 5).

Now, we will move on to feature engineering and enhance the road data with accident data and the following features:

- Maximum speed
- The distance of each road segment to a crossing
- Road segments containing a bridge
- Road segments containing a tunnel
- Road segments are under construction
- Average curvature of the road

We use the infrastructure dataset to obtain crossings. The accident data is already in the metric system EPSG:3044, so we transform the infrastructure table to it:

```
crossings = infrastructure \
    .where("class == 'crossing'") \
    .selectExpr(
        "id",
        "ST_Transform(geometry, 'epsg:4326', 'epsg:3044') AS geometry"
    )
```

Now we will enrich the road network data with the features mentioned before. We will focus on road segments (*https://oreil.ly/frXTv*) with classes such as motorway, trunk, primary, secondary, tertiary, and residential:

```
is_bridge = match_road_flag("is_bridge")(
    f.col("road_flags")
).alias("is_bridge")

is_tunnel = match_road_flag("is_tunnel")(
    f.col("road_flags")
).alias("is_tunnel")

is_under_construction = match_road_flag("is_under_construction")(
    f.col("road_flags")
).alias("is_under_construction")

road_classes = (
    'motorway',
    'trunk',
    'primary',
    'secondary',
    'tertiary',
    'residential'
)

enriched_transportation = transportation \
    .where(f"class in {road_classes}") \
    .withColumn(
        "geometry",
```

```
            f.expr("ST_Transform(geometry, 'epsg:4326', 'epsg:3044')")
    ) \
    .withColumn("width", widths_mapping_expr[f.col("class")]) \
    .withColumn(
        "max_speed",
        map_speed_limit(f.col("speed_limits"), f.col("class"))
    ) \
    .select(
        "id",
        "geometry",
        "width",
        "max_speed",
        is_bridge,
        is_tunnel,
        is_under_construction,
        get_average_curvature("geometry").alias("curvature"),
    "quality")
```

We use the match_road_flag function to determine whether a specific road segment has a bridge or tunnel or is under construction. To make the function efficient and easy to implement, we use the Arrow UDF defined in the following:

```
def match_road_flag(flag_value: str):
    @pandas_udf(BooleanType())
    def is_road_flag(road_flags: pd.Series) -> pd.Series:
        def contains_road_flag(flags: list) -> bool:
            if flags is None:
                return False

            for flag in flags:
                if flag_value in flag["values"]:
                    return True

            return False

        return road_flags.apply(lambda x: contains_road_flag(x))

    return is_road_flag
```

We use the currying function to make the function flexible and create an additional UDF for each feature. The match_road_flag function returns an Apache Arrow UDF based on the feature flag we pass to it. Inside the function, we map the pd.Series type and look for the flag inside the flag values. If it exists, we return True; otherwise, we return False.

Naturally, the input dataset contains empty values; many techniques exist to fill null values, such as average values or any other statistical measurement. We used the following map of max speed per road class to fill the max speed (KPH) empty values:

```
german_speed_limits = {
    'motorway': 130,
    'trunk': 100,
    'primary': 80,
    'secondary': 80,
    'tertiary': 50,
    'residential': 30
}
```

We understand that the current solution isn't ideal. For the exercise, you can use Apache Sedona to fill null values for maximum speed using the nearest neighbor average.

Like the `is_road_flag` UDF, we also use the Arrow UDF to get the max speed limit value and fill in the empty values:

```python
@pandas_udf(FloatType())
def map_speed_limit(rss: pd.Series,rcs: pd.Series) -> pd.Series:
    def first_non_empty(road_speed, road_cls):
        default = german_speed_limits[road_cls]
        if road_speed is None:
            return default

        for element in road_speed:
            max_speed = element.get("max_speed")
            if not max_speed:
                continue
            speed_value = max_speed.get("value")

            if speed_value:
                return speed_value

        return default

    df = pd.DataFrame({'road_class': rcs, 'road_speed': rss})

    return df.apply(lambda x: first_non_empty(
        x["road_speed"], x["road_class"]
    ), axis=1)
```

In our features, we also include the line segment curvature to assess whether the road is dangerous from a geometrical standpoint. There are many approaches to solving this problem, one of which is to divide the distance from the start to the end point by the length of the line. The complex lines might be misleading, so we will calculate the average angle for each of the three neighboring points. For that, we will use a GeoArrow-based UDF. To obtain the angle between two lines created by three points, we will calculate the slope of each line and use the following formulas to get the angle:

$$m1 = \frac{D_y(a,\,b)}{D_x(a,\,b)}$$

$$m2 = \frac{D_y(b,\,c)}{D_x(b,\,c)}$$

$$\text{angle} = \text{atan}\left(\frac{m2 - m1}{1 + (m1 \times m2)}\right).$$

where:

- $D_y(a,\,b)$ is the difference between point b and point a y-coordinates, $D_x(a,\,b)$ is the difference between point b and point a x-coordinates.
- atan is the arctangent, a trigonometry function.

Let's implement this in Python. The simplified version is as follows (for all edge cases, please refer to the notebooks):

```python
from sedona.spark.sql.functions import sedona_vectorized_udf

@sedona_vectorized_udf(return_type=FloatType())
def get_average_curvature(line: LineString):
    coords = list(line.coords)
    if len(coords) < 3:
        return 0

    from math import atan, pi

    def slope(p1, p2):
        dx = p2[0] - p1[0]
        dy = p2[1] - p1[1]
        return dy / dx

    def angle_between(a, b, c):
        m1 = slope(a, b)
        m2 = slope(b, c)

        denominator = 1 + m1 * m2

        tan_theta = (m2 - m1) / denominator
        angle = abs(atan(tan_theta))

        return angle

    angles = []
    for i in range(1, len(coords)-1):
        angle = angle_between(coords[i-1], coords[i], coords[i+1])
        angles.append(angle)

    return sum(angles) / len(angles)
```

Now, we need to find the accidents for each road segment. One possible solution is finding the nearest neighbor, but it's risky because some roads are wider, and the data might be outside. Using the following map, we decided to use the average road width for each road class. This will be used later to calculate the buffer and find the accidents for each road segment.

To map it, we could use the UDF, but there is a more efficient way to do that; we can create the native map in Apache Spark using the following code:

```
typical_widths = {
    "motorway": 25,
    "trunk": 20,
    "primary": 12,
    "secondary": 10,
    "tertiary": 8,
    "residential": 6,
    "service": 5

}
widths_mapping_expr = f.create_map(
    [f.lit(x) for pair in typical_widths.items() for x in pair]
)
```

Now we can enrich road segments with the accidents using the spatial join:

```
roads_with_accidents = enriched_transportation \
    .alias("t") \
    .join(
        accidents.alias("a"),
        on=f.expr("ST_DWithin(t.geometry, a.geometry, t.width)")
    ) \
    .selectExpr(
        "t.*",
        "a.lighting_condition",
        "a.accident_category",
        "a.promiles"
    )
```

The last part is to enrich the road segments with information about the distance to the closest crossing. This approach has a flaw, as we don't have information about which direction the sides of the accident were traveling; still, it's relevant information:

```
roads_feature_values = roads_with_accidents \
    .alias("ra") \
    .join(
        crossings.alias("c"),
        on=f.expr("ST_KNN(ra.geometry, c.geometry, 1)")
    ) \
    .selectExpr(
        "ra.id",
        "ra.geometry",
        "ra.max_speed AS ms",
```

```
        "ra.is_bridge AS is_b",
        "ra.is_tunnel AS is_t",
        "ra.is_under_construction AS is_uc",
        "ROUND(ra.curvature, 3) AS c",
        "ra.lighting_condition AS lc",
        "ra.accident_category AS ac",
        "ROUND(ST_Distance(c.geometry, ra.geometry), 2) AS distance",
        "ra.promiles",
        "ra.quality"
    )
```

id	ms	is_b	is_t	is_uc	c	lc	ac	distance	promiles	quality
0891faa02e6...	50.0	false	false	false	0.243	0	2	11.37	6	3
0891faa02e6...	50.0	false	false	false	0.243	2	3	11.37	0	3
0891faa02e6...	50.0	false	false	false	0.243	0	3	11.37	0	3
0891faa02e6...	50.0	false	false	false	0.243	0	3	11.37	0	3
0861fa80eff...	120.0	true	false	false	0.018	0	2	198.37	0	3
0861fa80eff...	120.0	true	false	false	0.018	0	2	198.37	2	3
0861fa80eff...	120.0	true	false	false	0.018	1	3	198.37	0	3
0861fa80eff...	120.0	true	false	false	0.018	2	3	198.37	0	3
0871faa785f...	50.0	false	false	false	0.009	0	3	6.4	0	5
0891f8c81d4...	50.0	false	false	false	0.318	1	3	3689.76	4	1

We cannot predict that the road segments where there are no accidents are safe. We can't assume that, so in the last step we will create a machine learning model where our thesis is what the risk of fatal, major, or minor injuries is for each road segment based on the assumption that an accident happens. With this thesis, we can assess which road segments might be dangerous. In this exercise, we focus on showing you the pipeline to produce the ML model rather than creating the best in the world model for assessing the probability of specific accidents on the road. In our exercise, we will use the XGBoost algorithm to train the model to predict the accident category. You can read more about the algorithm in the official docs (*https://oreil.ly/MYLjt*).

Before we dive into it, we need to solve the issue of multiple accidents on the road. For that, we will group the data and select the category with the most occurrences, and that's our label. We also need to create similar sample sizes for each accident category. We don't want to end up with an overfitted model. We have overrepresentation of low injury accidents, and we can even randomly say it is low injury all the time, and we will have good accuracy, but the usability of such a model is low. We will create around 1,000 samples for each accident type:

```
from pyspark.sql.window import Window
from pyspark.sql.functions import row_number

window_spec = Window.partitionBy("id").orderBy(f.desc("count"))
similar_size_buckets = Window.partitionBy("ac").orderBy("id")
```

```
roads_feature_values_ranked = roads_feature_values \
    .groupBy("id", "ac", "lc", "promiles") \
    .agg(
        f.col("id"),
        f.count("*").alias("count"),
        f.first("ms").alias("ms"),
        f.first("is_b").alias("is_b"),
        f.first("is_t").alias("is_t"),
        f.first("is_uc").alias("is_uc"),
        f.first("c").alias("c"),
        f.first("distance").alias("distance"),
        f.first("quality").alias("quality")
    ) \
    .withColumn("rank", row_number().over(window_spec)) \
    .where("rank == 1") \
    .withColumn("bucket_size", row_number().over(similar_size_buckets)) \
    .where("bucket_size < 1000") \
    .drop("rank", "bucket_size")
```

Before we use the XGBoost model, we need to convert a few of our columns properly:

- Boolean fields need to be cast to int 0, 1 values.

- We need to normalize float values to be in the range of 0 to 1.

- We need to one-hot encode categorized string values.

We will use the built-in Apache Spark MLlib functions for all needed transformations and close everything inside the pipeline:

```
from pyspark.ml import Pipeline
from pyspark.ml.feature import (
    StringIndexer, OneHotEncoder, VectorAssembler, MinMaxScaler
)
from pyspark.sql.functions import col

# Convert the boolean fields to 0, 1 integer values
roads_feature_values_transformed = roads_feature_values_ranked \
    .withColumn("is_b", col("is_b").cast("int")) \
    .withColumn("is_t", col("is_t").cast("int")) \
    .withColumn("is_uc", col("is_uc").cast("int"))

# Function to create the one hot encoded int values from string values
def index_string_column(column_name: str) -> list:
    indexer = StringIndexer(
        inputCol=column_name,
        outputCol=f"{column_name}_index"
    )

    encoder = OneHotEncoder(
        inputCol=f"{column_name}_index",
        outputCol=f"{column_name}_encoded"
```

```
        )

        return [indexer, encoder]


    # Function to convert the continuous values to range from 0 to 1
    def min_max_scale_column(column_name: str) -> list:
        ms_assembler = VectorAssembler(
            inputCols=[column_name],
            outputCol=f"{column_name}_vec"
        )

        ms_scaler = MinMaxScaler(
            inputCol=f"{column_name}_vec",
            outputCol=f"{column_name}_scaled"
        )

        return [ms_assembler, ms_scaler]

    # Convert label 'ac' to numeric
    label_indexer = StringIndexer(
        inputCol="ac",
        outputCol="label"
    )

    # Create vector used to train the model
    assembler = VectorAssembler(
        inputCols=[
            "lc_encoded",
            "ms_scaled",
            "is_b",
            "is_t",
            "is_uc",
            "c",
            "distance_scaled",
            "promiles_scaled",
            "quality_encoded"
        ],
        outputCol="features"
    )

    # Compose pipeline
    pipeline = Pipeline(stages=[
        *index_string_column("lc"),
        *index_string_column("quality"),
        label_indexer,
        *min_max_scale_column("distance"),
        *min_max_scale_column("promiles"),
        *min_max_scale_column("ms"),
        assembler,
    ])
```

```
# Fit and transform the input data to format model understands
model = pipeline.fit(roads_feature_values_transformed)
data_for_modelling = model.transform(roads_feature_values_transformed)
```

Now we can use the `SparkXGBClassifier` instance to train the model on the input data:

```
from xgboost.spark import SparkXGBClassifier

xgb_classifier = SparkXGBClassifier(
  features_col="features",
  label_col="label",
  num_workers=10,
)
```

To split the data into training and test datasets, we can use the `randomSplit` method in Apache Spark DataFrames:

```
train_df, test_df = data_for_modelling.randomSplit([0.8, 0.2], seed=42)
```

To fit the data, we can run the following code:

```
xgboost_model = xgb_classifier.fit(train_df)
```

Now to evaluate the classification model, we can use the following metrics:[4]

- Accuracy: 0.7375
- F1-score: 0.7379
- Recall: 0.7375

Summary

Apache Sedona provides you with the flexibility to run spatial machine learning algorithms at scale. In this chapter, you learned about the geospatial machine learning algorithms that Apache Sedona provides to you out of the box, like clustering using DBSCAN, outlier detection, hot spot detection, and autocorrelation using the Moran's I algorithm. Then we discussed how to combine Apache Sedona's raster data type to detect objects or segment images. One of the most significant benefits is the possibility to integrate geospatial processing and machine learning with the popular Apache Spark machine learning package, MLlib. We concluded the chapter by applying the concepts to analyze road accidents in Germany.

Each machine learning model benefits from reliable, clean, and available data. In the next chapter, we will utilize the Apache Parquet and Apache Iceberg formats in the geospatial data lakehouse architecture using Apache Sedona.

---

4 Read "A Guide to F1-Score" (*https://oreil.ly/kkYiT*) by Inna Logunova to learn more about F1-scores.

## CHAPTER 8

Building a Geospatial Data Lakehouse with Apache Parquet and Apache Iceberg

Geospatial data formats have been lagging behind the overall evolution of data analytics, which began in the mid-2010s. Apache Parquet and Apache ORC have lacked native support for geospatial data. People used binary formats like WKB to store geospatial data in Apache Parquet, but this didn't enable one of the biggest advantages of the Apache Parquet format: efficient data skipping based on statistics.

In late 2021, the idea of the GeoParquet file format specification emerged as a response to the lack of geospatial support in data lakes. Around this time, Apache Iceberg gained significant popularity. Apache Iceberg is a table format that addresses several key pain points in the data analytics space, including the lack of transactions, partial failures, and schema evolution. The era of the data lakehouse has begun. Nevertheless, despite the rise in popularity of file formats like Apache Iceberg, Delta Lake, and Apache Hudi, none of these supported geospatial data at the time. Then, thanks to the geospatial community, in early 2025, geospatial data types were added to Apache Parquet and Apache Iceberg. Still, the whole ecosystem needs to adapt and implement data readers and writers for the new specification. Apache Sedona is one of the pioneers in this space, so you will soon be able to load and store both the Apache Parquet and Apache Iceberg formats with Apache Sedona. We will update the book repository when we have all the integrations ready.

Overview of Data Lakehouse Architecture

The key difference between data lakes and data lakehouses is open table formats like Apache Iceberg and Delta Lake, which bring optimization techniques, transactions, and data versioning, making data lakehouses more efficient. If a data lake is an analog map, then a data lakehouse is a GPS navigation system. A map is a great tool that humanity has used for millennia, but finding the optimal route, especially for considerable distances, can be overwhelming, let alone time-consuming. On the other hand, a navigation system automatically provides you with an optimized route from point A to point B, including the current traffic information and your preferences, to make the journey easier and safer.

> This is not a book on data modeling; the data lakehouse architecture is a method of data instrumentation rather than modeling. There are great books on data modeling in a data lakehouse that we highly recommend.[1]

A key part of a data lakehouse is query engines, which can help you load and transform data. They can be used interchangeably thanks to unified file formats and table specifications, so you are no longer tied to one tool only, and you can choose the best tool for each use case. You can see the spatial data lakehouse components in Figure 8-1.

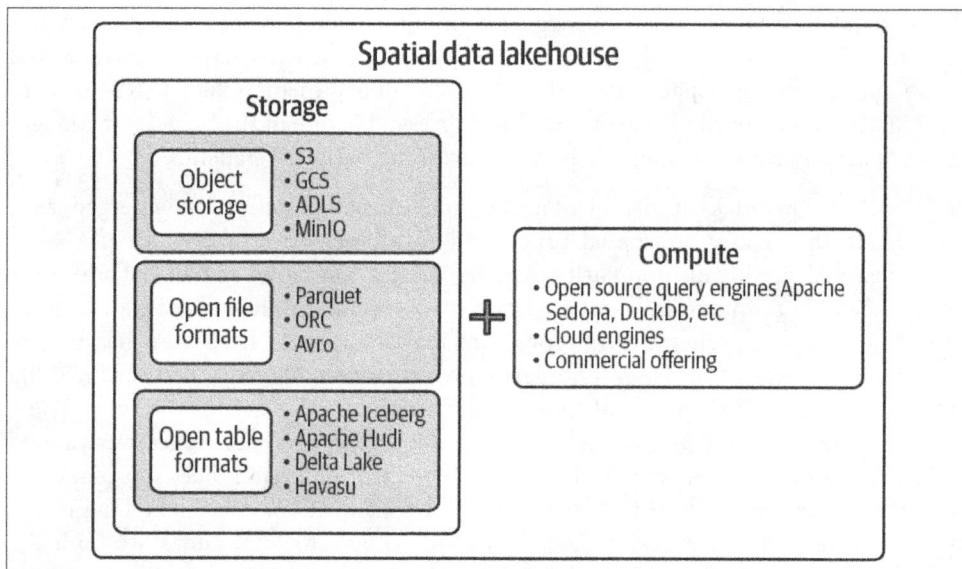

Figure 8-1. A data lakehouse consists of separated storage and compute, utilizing object storage (e.g., S3, GCS) and open file formats (e.g., Parquet, ORC) to help optimize queries and the costs of processing data[2]

---

1 See, e.g., *Building the Data Lakehouse* by Bill Inmon, Mary Levins, Ranjeet Srivastava (Technics Publications, 2021).

2 See *Practical Lakehouse Architecture* by Gaurav Ashok Thalpati (O'Reilly, 2024) for more on lakehouse architecture.

One of the most common design patterns in a data lakehouse is a medallion architecture (*https://oreil.ly/yEQ2R*). It consists of three layers: bronze, silver, and gold. Data quality, structure, and reliability improve with each layer, where bronze has raw data, like audio files, images, and unstructured files integrated from external systems. Silver has data that has been cleaned, structured, and tested. Gold is the layer with business aggregates, ready to be used by external teams, BI tools, or machine learning algorithms. Relating this to data products for the real estate industry, in the bronze layer, you might store raw satellite images, in silver, identified shapes of buildings, and in gold, buildings enriched with neighborhood data like access to public transportation.

Massive advancements have been made in data processing to make it more manageable and reliable. When we recall the data landscape in 2017, barely anyone cared about data quality or observability. Most were bothered by other problems, like making Apache Hadoop stable with grant control to users. But even with the advancements made since then, few have benefited from geospatial data management. Until recently, you couldn't define geometry or raster types in tables; metadata had no information about location data to speed up loading time. Basically, there was no native support for geospatial data in table formats like Apache Iceberg or Delta Lake. Now, thanks to the geospatial community, Apache Iceberg has geospatial data support.

But what makes a data lakehouse a geospatial data lakehouse? It definitely supports native geometry and raster data, as well as optimized queries based on geospatial statistics and indexing techniques. We need to include a compute engine that is capable of processing geospatial data and writing to efficient analytical formats that support spatial types. The compute engine needs to be able to utilize all the geospatial statistics to provide faster and more efficient reads. The compute engine also needs to be able to read legacy formats, such as shapefiles and geopackages, and provide a set of functions to transform both spatial and nonspatial data. Surely, Apache Sedona as a compute engine, Apache Parquet, and Apache Iceberg with spatial data types fulfill this requirement.

A data lakehouse is not only reliable, with noncrashed processes, but also provides valid and correct data. Many data and AI projects are failing due to data quality issues. You cannot train any reliable model on untrustworthy data. A simple linear model using cleaned and good-quality data beats even the most sophisticated neural network models based on garbage data. There is a saying: you can't pour from an empty cup, which in our case means that even the most capable person on Earth can't do the impossible.

When you travel or commute to a new place, you open the navigation app to find the route from your current location to your destination. Without this, you might get lost. You can ask a stranger for directions, but this takes longer, and you can get false information. You can also ask people in your organization where you can find a specific dataset, but similarly to asking a stranger for the way, you may struggle to find correct and precise information. Having a place to see what happens with the data and how it flows, and having alerts based on data quality issues, can prevent your data project from disaster.

Data governance is the process of making data in the organization visible, available, reliable, and secure. With the proper tooling and processes set up, data governance can help to understand how data is collected and processed, who currently has access to the data, and who should have proper permissions.[3] It's really important to keep the data safe and maintain the least privilege principle. Data governance can solve all those headache issues regarding your data. There are many components and processes that help bring the best data governance practices to the organization, including:

- Data quality
- Data lineage
- Data security

Similar to how you test your code before shipping it to production, you should test your data before you save it to the production schema. We are only human, and we make mistakes. You can have your ETL pipeline thoroughly tested and all possible branches covered, but the produced data may still be unreliable without a proper quality assurance process. To keep the data reliable and easy to discover by the team, we can use OpenLineage to store metadata about your data pipelines and data lakehouse.

Data lineage is a process of collecting metadata about your data pipelines to see how they flow over time. Imagine you found out that some of your data jobs are misbehaving. The output of column A has invalid values. You looked at the codebase, and the table from which the column originates was not created by your team. How do you track where that table was created and what the root cause of its misbehavior is? If you set up the data lineage for your spatial data pipelines in the organization, you can quickly use the tool to move backward to the root of the issue and try to ask the team responsible a question or even help them fix it. Data lineage helps you be aware of what's inside your organization's data platform. It improves team collaboration as you can quickly navigate and debug data inconsistencies.

---

3 Sara Gates, "5 Data Quality Tools—And Where You Should Start First" (*https://oreil.ly/1U3jl*), Monte Carlo Data, August 1, 2025.

Even if you take great care of your health, you still need regular blood tests to ensure that no hidden disease is threatening your life. In the same way, data security needs to be incorporated in your data platform before a threatening event occurs.

Data security is the process of securing your data from unauthorized usage, corruption, or theft throughout its whole lifecycle.[4] When is the best time for you to incorporate data security principles in your organization? From the beginning. When is the second best moment? Now. Data leakages might be disastrous for any organization. If they occur, lawsuits and loss of reputation are the least of your worries. As we previously mentioned, prevention is better than a cure.

But where to start? First, you can start with limitation of data usage.[5] The least privilege principle is best suited here. Disallow people from using the data by default, and grant it only to those who need it.

When data is not needed, don't move it to other tables. Take all you need, not all you have. This not only has security benefits but also helps you optimize disk space and processing time.

If you need sensitive data, mask or encrypt it to make it useless for possible threats. Never put sensitive data inside your tables if that's not needed. By sensitive data, we mean medical records, names, tax IDs, keys, passwords, etc. Audit your data pipelines with tools like data lineage to ensure you're not ingesting data that you shouldn't. Data security is not all about preventing data leakage; it's also about preventing data from being lost. Ensure that you are performing data backups and replication to avoid data loss.

Parquet Deep Dive

For a long time, geospatial analytics was behind data trends, until the concept of Geo-Parquet emerged. Until recently, people have used different techniques to store vast amounts of geospatial data, even in shapefiles, which are highly inefficient and not scalable. Another idea was to store data in Parquet with WKB or WKT, which gives no performance boost when using data-skipping techniques to reduce the amount of data loaded. There was even an idea to use Z-ordering with longitude and latitude, but it only works with points and does not give that much of an improvement anyway.

---

4 Tom Krantz and Alexandra Jonker, "What Is Data Security?" (*https://oreil.ly/a79UL*), IBM, August 1, 2025.

5 Kevin Gallagher, "Data Security and Privacy: Risks, Best Practices, and Compliance" (*https://oreil.ly/S6nPo*), Endpoint Protector, December 6, 2023.

Fortunately, the idea of GeoParquet emerged for cloud-native geospatial analytics. Apache Sedona is an early adopter of GeoParquet and one of the data processing engines leveraging its full potential.

GeoParquet is an Open Geospatial Consortium (OGC) standard that extends the Apache Parquet format with geospatial types (point, line, polygon) and optimization techniques to facilitate geospatial analytics. Apache Parquet, on the other hand, has added geospatial data types, including geometry and geography, to the specification.

In this section, we will review the Apache Parquet format, with a strong emphasis on its geospatial features, compare it to available alternatives, and thoroughly explain the GeoParquet standard. However, before that, let's discuss the difference between the columnar and row data formats as they are commonly used in analytical systems.

Columnar Versus Row Data Formats

As the names suggest, row data formats organize your data by rows and columnar formats by columns. Both columnar and row data formats are remarkable for their purposes. Some use cases are more suitable for row data formats, while others are better with columnar formats. It's essential to choose the right tool for the job at hand. Why do most RDBMS systems use row storage, while analytical systems tend to prefer columnar storage? We'll go through both data formats and explain their benefits and drawbacks, where to use them, and when to avoid one or the other.

The row data format stores all data related to a single entity close together. As a result, the previous entity is found just before the current one, and the next is found right after. As you can imagine, this brings simpler access to the data horizontally; it's beneficial for any workload highly dependent on data updates, removals, or appending. When the system needs high throughput during regular single-entity manipulation, this way of storing data might be optimal.

Consider, for example, a table with the locations of points with corresponding IDs:

id	geom
1	Point(69.680, 18.9129)
2	Point(35.685, 139.748)

The rows are stored as follows:

```
1   Point(69.680, 18.9129)   2   Point(35.685, 139.748)
```

There are many examples of systems using this method of storing data. *OLTP (online transaction processing)* often utilizes CRUD operations (create, read, update, delete) on single-row level RDBMSes focused on transaction processing. Financial services like banks or trading applications and other transactional systems rely on *ACID* (atomicity, consistency, isolation, durability; these properties will be described later in this chapter) capabilities, where data integrity and consistency are key. As mentioned in Chapter 3, RDBMS solutions, such as PostgreSQL (PostGIS), MySQL, and Oracle, are row-oriented. Apache Avro and Protobuf are row-based data formats used in analytics, primarily for real-time processing, to serialize messages sent on publish-subscribe systems like Apache Kafka.

Columnar data formats, on the other hand, store data about each column close together. This makes data skipping and faster data retrieval from a single column more efficient. This is beneficial for the world of analytics, where you filter tons of records based on a single column, aggregate a column's values, or select only a few columns for analysis.

Returning to the points table, the columnar way of storing data is stored as shown in the following:

```
1   2 Point(69.680, 18.9129)   Point(35.685, 139.748)
```

When you need to calculate the average distance to Delhi, India, for each point in the table, you don't have to load the ID field. One of the file formats that efficiently uses column storage is Apache Parquet.

Parquet Data Format

One significant component that helped commoditize analytics across organizations, anywhere from big tech companies to small start-ups, is the open file format to store and process data effectively.

Apache Parquet is an open source, column-oriented data file format that revolutionized data space with efficient data storage (small data size and significant compression) and retrieval (fast read times). It supports many languages, such as Java, Python, C++, Go, and more, which helps unify data analytics across many tools and languages.

The primary motivation behind the Apache Parquet project was to take advantage of compressed, efficient, and columnar data storage methods in the Hadoop ecosystem. One of the substantial advantages of Apache Parquet is its support for complex nested data structures. It helps to organize your data in the column space better, connecting entities with similar meanings. As an example, we can use an ecommerce domain; you can store product attributes in the product column, and nested inside are fields like identifier, name, iso code, etc. The schema might look like this:

```
-> product
    -> id: long
    -> name: string
    -> iso_code: string
-> offer
    -> id: long
    -> categories: array<string>
```

Apache Parquet is highly efficient for analytics OLAP use cases; you can leverage many optimizations like data skipping when loading a fraction of columns. Another optimization technique is using Apache Parquet metadata to skip files you don't need to load based on the predicates in your query (predicate pushdown). Imagine you have hundreds of Parquet files, and only six contain Australian market data. Thanks to Apache Parquet metadata, you don't have to load them all if you only wish to analyze Australian data.

Apache Parquet is well-built for cloud-native applications as it supports S3, GCS, Azure Blob storage, and more. Keep in mind that Apache Parquet helps you reduce the cost of your infrastructure and processing as it enables you to minimize storage (through compression) and I/O (through data skipping). It is built to store big data, structured tables, images, videos, and even documents. You can store all your data in one format in the data lakehouse.

Apache Parquet is not purely a column file format; it uses a hybrid approach; it supports both projection and predicates, where projection is the process of selecting columns, and predicates are the criteria used to skip/filter specific row groups. Now we will walk you through the internal architecture of Apache Parquet, which you can see in Figure 8-2.

Apache Parquet contains three main parts:

- Header
- Data
- Footer (metadata)

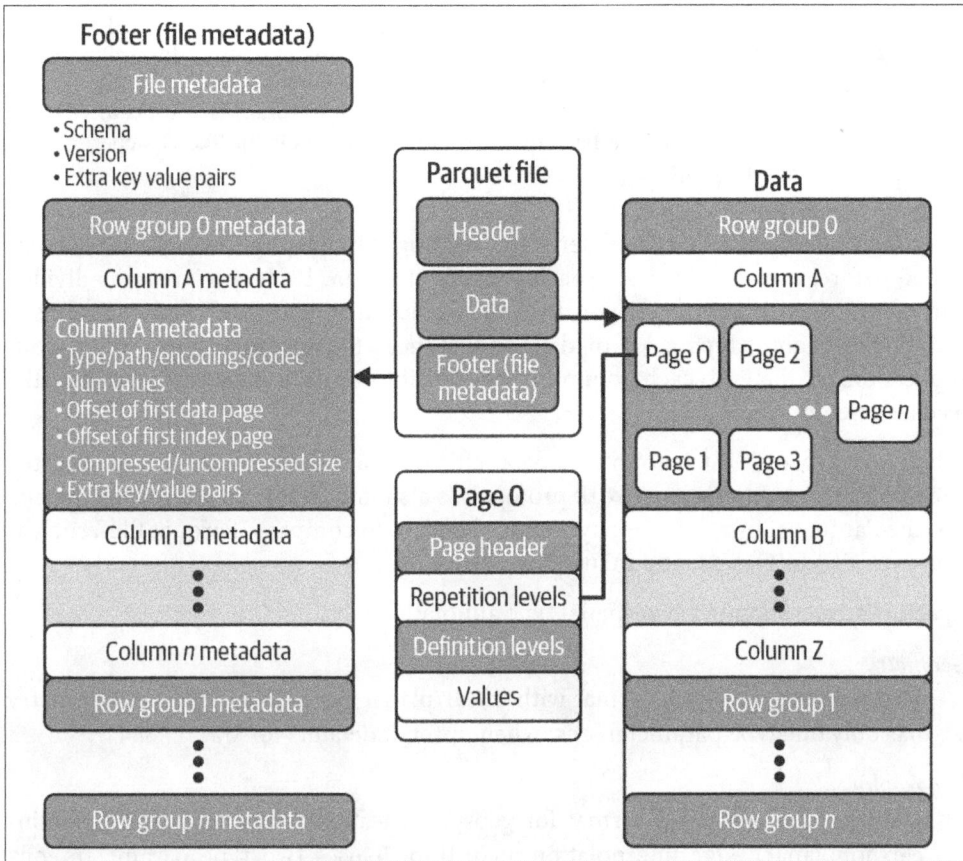

Figure 8-2. Apache Parquet internal architecture

When a reader reads the Parquet file, it starts from the header section to verify if it contains all the magic numbers, confirming that the file is, in fact, in the Apache Parquet file format. Next, it looks for a pointer to the metadata section of the Parquet file, aka the footer.

The footer keeps the metadata about the Parquet file, schema, version, and key-value pairs to store additional information. You can also find information regarding the row group and column metadata here. On the row-level group metadata, Parquet maintains the boundary box statistics to skip loading unnecessary data. The footer section is also critical for GeoParquet, which we will describe later in this chapter.

> When your dataset has a lot of columns, it is beneficial to group your columns into struct fields. It helps the engine reduce the scan time of the columns and may improve your query performance significantly. Also, remember to select only the columns you need, as not all engines have query optimizations built in, like Apache Spark does.

After digesting metadata, the reader starts reading the data itself, which, as we mentioned before, uses a hybrid approach to store the data. Each row group is divided into columns separately, so if you load only column A and don't need columns B and C, the engine skips a lot of data and reduces the memory footprint of your application. At the end, each column is divided into up to n pages to parallelize the reads efficiently.

When you process vast amounts of data, efficient data storage is essential, and the size of files you load using network protocols is also important. To reduce the impact, Apache Parquet allows using many standard codecs to compress Parquet files, such as Snappy, GZIP, LZO, LZ4, and many more.

Apache Parquet supports two spatial type annotations:

Geometry
    Defined with the WKB format with linear/planar edges interpolation. Geometry has only one type parameter, `crs`; when unset, it defaults to `'OGC:CRS84'`.

Geography
    Defined with the WKB format for geospatial features with an explicit (nonlinear/nonplanar) edge interpolation algorithm. It uses two type parameters, `crs` and `algorithm`. The `crs` argument is the same as in the geometry type. The `algorithm` parameter keeps information about the interpolation algorithm type; it is an enum with the following values: `'SPHERICAL'`, `'VINCENTY'`, `'THOMAS'`, `'ANDOYER'`, `'KARNEY'`. If unset, the algorithm defaults to `'SPHERICAL'`.

The Apache Parquet geospatial definition allows for CRS customization. The CRS values are strings in the format `'type: identifier'`, where type is one of `'srid'` and `'projjson'`. The identifier value depends on the type; for SRID, it is the SRID identifier, and for PROJJSON, it is the name of the file or table property where the PROJJSON string is stored.

One of the significant properties of the Apache Parquet data format is powerful statistics, which help filter data more efficiently. Apache Parquet supports geospatial statistics using a four-dimensional boundary box definition, comprising x, y, z, and m coordinates.

Now, let's examine the Apache Parquet file metadata, with an emphasis on the geospatial data types. We will use the PyArrow library for this purpose. When we inspect the column metadata for the geometry field, we can expect something similar:

```
<ParquetColumnSchema>
  name: geom
  path: geom
  max_definition_level: 1
  max_repetition_level: 0
  physical_type: BYTE_ARRAY
  logical_type: Geometry(crs=epsg:4326)
  converted_type (legacy): NONE
```

As you can see, the `logical_type` is `Geometry` and the `crs` is `EPSG:4326`. Now let's investigate the row group statistics for the geometry field:

```
<pyarrow._parquet.GeoStatistics object at 0x10e2bd760>
  geospatial_types: [1]
  xmin: -117.24608684094282, xmax: -115.31252839597236
  ymin: 32.53407674757135, ymax: 33.75001063107328
  zmin: None, zmax: None
  mmin: None, mmax: None
```

We are aware that you have been given a considerable volume of information to digest, but to make the process a little bit easier, we'll summarize the Apache Parquet advantages in a few bullet points:

- Support for geospatial data types, geometry and geography, and powerful geospatial statistics to improve query performance.

- Compression efficiency: Apache Parquet keeps extensive data small. You can use many compression codecs like Snappy, GZIP, or LZO.

- Data skipping helps make your applications faster and reduces the memory footprint.

- The columnar format is highly efficient for analytics workloads, as you can skip many columns and reduce your application's memory consumption.

- Static schema helps you with schema evolution; you don't need to infer schema or cast it in your code.

- Language agnostic: there is a variety of languages and frameworks supporting reading and writing to Apache Parquet.

GeoParquet

GeoParquet was created before native support for geospatial types in Apache Parquet and Apache Iceberg. Thus, many datasets are stored in the GeoParquet file format. Nevertheless, in upcoming years, we forecast more and more integration from data systems with the Apache Parquet and Iceberg geospatial types, as the aforementioned file formats are well designed to work together. Native geospatial types don't mean the GeoParquet will become obsolete: GeoParquet adds the geospatial metadata on the file level and Parquet geospatial on the row group level. They might compliment each other as the exchange format (Apache Iceberg is well designed for lakehouse, but GeoParquet might still be better suited for sharing files like Overture maps).

GeoParquet emerged from the need to process and analyze vast amounts of geospatial data in 2021. Shapefiles and GeoPackages, which dominate the desktop landscape for geospatial data storage, are not well suited for mid-to-large-scale analytics. There are a lot of drawbacks to using shapefiles for analytics:

- Lack of support for nested columns
- Not columnar
- 2GB size limit
- Column name limits
- Only one geometry field can be stored

Similar to shapefiles, GeoPackage is likewise inadequate for our use case due to the following drawbacks:

- Lack of support for nested columns
- Not partitioned
- Sequential access (you can create copies of files and read them in parallel, but it brings more harm than good)

GeoJSON is well designed for web development, but it is not distributed. Additionally, missing metadata requires scanning all files, and there are no features such as data skipping, column selection, or a predicate pushdown mechanism.

To address the problems mentioned earlier, the concept of GeoParquet emerged; however, these are not the only issues that GeoParquet resolves. GeoParquet is a unified standard that integrates frameworks, data processing engines, and warehouses. Currently, GeoParquet is supported by 84 systems, including Apache Sedona, Wherobots, Snowflake, Databricks, Carto, and others.

Key features of GeoParquet:

- Works with both planar and spherical coordinates
- Support for data files partitioning based on data locality
- Well suited for geospatial analytics, utilizing a Parquet columnar-oriented structure to speed up geospatial queries

- Support for multiple geometry columns
- Support for multiple spatial reference systems (CRS)

How does GeoParquet relate to Apache Parquet? GeoParquet extends the Apache Parquet file metadata (footer) with geospatial attributes that allow for faster data retrieval and data skipping. GeoParquet adds them on two levels: file and column.

On the file level, the GeoParquet specification defines three fields (all required), as shown in Table 8-1.

Table 8-1. GeoParquet file metadata consists of three metadata fields: version, primary column, and columns

Field name	Type	Description
version	string	Version of the GeoParquet specification.
primary_column	string	Name of the primary geometry column (GeoParquet supports multiple geometry columns, but one of them must be chosen as the primary one; this is an important hint for the reader during optimization processes, such as partition pruning).
columns	object<string, ColumnMetadata>	Metadata about the columns: each key is the name of the geometry column.

For geometry columns, GeoParquet defines the properties shown in Table 8-2: encoding and geometry_types are the only required fields.

Table 8-2. GeoParquet column metadata specification

Field name	Type	Description
encoding	string	How the geometry column is encoded: the currently supported types are WKB, point, linestring, polygon, multipoint, multilinestring, and multipolygon.
geometry_types	[string]	Geometry types of all geometries or an empty array if they are unknown.
crs	object|null	PROJJSON of the geometry column: if the value is not provided, then by default OGC:CRS84 is selected, which means the data needs to be stored in WGS84 datum (longitude, latitude).
orientation	string	Order of the coordinates for an exterior ring of polygons. If present, it has to be "counterclockwise"; for interior rings (holes), it has to be "clockwise".
edges	string	Name of the coordinate system for the edges; there are two possible values, "planar" and "spherical". The default value is "planar".
bbox	[number]	The bounding box of the geometries in the file; it's crucial for file skipping when using query predicates in Apache Sedona.
epoch	number	Coordinate epoch for the dynamic CRS, expressed in the decimal year.
covering	object	Object containing the bounding box column names, helps to speed up reading the spatial data.

Apache Sedona was one of the first data processing engines that added support for the GeoParquet reader and writer. Full specifications of GeoParquet can be found in the official GeoParquet repository on GitHub (*https://oreil.ly/uW2jV*).

You already know from Chapter 3 how to load and write to the GeoParquet file format. Now, let's dive into the GeoParquet metadata with Apache Sedona. To read it, use the `geoparquet.metadata` data source:

```
sedona \
    .read \
    .format("geoparquet.metadata") \
    .load(path) \
    .show()
```

There are four main columns: path, version, primary geometry column name, and metadata for the columns:

```
+-------------------+-------+--------------+-------------------+
|               path|version|primary_column|            columns|
+-------------------+-------+--------------+-------------------+
|s3a://bucket/aust...|  1.1.0|      geometry|{geometry -> {WKB...|
|s3a://bucket/aust...|  1.1.0|      geometry|{geometry -> {WKB...|
|s3a://bucket/aust...|  1.1.0|      geometry|{geometry -> {WKB...|
|s3a://bucket/aust...|  1.1.0|      geometry|{geometry -> {WKB...|
|s3a://bucket/aust...|  1.1.0|      geometry|{geometry -> {WKB...|
+-------------------+-------+--------------+-------------------+
```

The most interesting part is what's inside the column's metadata. Let's look at GeoParquet metadata in the DataFrame schema:

```
root
 |-- path: string (nullable = true)
 |-- version: string (nullable = true)
 |-- primary_column: string (nullable = true)
 |-- columns: map (nullable = true)
 |    |-- key: string
 |    |-- value: struct (valueContainsNull = true)
 |    |    |-- encoding: string (nullable = true)
 |    |    |-- geometry_types: array (nullable = true)
 |    |    |    |-- element: string (containsNull = true)
 |    |    |-- bbox: array (nullable = true)
 |    |    |    |-- element: double (containsNull = true)
 |    |    |-- crs: string (nullable = true)
 |    |    |-- covering: string (nullable = true)
```

You can see familiar metadata columns, which we mentioned earlier in the GeoParquet section (path, version, primary_column). Now we can look at the single record from the column columns to see what values are inside:

```
{
    geometry -> {
        encoding: WKB,
        geometry_types: [Polygon, MultiPolygon],
        bbox: [137.8166711, -38.8566971, 144.8431008, -33.7518239],
        crs: {"$schema":..."id":{"authority":"EPSG","code":"4326"}},
        covering: NULL}
}
```

Geometry is encoded using the WKB method. We have two types of geometry: Poly gon and MultiPolygon. The CRS is in PROJJSON format, in our case it's EPSG:4326. The most crucial piece of information is the bbox coordinates, which help to optimize spatial queries.

For a long time, geospatial analytics lacked the cohesive element to bind multiple systems together, the integration that helps data processing be more straightforward and robust.

Iceberg Tables

GeoParquet on its own is already an excellent data format, and Apache Sedona simplifies working with it even further. However, the lack of a few important features makes bare GeoParquet vulnerable to common data professional struggles, including data pipeline partial failures. Imagine the data pipeline to create a report for the board of directors failed in the middle of the process. You're a great engineer, so your process is idempotent. You use the overwrite method to store data with proper partitioning and geospatial boxes for your Parquet files. The dashboard achieves optimal query performance. Due to a failure, the dashboard stops working. With proper alerting and observability, you should have received an alert saying that the pipeline is broken and you must fix it. It looks like the solution isn't easy and you don't know how to patch the bug at first glance. You know that the board looks at the dashboard only once a week, and your job calculates daily, but you find an empty directory due to a failure. You're unsure of how to fix it quickly but must figure it out under time constraints. This would have never happened had you been using a table format like Apache Iceberg, which provides features such as ACID transactions (we'll cover that acronym shortly), time travel, versioning, and more to resolve common data professional headaches.

Data Transactions

One of the features that you take for granted in relational database systems is support for transactions. Many NoSQL databases also support them. One of the reasons for not adding transactions to distributed systems is that they are not well scalable and might result in slowing down systems designed for a larger scale. Furthermore, they are hard to implement for distributed systems. In some cases, transactions might be required, like for banking systems, where partial failures or lack of strong consistency guarantees are unacceptable when selecting the database system. For others, transactions are not a must-have, for example, in cases where high throughput is required and some data inconsistencies are not a dealbreaker.

The data reliability guarantees provided by transactions are defined using the acronym ACID: atomicity, consistency, isolation, and durability. The systems that do not fulfill these requirements use the acronym BASE, which is basically available, soft state, and eventual consistency. Eventual consistency[6] in distributed systems guarantees that the applied changes will eventually be reflected in all nodes that store the data. ACID is a strong consistency guarantee, and it's also one of the key features of table formats like Apache Iceberg. Now, let's explore what each component of the acronym means:

Atomicity

In concurrent programs, atomic means that one thread can't see the partial result of another thread modifying a piece of data.[7] In database systems, it means something slightly different. When you change a database entity like a table, there is no intermediate state; the transaction can either succeed or fail.

Consistency

When you write the data to a table, it should have integrity constraints. For example, the product's price can't be negative, and longitude coordinates can't exceed 180 degrees. In some database systems, you can use constraints to guarantee data integrity.[8] You can enforce the checks on the database level. For example, when a transaction tries to reduce the account balance below 0, it will be rejected, and none of the parts of the transaction will be applied. Some say consistency is not part of the database and that it's closer to the application level, as you can add data integrity checks before you save them.

Isolation

Databases, in most cases, are used by many concurrent applications. There are no issues as long as none of the applications are trying to modify the same records. Race conditions are among the greatest challenges to debug in a production application. Isolation prevents any possible issues when writing concurrently to the same record. It ensures that many transactions that run concurrently and modify the same record produce the same result if they run sequentially.

---

6 ScyllaDB, "Eventual Consistency" (*https://oreil.ly/vmdsx*).

7 Martin Kleppmann, *Designing Data-Intensive Applications: The Big Ideas Behind Reliable, Scalable, and Maintainable Systems* (O'Reilly, 2017).

8 BMC Software, "Database ACID Properties: Atomic, Consistent, Isolated, Durable" (*https://oreil.ly/Lx5wV*), BMC Software | Blogs, February 17, 2025.

Durability
> When a transaction succeeds, data systems guarantee that the result is safely stored and queryable by the application.

What is inevitable when creating production code is that it will sooner or later change due to a requirement change, new feature, or bug. In the data landscape, changed code often means a changed schema in the data. Schema changes over time are named schema evolution.

Schema Evolution

To prevent application failures due to schema evolution, there are defined rules, also known as compatibility types, for updating the schema to avoid application downtime:

Forward compatibility
> The producer creates a new schema that the consumer can read with an old schema. So, imagine you have a geospatial data pipeline with the process described as a directed acyclic graph (DAG) (Figure 8-3). When process A updates table A to make that change forward compatible, process B or C still needs to be able to read the new schema without adjusting their code. There are a few patterns to follow to make it possible, for example:

> - When you need to adjust an existing column in a breaking manner, add a new column that is not required instead of adjusting the existing one. By breaking change, we mean changing the data type or the column's meaning, such as different enumeration values.

> - Don't remove columns but rather make them deprecated and let clients adjust the code.

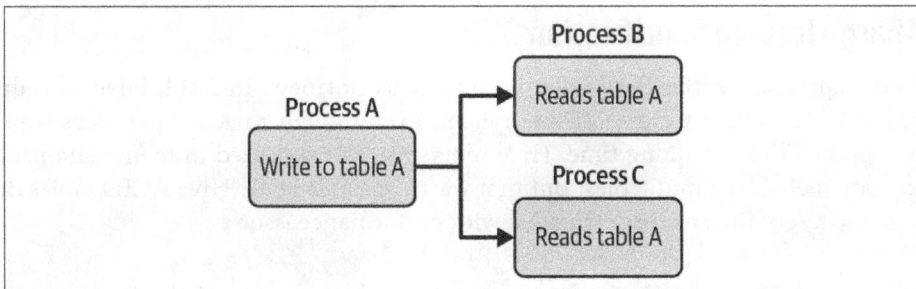

Figure 8-3. Data pipeline DAG

Backward compatibility

The data reader can adjust the schema and still be able to process the old, unchanged table. When you agree with another team on the schema, you can start incorporating that schema into your data pipeline without waiting for the producer to update the data. In the example from Figure 8-3, the schema will be backward compatible if process B or C adjusts the code and schema in a way that can still read nonchanged data from process A. Similarly to forward compatibility, there are patterns here to follow:

- When you update the schema on the reader side, ensure that you have a *coalesce* of columns; for example, you add a new nonrequired field B to replace field A first. You look at field A, which was previously used, and then at field B.

- Don't remove columns from the schema; just omit fields when writing your queries/ data pipelines.

- Don't change column data types; instead, add a new column with a new type and use logic to handle casting the previous column.

Sometimes, it is impossible to do this without breaking changes; they might be caused due to various reasons like business requirements changes or older processes that will backfill the previous data. In that case, it's crucial to adjust producers and consumers quickly. Effective communication between data teams, in the form of data contracts, is crucial. There must be one source of truth for the schema to avoid mismatches.

Coordinating teams for daily batch jobs is easier than managing streaming applications, where downtime is often necessary. Introducing the breaking schema changes is a last resort, so evaluate the necessity of this action thoughtfully before proceeding.

Apache Iceberg Specification

Updating tables in the Hadoop environment is not new; in 2014, Hive introduced ACID tables, which were ACID compliant. Even though Apache Spark was superior to Apache Hive for a long time, Hive Metastore was still used in many data projects to store metadata about tables. But that wasn't scalable at all. Hive ACID tables didn't pass the test of time as they struggled with performance issues.

> Apache Hive is a data warehouse built on top of the Hadoop ecosystem; it can use engines like MapReduce or Spark to process data.

This book is too short to cover this in detail, but you can find many great articles about the comparison of Hive ACID tables to Apache Iceberg.[9] Closer to 2018, a few solutions that came out in the data space got a lot of traction: Apache Iceberg, Apache Hudi, and Delta Lake. Each one offers similar capabilities, but Apache Iceberg is the most popular. It also supports geospatial types. In the next few sections, we will delve into the details of Apache Iceberg, but let's start with an overview of its most important features.

Apache Iceberg (*https://oreil.ly/FK_ce*) is an open table format designed to manage a large, slow-changing collection of files either in a distributed file system or in a key-value store, as a table. The project aims to achieve the following goals:

- No more partial failures, concurrent writes are separated from reads, and readers can only read from committed versions.
- When scanning table versions, Apache Iceberg uses $O(1)$ operation complexity to scan the data files, as metadata is stored in separate files, so the load times do not lose performance when the number of versions increases.
- As opposed to Hive's approach, Apache Iceberg is moving job planning to clients, not to centralized metadata stores.
- Schema evolution is natively built into the system.
- Support for many data files like Parquet, ORC.
- Partitioning is part of the table configuration. Thanks to this property, partitioning can evolve over time, and you can dynamically use partition filtering; we'll have more on this in the next section about Apache Iceberg features.

Now, let's go through how Apache Iceberg manages table data. The HDFS-distributed file store is used less and less often in data analytics. As an example, we will create a table on an S3-compatible MinIO bucket. Then, we will take data from the OSM project and save it as an Iceberg table.

You already know how to read data from the shapefile located on the S3 bucket using Apache Sedona, so we will skip this part (you can still reference it in the notebook prepared for this chapter). As of the writing of this book, there hasn't been a release of the reader/writer for the Apache Iceberg geospatial specs. In the examples, we will use the EWKB until the release is available. We will update the official book repository as soon as possible. Apache Iceberg has excellent integration with Spark SQL, so we will keep the data as a view. Apache Iceberg uses three-part table names separated by a dot, following the pattern *[catalog].[database].[table]*. Our code to save it to Apache Iceberg looks like this:

---

9 Yusuf Cattaneo and Emma Lullo, "Hive vs Iceberg: When to Migrate to Apache Iceberg" (*https://oreil.ly/PdaPq*), Starburst, May 16, 2023.

```
CREATE TABLE sedona.spatial.roads
USING iceberg
AS SELECT * FROM roads
```

Now let's follow the structure of how Apache Iceberg stores data; you can also follow Figure 8-4.

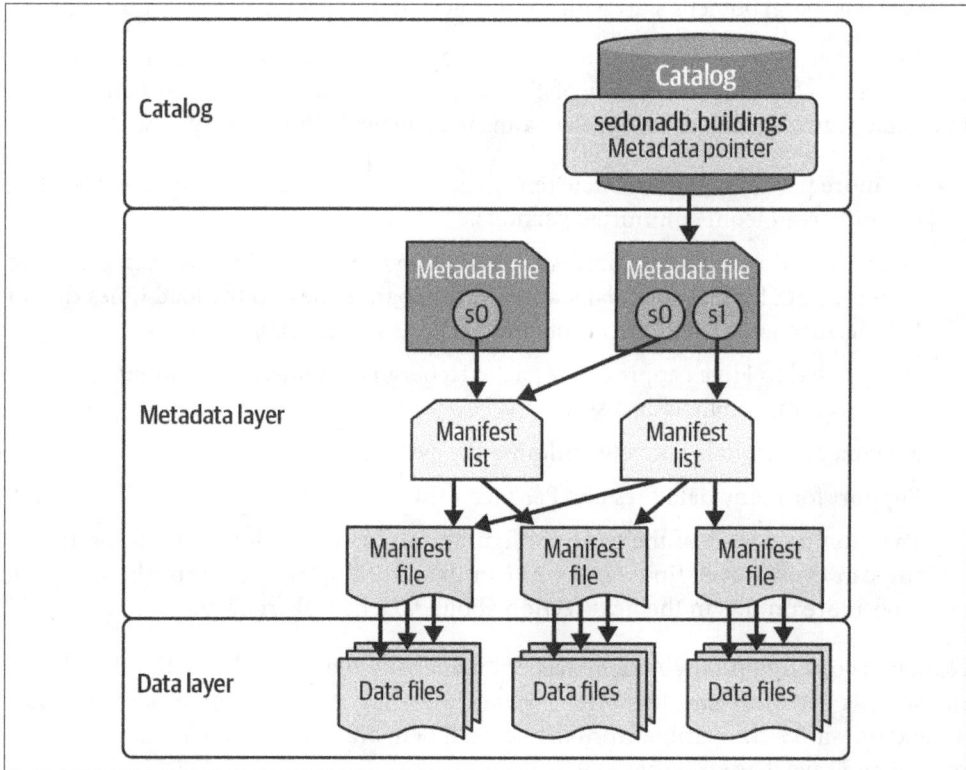

Figure 8-4. Apache Iceberg format overview[10]

Apache Iceberg splits the data into *data* and *metadata* paths. With this approach, the engine using Apache Iceberg can dramatically reduce listings of the files as all the hints and data skipping information are stored in the metadata directory, which is lighter and helps to get version files in O(1) time, assuming that filtering the manifest files is constant time. We will now explain why.

When you modify an Apache Iceberg table, a new version is created. Information about which version is currently the newest is stored in the *version-hint.text* file; there is only one number there, the version number. Apache Iceberg only has to read

---

10 Apache Software Foundation, "Apache Iceberg Table Spec" (*https://oreil.ly/FK_ce*).

this file to know which data files to read. This small file also helps to do atomic swaps, so that only when the new data has been successfully written can the engine writing the data quickly swap the version and not block the entire directory. The version number in *version-hint.text* corresponds to the table's current metadata file, *v${version_number}.metadata.json*, ensuring the engine locates the correct metadata file.

So far, the engine reading the Apache Iceberg table hasn't had to scan any file. Hence, as we previously mentioned, the complexity doesn't grow with the number of data files and versions. In the metadata file, you can find information about the schema of the table version and statistics that help to optimize the data reads. Also, there is a list of *manifest list* files whose names start with the *snap* prefix, which are stored in the Apache Avro file format. Data is stored in the table with columns containing information like the number of files added, added rows count, deleted rows count, partition, and manifest filepath. Using the steps of storing metadata as shown in Figure 8-4, we can reduce the number of overall files and reuse them. The metadata file on the right side points to the two manifest files. This is really useful as you update only one partition or a fraction of rows instead of the whole table. The manifest_file column points to the manifest file used. The manifest file is stored as Avro; the reason behind this is that Apache Avro is a row-based format that helps quickly scan the rows.

The manifest file in the data_file column stores nested fields containing the path to the data path and file statistics like:

- Record count
- Value counts for each column
- Lower bound for each column
- Upper bound for each column

Now we can see exactly which data files the version consists of, and so far, we haven't performed any listing of the files on the object storage.

You learned how the Apache Iceberg specification stores data in your data lakehouse. Now let's look at how Apache Iceberg can benefit you by going through its features.

Apache Iceberg Features

Apache Iceberg is entirely ACID compliant. Let's look at how it achieves this:

Atomicity
Apache Iceberg uses the version hint file to perform atomic swaps to either accept or reject the new version. If rejected, the files will be treated as orphans, and you can use automatic tools to clean them up.

Consistency

Apache Iceberg ensures that data is correctly saved based on the rules of the data lake, like if columns have valid types, keeping the nullability constraints, etc. It doesn't support the syntax for constraints like relational databases do.

Isolation

Apache Iceberg uses the optimistic locking mechanism to separate concurrent writes and readers can't see the partial state of the concurrent writes. Optimistic locking is a concurrency control mechanism that relies on the fact that conflicts are rare, and instead of using costly locks, it allows multiple concurrent writes to happen. It checks conflicts only during the commit phase. Each Apache Iceberg writer keeps the original version they've been using. If the version hasn't been changed when the writer tries to commit, then the transaction can be properly committed and our new version created. However, if a new version has been committed in the meantime by another writer, our transaction will fail and has to be retried.

Durability

When the write has been committed, the data is properly saved and ready to be served.

Apache Iceberg keeps the partitioning information on the metadata side. Thanks to this property, partitioning can evolve during your data lakehouse lifetime. Another outcome of this is hidden partitioning. Imagine when you partition Parquet files by date, and then the data consumer filters it by adding the hour predicate to the date, leading to a full data scan without using partitioning optimization. This is no longer an issue thanks to Apache Iceberg's hidden partitioning. Apache Iceberg knows the relation of your columns used for partitions, and there are many supported transformations when specifying the partitioning to give Iceberg hints like year, month, day, bucket, and truncate. An example query with the definition of the table with hidden days partitioning might look like this:

```
CREATE TABLE sedona.spatial.points (
    id bigint,
    geom geometry,
    ts timestamp)
USING iceberg
PARTITIONED BY (days(ts));
```

Now we will insert one row into the table:

```
INSERT INTO sedona.spatial.points
VALUES (
    1,
    ST_GeomFromText('Point(1 0)'),
    TIMESTAMP '2025-07-20 15:30:00'
)
```

When you look inside the data directory, you see a structure like this:

```
-> points
   -> data
      -> ts_day=2025-07-20
```

However, even in the loaded DataFrame, a timestamp column is available, and in the file metadata, Apache Iceberg recognizes that the partition columns are linked to the ts column:

```
+---+----------+-------------------+
| id|      geom|                 ts|
+---+----------+-------------------+
|  1|POINT (1 0)|2025-07-20 15:30:00|
+---+----------+-------------------+
```

So a query like the following, despite having a partition by date, won't scan the whole table but only one partition:

```
SELECT *
FROM sedona.spatial.points
WHERE ts BETWEEN '2025-07-20 15:00:00' AND '2025-07-20 16:00:00'
```

The append method of storing data by Apache Iceberg and versioning results in the great functionality of *time travel*. This mechanism enables you to select a version prior to the specified point in time. What if there are too many versions and the disk space has a lot of unnecessary data? You can tell Apache Iceberg to keep only a predefined number of versions to reduce the occupied space. To list all available versions run the following query:

```
SELECT *
FROM sedona.spatial.points.history;
```

```
+-------------------+-------------------+---------+-------------------+
|      made_current_at|        snapshot_id|parent_id|is_current_ancestor|
+-------------------+-------------------+---------+-------------------+
|2025-07-20 11:19:...|4015264917405324129|     NULL|               true|
+-------------------+-------------------+---------+-------------------+
```

Insert the new rows:

```
INSERT INTO sedona.spatial.points
VALUES
 (2, ST_GeomFromText('Point(1 3)'), TIMESTAMP '2025-07-20 15:30:00'),
 (3, ST_GeomFromText('Point(4 8)'), TIMESTAMP '2025-07-20 15:30:00')
```

The history table now has one additional record, which also has a non-NULL parent_id field:

```
+--------------------+----------------+----------------+------------------+
|     made_current_at|    snapshot_id|     parent_id|is_current_ancestor|
+--------------------+----------------+----------------+------------------+
|2025-07-20 11:19:...|4015264917405… |            NULL|              true|
|2025-07-20 11:35:...|5489915494028… |4015264917405… |              true|
+--------------------+----------------+----------------+------------------+
```

When you load the Apache Iceberg table, you load the most recent one. If you would like to read the previous version, like the initial table in our case, you can run the following query:

```
SELECT *
FROM sedona.spatial.points
VERSION AS OF 4015264917405324129
```

Or, using timestamps:

```
SELECT *
FROM sedona.spatial.points
TIMESTAMP AS OF '2025-07-20 11:19:52.145'
```

Apache Iceberg rich metadata can help you optimize queries and make your analytics pipelines quicker, cheaper, and more reliable. You can use not only Parquet files but also ORC or Avro depending on what suits you best.

The Apache Iceberg specification has three versions:

Analytics data tables (version 1)
When writing to the new version, the files affected are rewritten. This is an excellent choice for analytics where there are relatively many reads and fewer writes. You don't need to compact your data from time to time, as is the case in version 2.

Row-level tables (version 2)
The main difference from version 1 is support for deleted files. Now, when you remove records from the table, Apache Iceberg adds new deleted files that track the removed records' information. After many deletes, you might need to compact your data using compaction, which is the process of rewriting the data and creating a new version to make your data quicker to query.

Version 3
The third version includes geospatial types, row lineage tracking, binary deletion vectors, and more.

Last but not least is schema evolution. You can easily add columns and change data types, and Apache Iceberg maintains data integrity. Let's add a new column of type string to the points table:

```
ALTER TABLE sedona.spatial.points
ADD COLUMN type STRING
```

```
+---+-----------+-------------------+----+
| id|       geom|                 ts|type|
+---+-----------+-------------------+----+
|  1|POINT (1 0)|2025-07-20 15:30:00|NULL|
|  2|POINT (1 3)|2025-07-20 15:30:00|NULL|
|  3|POINT (4 8)|2025-07-20 15:30:00|NULL|
+---+-----------+-------------------+----+
```

The table has an additional field that is currently empty; if you would like to fill it, you can use many possible options, such as an INSERT OVERWRITE or MERGE INTO statement. MERGE INTO has the advantage of being flexible enough to handle deletes, updates, and inserts in a single powerful command. We will start with INSERT OVERWRITE. We have an additional table with categories, named categories, which has two fields: id (int) and type (string). The SQL query to update using INSERT OVERWRITE looks as follows:

```
INSERT OVERWRITE sedona.spatial.points
SELECT
    p.id,
    geom,
    ts,
    c.type
FROM sedona.spatial.points AS p
JOIN categories AS c ON c.id = p.id AND c.type IS NOT NULL
```

For the MERGE INTO statement, which we already mentioned is more flexible, we are using UPDATE SET, but we can also use DELETE or INSERT:

```
MERGE INTO sedona.spatial.points p
USING categories c
ON p.id = c.id
WHEN MATCHED AND c.type IS NOT NULL THEN UPDATE SET p.type = c.type
```

In all scenarios (INSERT OVERWRITE and MERGE), a new version of the table has been created.

Apache Iceberg has numerous exciting features, but unfortunately, this book is too brief to cover them all. We recommend further reading on the topic with the official documentation (*https://iceberg.apache.org*) and *Apache Iceberg: The Definitive Guide* by Tomer Shiran et al. (O'Reilly, 2024).

Iceberg Geospatial Types

Apache Iceberg supports both geometry and geography data types. The geometry type also keeps information about the CRS; if not specified, OGC:CRS84 is the default. Geography, in addition to CRS, stores information about the edge interpolation algorithm, which we previously covered in "Parquet Deep Dive" on page 231, including spherical, Vincenty, Thomas, Andoyer, and Karney. The CRS structure is the same as in the Apache Parquet type, `type:identifier`.

Both geometry and geography are stored using WKB serialization in the binary array. So we support all of the geometry and geography types specified in official OGC documents related to the WKB. The Apache Iceberg specification supports coordinate parts X, Y, Z, and M.

For the geography and geometry fields, Apache Iceberg stores metadata information about boundary boxes for each file. The boundary box is represented by the upper bounds and lower bounds for xmin, xmax, ymin, and ymax, which are also referred to as the westernmost, easternmost, southernmost, and northernmost points, respectively.

To create the Iceberg table with the geometry or geography type, you can reuse the following:

```
CREATE TABLE sedona.spatial.points (
    id bigint,
    geom geometry,
    ts timestamp)
USING iceberg
PARTITIONED BY (days(ts));
```

Or, if you want to specify the CRS:

```
CREATE TABLE sedona.spatial.points (
    id bigint,
    geom geometry('OGC:CRS84'),
    ts timestamp)
USING iceberg
PARTITIONED BY (days(ts));
```

Apache Iceberg tracks geospatial statistics at the file level, allowing you to improve even your geospatial Parquet files with better predicate pushdown efficiency. You can see the example file boundary boxes and query windows in Figure 8-5.

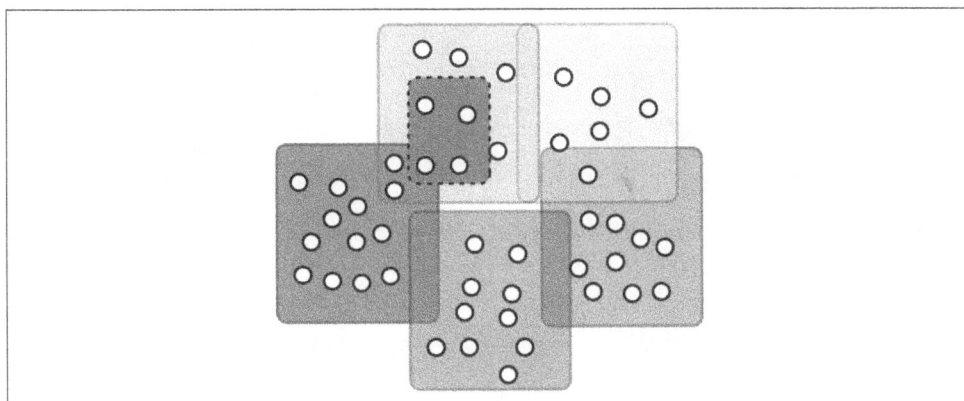

Figure 8-5. Apache Iceberg tracks the geospatial statistics of the Parquet files

Apache Iceberg, GeoParquet, and Apache Parquet greatly benefit from properly ordering and storing data in your data lake. We will cover how to efficiently store those files in Chapter 10, including indexing techniques such as Geohash or KDB trees to evenly distribute the data across the files.

Hands-On Use Case: Geospatial Data Lakehouse Deep Dive

In this section, we will focus on creating a geospatial data lakehouse architecture. We will use a medallion architecture to structure our lakehouse. Our gold layer is named prod, silver is named stg, and bronze is raw. We aim to create a Netherlands Road Risk Analysis table in production that might later be used for BI tools or further analytics. Only a subset of the code is printed in this book; however, the entire application code is also available on GitHub. We store the data on an S3-compatible MinIO bucket.

We will store all the data in the Apache Iceberg table data format. We will use the Apache Spark Airflow operator to schedule our data pipeline. After saving data to the staging layer, we will perform tests to make sure our data meets the standards we expect. When the data is neat and clean and passes all the tests, we will push it to the prod layer. The final step is simply rewriting the data, as we already know it is valid. As a result of Apache Iceberg properties, such as atomic swaps and versioning, the production data remains intact even during pipeline failures. Clients can continue to read the data without interruption. Moreover, we further mitigate this risk by rewriting the data and applying the index without applying major transformations, such as joins. More on optimizing Apache Iceberg with geospatial data can be found in Chapter 10. The simplified architecture is shown in Figure 8-6.

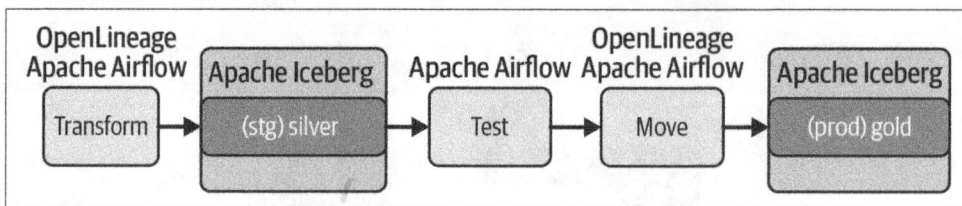

Figure 8-6. Example of a medallion architecture for a geospatial lakehouse

The final Apache Iceberg table we will create has a `risk_score` field, which is created based on the following features:

- Maximum speed for the road segment in the H3 cell
- Number of residential building centroids in the H3 cell
- Number of floods in the past 10, 50, and 100 years

We will use the Overture Maps Foundation dataset to get the maximum speed and number of buildings. For floods, we will use European Commission raster data.

The summary of the data we need is shown in the following bullet points:

- Overture Maps Foundation layers
  — Transportation
  — Buildings
- European Commission
  — River flood hazard maps

Our simplified version of the process is illustrated in Figure 8-7.

We will start by filtering the Overture administrative boundaries to the Netherlands, and we will store that shape in the Apache Iceberg format. This geometry will be used to filter the data to calculate other features.

To prepare our data, we will filter the transportation datasets by *motorway* class and the buildings by *residential* and *apartment* classes. For flood maps, the situation becomes more complicated. First, we will start by exploding the raster data into smaller tiles. We will keep the raster tiles relatively small to store the data directly in the Apache Iceberg table. To achieve this, we use the function:

```
RS_TileExplode(rast, 256, 256) AS (x, y, rast)
```

As a result, we get `rast` tiles that are no larger than 256 by 256 pixels. Our dataset consists of several bands, which are stored in separate GeoTIFF files. We also filter the data for floods in the past 10, 50, and 100 years.

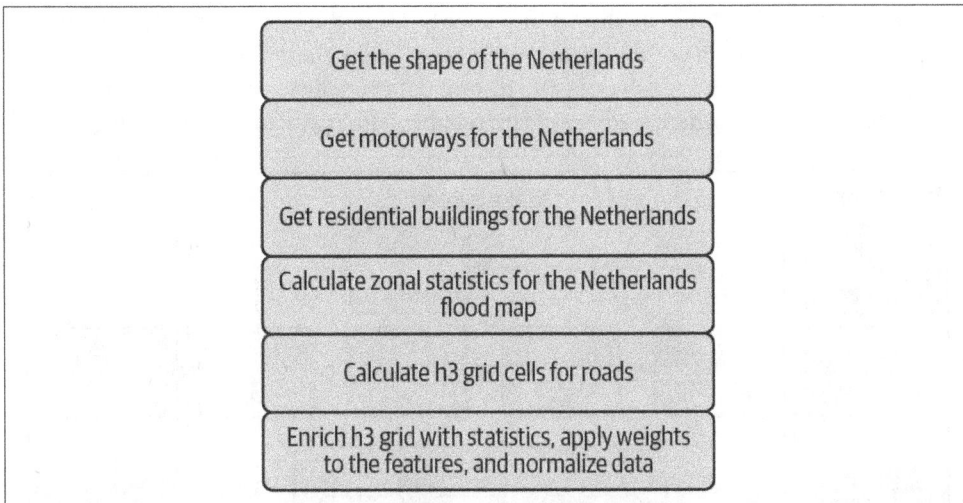

Figure 8-7. Process of creating a data product utilizing the geospatial lakehouse architecture

All three preprocessing steps are stored in separate tables. We also create separate Apache Airflow tasks for that. Although this requires additional effort, the maintainability it provides is critical for a production-ready application. Imagine you are running an Airflow job, but it fails in the middle. Now, you have to rerun everything from scratch. When cost reduction and delivery time are important, the initial effort of splitting the process into smaller pieces, as we are doing, is of great value. Breaking the process up into smaller steps is extremely helpful in meeting SLA requirements and reducing retries.

We will utilize Apache Sedona H3 functions to create grids over the Netherlands road network, based on which we will aggregate the values of each desired feature. To achieve this, we need a combination of two functions, ST_H3CellIDs and ST_H3ToGeom. We already used them in Chapter 3.

The last step is to use a spatial join to enrich H3 cells with the features and then normalize the data:

- For buildings, we take centroids and calculate the count in the grid cell.
- For the speed feature, we take the maximum speed for each of the cells.
- For floods, we use the RS_ZonalStats function to count the number of pixels with the flood inside the H3 index.

To make the features comparable, we normalize them using the formula (value – min /(max – min)) and apply weights based on their significance. Then, we add the values together to produce the final score.

Our final Airflow Dag looks as shown in Figure 8-8. On the left, you can see the bronze layer where our raw data comes from, and in the middle, there is all the processing and transformation in the stage/silver layer. In our data pipeline, prod/gold (right side of the figure) is the place where we have clean, reliable data ready to be consumed.

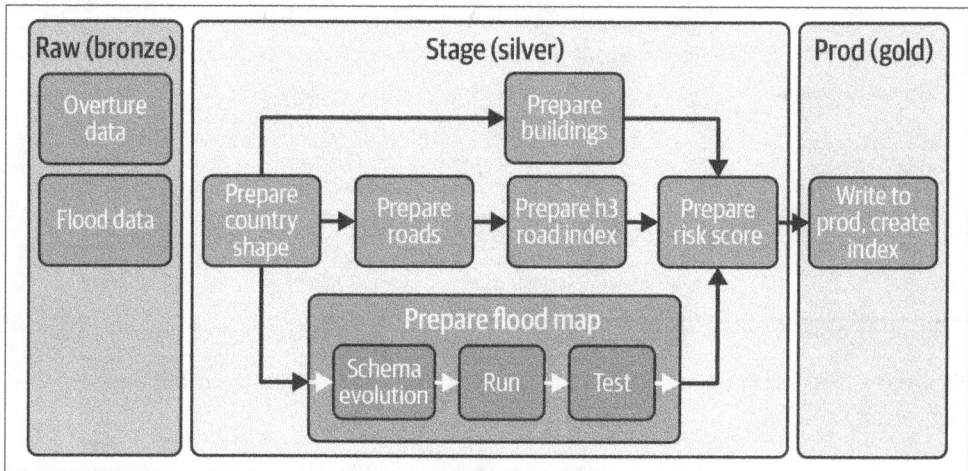

Figure 8-8. Visualization of the data pipeline

Apache Airflow exposes a feature named task group, which allows us to group similar tasks into one group. In our data lakehouse, it is beneficial to group, create a table, run the code, and then run tests.

Each task group consists of the following steps:

- Schema definition query (DDL and evolution). We use the `SparkSqlOperator`.
- A task that creates the Apache Iceberg table. We use the `SparkSubmitOperator`.
- A test to run against the created table. We use the `SparkSubmitOperator`.

Apache Iceberg provides resilience to your data pipelines, enabling high data availability and consistency. To achieve this, we run tests after key steps. Data exposed to consumers is only rewritten at the end from the staging table without major transformations, using techniques to store the data in Apache Iceberg format efficiently. You can find more on that in Chapter 10.

We extend each task in the Apache Airflow pipeline with the OpenLineage export to the external tool, which in our case is Marquez. This can help you understand your data, starting with the schema, column-level lineage, and integration with other systems, among other aspects.

Our table is ready for visualization and analytics. Now, you can use the benefits of Apache Iceberg, like geospatial predicate pushdown and data skipping.

Summary

The data lakehouse architecture improves the data lake by adding resilience to data pipelines. By combining Apache Parquet with Apache Iceberg's geospatial capabilities, you can create reliable, efficient, and maintainable spatial data pipelines. In this chapter, we covered a lot. We began with the data lakehouse architecture, then proceeded to a detailed explanation of Apache Parquet, including spatial types and GeoParquet. We then transitioned to Apache Iceberg table format, highlighting its advantages and explaining key topics, including schema evolution, ACID properties, time travel, and dynamic partitioning. In the previous section, we leveraged the knowledge we gathered to create a spatial data lakehouse based on Apache Sedona, Apache Iceberg, Apache Airflow, and OpenLineage.

Apache Sedona revolutionizes geospatial data analytics and pushes forward to make sure that spatial data is not a second-class citizen in the most powerful tools used for analytics and data processing. Many examples prove this, but the most recent is the adoption of geospatial datatypes for Apache Iceberg and Apache Parquet, as well as the quick adoption of GeoParquet, among others.

## CHAPTER 9

Using Apache Sedona with Cloud Data Providers

You can use Apache Sedona with many software-as-a-service (SaaS) and platform-as-a-service (PaaS) products from different cloud providers. In this chapter, we focus on integrating Sedona with the most common providers, including Databricks, AWS EMR and Glue, Microsoft Fabric, GCP Dataproc, and Wherobots Cloud. This chapter focuses on how to install and use Apache Sedona with different systems, but we can divide them into three groups based on the main system used:

- Apache Spark
- Apache Flink
- Snowflake (SedonaSnow)

We have covered Apache Sedona Spark from the ground up during this book, so for Apache Spark–based products, we focus primarily on installation. We also provide some examples and feature comparisons for SedonaSnow and Wherobots. If you use a system based on Apache Spark or Flink and can't find the installation process, please review the official Apache Sedona documentation. If the installation process is still missing in the official documentation, you can create an issue on the Apache Sedona repository or follow your system's official documentation.

Prerequisites

The only constant is change. Every system evolves over time. To make sure you are using the same version as we are, we use the following versions for the examples in this chapter:

- Apache Spark 3.5.x
- Scala 2.12
- Python 3.11
- Apache Sedona 1.8.0
- GeoTools 33.1
- Apache Flink 1.19.1
- Databricks runtime 16.4 LTS

If you haven't already, you need to install Apache Sedona on the Spark cluster. Then, add two jar files to your Apache Spark application. The first jar file contains all the geospatial extension logic provided to Apache Spark, such as KNN, spatial partitioning, GeoParquet reader, etc.:

```
org.apache.sedona:sedona-spark-shaded-{SPARK_V}_{SCALA_V}:jar:{SEDONA_V}
```

- SPARK_V is the `major.minor` version of Spark you are using, for example, 3.5.
- SCALA_V is the `major.minor` version of Scala you use, for example, 2.12.
- SEDONA_V is the `major.minor.patch` version of Sedona you use, for example, 1.8.0.

So, the jar file coordinates may look like the following for Spark 3.5, Scala 2.12, and Sedona 1.8.0:

```
org.apache.sedona:sedona-spark-shaded-3.5_2.12:jar:1.8.0
```

Apache Sedona uses GeoTools to provide operations on geometries, like the `inter sects` algorithm. Due to licensing reasons, we can't include it directly in the source code. Also, Apache Sedona needs a modified version of geotools, and that's why it's being kept in a separate Maven artifact than the official geotools. The jar that you need to provide in addition is:

```
org.datasyslab:geotools-wrapper:jar:{SEDONA_V}-{GEOTOOLS_V}
```

- SEDONA_V is the `major.minor.patch` version of Sedona you use, for example, 1.8.0.
- GEOTOOLS_V is the `major.minor` version of GeoTools used.

An example of jar coordinates for Apache Sedona 1.8.0 and GeoTools might look as follows:

```
org.datasyslab:geotools-wrapper:jar:1.8.0-33.1
```

When you add all the libraries, please ensure the Python library version matches the `geotools-wrapper` and `sedona-spark-shaded` jars. For Apache applications, we will call them `sedona-spark-shaded` and `geotools-wrapper`. And for Apache Flink applications, we have `flink-shaded`. Another key factor is matching the `SPARK_V` version and `SCALA_V` version with your Apache Spark installation.

You also need to install the apache-sedona PyPI package for the Python application. Each system, like Databricks and Google DataProc, has a different way of doing that; some use conda or pip.

Once your Apache Spark cluster has all the jar files needed and the Python interpreter has Apache Sedona installed, you must register all the additional types, functions, and optimizations. You can achieve that in two ways:

- Using `SedonaContext`
- Providing Sedona extensions to your Apache Spark application via Apache Spark config parameters:

```
spark.sql.extensions -> org.apache.sedona.sql.SedonaSqlExtensions
spark.serializer -> org.apache.spark.serializer.KryoSerializer
spark.kryo.registrator -> org.apache.sedona.core.serde.SedonaKryoRegistrator
```

Some Apache Spark SaaS and PaaS products create an Apache Spark session for you. In those cases, `SedonaContext` won't work; you will need to provide the extension parameters.

To add Apache Sedona to Flink you need to provide the `flink-shaded` jar:

```
org.apache.sedona:sedona-flink-shaded_{SCALA_V}:jar:{SEDONA_V}
```

Currently, Apache Sedona doesn't support version-specific jars for Apache Flink. Sedona uses Apache Flink version 1.19.1, and it only uses basic functionality, so it will likely be compatible with later Apache Flink versions.

Now that you've installed the prerequisites, let's dive into using Sedona Spark, SedonaSnow, and Sedona Flink with the major cloud providers.

Sedona Spark

Apache Sedona initially supported only Apache Spark, which resulted in the most mature support for this system. There are many Apache Spark providers where you can use Apache Sedona. In the book, we will cover:

- Databricks
- AWS EMR
- AWS Glue
- Microsoft Fabric
- GCP Dataproc

Databricks

Databricks is a company founded by the creators of Apache Spark. The Databricks platform is highly extensible and customizable. Since its release, many community efforts have been made to provide missing functionalities like geospatial or graph analytics. Apache Sedona is not the first and only solution for unlocking geospatial data processing in the Apache Spark environment; there is also Magellan, GeoMesa, or, recently, Databricks' Mosaic and spatial SQL in Databricks. Apache Sedona was initially created on top of Apache Spark, so performance is optimized in the Databricks environment.

Databricks offers several editions, which can be grouped into two tiers: the free tier (Community Edition) and the paid tier (Enterprise Edition, etc.). Each tier has distinct installation procedures for Apache Sedona. In this chapter, we focus on the enterprise version of Databricks.

The installation process for the paid tier consists of the following four steps:

1. *Download Apache Sedona jars.*
   First, download Apache Sedona jars to the DBFS directory (`sedona-spark-shaded` and `geotools-wrapper`).

2. *Create an `init` script.*
   Those jars need to be placed in */databricks/jars*. Creating the *init.sh* script is essential before creating the cluster; you can find it in the official Apache Sedona docs (*https://oreil.ly/GN9gj*).

3. *Set up the cluster configuration.*
   To use those jars in the Databricks cluster, the following Spark SQL options have to be applied (Cluster → Edit → Configuration → Advanced options → Spark); you need to paste the following Spark config properties:

```
spark.sql.extensions
org.apache.sedona.sql.SedonaSqlExtensions

spark.serializer
org.apache.spark.serializer.KryoSerializer

spark.kryo.registrator
org.apache.sedona.core.serde.SedonaKryoRegistrator
```

The `init` script must be included in the Spark cluster configuration before creating a new cluster (Cluster → Edit → Configuration → Advanced options → Init Scripts).

To enable Python, you do not need to configure the cluster in any additional way. You only need to install the required Python libraries: `apache-sedona` and the optional `geopandas`, `keplergl`, and `pydeck`.

4. *Verify the installation.*

To verify installation, you can try to use any of the Apache Sedona spatial functions, like the following:

```
spark.sql("SELECT ST_Point(21, 52)").show()
```

As you followed the installation instructions, you might have noticed that we didn't create the `SedonaContext` using the `SedonaRegistrator.registerAll(spark)` function. `SedonaSqlExtensions` automatically injects the additional Apache Sedona optimizers, functions, and data sources we passed to the `spark.sql.extensions` cluster parameter.

AWS EMR

Elastic MapReduce (EMR) is an ecosystem in AWS that allows users to efficiently run and scale Apache Spark, Hive, Presto, and other big data workloads.

When creating the EMR cluster, you must follow two steps to install Apache Sedona:

1. Add a bootstrap step for downloading and installing the packages (jar files, Python library).
2. Add a software configuration script.

The *init.sh* script in the bootstrap step needs to be placed into an S3 bucket to which EMR has access. The script might look as follows:

```
#!/bin/bash
# EMR clusters only have ephemeral local storage.
# It does not matter where we store the jars.
sudo mkdir /jars

# Download Sedona jar
```

```
sudo curl -o /jars/sedona-spark-shaded-3.5_2.12-1.8.0.jar \
  "https://repo1.maven.org/maven2/org/apache/sedona/
    sedona-spark-shaded-3.5_2.12/1.8.0/sedona-spark-shaded-3.5_2.12-1.8.0.jar"

# Download GeoTools jar
sudo curl -o /jars/geotools-wrapper-1.8.0-33.1.jar \
  "https://repo1.maven.org/maven2/org/datasyslab/geotools-wrapper/1.8.0-33.1/
    geotools-wrapper-1.8.0-33.1.jar"

# Install necessary python libraries
sudo python3 -m pip install apache-sedona==1.8.0 … other libraries you need
```

You need to provide the Spark config for the software configuration, which will extend the Apache Spark application on EMR. The properties you need to add to the configuration are as follows:

```
[
  {
    "Classification":"spark-defaults",
    "Properties":{
      "spark.jars": "sedona_location,geo_tools_location",
      "spark.serializer": "org.apache.spark.serializer.KryoSerializer",
      "spark.kryo.registrator": "kryo", ❶
      "spark.sql.extensions": "extensions" ❷
      }
  }
]
```

❶ Tells Spark to use an implementation of the SedonaKryoRegistrator.

❷ Sedona can be registered using the SedonaContext class or via the extensions. To enable it via extensions, use extensions like:

```
org.apache.sedona.sql.SedonaSqlExtensions
```

You can open a Jupyter Notebook on EMR and safely type:

```
sedona.sql('SELECT ST_POINT(21, 52) AS geom').\
    printSchema()
```

You can also run a new step, and Apache Sedona is available on your EMR cluster. To do so, click "step" in the UI or run the following new Spark step command:

```
aws emr add-steps --cluster-id your_cluster_id \ ❶
  --steps Type=Spark,Name="Apache Sedona",ActionOnFailure=CANCEL_AND_WAIT, \ ❷
Args=[--deploy-mode,cluster,--master,yarn,s3://${bucketName}/emr_app.py]
```

❶ The cluster-id is the identifier of the EMR cluster.

❷ --steps defines the step for the EMR cluster. Type=Spark tells EMR this is a Spark job. We then name the step Apache Sedona. On failure, we don't remove the cluster. We also pass additional variables like deploy mode (cluster[1]) and Apache Spark driver program (scheduler services like yarn or Kubernetes). Last, we pass the location of the script on the S3 bucket.

AWS Glue

Glue is an AWS data integration tool that helps you process, manage, and discover data from multiple sources. You can use Apache Sedona in Glue in two services:

- ETL jobs
- Notebooks

To run ETL jobs, you must add Apache Sedona artifacts to your job in the Advanced properties section when creating an ETL job:

- In the *job parameters* add `--additional-python-modules` with the value `apache-sedona==1.8.0`.
- In the *dependent jars path*, you must pass the comma-separated jar files from the S3 location. These are the same jar files that you downloaded in the EMR bootstrap script, `geotools-wrapper` and `sedona-spark-shaded`.

It gets trickier with notebooks. If you use the default notebook example, you must navigate and find the first cell with code similar to this:

```
%idle_timeout 2880
%glue_version 4.0
```

Next, add the Apache Sedona jar files from the S3 bucket and the Apache Sedona Python package:

```
%extra_jars sedona-spark-shaded, geotools-wrapper
%additional_python_modules apache-sedona==1.8.0
```

`sedona-spark-shaded` and `geotools-wrapper` are the full S3 paths to the jar files. So `geotools-wrapper` is:

```
s3://your_bucket/geotools-wrapper-1.8.0-33.1.jar
```

Then, run the default Glue code as follows:

```
from pyspark.context import SparkContext
from awsglue.context import GlueContext
from awsglue.job import Job

sc = SparkContext.getOrCreate()
```

---

1 For more information, see the Apache Spark official documentation (*https://oreil.ly/lTmoA*).

```
glueContext = GlueContext(sc)
spark = glueContext.spark_session
job = Job(glueContext)
```

Now you can register the Apache Sedona extension:

```
from sedona.spark import *

sedona = SedonaContext.create(spark)
```

You can run code that triggers Apache Sedona spatial functions to validate if it works:

```
sedona.sql("SELECT ST_POINT(1., 2.) as geom").show()
```

Microsoft Fabric

Microsoft Fabric is an end-to-end data analytics platform hosted on Azure that combines various Azure tools and services under a unified umbrella. It unifies data movement, processing, ingestion, transformation, real-time event routing, and report building. The services Microsoft Fabric provides are:

- Data engineering
- Data factory
- Data science
- Real-time intelligence
- Data warehouse
- Databases

You can install Apache Sedona in the data engineering service in four steps:

1. Create a data engineering environment with the desired Apache Spark version. Let's name it ApacheSedona.
2. Set up the environment.
   - Go to the Environment page, click the Home tab, and select the appropriate version of Apache Spark. Remember the version as you need it to install the correct version of Apache Sedona.
   - On the Environment page, click Public Libraries and provide apache-sedona. Ensure the installed PyPI package is the same version as the jar files you later included in the Apache Spark cluster.
   - Add the Spark properties to your cluster in the Spark properties tab.
     ```
     spark.sql.extensions:
     org.apache.sedona.sql.SedonaSqlExtensions

     spark.serializer: org.apache.spark.serializer.KryoSerializer
     spark.kryo.registrator: org.apache.sedona.core.serde.SedonaKryoRegistrator
     ```
   - This will enable Apache Sedona extensions, optimizations, and data types.
   - Click the Save and then Publish buttons to save and publish the environment. The publishing process will take about 10 minutes.

3. Provide jars for the notebook.

- Find the link to the Apache Sedona jar files needed for `geotools-wrapper` and `sedona-spark-shaded` from Apache Spark. Ensure your cluster's Spark and Apache Sedona Python versions are correct.

- You can install the jars in the notebook by running the following code. Replace the jars with the download links of the two jars we mentioned:

```
%%configure -f
{
    "jars": ["geotools-wrapper", "sedona-spark-shaded"]
}
```

- `sedona-spark-shaded` and `geotools-wrapper` are full HTTP paths to the Maven jar files. So, `sedona-spark-shaded` might be as follows:

```
https://repo1.maven.org/maven2/org/apache/sedona/
    sedona-spark-shaded-3.5_2.12/1.8.0/
    sedona-spark-shaded-3.5_2.12-1.8.0.jar
```

4. Verify the installation.

- To verify the correctness of the installation, run the following code in the notebook:

```
from sedona.spark import *

sedona = SedonaContext.create(spark)

sedona.sql("SELECT ST_GeomFromEWKT('POINT(12.49237 41.89017)')").show()
```

GCP Dataproc

Dataproc is a managed Apache Spark and Apache Hadoop service. It's a good choice when you migrate an on-premise Hadoop ecosystem to the Google Cloud Platform. You can run Apache Spark and Apache Sedona jobs on Dataproc. If you are unfamiliar with Dataproc and want to learn about it, you can use the free tier account in the GCP, which grants you $300 for 90 days. For the installation process, please follow the official documentation (*https://oreil.ly/L2May*).

You can install Apache Sedona in the Dataproc cluster in multiple ways:

1. An `init` script, which downloads the jar files and installs Apache Sedona Python on each node

2. Adding property flags to the create cluster command

3. Creating your own Docker image

4. Copying the artifacts from the bucket

Following the first method, the `init` script might look as follows. If you are using Dataproc for the first time, you might need to add access to the internet from your cluster (see the official documentation):

```bash
#!/bin/bash
set -e

#Download jar files and put them in the Spark jars directory
sudo curl \
  -o /usr/lib/spark/jars/sedona-spark-shaded-3.5_2.12-1.8.0.jar \
  "sedona_artifact_location"

sudo curl \
  -o /usr/lib/spark/jars/geotools-wrapper-1.8.0-33.1.jar \
  "geotools_artifact_location"

#Install necessary python libraries
pip install apache-sedona==1.8.0
```

Another way to install Apache Sedona in the Dataproc cluster is by using the additional properties flag:

```
-properties='^#^dataproc:pip.packages=apache-sedona==1.8.0'
```

Or you can use conda:

```
--properties='^#^dataproc:conda.packages=apache-sedona'
```

However, this approach still requires provisioning the jar files. You can also add the `init` script that downloads the Apache Sedona jar files. These methods, as mentioned earlier, require external traffic to be turned on.

To create your own Dataproc image, please follow the official GCP docs (*https://oreil.ly/DVmZ1*). Creating the image may take some time. You can reuse the `init` script for the `--customization-script`. Remember that the `pip` installed in the customization script might not install the packages into a directory used in the cluster. For image *2.2-ubuntu22*, we had to find which Python version was used in the cluster VM. Creating an image doesn't require access to the public internet so it might be a good approach from a security perspective.

After adjusting where we install Apache Sedona Python, use the following command:

```
/opt/conda/miniconda3/bin/python -m pip install apache-sedona==1.8.0
```

You can copy and install the artifacts from the GCS bucket, but the previous three approaches are more convenient.

For DataProc Serverless, we recommend following the official guidelines and creating a Docker image with Apache Sedona Python installed and the Apache Sedona jar files downloaded and copied to *ENV SPARK_EXTRA_JARS_DIR=/opt/spark/jars/* (see the GCP documentation (*https://oreil.ly/DVmZ1*)). To install Apache Sedona Python, add an apache-sedona entry in the Docker image when the Python packages, like pandas and Arrow, are installed.

Wherobots Cloud

Wherobots is the company founded by the creators of Apache Sedona. Apache Sedona is installed on Wherobots. This section will cover how to communicate with the platform so that you can integrate it with your existing data stack. We will use the community version of Wherobots Cloud for the following examples. You can communicate with the platform in three ways.

> To obtain a Wherobots API key, go to the account settings and select the API Keys tab. You can navigate to the settings by clicking on your account avatar in the bottom left corner. Then click on the button titled "Create New Key." Type the key's name and select the expiration date for the newly created key.

Notebook
> The Wherobots platform console UI allows you to start a notebook environment, which is great for collaboration and exploratory analysis. You can add Python dependencies from the PyPI repositories or a file.

SQL API
> This is a general-purpose way to integrate your data pipelines with Wherobots Cloud. You can use the Python DB-API driver, Harlequin-wherobots SQL IDE for your terminal, JDBC driver, or even the Wherobots SQL Driver TypeScript SDK. You can use the following code to interact with the platform using Python. To install the Wherobots Python driver API, type "pip install wherobots-python-dbapi" in the command line:

```
from wherobots.db import connect
from wherobots.db.region import Region
from wherobots.db.runtime import Runtime

api_key = '...'
host = 'api.cloud.wherobots.com'
sql_query = """
    SELECT *
    FROM wherobots_open_data.overture.places_place
    LIMIT 10
"""

with connect(
    host=host,
    api_key=api_key,
    runtime=Runtime.SEDONA,
    region=Region.AWS_US_WEST_2
```

```
    ) as conn:
        curr = conn.cursor()
        curr.execute(sql_query)
        results = curr.fetchall()
```

As a result, you get a pandas DataFrame. The first query may take longer as it's creating a WherobotsDB instance. When using the community version of Wherobots, turn off any notebook instances before you run the code, as you may hit the quota limit.

Wherobots Airflow operators

We covered the Airflow operator in Chapter 6. Airflow is the most mature and popular task scheduler, making it an excellent fit for automating your spatial data pipelines.

We used the SQL API for the examples of Chapter 6 (data schedulers). In this chapter we'll focus on the collaborative experience you get with notebooks.

Let's create and visualize a spatial application using the Apache Sedona Kepler package. We will take the buildings dataset from the Overture Maps dataset, which is pre-loaded in Wherobots Cloud. Let's assume that one of the partitions we are processing works slower than the rest. We were able to track that the partition is in Sydney. We suspect that we have errors in the dataset so we will filter buildings to Sydney and filter to the ones with more than 30 vertices.

In the Jupyter environment, you can create an Apache Sedona application in Python or Scala. You can access the terminal to run `spark-submit` from the notebook instance or the Apache Spark shell interactive console.

Wherobots notebooks use a custom version of the JupyterLab ecosystem. Once you log in, you can see a few plugins installed, like `jupyter-leaflet`, `keplergl-jupyter`, and `bqplot`.

Now, let's write some code. We chose the Python kernel for the Jupyter Notebook. The Apache Sedona context isn't created automatically. You can simply use the following code in the notebook to make one:

```
from sedona.spark import SedonaContext

config = SedonaContext \
    .builder() \
    .appName('WherobotsExample') \
    .getOrCreate()

sedona = SedonaContext.create(config)
```

Let's load the building dataset from the Overture Maps Foundation (*https://oreil.ly/ JwnqG*) and filter it to the Sydney boundary box:

```
sydney_wkt = "POLYGON(...)"#
schema = "overture_maps_foundation"
catalog = "wherobots_open_data"

buildings = sedona.sql(
    f"""
        SELECT *
        FROM {catalog}.{schema}.buildings_building
        WHERE ST_Intersects(geometry, ST_GeomFromText("{sydney_wkt}"))
    """
)
```

Now let's use the `ST_NPoints` function to filter the buildings to more complex ones with more than 30 vertices in the building polygon:

```
complex_buildings = buildings \
    .selectExpr("id", "class", "geometry") \
    .where("ST_NPoints(geometry) > 30")
```

We also select `id`, `class`, and `geometry`, which we will use later for visualization:

```
from sedona.spark import SedonaKepler
SedonaKepler.create_map(complex_buildings)
```

Now, show me the map (Figure 9-1)!

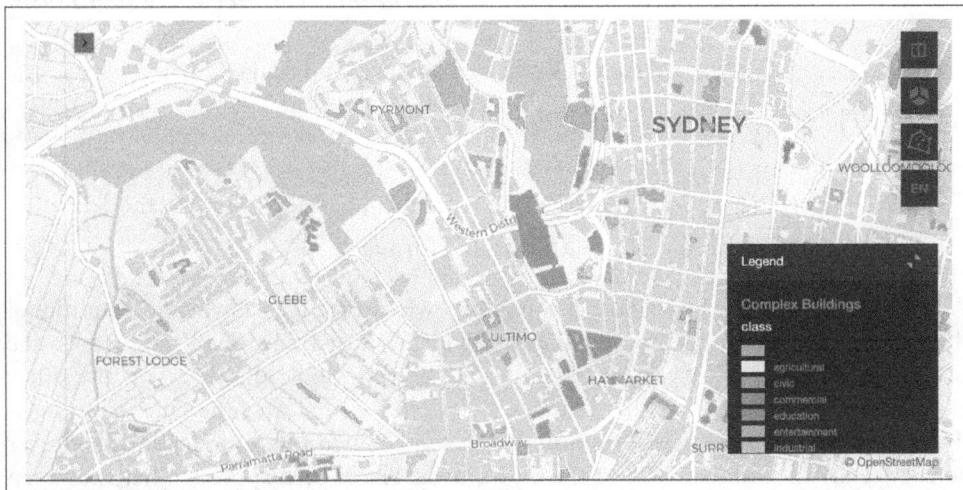

Figure 9-1. Visualization of complex buildings from Overture Maps, categorized by class

We can't see anything suspicious. Let's show the maximum value; it's 456, and the number of buildings with over 30 vertices is only 2,494, so it's not the reason for our slower ETL job. There is no strict threshold for a number of vertices, but getting around a hundred thousand points for geometry will slow down the job and cause a data skew problem. It was an example, but you can see how easy exploratory analysis is in the Wherobots notebook environment.

The code looks simple, and that's the aim of Wherobots: to simplify complex geospatial processing. When we loaded our data, we used spatial pruning and SQL ST functions, and in the end, we visualized the data in around 20 lines of code.

SedonaSnow in Snowflake

Snowflake is a rich and robust product with many features regarding data storage, processing, compliance, and AI. Plenty of suitable materials are available to learn about the platform; please review other sources to familiarize yourself with this solution. We focus on geospatial support in Snowflake and provide a brief introduction to the Snowflake platform.

Snowflake is a data platform as a self-managed service. It means there is no hardware to select, install, or configure. You don't have to manage any platform like with Hadoop; Snowflake handles all the maintenance, management, and upgrades.

Snowflake offers a comprehensive ecosystem replete with a myriad of features:

- Built-in data governance
- Feature-rich SQL: transactions, Iceberg tables, geospatial support, stored procedures, window functions, and more
- Language integrations: APIs for Python, SQL, Java, and Scala
- Tool integrations: Spark connector
- Data sharing
- LLM models to ease your analytics and a platform to build your ML models
- Data integration from many platforms and formats

When we look into the Snowflake architecture, we can see it as a hybrid of traditional shared-disk and share-nothing databases. Like the shared-disk databases, it has one centralized data repository from which compute nodes take the data. On the other hand, like in the shared-nothing databases, Snowflake processes the data using massively parallel processing (MPP) compute clusters. All compute nodes in the cluster persist locally in some amount of the entire data. The hybrid approach helps to keep the simplicity of managing the data (shared-disk) with excellent scaling capabilities and performance (shared-nothing).

Snowflake natively supports only geometry and geography data types for vector data. The raster data type is unavailable natively or via the Apache Sedona extension. Snowflake supports a limited number of ST functions without 3D support; it has around one hundred ST functions, and around half support only the geography data type.

To load the geospatial data to Snowflake, you must store the geometry/geography in the proper data format, like WKB, WKT, or GeoJSON. Snowflake doesn't support natively loading GeoParquet or any popular spatial format. It's clear that geospatial data may not be Snowflake's primary focus. That's why you need SedonaSnow, with over two hundred efficient functions at your disposal.

You can install the SedonaSnow extension on Snowflake in two ways: manually or using the Snowflake marketplace offering provided by Wherobots. For manual installation, please follow the official documentation (*https://oreil.ly/uNggE*).

> When you install the Apache Sedona spatial extension in Snowflake, remember to keep the schema name for registered functions different from DEFAULT. You can use, for example, the schema name SEDONA to avoid spatial function name conflicts. Then, to call the Apache Sedona extension function, you can use syntax like SEDONA.*[ST_Function]*, where [ST_Function] is the name of the function. When you install it from the marketplace, the default name for the namespace where Apache Sedona ST functions is SEDONA.

The Snowflake API doesn't allow user-defined data types, unlike Apache Spark. There are two versions of the Apache Sedona UDF functions in Snowflake:

- Using EWKB as serialization
- Using the geometry/geography Snowflake data type, but with a slower GeoJSON serialization method

To create a SedonaSnow geometry object (EWKB serialization), you can use a constructor function like the following, which converts the WKT string to SedonaSnow geometry:

```
SELECT SEDONA.ST_GeomFromText('POINT(45.811357 6.967252)') AS geom
```

To create a Snowflake geometry type from SedonaSnow vector data, you can simply use the `to_geometry` function:

```
SELECT to_geometry(geom) FROM point;
```

You can use SedonaSnow geospatial functions interchangeably with Snowflake's built-in geospatial functions. You can combine SedonaSnow spatial functions with Snowflake's built-in functions in two ways. It depends on whether you operate on SedonaSnow EWKB-based or GeoJSON-based functions.

Sedona EWKB-Encoded Geometry Constructor Functions

In this scenario, you use SedonaSnow constructor functions like SEDONA.ST_Geom FromWKT to create geometry objects. To use Snowflake spatial functions, you must transform EWKB to the Snowflake geometry or geography data type. To cast it to a geometry data type, you can use the to_geometry function:

```
SELECT to_geometry(geom) FROM point;
```

To cast it to a geography data type, change to_geometry to to_geography:

```
SELECT to_geography(geom) FROM point;
```

To convert the Snowflake geometry or geography data type to the SedonaSnow EWKB-encoded geometry data type:

```
SELECT ST_AsEWKB(geom) AS geom FROM snowflake_point;
```

You won't lose the SRID information when you use any of these conversions between the SedonaSnow geometry and Snowflake geography/geometry types. Now, let's explore an example. We will create a SedonaSnow geometry based on the WKT string and auto-assign the 4326 SRID code to the geometry:

```
SELECT SEDONA.ST_GeomFromText(
    'POINT(-122.116188 37.507550)',
    4326
) as geom
```

The point geometry we created in the previous code snippet is stored in the table point_srid. When we call the SEDONA.ST_SRID function to get the SRID code, the value is still 4326. Next, we can transform it to the 3857 SRID, where the unit of measure is a meter. After the transformation, we apply the ST_Buffer function to create a 250-meter buffer:

```
SELECT
    SEDONA.ST_Buffer(
        SEDONA.ST_TRANSFORM(
            geom, 'epsg:4326', 'epsg:3857'
        ),
        250
    )
FROM point_srid
```

Despite many transformations, the SRID information has not been lost, and the SEDONA.ST_SRID function now returns 3857. When you apply the to_geometry function on the return from the previous code snippet, the ST_Srid functions still return the epsg:3857 code.

If you need to use multiple Sedona functions, this WKB serialization method is more efficient and might bring about a 2X performance improvement.

Snowflake also provides the possibility to define UDFs based on the internal geometry and geography objects (see the Snowflake documentation (*https://oreil.ly/S1L_P*)). The issue is that it exposes only GeoJSON objects, which are slow in decoding and encoding. Another disadvantage is that during those conversions, you will lose information about SRID:

```
-- losing SRID
SELECT
    SEDONA.ST_SRID(
        ST_GeomFromText('POINT(45.811357 6.967252)', 4326)
    ) AS geom

-- preserving SRID
SELECT SEDONA.ST_SRID(
    ST_ASEWKB(
        ST_GeomFromText('POINT(45.811357 6.967252)', 4326)
    )
) AS geom
```

Snowflake GeoJSON-Encoded Geometry Constructor Functions

Snowflake encodes geometry and geography data types as GeoJSON strings for UDFs. The GeoJSON standard doesn't keep the information about the CRS, as it's not designed to handle the serialization and deserialization of geospatial data. SedonaSnow also provides a version of ST functions that operate on the GeoJSON data type when you create the geometry or geography objects using Snowflake. You can use them without any transformations. SEDONA.ST_DumpPoints is a SedonaSnow function that does not exist in the Snowflake geospatial function catalog. ST_Dump Points creates a multipoint geometry from the linestring:

```
SELECT SEDONA.ST_DumpPoints(ST_GeomFromText('LINESTRING (0 0, 1 1, 1 0)'))
```

During installation, SedonaSnow creates two versions for each spatial function: one takes the EWKB as input and the second takes the GeoJSON input. That's why the previous example is valid, as SEDONA.ST_DumpPoints can accept different types of input parameters. It's more convenient not to use additional transformations like to_geometry or ST_AsEWKB, but you are losing the SRID code in the process, and the GeoJSON string processing is much slower than EWKB.

SedonaSnow is utilizing the user-defined table functions to provide you with more handy and powerful functions. For example, ST_Collect creates a geometry, multigeometry (multipoint, multipolygon, etc.), or geometry collection based on the geometries in the aggregation rows.

A user-defined table function (UDTF) is a UDF that can return zero or more rows for an input row with at least one column. Apache Sedona uses UDTFs to provide aggregation functions that operate on the whole table.

A UDTF can be accessed in the FROM clause of a query:

```
WITH PLACES AS (
    SELECT
        sedona.ST_GeomFromText('POINT (37.356569 -3.070110)') AS geom,
        'Africa' AS continent
    UNION
    SELECT
        sedona.ST_GeomFromText('POINT (25.853491 -17.924335)') AS geom,
        'Africa' AS continent
    UNION
    SELECT
        sedona.ST_GeomFromText('POINT (78.042126 27.174978)') AS geom,
        'Asia' AS continent

)
SELECT collection AS geom, continent
FROM PLACES,
TABLE(sedona.ST_Collect(PLACES.geom) OVER (PARTITION BY continent));
```

In the example, we create a table of locations of known tourist attractions in Africa and Asia. Then we aggregate it by continent (PARTITION BY continent), and based on the aggregated row groups, we apply the SEDONA.ST_Collect function. The result should look as follows:

geom	continent
MULTIPOINT ((37.356569 -3.07011), (25.853491 -17.924335))	Africa
MULTIPOINT ((78.042126 27.174978))	Asia

ST_Dump returns a new row for each geometry composing the multigeometry or geometry collection. We will reuse the table created by the example for ST_Collect:

```
SELECT m.geom, c.continent
FROM
    collected AS c,
    table(SEDONA.ST_Dump(geom) OVER (PARTITION BY continent)) AS m;
```

The result is the same as the input for the ST_Collect function example.

`ST_Union_Aggr` is an aggregation function that returns the union of all the polygons in the row group. We will use a table with the data shown in Figure 9-2.

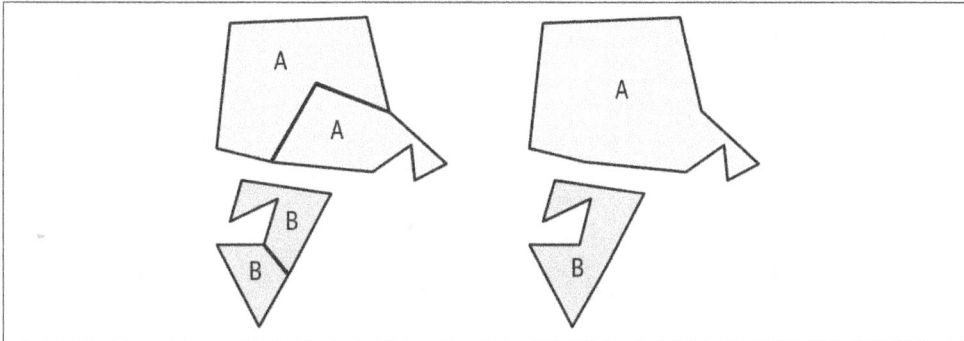

Figure 9-2. Left: the polygons with IDs A and B used for the `ST_Union_Aggr` function; right: the result of merging the polygons based on grouping by ID

The table has two fields: geom (EWKB) and id (A or B). The following code transforms the result from the left side of Figure 9-2 to the aggregation on the right side:

```
SELECT id, unioned
FROM polygons,
TABLE(SEDONA.ST_Union_Aggr(polygons.geom) OVER (PARTITION BY id));
```

You can follow the official SedonaSnow documentation (*https://oreil.ly/EDdfb*) to find more spatial SQL examples in Snowflake.

Spatial Joins

Spatial joins are critical to many geospatial applications that process vector data. Apache Sedona Spark optimizes many complex spatial queries like range and distance join queries out of the box. With SedonaSnow, you can write a query to perform a range join query:

```
SELECT *
FROM polygondf, pointdf
WHERE ST_Contains(polygondf.polygonshape,pointdf.pointshape)
```

You can also write a distance join query:

```
SELECT *
FROM pointdf1, pointdf2
WHERE ST_Distance(pointdf1.pointshape1,pointdf2.pointshape2) < 2
```

Executing the previous queries will yield valid results, though at the cost of increased processing time and resource consumption. Snowflake doesn't expose any API for optimizing operations between more than one table, so the spatial join queries (distance and range join) will utilize the Cartesian product, which is highly inefficient.

To improve the query time, use the optimized GeoJoin exposed by Snowflake's built-in geospatial functionality or write an S2, H3, or Geohash-based spatial join using SedonaSnow or Snowflake. You can read more about the optimizations in Chapter 10, which discusses optimizing Apache Sedona applications.

> SedonaSnow doesn't add the H3 functions, as the Snowflake API doesn't allow the inclusion of embedded C code in a UDF.

Sedona Flink (Ververica)

Apache Flink is a framework and engine for batch and stream data processing. Plenty of platforms allow you to run Apache Flink in a cloud environment. In this chapter, we stick to the platform created by the original creators of Apache Flink, Ververica.

To run Apache Sedona with Ververica, add the jar artifacts on the Ververica platform:

- `flink-shaded`
- `geotools-wrapper`

Then, in the deployment, reference them in the "Additional Dependencies" section so they are visible to your PyFlink application. Next, add your Python application and the Apache Sedona Flink Python library. To do that, in the "Python Libraries" section, type "apache-sedona".

To unlock spatial functions in your PyFlink application, register all the additional functions Apache Sedona provides using the `SedonaContext` object:

```
stream_env: StreamExecutionEnvironment ...
flink_settings: EnvironmentSettings ...

table_env = SedonaContext.create(stream_env, flink_settings)

buffer_table = table_env.sql_query(
    "SELECT ST_Buffer(ST_Point(1.0, 2.0), 1.0) AS buffer"
)
```

Summary

We discussed three major data processing engines that can be extended using Apache Sedona:

- Apache Spark
- Apache Flink
- Snowflake

Using different engines can result in significant differences and performance considerations. Apache Sedona initially supported only Apache Spark, which resulted in the most mature support for this system. We highly recommend using Apache Spark when you use Apache Sedona. Table 9-1 compares the significant Apache Sedona features available with the three data processing engines.

Table 9-1. Comparison of Apache Sedona features available with Spark, Flink, and Snowflake

	Apache Spark	Apache Flink	Sedona Snowflake
Spatial join	Optimized with spatial partitioning, spatial join including indexes H3, S2, Geohash	Using H3, Geohash, S2 indexes	Using Geohash, S2 indexes
Spatial formats	GeoParquet, spatial Parquet, Iceberg, OSM PBF, GeoPackage, shapefile	No	No
Spatial Apache Iceberg	Yes	No	No
GeoParquet	Yes	No	No
KNN	Yes, distributed KNN, including many to many	No	Nonoptimized
ST functions	Yes	Yes	Not all
H3 indexes	Yes	Yes	No (native Snowflake supports H3)
S2 indexes	Yes	Yes	Yes
Geohash indexes	Yes	Yes	Yes
Geostatistics	Yes	No	No
Raster format	Yes	No	No

We covered the majority of Apache Sedona features, so let's move to the next chapter, which focuses on how you can make the Apache Sedona application efficient. Chapter 10 focuses on optimizing your Apache Sedona code and data modeling to make your distributed spatial applications reliable, fast, and memory efficient.

## CHAPTER 10

Optimizing Apache Sedona Applications

Apache Sedona is a constantly evolving project; numerous improvements are underway, including Apache Iceberg geospatial data types, spatial Parquet, and GeoArrow integrations. It's good to understand which functionalities are recommended to make your application reliable, performant, faster, and more memory efficient. In this chapter, you will learn how to optimize your spatial join queries, accelerate your Apache Sedona Python application, and efficiently store data in Parquet and Apache Iceberg formats.

We will utilize publicly available data, primarily from the Overture Maps Foundation, and will randomly generate it using the Apache Sedona Spider dataset. All tests were performed on an Apple MacBook Pro with an M3 Pro processor (11 cores) and 36 GB of RAM. We prepared numerous examples in the Jupyter Notebook environment.

Optimizing the Apache Sedona Program

Apache Sedona heavily relies on partitioning and parallel data processing; the data must be serialized and transferred across the nodes of your Apache Spark cluster. For smaller datasets, this doesn't make much of a difference. Still, as the scale increases, the large number of columns in your query can negatively impact query performance, CPU usage, and memory usage, especially when you cache or store partial results on disk.

Select Only the Needed Columns

In multispatial join queries or spatial aggregations, it is best to retain only the necessary columns to optimize performance. Another advantage is that it is more reliable for applications if you, at the beginning, explicitly select only the columns needed; your application will fail fast when the expected data doesn't have the required columns with the expected column types. If you utilize `SELECT *` like expressions, you can end up with errors like:

- Caching a large amount of data, as you don't assert what you are taking
- Processing too much data
- Unpredictable processing of data, such as when data is partially valid, which may result in a partial outcome, with only a portion of the tables being properly saved

If you store data in Parquet, which is later used by a different process, ensure that you only save the data you truly need. If you're worried about future use cases, you can extend your schema later with the field you need. The smallest possible schema will expedite the process and reduce the space required in your data lakehouse.

Filter Early

If you load data only for a specific region, make sure that a spatial predicate like `ST_Within` or `ST_Intersects` is at the top of your query, not at the end of your transformation. The Apache Spark predicates pushdown mechanism is smart, but it may not continually optimize your query; that's why it's good to do it explicitly in your application. In the following example, we will use the Overture Maps Foundation buildings dataset for the state of California in the US. We also use the H3 grid for the same region on the ninth level. We will calculate the number of buildings by subtype in the H3 grid. In the first query, we will filter at the end, and in the second query, we will filter at the beginning.

`smaller_area` is part of the interpolated string in Python, and the WKT for it is:

```
POLYGON (
  (-121.86 37.30,
  -121.86 37.42,
  -121.98 37.42,
  -121.98 37.30,
  -121.86 37.30)
)
```

This query with late spatial filtering takes six times longer than the query with early filtering:

```
WITH spatial_join AS (
    SELECT
        b.geometry,
        h.geometry AS h3_geom,
        h.h3_id,
        b.subtype
    FROM buildings AS b
    JOIN h3_cells AS h ON ST_Intersects(b.geometry, h.geometry)
), aggregated AS (
    SELECT
```

```
        h3_id,
        subtype,
        FIRST(h3_geom) AS geometry,
        COUNT(*) AS count
    FROM spatial_join
    GROUP BY h3_id, subtype
)
SELECT
    *
FROM aggregated
WHERE ST_Contains(ST_GeomFromText('{smaller_area}'), geometry)
```

Next, we filter early, for tables, buildings, and H3 cells. We also use the intersects predicate for the buildings to include those that touch the H3 cells but are not contained within the smaller polygon area:

```
WITH h3_filtered AS (
    SELECT
        *
    FROM h3_cells
    WHERE ST_Contains(ST_GeomFromText('{smaller_area}'), geometry)
), buildings_filtered AS (
    SELECT
        *
    FROM buildings
    WHERE ST_Intersects(ST_GeomFromText('{smaller_area}'), geometry)
), spatial_join AS (
    SELECT
        b.geometry,
        h.geometry AS h3_geom,
        h.h3_id,
        b.subtype
    FROM buildings_filtered AS b
    JOIN h3_filtered AS h ON ST_Intersects(b.geometry, h.geometry)
)
    SELECT
        h3_id,
        subtype,
        FIRST(h3_geom) AS geometry,
        COUNT(*) AS count
    FROM spatial_join
    GROUP BY h3_id, subtype
```

Reduce the Number of Vertices

When you process polygon or linestring geometries that are complex, or you don't need an exact result, use the ST_Simplify or ST_SimplifyPreserveTopology functions to reduce the number of vertices in your query. When is the number of vertices too large? It depends on the specific use case, but if the data you are processing has tens of points representing a straight line, then it might be a good use case to utilize simplifying functions.

Limit Spheroid Distance Use in Joins

Unless it is necessary, avoid using the sphere distance function in the join condition and use planar distance in the CRS where your table is located. We will compare two simple queries: one that transforms the data to the metric CRS and uses planar distance, and another that uses the spherical distance in the ST_DWithin function. Let's start with one that transforms the CRSes:

```
WITH transformed AS (
    SELECT
        id,
        ST_Transform(geometry, 'EPSG:4326', 'EPSG:2229') AS geometry
    FROM buildings
)
SELECT
    b1.*,
    b2.*
FROM transformed AS b1
JOIN transformed AS b2 ON ST_DWithin(b1.geometry, b2.geometry, 500)
```

This query appears more complex than the one that follows, yet it takes around 12 minutes to complete. The following utilizes the spherical distance:

```
SELECT
    b1.*,
    b2.*
FROM buildings AS b1
JOIN buildings AS b2 ON ST_DWithin(b1.geometry, b2.geometry, 500, TRUE)
```

The query is more straightforward, but it takes *five hours* to complete.

Cache Reused DataFrames

When you reuse the same data multiple times in different query parts, consider utilizing the caching mechanism provided by Apache Spark, which can significantly enhance performance. If you don't have enough RAM, part of your intermediate result will be spilled to disk, which will slightly slow down the process. However, it might still significantly improve query performance, as you won't have to repeat the same process multiple times. Let's assume we have a complicated query like the following, which calculates the common water type within a 500m radius of the buildings dataset, which is filtered to a predefined smaller area.

We start by filtering buildings and properly transforming them to the metric CRS system:

```
SELECT
    id,
    ST_Buffer(
        ST_Transform(
            geometry,
```

```
            'EPSG:4326',
            'EPSG:2229'
        ),
        500
    ) AS geometry
FROM buildings
WHERE ST_Intersects(geometry, ST_GeomFromText('{smaller_area}'))
```

For water, we need to only transform to the common CRS. We can also use the previously mentioned tip and select the columns we will need in our processing:

```
SELECT
    ST_Transform(geometry,  'EPSG:4326', 'EPSG:2229') AS geometry,
    subtype
FROM water
```

One of many advantages of the Apache Sedona and Apache Spark ecosystems is how easily you can switch between Python and SQL code for improved readability, performance, and any other reason you may decide to mix SQL code with Python in the same application. For spatial joins, we will group the data by building an ID and water subtype and then find the most common occurrence using a window function written as a combination of Python and SQL code:

We will start by spatially joining buildings and water, then group by ID and water subtype:

```
buildings_water = buildings_spatially_filtered.alias("b") \
    .join(
        water_pretransformed.alias("w"),
        f.expr("ST_Intersects(w.geometry, b.geometry)")
    ) \
    .selectExpr(
        "b.id",
        "b.geometry AS b_geometry",
        "w.subtype"
    ) \
    .groupBy("id", "subtype") \
    .agg(
        f.expr("COUNT(*) AS count"),
        f.expr("FIRST(b_geometry) AS geometry")
    )
```

Here is the window expression:

```
most_common_water_type = buildings_water \
    withColumn("rank", f.expr("RANK() OVER (PARTITION BY id ORDER BY count)"))
```

We perform numerous complex computations, including spatial joins, grouping, and window functions. Based on the results, we enrich three additional tables—infrastructure, places, and segment—with the results from the previous query. Without caching, we would need to calculate the most_common_water_type three times! With caching, we can persist the partial result in RAM or on disk. Cache operations, similar to select, do not invoke an action in Apache Spark. This is essential because the first calculation will invoke the transformation to obtain the most_common_water_type table and store it in memory or on disk, eliminating the need for an additional step:

```
most_common_water_type.cache()

# computation below caches the most_common_water_type table
infrastructure.alias("i").join(
    most_common_water_type.alias("m"), f.expr("SPATIAL JOIN CONDITION")
).count()

places.alias("p").join(
    most_common_water_type.alias("m"), f.expr("SPATIAL JOIN CONDITION")
).count()

segment.alias("s").join(
    most_common_water_type.alias("m"), f.expr("SPATIAL JOIN CONDITION")
).count()
```

Please refer to the notebooks in the book's repository for the complete code example. With caching, we were able to reduce computation time by 25 percent. If you have a data pipeline with many steps, it's worth considering storing intermediate steps in tables, as it gives you the following advantages:

- Easier debugging, as you have partial results stored, which is helpful in complex data pipelines
- More reliable processing (cache might be overwhelming for the application if the data is enormous) and reduction of repeated computations
- Simpler retries when failure occurs, as you need to retry only failed steps, not the whole data pipeline

Modify the Partition Number for Join Operations

Manipulate the number of partitions for large datasets to calculate the result efficiently and without errors. To increase the parallelism of the spatial join operation, modify the Apache Sedona sedona.join.numpartition parameter in the configuration and set it to the desired value. The higher the value, the more spatial partitions will be created to run the spatial join operation. The default is –1, which means use the existing partitions, which in recent Spark versions (for example, 3.5) is driven by the Apache Spark adaptive query execution mechanism. See the Spark documentation (*https://oreil.ly/V1pAJ*) for more on tuning partitions.

Avoid Unnecessary Shuffling

Avoid shuffling if it's not necessary. Adding the additional repartition after each Data-Frame might cause more harm than good. If you want to bump the partition number in the spatial joins, please use the Apache Sedona config parameter `sedona.join.num partition`, like we mentioned in the preceding section.

Avoid Wide Operations

Avoid wide transformations and try to solve your problem by using narrow operations. In some scenarios, joining or grouping transformations can be replaced with a simple mapping operation. When your data is small, such as tens of thousands of records, this improvement for a typical dataset doesn't make a significant difference. However, with larger datasets, it reduces the memory footprint and the time required to obtain the result. Let's use the example of the dataset with the following schema:

```
root
 |-- id: string (nullable = true)
 |-- geometry: geometry (nullable = true)
 |-- neighbors: array (nullable = true)
 |    |-- element: struct (containsNull = true)
 |    |    |-- id: string (nullable = true)
 |    |    |-- geometry: geometry (nullable = true)
```

We have point locations from the Overture Maps Foundation aggregated so that each element in the neighbor's array is one of the five closest neighbors, excluding self. Our goal is to create a convex hull from the neighboring points. Apache Sedona exposes the `ST_ConvexHull` function, which takes the geometry type as input. We have a list of objects, and there is no matching function for the use case. We can use the `GroupBy` statement in conjunction with the `EXPLODE` function. This is an example of wide operation; we need to reshuffle our data by the ID key, which is a costly operation, especially for larger datasets:

```
SELECT
    id,
    ST_ConvexHull(
        ST_Union_Aggr(neighbor_geom)
    ) AS convex_hull
FROM (
    SELECT
        id,
        geometry,
        n.geometry AS neighbor_geom
    FROM places_neighbors
    LATERAL VIEW EXPLODE(neighbors) AS n
) AS r
GROUP BY r.id
```

When we used a dataset with 7 million rows, the processing of the query took, on average, two times slower than with the narrow operation:

```
SELECT
    id,
    ST_ConvexHull(
        ST_Union(
            Transform(neighbors, n->n.geometry)
        )
    ) AS convex_hull
FROM places_neighbors
```

Avoid Collecting Large Amounts of Data for Your Application Driver

Avoid the `collect` or `toPandas` function, which transfers all of the data from your worker nodes and moves it to the driver. This kills parallelization, may require a significant amount of memory, and can result in memory errors. Apache Sedona heavily utilizes distributed algorithms and is designed to run on multiple machines. When your data exceeds the size of your driver node, pulling the data to the driver node will cause your application to crash. When data isn't extensive and you need to use a GeoPandas algorithm, use the GeoArrow conversion. Please follow the latter part of this chapter, which discusses transferring a spatial DataFrame between the Python ecosystem and Apache Sedona's internal format.

Use Window Functions Over GROUP BY and JOIN

Use window functions instead of `JOIN` and `GROUP BY`. For example, we will use the fake property listing data. The dataset has four columns: ID, geometry, price, and listing date. Our processing needs the most recent listings. We can start by using the `GROUP BY` statement to select the largest date. We need an additional join to retrieve the matching price as in `GROUP BY`, we can't preserve the current row for the maximum date:

```
SELECT
    o.*
FROM (
    SELECT
        id,
        max(date) AS date
    FROM observations
    GROUP BY id
) AS r
JOIN observations AS o ON o.id = r.id AND o.date = r.date
```

In the preceding query, we need to aggregate the data by ID and then rejoin it to obtain the record with the maximum date for each ID. We need to shuffle the data on grouping and when performing the `JOIN`. Another disadvantage is that we have two conditions for joining. The alternative approach is using a window function, called `row_number`:

```
SELECT
    id,
    geometry,
    price,
    date
FROM (
    SELECT
        *,
        row_number() OVER (PARTITION BY id ORDER BY date DESC) AS rank
    FROM observations
) AS r
WHERE rank = 1
```

The query needs to shuffle the data only once; then, we have a narrow operation, filtering. In the query, we partition by ID and order by date in descending order, so we retrieve the most recent one. The last part is to filter the rank, which equals 1. On average, for sample data, when using the window function we improved the time by 40%.

Use Native Apache Sedona Methods

Use native functions and methods, which are available out of the box and are optimized and, most of the time, faster than UDFs in Python. We provide benchmarks on real data in "Apache Sedona Python" on page 295.

Use Apache Sedona Serializers

Apache Sedona implements custom serializers to reduce the memory footprint of your spatial application. If you follow the recommended approach for creating a SedonaContext, as shown in the following code, spark.kryo.registrator and spark.serializer are assigned to KryoSerializer and SedonaKryoRegistrator, respectively:

```
from sedona.spark import SedonaContext

sedona_spark = "org.apache.sedona:sedona-spark-3.5_2.12:1.8.0"
geotools = "org.datasyslab:geotools-wrapper:1.8.0-33.1"

config = SedonaContext.builder() \
    .config("spark.jars.packages", f"{sedona_spark},{geotools}")

sedona = SedonaContext.create(config.getOrCreate())
```

Avoiding Skew Joins

In distributed analytical systems, skew joins can cause your job to run slower, take more memory, and block the usage of your resources for other applications. It's easy to say to avoid skew joins, but the reality is that it's impossible to avoid them. Apache Spark, for key shuffle operations such as join or group by, introduced AQE (*https://oreil.ly/WqWyA*) in recent versions, which works well for nonspatial columns. When running H3 or S2 joins, ensure that `spark.sql.adaptive.enable` is enabled (it is enabled by default).

Spatial Partitioning

Depending on the data size and complexity, decreasing the number of partitions may slow your Apache Sedona application or even render calculations impossible due to errors such as `java.lang.OutOfMemoryError: Java heap space` when you don't have enough memory in your Apache Spark executors. It can also significantly increase performance when most partitions are too small and you encounter the lazy executor problem. In some cases, increasing the number of partitions can lead to better parallelization of your job, or even make it possible for your Apache Sedona job to be finished without errors.

For example, with one million points, 10 million polygons, and 200 partitions, we obtain a runtime of roughly 42 seconds to perform the spatial join. When we decrease the number of partitions to five, we encounter the Java heap space exception. For 100 partitions, the result is slightly worse, around 46 seconds. For 60 partitions, we obtain approximately 49 seconds. However, changing it to a significant value, such as 10,000, makes it longer, and it takes around 78 seconds.

The number of partitions can affect the speed of your application, or you may overwhelm the Apache Spark driver with too many processes, making it prone to errors. You can modify the number of partitions used in a spatial join using the property `sedona.join.numpartition`. The number of partitions might not be the same as you set it by using this property because Apache Sedona tries to optimize the number of records per partition to avoid skewed joins.

Another property that you can set for spatial partitioning is the partitioner type, which can be either KDB-tree or quadtree. To change it, use the `sedona.join.grid type` parameter when you create the application. By default, Apache Sedona uses the KDB-tree.

A KDB-tree is well suited for spatial joins, as it splits data evenly, leading to improved parallelization and reduced skew in joins. With a basic H3 or S2 join, the issue may arise due to skewed partitions or larger data sizes for polygons or lines, as a polygon may be located within many H3 grids. You can improve the H3 or S2 join by splitting cells with a larger amount of data or merging those with smaller amounts. To achieve this, you need to take a similar approach to Apache Sedona's, but you will still not achieve even splitting, as seen in a KDB-tree, for instance. This involves creating a sample dataset and attempting to generate data grids with no hot partitions, which means avoiding situations where one grid ID contains too many geometries from the left and right side compared to other grids, as we might end up with a skewed join.

Let's compare the KDB-tree with the quadtree in Apache Sedona by comparing the standard deviation of the number of features for each partition for the left part of the join, the right part, and the ratio between them. For that, we will reuse the building dataset from the Overture Maps Foundation and places for the California region. The comparison table for the spatial join using the KDB-tree and quadtree looks like this:

```
+--------------+----------------+--------------+--------------+
|num_partitions|         measure|kdbtree_value|quadtree_value|
+--------------+----------------+--------------+--------------+
|            10|        avg_time|         28.35|         21.77|
|            10|       diff_stdev|        263.76|        402.13|
|            10|stddev_buildings|     258959.19|     398814.72|
|            10|   stddev_places|      29483.42|      43735.72|
|            20|        avg_time|         24.92|         29.59|
|            20|       diff_stdev|        346.23|        394.03|
|            20|stddev_buildings|     109067.41|      164243.0|
|            20|   stddev_places|      22056.69|      22224.03|
|            40|        avg_time|         28.74|         25.76|
|            40|       diff_stdev|        385.25|        508.54|
|            40|stddev_buildings|      45306.39|     110093.51|
|            40|   stddev_places|       9866.39|      14053.29|
|           100|        avg_time|         28.74|         24.49|
|           100|       diff_stdev|        460.56|        920.92|
|           100|stddev_buildings|      20935.73|      41951.82|
|           100|   stddev_places|       5120.79|       5761.24|
|           200|        avg_time|         17.23|         18.56|
|           200|       diff_stdev|        771.45|       1113.24|
|           200|stddev_buildings|      11781.74|      21227.85|
|           200|   stddev_places|       3170.64|       3117.01|
+--------------+----------------+--------------+--------------+
```

We compared the processing time (average from four tries), the standard deviation for the number of features for buildings (stddev_buildings) and places (stddev_places), and the standard deviation value based on the ratio between the number of places and building features in each partition.

If the left data is evenly distributed in the planar space and the right side of the join is also evenly distributed but only covers a small part of the left dataset's space, consider changing `sedona.join.spa titionside` to right (default is left). This is because the spatial partitions will be built on top of the left side of the join, resulting in a skewed join, as a small percentage of the left partitions will need to process almost all the data from the right side. If you ever wondered why the last partitions take a large amount of processing time, this might be a sign that you should switch the partition side to the opposite side. For example, joining the buildings that cover the California region and a subset representing the Los Angeles neighborhood took two times longer when building partitions in California, rather than in Los Angeles.

Spatial Join

Spatial join optimization is a crucial part of the Apache Sedona Spark library. You must focus on numerous optimizations to make your application faster and more memory-efficient. Let's start with the most critical part: verifying that the optimization was applied correctly in your Apache Sedona code. To test spatial join, we used randomly generated polygons and points using the Apache Sedona Spider dataset.

When you run a spatial join transformation, examine the Spark logical plan to determine if it contains an optimized plan keyword, such as `RangeJoin`:

```
== Physical Plan ==
*(3) Project [id#646L, geometry#647]
+- RangeJoin geometry#647: geometry, geometry#651: geometry, INTERSECTS
   :- *(1) Project [id#646L, geometry#647]
   :  +- *(1) Filter isnotnull(geometry#647)
   :     +- BatchScan spider[id#646L, geometry#647]
   :        class org.apache.sedona.sql.datasources.spider
   :           .SpiderScanBuilder$$anon$1
   :        RuntimeFilters: []
   +- *(2) Project [geometry#651]
      +- *(2) Filter isnotnull(geometry#651)
         +- BatchScan spider[id#650L, geometry#651]
            class org.apache.sedona.sql.datasources.spider
               .SpiderScanBuilder$$anon$1
            RuntimeFilters: []
```

When running Apache Sedona, you can disable spatial join optimizations using the `sedona.join` optimization mode and value none. But we don't recommend doing that:

```
== Physical Plan ==
*(3) Project [id#914L, geometry#915]
+- CartesianProduct
   org.apache.spark.sql.sedona_sql.expressions.ST_Intersects
```

```
:- *(1) Project [id#914L, geometry#915]
:  +- *(1) Filter isnotnull(geometry#915)
:     +- BatchScan spider[id#914L, geometry#915]
:        class org.apache.sedona.sql.datasources.spider
:           .SpiderScanBuilder$$anon$1
:        RuntimeFilters: []
+- *(2) Project [geometry#919]
   +- *(2) Filter isnotnull(geometry#919)
      +- BatchScan spider[id#918L, geometry#919]
         class org.apache.sedona.sql.datasources.spider
            .SpiderScanBuilder$$anon$1
         RuntimeFilters: []
```

CartesianProduct is what you want to avoid at all costs in spatial join; it's joining each row from the left table with all rows from the right table.

Now, let's compare the times for running the same query, within the left dataset (10,000 polygons) and in the right (10,000 points):

- The average time needed for a nonoptimized join (Cartesian JOIN) is 13.74 seconds.

- The average time needed for an optimized spatial join is 0.08 seconds.

We covered how a broadcast join works in Chapter 4. When one side of the join is small enough, one of the datasets will be copied to all the executor machines instead of running spatial partitioning. Thus, the data doesn't have to be shuffled. When you run a broadcast spatial join, ensure that your transformation plan resembles the following and contains the BroadcastIndexJoin keyword:

```
== Physical Plan ==
*(3) Project [id#1409L, geometry#1410]
+- BroadcastIndexJoin geometry#1410: geometry, RightSide, LeftSide, Inner,
   INTERSECTS ST_INTERSECTS(geometry#1410, geometry#1414)
   :- *(1) Project [id#1409L, geometry#1410]
   :  +- *(1) Filter isnotnull(geometry#1410)
   :     +- BatchScan spider[id#1409L, geometry#1410]
   :        class org.apache.sedona.sql.datasources.spider
   :           .SpiderScanBuilder$$anon$1
   :        RuntimeFilters: []
   +- SpatialIndex geometry#1414: geometry, RTREE, false, false
      +- *(2) Project [geometry#1414]
         +- *(2) Filter isnotnull(geometry#1414)
            +- BatchScan spider[id#1413L, geometry#1414]
               class org.apache.sedona.sql.datasources.spider
                  .SpiderScanBuilder$$anon$1
               RuntimeFilters: []
```

To increase the spatial broadcast join threshold size, use the Apache Sedona property sedona.join.autoBroadcastJoinThreshold. The property uses integer values and the suffix with the unit, such as 10 MB. To enforce broadcasting of one side of the join, you can use the broadcast function, like in the following Sedona code snippet:

```
import pyspark.sql.functions as f

left.alias("l") \
    .join(
        f.broadcast(right.alias("r")),
        f.expr("ST_Intersects(l.geometry, r.geometry)")
    ) \
    .select("l.id", "l.geometry")
```

Or using SQL:

```
SELECT
    /*+ BROADCASTJOIN (l) */
    l.id,
    l.geometry
FROM right AS r
JOIN left AS l ON ST_Intersects(r.geometry, l.geometry)
```

To enforce a nonbroadcast join, we set `sedona.join.autoBroadcastJoinThres hold=-1`. Keep in mind that we need to perform costly shuffling, so for a non-broadcast join, we also need to bump the memory for worker nodes up using the `spark.executor.memory` property.

Let's compare a spatial join between polygons with 100 million records and points with 10 thousand elements. On average, the broadcast join took 27.4 seconds and the nonbroadcast 88.5 seconds.

Apache Sedona optimizes the spatial join by using a subset of your data to create the proper spatial partitioning. The number of spatial partitions depends on several factors, including the data size and the properties applied to your Apache Sedona application and input data partitions.

When the number of spatial partitions isn't that large, you might turn off the global index, which is turned on by default. To do that, you can use the `sedona.global.index` property and set it to `False`. When your data is small, such as hundreds of records, the difference between the global spatial index being turned on and off isn't significant in absolute numbers. With a larger number of partitions, `sedona.global.index` gives a significant performance boost.

To test the global index parameter, we used 100,000 points and 1,000,000 polygons. When the global index was turned off, we got on average a processing time of 22.8 seconds, and when it was turned on, the time was reduced to 1.5 seconds on average.

Apache Sedona uses R-tree by default to create a global index. It is great for verifying the intersection between geometries. You can also use a quadtree by setting the `sedona.global.indextype` property.

Apache Sedona Python

If Apache Sedona Python is used carefully, it is as performant as the native Java/Scala API. We explained in Chapter 6 that using the native Apache Sedona function is the recommended way to transform the data. Let's compare a few application types:

- Python (vectorized) UDF versus using the Apache Sedona SQL function
- Apache Sedona DataFrame to GeoPandas with and without GeoArrow
- GeoPandas DataFrame to Apache Sedona DataFrame with and without GeoArrow

In this section, we will utilize the Overture Maps Foundation buildings dataset for the US region. The WKT polygon is as follows:

```
POLYGON(
  (-124.30 31.63,
  -124.30 48.67,
  -61.56 48.67,
  -61.56 31.63,
  -124.30 31.63)
)
```

Python (Vectorized) UDF Versus Using Apache Sedona SQL Function

Python UDFs are handy for solving uncommon problems, but they come with a significant cost, as they require serializing internal Apache Sedona geometries into Python Shapely objects. We begin with the UDF, which converts geometry into an area. We call the function on the building dataset on the geometry column. We sum the entire area, and for each processing, we repeat the operation 10 times to obtain the average:

For the Python UDF function, we get on average 15.7 seconds:

```
def get_area(s: b.BaseGeometry) -> float:
    return s.area

get_area_udf = f.udf(get_area, t.DoubleType())

sedona.udf.register("GetArea", get_area_udf)
```

For the Python vectorized version, we can reduce the time to as little as 11.4 seconds, which is better. The improvement stems from the faster serialization between Spark and Python using Apache Arrow; additionally, we utilize pandas DataFrames instead of calculating row by row. However, what happens when we call the native Apache Sedona function?

```
@sedona_vectorized_udf(
    udf_type=SedonaUDFType.GEO_SERIES,
    return_type="double"
)
def get_area_vectorized(geom: gpd.GeoDataFrame):
    return geom.area
```

The internal Apache Sedona SQL function ST_Area performs the computation in around 2.4 seconds, which is significantly faster. The Apache Sedona community is working extensively on improving Apache Arrow integrations. When you read this book, the Sedona vectorized UDF may be even more performant. To keep up to date, follow the official docs and the notebooks for this chapter.

If you know how to program in Scala or Java, you can follow the examples on how to create a Scala UDF and register it with Python in the official repository prepared for the book. You should achieve a similar average time to calculate the result as with native Apache Sedona functions, around 2.4 seconds, using our dataset. The UDF to calculate the area looks as follows:

```
object UDFFunction {

  def register(sparkSession: SparkSession): Unit = {

    val areaUDF = (s: Geometry) => s.getArea

    sparkSession.udf.register("ST_AreaUDF", areaUDF)
  }
}
```

And in Python:

```
sedona._jvm.org.sedona.sql.UDFFunction.register(sedona._jsparkSession)
```

where Sedona is a SparkSession instance and sedona.sql.UDFFunction.register is the location of the Scala code.

Apache Sedona DataFrame to GeoPandas With and Without GeoArrow

Natively, when you call toPandas() on an Apache Sedona spatial DataFrame, each row is serialized to Sedona's internal serialization format and then deserialized into Python Shapely objects using Sedona's custom C bindings. The process is not ideal, as we need to:

- Serialize the DataFrame rows to binary data.
- Use the Py4J library, which allows us to transfer data between the JVM and Python.

- Deserialize it using the C bindings to Shapely objects.
- Construct the pandas DataFrame object based on Python objects, which is additional overhead.

The process involves several steps, during which we have extensive communication between the JVM and Python (which is performed for each row of the data). We can simplify this process by utilizing Apache Arrow, which drastically reduces the memory footprint and the time required to transform the Apache Sedona spatial DataFrame into GeoPandas. The process simplifies to the following:

- Convert Apache Spark to an efficient Arrow format (zero-copy, columnar format)
- Efficiently load Apache Arrow to GeoPandas directly.

For the following GeoArrow examples, we will be using three dataset sizes: small (10,000 rows), medium (500,000 rows), and large (10,000,000 rows). In the example, we use the building dataset from the Overture Maps Foundation.

We no longer incur the JVM-to-Python translation penalty; instead, we construct the GeoPandas DataFrame efficiently from Arrow. To show the difference, we will monitor application memory usage and the time needed to translate the data to GeoPandas from the Apache Sedona spatial DataFrame.

We will compare the aforementioned dataset sizes with the native `toPandas()` method and a custom method in Apache Sedona, which uses the efficient GeoArrow conversion. We use a Python script that loads data from the GeoParquet format and converts it to GeoPandas. We repeat the procedure 10 times. The GeoParquet file represents the building dataset from California from the Overture Maps Foundation dataset. We use the following functions to convert an Apache Sedona spatial Data-Frame to a GeoPandas DataFrame.

In the benchmark for converting GeoPandas to Apache Sedona DataFrame and from Sedona DataFrame to GeoPandas, we use 10 repetitions. The peak memory usage does not refer to one translation: it's also not the sum of all; it's the maximum during 10 repetitions, as Python does not clear the memory instantly with the built-in garbage collector (GC).

GeoArrow

```
def convert_using_arrow(df):
    return gpd.GeoDataFrame.from_arrow(
        dataframe_to_arrow(df)
    )
```

Default toPandas() *method*

```
def convert_using_non_arrow(df):
    return gpd.GeoDataFrame(
        df.toPandas(),
        geometry="geometry"
    )
```

Using GeoArrow with a small dataset (10,000 rows), on average, over 10 tries, we achieve 0.68 seconds, and at peak, the application utilizes 225.58 MB of RAM.

On the same small dataset, when we are not using the Arrow conversion, we obtain a similar average time required for one processing loop, 0.64 seconds, and a memory usage peak of 233.55 MB of RAM.

For the medium dataset (500,000 rows), we begin to see a performance boost and reduced memory usage for GeoArrow conversion.

With GeoArrow, the transformation is three times faster compared to not using GeoArrow. Additionally, we require less memory to convert to GeoPandas, with a peak of 2.61 GB. For non-GeoArrow conversion, memory consumption at peak reaches 3.4 GB, so we need 50% more RAM.

For larger datasets (10,000,000 rows), we observe an enormous improvement; the GeoArrow conversion is nine times faster than the non-GeoArrow conversion and requires half the memory in peak. For a large dataset, the data becomes so extensive that we need to utilize Apache Spark's spark.driver.maxResultSize property and set it to 6 GB, allowing extensive data to be stored in the driver's RAM.

GeoPandas DataFrame to Apache Sedona DataFrame With and Without GeoArrow

The Apache Spark session object has a createDataFrame() method, which, for example, takes a pandas DataFrame and creates an Apache Spark spatial DataFrame. As we mentioned earlier in the Apache Sedona to GeoPandas DataFrame transformation, this scenario also involves translating from Python to JVM and deserializing each GeoPandas row into Python objects at a significant cost. Another drawback is the lack of batch support; we convert the data row by row.

We will also track the memory usage and the time needed to transform the GeoPandas DataFrame to the Apache Sedona spatial DataFrame. We load the data using GeoPandas from GeoParquet and also create an Apache Sedona DataFrame, loading it into a GeoPandas DataFrame.

We use the following functions to convert a GeoPandas DataFrame to Apache Sedona.

When converting the GeoPandas DataFrame using Sedona, the `createDataFrame` method required us to provide the schema explicitly due to casting issues, which resulted in an application crash.

GeoArrow

```
df = create_spatial_dataframe(sedona, gdf)
```

Default `sedona.createDataFrame()` *method*

```
df = sedona.createDataFrame(gdf, schema=schema)
```

Similar to the conversion of an Apache Sedona DataFrame to GeoPandas, for smaller datasets, the difference is not impactful.

Using GeoArrow, the small dataset, in 10 runs, averages 0.51 seconds per run, and at peak, it uses 206.52 MB. For non-GeoArrow conversion, the average time was 0.83 seconds, and memory usage increased to 239.50 MB.

To be able to run the non-GeoArrow conversion with the medium dataset, we had to bump the Spark configuration parameters up, because our data is quite heavy and needs time to be transferred appropriately to a Apache Sedona DataFrame:

- `spark.network.timeout` to `"1000s"`
- `spark.rpc.askTimeout` to `"1000s"`
- `spark.executor.heartbeatInterval` to `"60s"`

However, from time to time, we get the `java.net.SocketException: Connection reset` error.

The average time using GeoArrow is 3.11 seconds, and the RAM usage peaked at 1.51 GB. The processing time without GeoArrow is significantly slower, over three times slower at 11.04, and it utilizes twice as much memory, 2.6 GB.

The average run time for the large dataset using GeoArrow is 63.15 seconds, and the memory usage at peak is 11.52 GB. For the large dataset, we struggled to create a DataFrame object from the GeoPandas DataFrame without Arrow successfully.

GeoParquet and Spatial Parquet

Spatial Parquet and GeoParquet, as we discussed in Chapter 6, can significantly improve the speed of your spatial application. Apache Parquet now supports geospatial data types in its specifications: geometry and geography. The current improvement stems from the fact that we can filter out unused data early using row group filtering and file metadata filtering in GeoParquet. However, to fully optimize your application, you also need to consider nonspatial optimizations of the Apache Parquet file format.

When working with analytical columnar file formats like Apache Parquet, keep in mind that a few operations might significantly slow your application:

- Loading all columns if you don't need them all. Apache Parquet is a columnar format: its advantage is to work on a *set* of columns to reduce the memory footprint and accelerate your application.

- Many small files can lead to a significant slowdown of the application, as a considerable amount of time is spent on file scanning operations, followed by merging and rearranging data. There is no strict rule on this, but files from 128 MB to 512 MB are preferred.

- If you work with wider datasets, consider grouping columns using nested structures, such as structs, lists, or maps. This will reduce the amount of data scans, especially when you select only a subset of columns.

- In read-heavy applications, utilize geospatial indexing and sort the data accordingly to preserve data locality and enhance the spatial predicates pushdown mechanism.

- The simplest approach is to use the Geohash algorithm; however, this will not result in evenly distributed files. You can see the partitions on the map in Figure 10-1. We get a standard deviation of 107538.26, which is a large value for 25 files. In the file, we would expect on average 400,000 records per file. The smallest file is 50,064 and the largest is 542,303. To store the data partitioned by Geohash, you can use the following code:

```
SELECT
    col1,
    col2,
    geom,
    ST_GeoHash(geom, 5) as geohash
FROM spatialDf
ORDER BY geohash
```

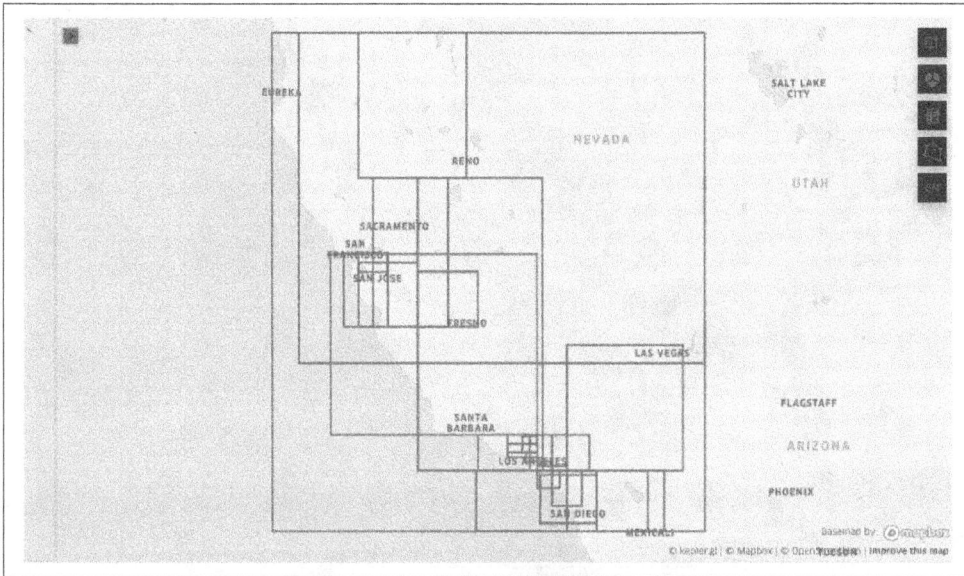

Figure 10-1. Geohash-based distribution of records inside the Parquet files

Apache Sedona exposes the possibility of using the KDB-tree partitioning used in the examples of evenly distributing rows in a spatial join. To achieve this, you can reuse the Python code. The KDB-tree partitioning of Parquet files is in Figure 10-2. The standard deviation dropped to 70,118.39, where the minimum value is 239,236 and the maximum is 462,412 records per partition.

```python
from pyspark.sql import DataFrame
from sedona.utils.structured_adapter import StructuredAdapter
from sedona.core.enums import GridType

def repartition(df: DataFrame):
    spatial_rdd = StructuredAdapter.toSpatialRdd(
        df, "geometry"
    )

    spatial_rdd.analyze()

    spatial_rdd.spatialPartitioningWithoutDuplicates(
        GridType.KDBTREE,
        20
    )

    return StructuredAdapter.toSpatialPartitionedDf(
        spatial_rdd,
        df.sparkSession
    )

input_dataframe.\
```

```
transform(repartition).\
write.\
format("geoparquet").\
mode("overwrite").\
save("path")
```

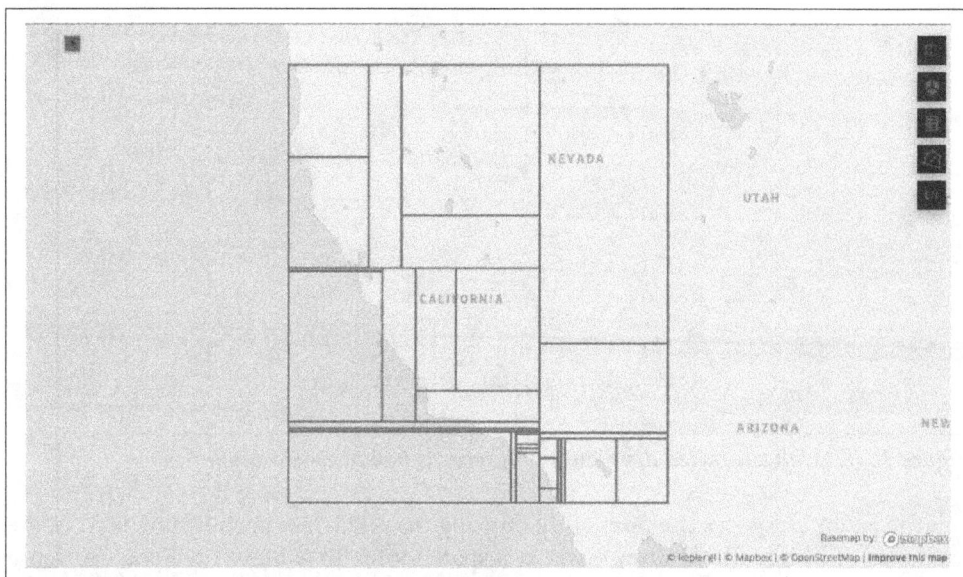

Figure 10-2. In KDB-based partitioning, partitions have no overlaps

To preserve locality for Parquet on the row group level, you can consider combining the KDB with Geohash. To do that, you can use Apache Spark's `sortWithinParti tions` function to also order the data inside the partition:

```
partitioned.\
    transform(repartition).\
    withColumn("geohash", f.expr("ST_GeoHash(geometry, 5)")).\
    sortWithinPartitions("geohash").\
    write.\
    format("parquet").\
    mode("overwrite").\
    save("path")
```

To improve the spatial predicate pushdown mechanism, consider adjusting the size of the row groups in your Parquet files and the overall file size to optimize performance. There is no exact mechanism in Apache Spark to save files of equal size, but you can achieve that with a few Apache Spark configuration parameters, like:

- `spark.sql.files.maxRecordsPerFile` (default 0)
- `spark.sql.files.maxPartitionNum` (default None)

Apache Iceberg

Apache Iceberg recently introduced geospatial data types to the table specification: geometry and geography types. Similar to GeoParquet, Apache Iceberg adds file-level statistics, which help reduce the number of files that need to be loaded into your spatial application. When you are using Apache Iceberg tables, consider the following points:

- If you are using a different engine than Apache Sedona, ensure it supports geospatial statistics for both write and read operations.

- Geospatial statistics are well suited for Apache Iceberg, but if you don't order the files to preserve spatial locality, then all the files will contain data within similar boundaries. Ensure that you order your data by a geospatial index, such as Geohash or KDB-tree, for which we provided examples in the previous section, to preserve locality. Then, each file represents a different region, and the predicate pushdown mechanism helps improve your application's performance.

- Use data compaction to even out the file sizes in Apache Iceberg. With numerous updates and other operations, you may end up with many smaller files, which can compromise performance and lead to data skew.

- To reap the benefits of Apache Parquet performance and Apache Iceberg, ensure your data files are of optimal size. Use parameters such as `target-file-size-bytes` to maintain an optimal size.

Apache Iceberg has a great book that covers, in great detail, how to optimize your data, with a strong emphasis on nonspatial data. If you are interested in learning more about this topic, read *Apache Iceberg: The Definitive Guide* by Tomer Shiran et al. (O'Reilly, 2024).

Summary

Apache Sedona simplifies many of your spatial daily tasks; you don't have to worry about writing distributed spatial join queries or saving data to spatial Parquet, GeoParquet, or Apache Iceberg. The Apache Sedona community has prepared numerous query optimizations, but if you select the wrong tools or data modeling techniques, your application will not perform optimally. In this chapter, we discussed possible Apache Sedona application optimizations, and then we talked about improving two crucial parts of the Apache Sedona framework, spatial partitioning and spatial join.

Apache Sedona Python is more convenient to use because of Python's simplicity compared to Java or Scala. However, it comes at the cost of performance when used improperly. We covered how to utilize GeoArrow optimizations to fasten your UDFs or transform datasets between Python and internal Apache Sedona.

Each spatial application needs to persist data to allow further analytics or training of machine learning models. In the last section, we discussed how you can optimize spatial Parquet, GeoParquet, and Apache Iceberg tables.

Index

A

ACID (atomicity, consistency, isolation, durability), 233, 242, 244, 247
Adaptive Query Execution (AQE), 11, 290
add_binary_distance_band_column function, 198
add_distance_band_column function, 198
affine transformation, 116, 117
aggregations, spatial SQL functions as, 32
AirflowException, 172
algorithm parameter, 236
allTouched (Boolean) parameter, 133
Amazon DynamoDB, 55
Apache Airflow, 170-174, 253-256, 270
Apache Arrow, 160, 163, 218, 296, 297
Apache Avro, 233, 247
Apache Flink, 7, 261
Apache Hadoop jar files, 9
Apache Hive, 69, 244
Apache Iceberg, 42
    data transactions, 241-243
    features, 247-251
    geospatial types, 252-253
    optimizing, 303
    schema evolution, 243-244
    specification, 244-247
Apache Kafka, 233
Apache Parquet, 18, 40
    columnar versus row data formats, 232
    data format, 233-237
    GeoParquet, 237-241
    saving data to, 24-25
    spatial types, 236
Apache Sedona
    architecture and components, 12-14
    developer community, 18
    developer experience, 16-18
    Discord server, 19
    getting started with
        DataFrame API, 34
        Docker image, 27-29
        Jupyter Notebook environment, 29
        Python program, 22-27
        spatial DataFrame, 30
        spatial SQL, 31-34
    industry adoption of, 18
    integration with Apache Spark ecosystem, 15
    resources, 19
    scalability, 15
    use of by data analysts, engineers, and scientists, 16
    visualization, 35
Apache Sedona applications
    optimizing
        Apache Iceberg, 303
        Apache Sedona Python, 295-299
        avoiding large data for application driver, 288
        avoiding shuffling, 287
        avoiding skew joins, 290
        avoiding spheroid distance in joins, 284
        avoiding wide operations, 287
        caching reused DataFrames, 284-286
        filtering early, 282-283
        GeoParquet and Spatial Parquet, 300-302

coalesce function, 212

collect() method, 9, 124, 158, 159, 160, 165, 166, 288

collect_list function, 34, 113

color raster, 115

columnar versus row data formats, 232

columns, grouping into struct fields, 235

comma-separated values (CSV)
  datasets, 42
  loading data from CSV files, 23

compute engine, in geospatial data lakehouses, 229

computer vision, 203-207

concurrency control, in Apache Iceberg, 248

config parameters, Apache Spark, 261

conic projections, 80

constructors, spatial SQL functions as, 32

context parameter, of poke method, 171

contextily library, 184

convex hull, 87, 287

convex set, 87

coordinate reference system (CRS), 78
  in Apache Iceberg, 252
  for distance measurement, 84
  planar distance in, 284
  and raster data, 116, 144
  vs. spatial reference identifier (SRID), 83

coordinate systems, overview of, 4

core points, in DBSCAN, 190, 191

CouchBase, 55

count action, 10

COUNT aggregation function, 154

covering field, 49

createDataFrame method, 26, 162, 298

create_map function, 183

crowd-sourced datasets, 2

crs parameter, 236

crs_wkt parameter, 167

curvilinear coordinate, 79

cylindrical projections, 80

D

Dags, 170-174

data analysts, use of Apache Sedona by, 17

data array, 122

data built tool (dbt)
  testing applications, 179-181
  writing applications, 175-179

data engineers, use of Apache Sedona by, 16

data governance, geospatial data lakehouses and, 230

data lakehouse architecture, 227-231
  (see also geospatial data lakehouse)

data lineage, geospatial data lakehouses and, 230

data quality, geospatial data lakehouses and, 229

data scheduling tools, 170-174

data skew, 11, 99

data structures, 12

data synchronization, 59

data transactions, 241-243

data transfer, minimizing, 5

data warehouses, 6

databases
  CDC with PostgreSQL to GeoParquet source, 60-62
  data synchronization, 59
  reading from MongoDB, 58
  reading from MySQL, 57
  reading from PostgreSQL (PostGIS), 56
  replication of, 59

Databricks, 262-263

DataFrame API, 8, 11, 30, 34

DataFrame.collect(), 159

DataFrame.toPandas(), 159

DataFrames, Apache Sedona
  caching reused, 284-286
  to GeoPandas, 296-298
  GeoPandas DataFrame to, 298-299

DataFrames, GeoPandas (see GeoPandas Data-Frames)

DataFrames, pandas, 9, 160, 295

dataframe_to_arrow function, 160

DataSourceV2, for GeoPackage, 47

datum, 79

.dbf file format, 43

dbscan function, 191

dbt_expectations plugin extension, 179

Debezium library, 59, 60

deck.gl, 13

density-based spatial clustering of applications with noise (DBSCAN), 189-192

df.cache(), 10

Dimensionally Extended 9-Intersection Model (DE-9IM), 76-78

display_image function, 131

distance join optimization, 101

loading from databases
    CDC with PostgreSQL to GeoParquet
        source, 60-62
    data synchronization, 59
    MongoDB, 58
    MySQL, 57
    PostgreSQL (PostGIS), 56
loading vector data formats
    distributed vs. nondistributed files, 42
    flat files, 42-43
    format differences, 40
    GeoJSON, 44-46
    GeoPackage, 47-48
    GeoParquet, 48-52
    serialization methods, 38-40
    shapefiles, 43
New York Taxi data analysis, 63-67
processing rasters, 53-55
raster data formats (GeoTIFF), 52
sources of, 2
spatial data vs., 3
geospatial data lakehouse
    Apache Iceberg
        data transactions, 241-243
        features, 247-251
        geospatial types, 252-253
        schema evolution, 243-244
        specification, 244-247
    Apache Parquet
        columnar vs. row data formats, 232
        data format, 233-237
        GeoParquet, 237-241
        spatial types, 236
    architecture, 227-231
    data governance and, 230
    data lineage and, 230
    data quality and, 229
    use case, 253-256
geospatial data science
    autocorrelation, 201-203
    clustering, 189-192
    creating geospatial machine learning mod-
        els, 207-213
    getting vector objects from raster data,
        203-207
    hot spot analysis, 197-200
    outlier detection, 193-197
    road accidents in Germany use case,
        213-225

geospatial indexing, 4, 300
geospatial machine learning models, 207-213
geospatial statistics
    in Apache Iceberg, 303
    in Apache Parquet, 236
geospatial vector data manipulation, 158
GeoTIFF, 13, 53, 146, 186
GeoTools, 260
geotools-wrapper, 265
get_possible_releases method, 172
GitHub, Apache Sedona on, 19
global index parameter, 294
Global Moran's I, 201-203
global.index configuration value, 103
Glue, AWS, 265-266
GPS data, 2
GraphFrames, 191
GridGeometry2D object, 117
GROUP BY statement, 288
groupBy, 52, 212
g_local function, 197, 198, 199, 215

H

H3 indexes, 65-67, 97, 176
handleTies, 197
hash indexes, 4
hash join, 89
hash maps, 90
hash tables, 89
Haversine/great circle distance, 84
.head() method, 166
header section, of Apache Parquet, 235
heap memory issues, 46
heap space errors, 54, 91, 290
heat maps, 182, 185
Helmert transformation, 81
hexagon grids, 65
hidden partitioning, 248
hint method, 90
Hive Metastore, 244
holes, in polygons, 70
hot spots, 4, 197-200, 214

I

idempotency, 60
IllegalArgumentException, 133
image classification, 203
image segmentation, 203
include_self parameter, 214

indb method, 165
InDbSedonaRaster object, 166-169
indexing (see spatial indexes)
INSERT OVERWRITE statement, 251
insurance risk modeling use case
    closest police and fire departments, 153
    fire risk, 152
    flood risk, 151
    overview, 148-150
    population density, 150
    residential building density, 154-155
interior, defined, 71
intersects algorithm, 260
inverse distance weighted (IDW) method, 128
ISO/IEC 13249-3:2016 standard, 38
isWithinXRange variable, 141
isWithinYRange variable, 141
itertools.chain from_iterable function, 122

J

Java heap space errors, 54, 91, 130, 290
JDBC (Java Database Connectivity), 56, 60
Jiffle language, 137
JOIN keyword, 101, 102
join operations
    modifying partition number for, 286
    spheroid distance in, 284
joining raster data, 143-148
Joint Research Centre (JRC), 145, 149
JSON format, 44-46
Jupyter Notebook environment, 10, 14, 29
JVM, 158, 160, 163, 298

K

k nearest neighbors, 13
K-means algorithm, 207-213
Kafka Connect, 59
KD-trees, 96
KDB-trees, 96, 100, 291, 301, 303
Kepler.gl, 8, 13, 150, 182
KryoSerializer, 289

L

LATERAL VIEW command, 124
lazy evaluation, 52
Leaflet JS library, 184
least privilege principle, 231
leaves, in tree data structure, 94

lenient (Boolean) parameter, 133
linestrings, 69
    components of, 71
    defined, 70
Local Getis-Ord Gi(*), 197-200
local mode, Apache Spark, 8
Local Outlier Factor (LOF), 193-197
local reachability density (LRD) ratio, 193
local_outlier_factor function, 194, 196
longitude, 78

M

M value, 70
machine learning
    computer vision, 203-207
    creating models with MLlib, 207-213
    DBSCAN, 189-192
    Local Outlier Factor (LOF), 193-197
map algebra, 136-143
map projections, 80-81
mapping, 11
MapReduce, 69
massively parallel processing (MPP) compute
    clusters, 272
Matplotlib, 13, 183
maxRadiusOrMinPoints, 128
MBR (minimal boundary rectangle), 94, 103
means.fit method, 213
medallion architecture, of data lakehouses, 229,
    253
memory issues, 46
Mercator, 80
MERGE INTO statement, 251
meridians, 80
metadata, 51
    in Apache Iceberg, 246-247, 250, 252
    in Apache Parquet, 234, 235, 237
    in GeoParquet, 239-240
    in geospatial data lakehouses, 230
    about rasters, 126
Microsoft Fabric, 266-267
minimal boundary rectangle (MBR), 94, 103
Minio, 23
minPts parameter, 190
min_pts parameter, 192
MLlib, 207-213, 223
model.transform method, 213
MongoDB, 55, 58

MPP (massively parallel processing) compute clusters, 272
(multi)linestring collection, 70, 82
(multi)point collection, 70, 82
(multi)polygon collection, 70, 82
multiple-band rasters, 116
MultiPolygon, 210, 241
__mul__ method, 118
MySQL, 57, 233

N

narrow operations, 11, 89
NetCDF/HDF, 13
New York Taxi data analysis, 63-67
NoData values, 116
nodes, in tree data structure, 94
noise points, in DBSCAN, 190
nonbroadcast spatial joins, 11
nondistributed versus distributed files, 42
Normalized Burn Ratio (NBR) index, 142
NoSQL (Not Only SQL), 55
numBands, 121
numPointsOrRadius, 128
NumPy library, 168

O

object detection, 203
oblate spheroid, 78
odbc (Open Database Connectivity interface), 175
OGC Simple Feature specification, 70
OLTP (online transaction processing), 233
Open Geospatial Consortium (OGC), 15, 38
Open Route Service (ORS), 209
open source tools, 5
OpenLineage, 230, 256
OpenStreetMap (OSM), 2, 41, 183
optimistic locking, 248
optimized spatial joins, 97-98
Oracle, 233
OSM pbf format, 41
outlier detection, 193-197
Overture Maps dataset, 49, 108, 149, 208, 254, 270, 291, 295, 297

P

--packages flag, 27
pair coordinates, 70

PARTITION BY, 111
partition number for join operations, 286
partitioning, 4, 10
 (see also spatial partitioning)
 hidden, in Apache Iceberg, 248
 optimization of, 248
pivot function, 212
pixels, 52, 115
 centroid of, 115
 classifying with image segmentation, 204
 converting pixel coordinates into real-world coordinates, 117-120
planar projections, 81
plot method, 183, 184
points, 69
 defined, 70
 finding out if two points intersect, 85
 finite number of, 70
poke function, 171, 172
Polygon type, 241
polygons, 33, 69
 components of, 71
 defined, 70
 holes in, 70
polynomial transformations, 116
PostGIS, 5, 6, 13, 55, 56-57, 60
PostgreSQL, 233
 CDC to GeoParquet source, 60-62
 reading from, 56, 60
predicates
 in Apache Parquet, 234
 predicate pushdown, 8, 49-52, 282, 300, 302
 spatial SQL functions as, 32
printSchema(), 31, 82
.prj file format, 43
projected coordinate systems, 4
projection, in Apache Parquet, 234
projective transformation, 116
PROJJSON, 236, 241
Protobuf, 233
Py4J library, 158, 296
PyArrow library, 237
PyData ecosystem, 14, 16
 data scheduling tools, 170-174
 GeoPandas and Shapely, 158-165
 manipulating geospatial vector data, 158
 raster data tools, 165-169
 raster geospatial visualization, 186
 transforming geospatial data with dbt

overview, 174
testing applications, 179-181
writing applications, 175-179
vector geospatial visualization
GeoPandas, 183-184
Kepler.gl, 182
overview, 181-182
PyDeck, 185
PyDeck, 185
PySpark dependencies, 22
pytest framework, 25-27
Python, 29
(see also Apache Sedona Python)
benefits of, 157
libraries, 6, 14
mixing with SQL in same application, 285
UDF function, 295-296
PyTorch, 204

Q

QGIS, 5
quadtrees, 4, 105, 290, 294
query engines, data lakehouses and, 228
query optimization, 8
query processing, 7

R

R-trees, 4, 95, 97, 103, 104, 294
randomSplit method, 225
range join, 102
RangeJoin keyword, 144
raster data, 5
formats for, 52
getting vector objects from, 203-207
insurance risk modeling use case
closest police and fire departments, 153
fire risk, 152
flood risk, 151
overview, 148-150
population density, 150
residential building density, 154-155
joining raster data, 143-148
map algebra, 136-143
overview of, 3
processing, 53-55
raster data model, 115-120
SQL and data manipulation
geometry functions, 125
pixel functions, 124

raster accessors, 126
raster band accessors, 126
raster loader, 120-122
raster predicates, 127
raster tiles, 130
raster visualization, 131
raster-based operators, 127-129
writing to raster formats, 123-124
tools, 165-169
zonal statistics, 132-136
raster geospatial visualization, 186
raster spatial (RS) functions, 19
Rasterio library, 6, 14, 16, 130, 165, 168
converting Rasterio object into geometry
collection, 206
transferring InDbSedonaRaster into, 168
RasterType, 158, 165
raster_df, 122
raycasting algorithm, 85
real estate analysis use case, 107-113
reflection, 120
refRaster, 122
relational database management systems
(RDBMS), 55
Resilient Distributed Datasets (RDDs), 11, 103
rich spatial operations, 15
road accidents in Germany use case, 213-225
root, in tree data structure, 94
rotation, of rasters, 119
row versus columnar data formats, 232
row_number function, 111
RS (raster spatial) functions, 19
RS prefix, 32, 120
RS_AddBand function, 127
RS_AsBase64 function, 131
RS_AsGeoTiff function, 123
RS_AsImage function, 131
RS_AsMatrix function, 131
RS_Clip function, 127, 134
RS_Contains raster predicate, 127, 143, 144
RS_ConvexHull function, 125
RS_Count function, 126
RS_Envelope function, 125
RS_FromArcInfoAsciiGrid function, 120
RS_FromGeoTiff function, 53, 120, 205
RS_FromNetCDF function, 120
RS_Interpolate function, 128
RS_Intersects function, 127, 143, 144, 147, 150
RS_MakeEmptyRaster function, 121, 125

About the Authors

Paweł Tokaj is a staff software engineer at Splunk and a PMC member of the Apache Sedona project who enjoys writing reliable, efficient software that helps others. His love for geospatial data started at the Warsaw University of Technology, where he graduated in geodesy and cartography.

Paweł's primary focus areas are distributed databases and systems, cloud computing, and geospatial data processing. He believes that open source projects make knowledge more accessible; he has contributed to Apache Sedona, Open Lineage, and Airbyte. He attends various conferences or meetups where he shares his knowledge as a speaker or participant. He is a technology nerd, spending a lot of his spare time reading books and articles and developing open source software.

Jia Yu is a cofounder of Wherobots, a venture-backed company for helping businesses to drive insights from spatiotemporal data. He was a tenure-track assistant professor of computer science at Washington State University from 2020 to 2023. He obtained his Ph.D. in computer science from Arizona State University.

Jia's research focuses on large-scale database systems and geospatial data management. In particular, he worked on distributed geospatial data management systems, database indexing, and geospatial data visualization. Jia's research outcomes have appeared in the most prestigious database/GIS conferences and journals, including SIGMOD, VLDB, ICDE, SIGSPATIAL and *VLDB Journal*. He is also the main contributor on several open sourced research projects, such as Apache Sedona, a cluster computing framework for processing big spatial data, which receives one million downloads per month and has users/contributors from major companies.

Mo Sarwat is the CEO of Wherobots and cocreator of Apache Sedona. At Wherobots he is spearheading a team developing a cloud data platform equipped with a brain and memory for our planet to solve the world's most pressing issues. Wherobots is founded by the creators of Apache Sedona, an open source framework designed for large-scale spatial data processing in cloud and on-prem deployments.

Mo taught and conducted research at Arizona State University in the fields of large-scale data processing, databases, data analytics, and AI data infrastructure. With over a decade of experience in academia and industry, Mo has published more than 60 peer-reviewed papers, received two best research paper awards, and been named an Early Career Distinguished Lecturer by the IEEE Mobile Data Management community. Mo is also a recipient of the 2019 National Science Foundation CAREER award, one of the most prestigious honors for young faculty members.

His mission is to advance the state of the art in data management and AI to empower data-driven decision making for a wide range of applications, such as transportation, mobility, and environmental monitoring. He is passionate about developing robust and scalable data systems that can handle complex and massive datasets and leverage AI and machine learning techniques to extract valuable insights and patterns.

Colophon

The animal on the cover of *Cloud Native Geospatial Analytics with Apache Sedona* is the yellow-billed cuckoo (*Coccyzus americanus*), also known as a rain or storm crow.

This nickname comes from their tendency to perform calls in the warm days that are sometimes harbingers of stormy weather. As their scientific name suggests, they are native to America, primarily living in North America and migrating south to Central America and northern South America. Their migration pattern is a loop migration, meaning that they sometimes take a different path north than they did south. This habit suggests that they are sensitive to weather and other environmental factors that contribute to better flight paths.

Forests are their preferred habitat, and they primarily eat insects, particularly tent caterpillars. Their voracious appetites mean that sometimes they gravitate toward areas with infestations: they can eat up to 100 caterpillars in a sitting. These caterpillars, however, do not go down easy: their setae, or bristles, get stuck in the stomach lining of the cuckoo. But this doesn't cause a problem! The cuckoo sheds the stomach lining, regurgitates it, and is left with a fresh lining.

Their nests are not particularly sturdy (and occasionally they steal nests from other birds), but the lack of solid structure makes sense given that they have one of the shortest nesting cycles among birds. From egg-laying to fledging can take just 17 days. Males and females work together during this nesting cycle. With three to four eggs in a clutch, the female lays the eggs asynchronously, so sibling cuckoos can vary in age by days. If food is scarce once the fledglings are born, the youngest cuckoo will get booted from the nest.

Many of the animals on O'Reilly covers are endangered; all of them are important to the world.

The cover illustration is by José Marzan Jr., based on an antique line engraving from *British Birds*. The series design is by Edie Freedman, Ellie Volckhausen, and Karen Montgomery. The cover fonts are Gilroy Semibold and Guardian Sans. The text font is Adobe Minion Pro; the heading font is Adobe Myriad Condensed; and the code font is Dalton Maag's Ubuntu Mono.

O'REILLY®

Learn from experts.
Become one yourself.

60,000+ titles | Live events with experts | Role-based courses
Interactive learning | Certification preparation

**Try the O'Reilly learning platform
free for 10 days.**

www.ingramcontent.com/pod-product-compliance
Lightning Source LLC
Chambersburg PA
CBHW080919220326
41598CB00034B/5618

* 9 7 8 1 0 9 8 1 7 3 9 9 9 *